This book is dedicated to the memory of

Gail Cruickshank

*the last 'Mehitabel and my personal assistant
for six years. Dedicated, she kept me ticking,
making my overseas travel a pleasure.
After devoting long hours to deciphering my
erratic scribble, using her word processor,
she gave this book a sense of order.*

*A tree has been planted in her memory
on Primrose Hill.*

JG

Gail arranging creepy-crawlies in Taiwan

1

JAMES GARDNER

The ARTful designer

Ideas off the drawing board by James Gardner

This book was written in hotel bedrooms, between flights from A to B, and illustrated when I should have been concentrating on other work

A number of chapters are developed from *Elephants in the Attic*, published in 1983 by Orbis.

The text was prepared by Jennie Barlow, who also corrected my erratic spelling. Diane Allard laid out the pages for printing by Centurion Press Limited, London.

Distributed by Lavis Marketing.

British Library Catalogue-in-Publication Data.
A catalogue record for this book is available
from The British Library.

ISBN 0 9521277 0 9

Some years ago I was asked by *Designer* magazine to draw a portrait of James Gardner and I portrayed him as Leonardo da Vinci based on the drawing that comes to mind when we conjure up a mental picture of the great Renaissance painter, architect, engineer and inventor.

The excellence of James Gardner's intellect is also beyond doubt, and may, if the conditions are right, even make many among us reach out to heaven. It may even make some of them reach for their revolvers. But that's another story. Because it's that kind of intellect. Nothing you can tie down. No conventional training of the 'processed' kind which makes company men out of most.

He has that peculiar kind of mind which retains oddness and values perception, seizing every opportunity to exploit an idea in the most practical way. He is the only man I know who can describe circlets for courtesans' thighs in the same breath as a design for an aircraft seat.

Ralph STEADman

FIELDS OF KENT, ENGLAND

Contents

The 20's

The secret place
The currency of adoration

Meanwhile . . .

Woolworth Building – first skyscraper

Titanic hits iceberg

Zeppelins bomb London

First Tank Battle, at Cambrai

Mary Pickford in *The Little Princess*

Lindbergh flies Atlantic

Al Jolson in first 'talkie'

The great Paris World Fair opens

Diaghilev's Russian Ballet in London

Girls dance the Charleston

Le Corbusier: *Towards a New Architecture*

World's first public radio – 2LO

Hitler is writing *Mein Kampf*

Ford produces 15 millionth Model 'T'

Picasso's surrealist period

German mark nosedives

Felix kept on walking

The secret place

A sultry afternoon. Down on the street there is the steady judder of car engines as the traffic creeps forward, stop-go, each driver wearily loathing the rear of the car in front, but up in the cosy cafe behind the balcony of the Stoll Cinema all is quiet. Time stands still.

In the darkness one can just make out a lanky young man with tousled hair peering intently at flickers of light picked up by the bevelled glazing of the auditorium doors. Difficult to discern from those reflected clues what epic is 'Now Showing' on the giant screen.

A motherly old waitress moves out of the shadows to whisper confidentially, "In you go, dearie, it's all the same to me."

A burst of cinematic sound as he slides through the swing doors and eases into a back seat.

On the screen the camera has zoomed in to give a black and white close-up; slender hand seductively stroking a superlative silk-clad shin. (Superlative? Surely, those particular legs are said to be insured at Lloyds for £1,000,000.)

It's Marlene Dietrich in *The Blue Angel.*

By the second reel our interloper is no longer in the cinema, but backstage at a Berlin Cabaret, entrapped, as the goddess drawls in her velvety voice:

"Falling in love again,
Never wanted to,
What am I to do?
I c-a-n-'t help it."

Suddenly the picture blacks out and a hastily scribbled message appears, right across the screen.

Hell!

He takes the exit stairs three at a time, arriving at the studio breathless, to be informed that he is about to design a poster. Not an abstract in the manner of his Master of the moment, E. McKnight Kauffer, who favours the Continental Modernist style, but a realistic full sixteen-sheet rendering of a suet pudding. Not any suet pudding but an *Atora* suet pudding . . . with jam on it.

This pudding incident occurred in the twenties, before intrusive guys with cameras slung round their necks arrived to picture anything and everything with a click. Impersonal.

Making actuality appear more comfortable to live with by artwork is one of the oldest trades, and the artist involved must be happy to observe and draw anything and everything, as a way of life. As the young artist concerned, I rarely drew people. In a sense they were the enemy, performers in some accepted ritual, which I would observe from the margin – as a 'wallflower' might at a village hall dance.

The trick of rendering things by artwork was my release.

I had no ambition even to own a car, but to draw one in my own way made it, for that moment, friendly.

In Art, painting a pudding has equal status with a nude backside, it's the same conjuring trick. After all, indecently realistic renderings of food by the Dutch Masters are hung in the top museums. This young artist (bow-tie is a clue) has already forgotten his recent celluloid romance. A sixteen-sheet poster, that's BIG. Jam creeping over a suet pudding?

No big deal. First a wash of carmine then, for the inner reflected glow, a dab of opaque white with, when dry, a glazing of rose cartham, then a quick flick of varnish and hey presto, a cabochon ruby, lipstick lips – or jam.

I've looked myself up in *Who's Who,*
but it doesn't say *why*

I guess I was not born specifically to fit into this Art niche, as a young wood-louse crawling out from under a stone is designed to fit into his, but then a wood-louse can trace its ancestry and way of life back for a hundred million years.

I can only trace mine as far back as Willesden Junction, a scrap of sooty no-man's land that got lost when the London jigsaw took over the countryside.

Not quite true, as on my mother's side there was an uncle, twice removed, who lived in Windsor Castle. His job was to go on ahead when the Queen planned a Royal Visit, to remind her would-be hosts of their P's and Q's, warn them to conceal any fine china she might take a liking to, and then discreetly creep upstairs to fit a red velvet cover on a lavatory seat, so it would not be kissed by the Royal behind.

Alas, my old man, who could not even mend a lavatory seat, had failure built in. This became apparent when he married my Ma. Nevertheless, he was able to talk two spinster sisters, who ran a genteel kindergarten, into the notion that I could be converted into a little gentleman.

This abortive experiment came to mind later, when Jacob Bronowski (the physicist who practically invented the universe and was kindly explaining how it ticked) discovered that I couldn't do the simplest sum without counting on my fingers.

"The brain," he told me, "operates by rules of logic that mirror the logic of Nature, so it is inherently mathematical." Then he gave me a worried look, as though my feet pointed to the back instead of to the front. Here was an anomaly.

"I am afraid, G, that someone must have muddled the mathematical linkages in your brain at a very early age."

I suddenly felt something was missing in my head. Maybe those spinster sisters' three commandments – wear your gloves, no running, no shouting in the street – had taken precedence over maths.

I made such a poor showing at tasks which demanded programmed thinking, (spelling, for instance), that my old man became desperate and decided to risk all on a gamble. He paid a genuine artist to coach me.

It was immediately apparent from this character's poetic far-away looks and long lank hair that he was a *real artist*. So I would spend hourly sessions dabbing a canvas (and my velveteen nicks) with oils, while he trilled grace-notes with spidery fingers on a white grand piano.

Painting in backgrounds for his reproduction pot-boilers, turned out in batches of five at a time, was my earliest and only adventure into 'Art Gallery' art.

Sounds of battle, off stage

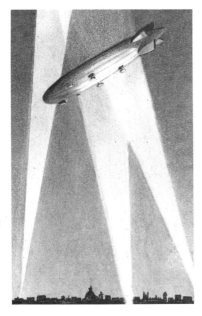

At that time the First World War was in its second year of grim stalemate, the invention of the machine-gun having forced the opposing sides to dig themselves into the mud and then shoot at anything that moved. But to us kids, a war was the natural order of things. Rather exciting, at night, to huddle under the dining-table to the drone of a great Zeppelin, the crump of distant bombs and the angry response from an anti-aircraft gun mounted on nearby Dead Man's Hill.

A stately Zeppelin floating quietly overhead through the beams of searchlights was beautiful. As though it were yesterday, excitement when I was taken to view the pitiful wreck of the first to be shot down – by a pilot in a little prop-plane – and sadness at the ignominious death of such a lovely thing.

While the French Army was making a last stand, beleaguered at Verdun, my old man also hit a low and parcelled me off to a local school and, as he was too hard up to buy me new footwear, in button boots.

This gave the school knockabouts good reason to treat me as a lamb offered up for slaughter until I learned to ape the norm, while observing their group behaviour curiously, as from a distance. An attitude I acquired for life.

The cream of the teaching profession had been shipped over to France to be gassed and shot at, so we children were crammed sixty or more to a class. This enabled me to keep my head down and avoid questioning.

Unfortunately, when mark-up time came, I would be nowhere.

Nemesis occurred when an irate master held me by the ear in front of the class and said, "This chap, Gardner," a prod with the cane, "is no good at . . ." He then ran through the complete curriculum, terminating with the final damning remark, "He's not even any use at sports."

Five strokes with the stick, which he artfully named Fido, and so back to my desk with aching fingers and a false grin to impress the mob – as a French aristocrat would be in honour bound to do when led to the guillotine.

In button boots.

I then discovered that a questionable status could be achieved by peeing higher than others at the lavatory ceiling, or putting out street lamps with a catapult.

For pocket-money, I constructed rabbit hutches from old ammunition boxes, squandering the proceeds on stale doughnuts, which proved to be somewhat sweaty, and 'bangers', which placed judiciously on tramway lines gave a dramatic return for my investment.

Outlets for what copycat sociologists term *creativity*, would be renderings of bi-planes bombing U-boats, and U-boats torpedoing battle-cruisers in the margins of my exercise book.
I also specialised in cartoons depicting aberrant, but imaginative, sexual behaviour, to be passed surreptitiously round the class.

I doubt there is an artist living so dull that he has not essayed into 'naughty' drawings; I just started early.

The inscrutable bowler hat

The British Establishment, from the Queen Mother down, has ever been brutishly indifferent to Art and this went for our tight-minded teachers, who considered drawing a childish activity on a par with skipping or bowling a hoop.

Nevertheless, come Friday afternoon, with a lazy week-end in view, they would keep us captives quiet with a period they termed *Art*.

On one such afternoon the master, at a loss for a subject, set this up as the object to be copied.

A bowler hat happens to be one of the most subtle forms civilised man has devised. Its top is nearly, but not quite, flat. The sides curve very slightly inwards to meet the brim. The brim is a stiff Rococo curve within a curve that must be delineated exactly, or the hat's character and dignity is lost. Also, it is black, which would have floored even a Leonardo.

I never hit the lavatory ceiling, but when it came to drawing I could lead the pack and made such a good rendering of this smug symbol of authority its gratified owner let me off compulsory games. Instead I was free to stand on the touch-line and produce cartoons of our football team cavorting in the mud.

After correcting the word 'careless', which I had carelessly misspelt, the finished artwork was hung in the Assembly Hall, a place of honour in that small world.

My poor mother, seeing this as fame, chivvied the authorities until, at last, losing patience, they awarded me a scholarship to a genuine art school. A narrow squeak. But for that bowler hat, I would probably have ended up doing a postman's rounds or serving – as did one of my buddies – behind the bacon counter in the local store.

At art school, the unteachable were free to teach themselves or, of course, end up behind the bacon counter.

Oh, to be an artist now that spring is here

Having devoted what educationalists term the formative years just growing out of my clothes, I now found myself in a world where if you could draw you were IN. As I could draw almost anything without even thinking, maybe I had been tooled up for a purpose . . . *I was to be an artist!*

I no longer bit my fingernails worrying about whether x x $2 + 3 = 15 \therefore x = 6$, or the names of the rivers down the east coast of Africa, but set about programming my eye and hand to become precision instruments. But for what?

Watched by groups of curious cows, I would attempt a water-colour of Harrow-on-the-Hill. Damp the paper, flood on colour, guide it around a bit, tipping the board so it ran right – keeping it wet like the English weather. All weathers.

Winter would find me, collapsible stool in the snow, as I rendered Canterbury Cathedral, its spires iced like a Christmas cake, numb fingers gripping that most sensitive tool, a 2B pencil.

Pretty postcard stuff, even old girls do it, so what next?

I am sketching tired passengers on the Inner Circle Subway late at night, or looking giddily down into the lobby of the Victoria & Albert Museum from a gallery high up in the dome, attempting an upside-down view of classical columns and (impossible) of the elaborate curlicues of the great chandelier.

I was soon versed in the laws of precise perspective and could now do it intuitively and, so, avoid the geometry. We Westerners take perspective for granted, but when Leonardo painted *The Last Supper* he would not be so interested in the figures – routine character illustration to please the patron – as to demonstrate the newly developed trick of painting in perspective. The figures are seated in a deep chamber at eye-level, so a viewer feels he can actually walk into it. As remarkable then as the first showing of a film in Technicolor must have been to an audience in the thirties.

At first, to keep us in our place, we were only permitted to mix three basic colours; carmine red, Prussian blue and Indian yellow. As the latter is ground from camels' piss congealed in sand, one must resist licking the brush – useful training.

A 2B pencil rendering of Chelsea old church, before it was hit by a bomb in World War II.

We were all put through the mill. First shade and shadow on white cylinders and cubes, a sort of three-dimensional ABC. Then *still life*, which might be some grinning skull poised on an ancient book, or glassware, so we could chase highlights – fun using flake white.

Next the *antique*, plaster-casts of chopped-off ears and feet and, if we performed as expected, full-sized Greek statuary, the *Discus Thrower* or *Venus de Milo*, our replica of which was incongruously topped off with a floppy straw hat.

She was painted white, of course, to simulate marble. Painted to represent flesh, she would not be classed as ART.

Rather a joke, as when that stolid matron was in business as the figurehead of a Grecian ship, she would display rouge-red lips, blush-tinted cheeks and eye-shadow.

Innocently accepting marble as 'Art', I made a passable drawing of her (without the straw hat) and was moved up to Room 13 for *life drawing*, to be faced with unclothed human beings – maybe the crown of creation, in God's image, but damned difficult to draw. Warning. One can get away with a casual rendering of a boat or a bucket, but people, being secretly in love with their bodies, are 'experts' in that field.

What the Calvinists were so ashamed of

Rather a let down, to be faced with a sad middle-aged dear with sagging breasts, blobby body spreading on the plinth like a bladder of lard, her legs blotched as her blood gives up the effort of circulation. Difficult to locate the Greek ordered, muscular pattern under this blurred pink landscape; the only

A rather stolid dame in plaster.

18

visible point of reference being a prickly patch of pubic hair.

It can be done, I guess, if you are sufficiently obsessed with the image. A genius like Leli could render female thighs and behinds to simulate the delicacy of powder-dusted rose petals. However closely I placed my nose to the canvas, I could never detect how he managed it.

In one session, after I had flogged away at a charcoal rendering of a male model for an hour, while a little dribble of sweat slowly made its way down from his armpit, the instructor looked over my shoulder and remarked, "Really, Gardner, is THAT all you can see?"

Ants crept up my spine. Drawing should be an adventure of observation and discovery.

Stolen apples taste best

After the boring business of triangulating the outline of a hired model before she wobbled out of pose, another student and I would chivvy our 'donkeys' (stools designed to support a drawing board) near the windows hoping to catch a glimpse, through net curtains across the road, of a prim madam performing her afternoon toilet.

The model, posing ten feet away under an arc lamp with out-thrust hip and firm upturned breasts, was ignored, as a given.

The interpretation of what one *sees* depends on context. I discovered that even such a low form of life as a girl art student could, on occasion, trigger off a sense of arousal. Noticeable, when the more adventurous flirts discarded the then universal black stockings for flesh coloured, a break-through that put the geese in command for a while. Not at ease with real girls, I would fantasise — a rare exotic I had glimpsed poised on stiletto heels as she strutted proudly by with a flick of her silk clad buttocks — a demonstration of applied art, but beyond my reach like rosy apples in someone else's orchard.

One day I ventured a critical remark concerning one of the more extrovert student's girlfriends. This resulted in a fistfight in the snow in a quadrangle

called Bolton's Yard, organised by the school bully, when both protagonists acquired black eyes. All this to indicate that no one's life can be devoted entirely to art.

Though most of the students were struggling with juicy artwork in colour, I preferred working in line and tone, treating colours as an 'optional extra'. I have since learned that in this I was correct, as the bit of brain behind the eye is limited to *line*, *direction* and *angle*, for recognition. This may explain why young children first instinctively draw what they see in line, how a circle, two dots and a tick produce an immediate visual response, against which even a portrait by Rembrandt ends up as a lump of well-preserved meat. (We view it with prejudice, however, as it is a rendering of US.)

Prima donnas called experts

From time to time some art historian would turn up to manipulate us so that, with what intelligence we could muster, we conformed. *This* was accepted as good art, *that* was not. He would classify paintings like a bug hunter, explain how artist A had worked under the influence of artist B, when as likely as not it was under the influence of drink. He would expound at length, in the Ruskin manner, how a figure group or romantic setting had been composed by the artist to form a triangle that led the eye to a focal point. What the eye did after that was not revealed.

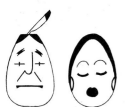

Stereotype characters.
Simple line treatment for an
exhibit in the Museum of Tolerance
(meaning intolerance) in Los Angeles.
The animated heads pop-up to
air their prejudices on sound.
Left to right: American Indian,
South American, WASP, Afro,
Orthodox, Opinionator,
Ditherer, Redneck.

A gaggle of youngsters learning to actually paint, we would refer to this as the 'fuck-all' point and, for light relief, pop a tablet of soap in the lecturer's tea-kettle.

We students were not aware of it at the time, but this guy was way off beam. Over in Paris, the Impressionists had already jettisoned contrived compositions. Why flog at realism now made too bloody mundane and completely 'unintellectual' by photography? So, they went over to paint-painting, using brilliant colours squeezed straight from the tube and, as cribs, adopting the happy accidents that occur in snapshots – with gratifying results.

Starting a students' monthly, named 'IT', and finding most students too lazy to submit the sophisticated and critical articles I had hoped for, I once inserted the following G-theory, between the obscure poems.

The grind-it-yourself period

Grinding each colour as one went along, and applying it with yolk of egg would result in the early painters filling in a mosaic of selected areas, using the colours they had just prepared. Then they would grind and lay an area with the next colour, and so on. This resulted in carefully mapped-out formal compositions, a sense of authority and control. Suitable for the accepted pagan and religious offerings of that time.

The oil-and-turps period

When the Venetians introduced oil as a medium, colours could be mixed on a palette as one worked. No constraints, so one could paint what one actually saw. The stiff, formal Virgin would now be posed by a compliant serving-girl.

Canaletto could sit in his blacked-out tent, overpainting an image of the Grand Canal projected onto his canvas through a lens, while the unromantic Dutch went for meaty portraits, household possessions and heavy compositions made up of rich food. As the food stayed still, they could take their time and render even the bloom on a grape.

The squeeze-a-tube period

Revolutions have often been triggered off by tradesmen.

Gütenberg invented printing and soon every man could interpret the Christian God to his own taste.

Winsor & Newton invented ready-mixed colours in lead tubes (with pretty labels), and soon anyone could interpret Art to their own taste.

No need to contrive settings in the studio, when one could grab a handful of tubes and paint landscape, or whatever, *on-the-spot.*

Painting became a genteel pastime for ladies including – when not being not amused – Queen Victoria and, not to be outdone, Winston Churchill during the Second World War – when not playing at soldiers.

Paint-as-paint period

Brilliant hues oozing out of tubes, dabs of colour, dazzle and light, paintings which made the solidly-shaded oils appear so heavy by contrast, they would never again be hung together in the same gallery.

Art gallery art was okay for students with a rich uncle or money in the bank. As my spending-money was limited to a few shillings a week – for cleaning mud off the rather smelly boots of two rednecks who were working on a nearby construction site and lodged with us – I concentrated on what was then termed 'commercial art'.

I had already come to the (erroneous) conclusion that what was worth doing artwise had already been priced, framed and hung, so why flog a dead horse?

To be fair, in Britain at that time art with a capital 'A' was at an all time low, while artwork for reproduction was developing apace.

Knocked way off track

One afternoon, I was happily dabbing away in a clutter of poster paints when I was interrupted by a messenger from fate, a school inspector breathing heavily in my ear, "Young man, would you like a job?"

Damn. I guessed at once that all this dedicated preparation had been no more than a dream, just as young girls who dream of becoming a leader in the *corps de ballet* end up mums – probably very nice mums, but that's not the point.

In a world apparently run by plump, comfortably-dressed school examiners, I was to take my place as, of all things, a *jewellery designer*. I experienced what my dog must feel when he gets above himself and is admonished with the order "Basket."

For Basket, read *Cartier* of Bond Street.

My stars may have been in collision just then. I was waiting at a street corner for a tramcar with my old man, when fate's second messenger arrived in the form of a demoniac tramp with piercing eyes, carrying a sign THE END OF THE WORLD IS NIGH. He accosted my Dad with, "Are you going to heaven?"

"No," was the response. "We are going to Wembley."

Pragmatic.

When my mother died, unexpectedly, a few days later, my old man, practised at evading the inevitable, trimmed his sails and made course for a monied widow. She turned out to be all of six feet tall, broad to boot, and would collapse heavily on the nearest sofa whenever I was around.

I took the hint and decamped – to go it alone among the eight million other creepy-crawlers that infest the sprawling chimney-potted brickery called London.

THE POSTER PAINT STYLE
An on-the-spot rendering of Paddington Station in the steam age.
This technique demanded bold placing of blocks of flat colour;
in this example, on a background of brown packing paper. Alas,
I would soon be devoting my time to placing precious stones
for the necks and arms of wealthy women.

MISDIRECTION

The currency of adoration

It was 1923. I had reached the mature age of fifteen and had two stolen treasures – a black woolly rug, painstakingly made by my Gran, and a capacious Gladstone bag.

This last friendly object only comes into the story as a reminder that I had what is called a background, but this job, for lack of other commitments, soon became my life.

At that time I was unaware of the existence of an exotic world where the Establishment acted out an expensive charade.

To be seen entering Cartier of Bond Street was a mark of status for the gentry, or money-men and their courtesans. To the latter 'diamonds were a girl's best friend', their ornamental purpose a side issue. A pity, as Cartier designs had a distinctive style.

Jacques Cartier, who ran the London branch, decided to train a young designer in that style. The Paris branch offered a thoroughbred French boy, but Jacques saw no reason why a local boy would not do as well. In fact, he rather liked the reserve of the Englishmen he had met.

So, one bleak Monday morning, unaware that I was to be Jacques Cartier's stake in the future, I arrived at the front entrance (my first mistake) wearing a reach-me-down suit and stiff collar that rode high and chafed my neck (my second mistake). To a Frenchman I was an artist, and artists need not subscribe to what the bourgeoisie consider proper.

Monsieur Boulangier, the chief salesman (who, two years later, was knocked on the head for a tray full of rings by an old Etonian of good family) averted his eyes and I was quickly steered into the inner room. To him I was "just one of Jacques Cartier's crazy ideas." At least Jacques Cartier had ideas.

I was set up in a corner of his private office, which was rather like an antechamber to a Louis XVI boudoir, to work at a little *ormolu* table under a pink-ruched, silk-shaded lamp, within range of the maestro's enquiring eye. Though scared

Drawn under stress for a BBC documentary, an intrusive TV camera peering close-up over my shoulder!

The subtle planes of a human figure,
seen as a series of cylinders and cubes.

stiff, I soon found something I could hang onto. Jacques was what we then called a gentleman. He was excitable, had compassion (or I wouldn't have survived) and he lived for design. Beauty of form conceived for no other purpose than to decorate women's bodies – and look expensive – was an unexpected angle that more than alarmed me. I soon discovered that a young apprentice was not expected to conjure loveliness out of space – only God can do that.

I must learn to use cribs. Everything grows from something that grew before and the room contained a library of things that had gone before; Chinese carpets, Celtic bronze-work, Japanese sword hilts, arabesques – designed to delight emperors, samurai and caliphs.

Meanwhile, Jacques Cartier would greet notable visitors in the manner of an ambassador, but he was more concerned with design than with people.

In the middle of a polite conversation with some expensive female, he would glance at my labours in the corner, then stride over and exclaim, "What is that you are doing, Gardinier? *Dis-donc* that is not a c-u-r-v-e. See, a curve has purpose, it starts here – so – but it expresses, how you say – an intention."

Ignoring the spoiled lady, now busy with a jewelled vanity case and intent on the care of her eyelashes, he would open the glazed bookcase, bring down a leather-bound volume of *Meubles Chinois*, and open it at an illustration of a black lacquered table. I must observe how the legs terminated. They were not amputated with a saw, but shaped with three tight little curves, which touched the floor lightly, as though politely saying, "I am a table poised in my own space and time; alter one line and I will become just an assembly of bits like all those other assemblies of bits."

"Tight curves that are enclosing, as on my finger nail, you see?" he would exclaim. In fact, he had flat finger nails, but I would do my damnedest to see.

Jacques would then return to the lady, as though such diversions were the most natural thing in the world.

Under his tuition, I soon became so involved in the meaning of line that I had no time to worry about the meaning of life, at least not from nine-to-six weekdays and half-day Saturday.

After the free run at art school, sticking little bits of glass on black wax while the great world outside went by was closing my mind, so of an evening I would be found maybe in the Life Room at Westminster where, to the distant boom of Big Ben, Meninsky interpreted the model as a bold construction of cylinders and cubes. He had something.

The model the next night would be in costume, to my relief, and Randolph Schwab would mince over, pin a fresh sheet of paper over my tentative effort and, commencing with the left foot, slowly work up the figure to produce a drawing as precise as silver-point – like a conjuring trick. He had something.

Or I would be miserably preoccupied with a pile of tin cans and scraps of lino, trying to translate them into a painting in the abstract manner. Miserably, because I did not wish to disappoint my instructor and god of the moment, E. McKnight Kauffer, who had surprised England with bold avant-garde poster techniques, then seen only on the Continent.

I had come to realise that seeing comes from what goes on in the mind. Drawing leads to *seeing*, so I kept on doing it until I got migraine and was advised to take a few nights off and practice leisure.

I have always considered leisure to be retirement (God forbid) on the instalment plan, so I would read books on philosophy under the mistaken impression that they held a clue to the meaning of the Universe.

At last Jacques Cartier gave me his seal of approval and moved me up to the design department. Here I was to sit on a stool perched on a girder which, I discovered, supported the great clock that used to hang out over Bond Street.

I sat there so long I got to recognise street girls on their regular Bond Street beat, strutting like wader birds at the Zoo.

To my innocent eye, they appeared to be identical with the 'real' ladies who entered our shop – until they spoke, "Hello, dearie."

Innocent in a blunderland

Now a complete loner, I was startled to read in the newspaper that my old man had been taken to court for breach of promise. 'He was an expert in love.' A journalistic phrase was, alas, his only claim to fame. Considering this previously unrevealed

E. McKNIGHT KAUFFER POSTER
Once, visiting Pick – a poster for the underground – waiting in reception. Pick called me in having mistaken me for McKnight Kauffer. Was I thrilled!

talent on my father's side, I decided it was time I took my place as a man of the world. (Pause, for laughter.)

After conning various street girls, some old enough to be my mother, I inveigled the one in the fur coat and highest heels up a secret stairway, lined with posters, to my apartment. Black waxed oak, scarlet enamelled floor, midnight blue walls and a mix of art books.

I donned a silk dressing gown and puffed my pipe in the manner of Sherlock Holmes.

But the sight of that insolent white body laid out as an offering on my woolly rug was like being challenged by a superior enemy, and with no retreat. Never again.

So I remained bounded by four walls, a drawing board and a collection of second-hand books – that is until one of Cartier's designers, a Miss Winter, decided I needed a push out into the real world. Twenty years my senior, she mixed with the St John's Wood intellectuals, considered herself avant-garde and didn't mind showing it – a wide-brimmed black hat, flowing cloak and monocle. She introduced me to the Diaghilev Ballet and the latest up-market ideas on religion, socialism and sex, about which, to my astonishment, people held different opinions.

I did once brush with a 'pie-in-the-sky' group called The Friends of Russia, as this made me eligible for a free trip to the Paris World Fair, including morning hand-outs of caviare and vodka. But everything must be paid for, even in a Peoples' Republic, so I must march round a cycle-track to the applause of a crowd of devotees, one clenched fist in the air as I sang (my version of) the *Internationale.*

> '*The Peoples' flag in palest pink,*
> *It's not as red as you would think'*

Unfortunately, the effect was rather spoiled, our muddle-minded lot having mislaid their red flag.

No red flags at Cartier's, but they occasionally hit problems.

In Cartier's showroom, the salesmen and their acolytes, who stood by to keep a watchful eye on the trays of jewels, would be impeccably tailored like successful bankers. I would be wearing a red bow tie and Harris tweeds (obtained through a back street trader in gentlemen's cast-off suits) having learned, while serving a short apprenticeship at the rue de la Paix in Paris, that the French prefer an artist to look like an artist. I am called to the showroom.

After scrubbing my finger nails and checking that my fly is in order, I stand with diffidence, one pace back, free to observe the goings on of the 'upper crust'.

The avant garde Miss Winter, who later let the side down by marrying a suburban stockbroker.

Visitors

There might be a smart female in a cloche hat, with sleek legs, arching her instep to show off a beautiful hand-made shoe by Rayne. After admiring the silk-clad shin, the dapper assistant would slip off-stage to check the lady's financial standing at her . . . or her boyfriend's bank. Onc of his tasks was to know who knew who in *Who's Who* and, if it came to it, in Debrett's *Peerage.*

They would be discussing anything but diamonds. The season at Deauville, dear Lady Astor, or the scandalous behaviour of Isadora Duncan, the unorthodox ballet dancer who occasionally revealed her body parts but, alas, died tragically when her flowing scarf wrapped round the rear wheel of a Bugatti sports car.

Or I would find the Meyers examining designs for diamond halters to hang round the necks of their three full-busted daughters. The old man, a diamond dealer in a silk top hat, would doze off. Beady-eyed Mrs Meyer, dressed in a full skirt like a character from a Dickens novel and very much awake, would mutter, "Still more diamonds you say? Batons and navettes?" Then, coolly hitching up her voluminous skirt to

Elegant and untouchable, with the essential wealthy boyfriend . . . and handmade shoes by Rayne.

reveal a similar silk undergarment, she would thrust her hand into a concealed pocket to lay on the table a row of little white envelopes containing the diamonds.

I soon learned that, in spite of their chic and exquisite manners, many of our clients were hard centred and, used to the genteel behaviour obligatory for the under-privileged classes, I would be quite shocked by the goings on of people self-confident enough to ignore criticism . . . and guys like me.

I was instructed not to speak unless spoken to and then only to express an opinion on design. Nevertheless, it could sometimes be a near thing.

I once designed a tiara for the great prima donna – Dame Nellie Melba – but she requested white sapphires, not diamonds. These would sparkle well enough under the theatrical spotlights, but off-stage anyone with half an eye would recognise them for what they were. She chatted to me quite knowledgeably about the design then, in a quick aside, said, "They will look just like real diamonds, won't they?" Boulangier, who was negotiating the deal, prickled with apprehension, fearful of a later accusation that we had misled her.

I doubted that the famous singer would even think of such a trick, but Cartier, open to this kind of ploy, could not afford an adverse whispering campaign in the powder room, where autocratic 'ladies' let their hair down.

Top people would be ushered into Jacques' inner sanctuary where he would greet them like family. A wealthy Parsee?

"How do you do, Mr Baba, and how are Mrs Baba and all the little Babas?"

Jacques was not, of course, aware that the cheeky switchboard girl on the top floor would at that moment be answering calls with her skirt over her face, while one of the younger salesmen, a *Cresta Run* athlete, was panting with exertion between her legs. Very polite, "Cartier here. Lady Cab . . . sorry, Lady Cabstanley. Would you . . . please . . . hold for a moment while I . . . while I connect you to Mr Fin . . . Finster . . . stop it! . . . Finstervaldt. You're through." Click.

The staff photographer and invited guests would be viewing this daily affair through an aperture in the dark-room partition. While this innocent diversion was being enacted on the top floor, down below the dignified doorman would be bowing in an Indian Prince.

Head ornament of the period.
Not for Dame Nelly Melba, but a dream goddess.

The Gaekwar of Baroda? I had fun designing his crown jewels, the headpiece dominated by the largest diamond I had ever seen, shallow and yellowish, but it would sparkle well enough in the Indian sun. This heavy, jewelled crown was designed round a traditional Baroda turban that looked for all the world like a pink trussed chicken, but I did my best with it and guess it has now been relegated to some dusty museum with other symbols of Empire.

Next, an Indian Prince of high standing who had been given the golden handshake – two bodyguards, typecast in oversized raincoats, patrolling the street outside. In India it is the custom for a man to wear a single large earring, and I would hold my breath as the prince screwed one more and more tightly into his equerry's ear to check how much pain the man could endure without showing it. A nice guy, who had an artificial hill constructed in his palace grounds, so that his spoiled son could charge up it at full throttle in his Lancia car – that is, when he was not busy fucking himself into an early grave between the knees of the girl population within a twenty mile radius.

In contrast, the Prince of Wales, diffident and no bodyguards, purchasing a jewellery piece which, we would discover later, was for the pleasure of a certain lady in the USA.

Any trifling incident can become a crisis when one is fiddling around with little pieces of cut diamond. One lunchtime, alone in the design office, it was rather too hot for comfort. Climbing onto my desk to open the skylight, carefully placing my feet to avoid the little trays of assorted diamonds with which it was littered, I found the wretched catch had jammed.

I gave it a real clout. It sprang free, only to fall back with a crash, scattering fragments of window pane and diamonds, sparkling as they filtered through a beam of sunlight. Then all was still.

Most of the stones were small 'batons' (little rectangular cut diamonds easily confused with the bits of glass) and 'mêlée' diamonds, so small that they needed to be weighed in bulk on a jeweller's balance.

Faced with the kind of impossible task witches set little girls in *Grimm's Fairy Tales*, I thought for a bit and devised a system. After locking the door I took off my clothes, shaking out a shower of sparklers in the process, then meticulously wiped every surface, peeling up the lino to chivvy years of accumulated dust from the cracks, pausing now and again to retrieve stray stones that stuck to my bare feet. Only then did I open the door and a team of us set about separating the glitter from dust and diamonds from glass. Quite a few escaped us.

What was I doing getting into such a state over little chips of carbon? But working with skilled craftsmen in any trade is worthwhile and the men in the workshop were top in their profession, mounting stones in platinum which was hardly revealed from the front, but the reverse would be a beautiful exercise in miniature engineering.

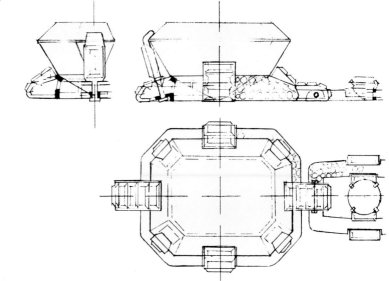

Mount for the centre stone of the Emerald Collection. I was permitted to observe the craftsman on a quiet Saturday, as he mounted the claws so as not to put undue pressure on the fragile stone . . . and make the tea.

No buyers existed for some of the collections, which Jacques, in his enthusiasm, would have elegantly mounted. The few men on this planet who could afford them would be more interested in the money-market than beautifying women.

Living in a world of visual images, I found the girls of my own age group disconcertingly unlike goddesses; they didn't trouble about how they walked, or straightened a twisted stocking. They even whistled.

When a goddess did make an appearance in the showroom, her manners and mode of talk would be of another world. The barrier between my visual image of beauty and reality was as impenetrable as the plate glass windows of the London stores that separated the static mannequins, exotically posed, from the meaty females who strutted like hens on the littered pavements outside.

One autumn, Cartier and Worth got together a collection and put on a mannequin show at the Mayfair, then the top hotel. I was deputed to apply the selected ornaments, under the cynical eye of a hired detective.

In the twenties, it was cheeky to roll a silk stocking to just below the knee, so it would be revealed occasionally by the swing of a slit skirt. Jacques Cartier decided to gild the lily, so next evening I knelt in a private dressing room while one of the goddesses rolled down a sheer stocking and posed, pointing a powdered knee. My job was to decorate each knee-cap with a pretty picture. I decided on romantic vignettes in the Worcester China style – Windsor Castle from the river, and Arundel in its setting of verdant trees.

She paused for a moment to give me a private view.

34

I took a deep breath, then, heady with perfume vaporised by the warmth of her body, experimentally stroked her knee-cap with a trembling thumb – to discover that the flesh on a goddess's knee-joint puckers with a cobweb of tiny creases, then stretches taut like any other. This posed a problem, but by wiping the area with alcohol, then mixing ox-gall with the paint, and taking my time, I made quite a neat job of it. After I had blown gently on each knee until the decoration was dry, the gilded lily swung about to examine the effect in a mirror, while I knelt – acutely aware of a little mole that moved disturbingly when she tensioned her calf.

She paused, knees together for a moment, to give me a private view, then minced off, slender ankles delicately flicking as she balanced her weight on the highest of heels, with the practised poise which comes naturally to any African village woman – or a dairy cow for that matter.

As I collected my paints and wiped the smudges off the floor with a grubby handkerchief, I had a depressing feeling that I was at the wrong end of the whole business.

For six years I had been designing costly halters for the necks of status seekers' wives, delicate chains dangling phallic symbols to circle the thighs of their mistresses, showy regalia for princes and, at the cheaper end of the trade, rings for the fat fingers of bishops.

Now I had seen my work decorating the bodies of beautiful women – pity it had to be professional models at ten guineas an hour, plus expenses.

I decided to give it all up and go on tramp.

I aired this notion so often in the following months that one of my fellow designers lost patience, "G," he said, "either go or shut up about it." At this moment we were taking a short-cut past the rear of some commercial buildings. I stopped in my tracks, pointed to an iron fire escape that zigzagged up the back of one and said, "I swear by that there fire escape that I will be gone in two weeks."

The die had been cast.

The 30's

LONER HITS LUCKY

No man had yet invented the jet
Innocence in a still innocent world
Landed, like a hooked fish
Adventure into flight

Meanwhile . . .

Film: *Gone with the Wind*

Lindbergh baby kidnapped

Duke of Windsor abdicates

Pop song: 'The Lady is a Tramp'

Picasso's *Guernica*

Empire State Building completed

Marlene Dietrich in *The Blue Angel*

The first jet: Frank Whittle

Hindenberg airship disaster

FBI shoots Dillinger

Sophie Loren is born

Disney's *Snow White and the Seven Dwarfs*

SS *Queen Mary* launched

Hitler guarantees not to attack USSR

Stalin triggers famine in the USSR

Huxley's *Brave New World*

New York defeats Cincinnatti in World Series

Hannibal, one of the bi-planes that did the regular cross Channel trip from
Croydon to Paris. I knew them intimately from the engineer who designed them,
by drawing them, but could not afford to be a passenger.

No man had yet invented the jet

True, a few of the leisured well-to-do would hop over to the Continent by air from a grass field called an aerodrome, recognised by the windsock hanging from a mast at one corner. Once aboard the heavy prop bi-plane, they would be tended, like queen ants, by debutantes, the daughters of real ladies – who were not yet extinct.

When Cartier dispatched me to Paris the Continent of Europe was still 'picture postcard' territory. To a callow youth of my class, accustomed to streets patrolled by the comfortable English 'bobby' and to looking on the occasional motor car as an interesting novelty, not to ride in let alone possess, the journey had been as remarkable as, I suppose, falling off the edge of the earth would be to a 'flat-earther'.

First, smoke flipping past the window to the clickety-click of a steam train. Then Dover and a slow ferry across the Channel, to end up in the dining car of a wagon-lit express, where lunch was not a refuelling chore, but a leisurely and considered titillation of well-trained taste buds. The brown sugar I piled on my melon proved to be ginger, which made my hair stand on end.

Arriving was like Alice stepping *Through the Looking Glass*, everything the same . . .

yet somehow different

More to the point, as disconcerting as finding myself in the second reel of a foreign film, all the characters spoke rapidly in French, but with no subtitles.

In those days tramping was an exercise only practised by the inveterate moneyless hobo, so I faced the idea of tramping across a Europe full of foreigners with some trepidation.

SAN GIMIGNANO
*Carbon pencil
on Fabriano paper,
background acrylic wash.*

40

Innocence in a still innocent world

A lift to Tunis on the ferry. Not a penny in his pocket, but appears unconcerned.

In a Jermyn Street window a pair of boots, ankle deep in a tank of water and looking very expensive, grinned up at me as I passed by, and for good reason. They carried the recommendation of a guy who had foot-slogged across the Gobi Desert. An omen. I dived in and squandered twenty per cent of my wherewithal, then a natty skiing jacket, cavalry twill trousers, a Bergen rucksack. I crossed my fingers and risked the fare, third class, to Florence.

From then on I would walk, conscience riding on my back in the form of a drawing-board. A reminder that I pretend to be an artist.

In those days there were few cars and no tourists, so I had the Italian landscape (and myself) to myself.

For the next year I followed tracks from one hill village to the next and occasionally, when motivated by a sense of guilt, sketching.

My first effort was triggered off by the sight of the towers of San Gimignano, a medieval Manhattan. Climbing the steps into an empty, echoing town hall and after some hairy moments on rickety ladders, I arrived at the top of the highest tower to find it ruined and grass-grown. Sitting, legs over the edge and gripping my drawing-board against the buffeting wind, I managed to produce a fair 'looking down' perspective.

Not too many such breaks, as I planned to make twenty to thirty miles a day, completing a half of it before breakfast so I could observe whatever the afternoon dealt me.

I soon got the hang of the tramper's rhythm, pace following pace in those seven league boots, but when the path crossed a stream I would allow myself to rest a while, and maybe inspect the map. However desolate a spot, the track would be marked in with a cartographer's care. Someone had been there before me. Friendly.

Something of an honour to be walking through history. To stand alone where Leonardo had stood when he watched his obedient assistant flap the bat-like wings of his bird-machine. I see it rise, stall and then, with his hopes, crash. To pause at a stone marking the spot where the early Christians met St Paul on the path to Rome, then relax and make a drawing of an ancient oak *(The Golden Bough)* on the verge of Lake Nemi, home of the pagan gods. No gods, but the lake still as a mirror.

The ancient Italian villages were invariably perched picturesquely on steep hill tops, against marauders with picks and axes, I guess, but a test of endurance for the footslogger.

By the cool of evening I would wearily climb up to such a village, rather like the Pied Piper of Hamelin, accompanied by a band of cheeky urchins and disreputable dogs, excited at the sight of this blond stranger from nowhere humping a pack – then, at a given moment, they would race on ahead to announce my approach.

The peasants, who would gaze balefully at any group of 'outsiders', were friendly enough to a loner. He posed no threat. In the dusk, field workers, dressed in drab black and perched on the back-ends of diminutive donkeys, would be making their way up from the valleys for their evening meal – to be away again at the first glimmer of dawn.

The Dante Bridge at Florence.
Prout's brown ink in a Waterman pen,
brush washed in some areas.

PONTE DI ST. TRINITA - FLORENCE.

Handsome, sun-browned young men throwing cheeky remarks at the girls who, graceful as madonnas, have, alas, spent the day destroying their slender beauty breaking rough ground in the burning sun. The older females, their lined faces hooded with black drapes follow on, folded umbrellas balanced on their heads. A long way from the cosmetic artifices of Bond Street.

Locating an inn, which might be in a narrow entry down a flight of rough steps, I find, under a low vaulted ceiling, a tiled kitchen illuminated by an open log fire, over which an enormous black pot hangs by a chain – supper. An old crone with hooked nose and shaggy white hair chases the screaming kids back up the steps with a switch broom. A witch? For me, if lucky, a scalding hot bowl of chestnut and rabbit stew, using my own knife on the coarse bread. A few lira on the table, I then find my way to the edge of the village to set up my minuscule tinker-tent, which I had camouflaged with an abstract of greens and browns, so it would merge into the background. This did not prevent my having to throw stones to deter hysterical dogs.

Anyone on tramp soon learns to detest dogs.

A domestic interior at Sienna,
as full of history as a museum.
Carbon pencil and colour wash
on pale grey paper.

Haunted by Benvenuto

Prior to sleeping and for continuity, I was re-reading Benvenuto Cellini's autobiography. What a guy. A braggadocio who, when not bedding compliant females, would be fending off competitors with sword-play, sculpting figures for Louis IV or designing jewellery for the Medici.

In those days designers had *cultured* clients – and, apparently, a whale of a time.

He describes in detail how, when casting the first large bronze figure ever, the metal wouldn't set. Cursing his assistants he rose from his bed, broke into a friend's house, took all the pewter he could find and threw it into the mix. Then the thatch of his workshop caught fire, but, alas, when the mould was broken away, the figure – *Perseus holding the head of Medusa* – lacked one foot. So he modelled and cast a replacement, annealing it invisibly in place.

Another of his tall stories?

PROUT'S BROWN INK AGAIN
Recording interesting details builds up
a store of images in one's sub-conscious
– maybe to pop up later, modified,
as an IDEA. Essential.

Cellini's Perseus at Florence.
Arrow indicates where foot was annealed,
as described in his autobiography.

When in Florence examining the statue, I could just make out a line of lighter bronze round one ankle. Gosh, one could see him doing it.

He describes how, when riding in haste from Rome to escape an enticing maiden whose grasping mother was greedy for money, he met up with a young man named Solosmeo. This guy invited him up to the nearby monastery at Monte Casino, where he was working on a sculpture.

By an amazing chance I passed down that same road next day. A spurious twentieth century shadow of Cellini, I climbed up to the monastery perched on a hill top, as ever, to be bedded in a simple cell for the night. The only decoration, a small crucifix. Next morning a monk, for a few lira, led me to view Solosmeo's work.

Ten years later I happened to pass by Monte Casino once again, but in uniform and following a white tape to avoid stepping on land mines. This was shortly after the Allies had captured the Mount, a shattered ruin in a landscape of shell holes and blasted trees. Frogs were croaking happily in fetid pools, stinking from the litter of decaying corpses.

No corpses on this trip, as I tramped slowly down the map of Italy, once following the line of the ancient Appian Way. Between the grasses, cobbles showed grooves worn by Roman wagons. But an omen, as two of dictator Mussolini's fighter planes circled above against the blue sky like brightly coloured insects.

This Roman road ran so straight that I felt like an insect myself, creeping slowly down a line scored across the landscape by some ancient giant.

Pausing to sketch, I soon discovered that most Italians are programmed to enjoy the visual arts from childhood. This gave me a sense of belonging, but could also be rather a bore.

When I settled on a pile of bricks to produce a rendering of the Forum in Rome, such a crowd of interested idlers gathered around me that two city policemen – full musical comedy regalia, Napoleonic headgear, fierce moustaches and voluminous capes – stood imperiously to either side, arms outstretched to prevent the press of onlookers obstructing my line of sight. Disconcerted, I doodled a bit just for show, then collapsed my folding easel, slung the drawing board on my back and walked as calmly as possible off stage.

Turning a corner, I glanced over my shoulder to see them still there, myopically observing my retreat. A critical lot; thank goodness it wasn't a bad drawing.

Every day developed a pattern of its own. Routine was once interrupted when I covered five miles, but only advanced two, as I joined a peasant steering an obstinate bull in the way it should go. As a result I arrived at my destination after dark. Too late to erect the tinker-tent, I wandered up the village street which, in the moonlight, looked for all the world like the stage setting of a modern ballet; whitewashed walls with the occasional wrought iron window grille and patterned with angular black shadows.

A solitary mule tied to a rail indicated the inn, so I entered by a small doorway to face, in the warm light, the largest bar I had ever seen. A sudden silence as the occupants all stared at this odd intruder.

Selecting an imposing guy in a flat-brimmed hat and with a pronounced belly I asked, in my best Italian, could he please give me supper and a bed for the night. No response. I tried it again with clearer articulation, but he shook his head. Nothing for it but to go into the mime routine, pointing to my mouth then closing my eyes with head resting on hands to indicate 'sleep'.

Ten years later, Monte Cassino devastated.

45

Uproarious laughter.

I was shocked. Country people have natural manners and would never ridicule a lone visitor. The imposing guy at whom I had aimed this performance then pointed to my side where, previously unnoticed, the tubby little innkeeper was grinning up at me.

The penny dropped. I had come in by the wrong door and, standing *behind* the bar, was doing my mime act at the sheriff. No charge.

My memory of the aftermath is hazy, but I recall the innkeeper and I peeing against one of those white 'ballet setting' walls in the moonlight, after he had shown me off round the village as one would a performing bear – wine wherever we stopped – then staggering back to the inn. Here he doused his armpits with perfume while describing the virtues (if that is the correct word) of some likely girls he had on tap. Thrusting him onto his bed, repeatedly saying *"mañana"* (which, come to think of it, is Spanish) until he lay still, I wedged a chair against the double doors of my own vaulted room in case he came to . . . and slept.

Next morning the only sign of life in the inn was the buzzing of bluebottles, which signalled the purpose of an angle at the dead-end of a tiled corridor. Leaving a few lira on the bar top, I decided that in future I must avoid involvement with those intrusive organisms called *people.*

Food for the ants?

Chased by scudding clouds, I trudged mountain tracks to the cacophony of barking guard-dogs excited at my intrusion. Slithering feet first down a stony scree I end up walled in by a volcanic crater I had not noticed on the map. I take shelter in a rock cleft like a half drowned rat, while lightning crackles around me and thunder rebounds from the crater walls as though the elements aim to scare me . . . they do.

Cheered by a glimpse of sunlight, I decide on a diversion and follow the trace of a road which, if I have it right on the map, will take me over a pass in the mountains. This being hard earth and not a map, the road, after twisting round rock outcrops for some miles . . . peters out.

I am unexpectedly faced with three tough-looking unshaven desperados squatting, with guns across their knees, at the base of what, I guess, was once a fortified dwelling. They focus on me as I approach with half closed eyes. Maybe they aim to shoot rabbits but, just in case they take me for a rabbit, I slope 'purposefully' off to the left, to discover in no time at all that I am blindly following goat tracks that lead nowhere.

Hill tops also lead nowhere, so there is nothing for it but to make my way up a steep incline, over its rocky top and slither down the reverse slope to land knee deep in a stream. I climb the next, to slide feet first down its other side – throwing my pack ahead to make a way through the prickly vegetation – and end up ankle deep in the next stream. A pause for breath as I size up the next obstacle and so on, and so on, and on; realising too late that no man attempts a diagonal path across the steep foothills of a mountain range.

After some hours I pass a long-deserted woodman's hut. No tracks. By dusk I am taking short spurts, say, to that tree and flop, then to that distant rock and just make it. No option but to struggle on, or be food for the ants.

It is now dark and I must have covered fifteen miles as the crow flies (lucky bird) until at dusk I finally collapse by what at last might be a hilltop track.

Blundering into the fifteenth century

I come to, to the clop-clop of an approaching horse, then make out its rider in dark silhouette. He dismounts, tut-tuts, humps my pack on his saddle and leads me – clinging to a stirrup – to a low farmstead set in the mountain side. Biblical.

A barn-like interior, lit by a log fire, inhabited by three generations of family, a cow, two goats, a flurry of hens and – a manger.

They accept me, as in scattered areas any isolated farmhouse will serve as a hostelry. Soon revived by a bowl of piping hot soup and that coarse grey bread I find difficult to swallow, I am scribbling in my diary in the light of a small still flame under an icon of the Virgin and Child.

Then up a ladder to the hay loft, where I am politely handed a wooden rake to make my bed alongside other sleeping males.

The Castel del Ova,
Vesuvius smoking in the background.
Ink and colour wash on tinted paper.

Disturbed by a whispering and muttering below, I peep down to see two shadowy figures emptying my pack in the flickering firelight.

The cotton tinker tent, woollen socks, a book, paints and pencils and finally my bank, comprising a column of coins tied in a handkerchief to form a neat cylinder. To them a small fortune.

To these peasants travellers cheques were unknown and the wealth of silver coins I carried, each valued at five dollars, were a complete rarity.

I hold my breath as they weigh it in their hands . . . then to my relief, replace everything as they found it. Curiosity.

Come morning and the place is deserted except for the older women tending animals and children. Granddad, in spite of his arched back, reaches up to a dusty bottle in a secret niche and pours me a thimble of sweet liqueur. Such an honourable gesture I feel a lump in my throat.

A young goatherd is waiting to see me on my way and I soon realise that I may be good at artwork, but am useless when it comes to driving goats. At a drinking hole I present him with my spare Swiss penknife. He is at a loss for words – comparable at home to presenting a complete stranger with a new Mercedes car.

Way below, a beautiful valley, cultivated patches, scattered hamlets and the cypress-lined road leading south, all swept by the slow moving shadows of fleecy clouds.

Some hours later, after zigzagging down innumerable tumbled-down terraces, I have dumped my pack and am sunning myself at rest on the coping of an ancient village fountain, sketching some architectural detail to the untranslatable chatter of a group of heavily draped village dames. They pause from flogging wet washing to stare, as an arrogant youth in Fascist uniform saunters over, *"La sua carta d'identita signore, per favore."* Where am I going and for what purpose?

A threat? No. I am a stranger on the scene and unaccountable. Everyone in a Fascist state must be accounted for. My route to date is probably pegged out at Security HQ, as Mussolini, like the Vatican's God before him, even records the fall of a sparrow.

If there is such a map, they must have lost me as I approached Naples when, at long last, after months of tramping and minor adventures, I avoided a mile of city slums by boarding a tramcar. The sense of speed was exhilarating. What unimagined luxury. And what a lovely way to arrive, casually stepping off the tram like a local.

See Naples and die

I guess I'll die anyway, but thrilled at the prospect of spending my first night in civilised comfort I scanned 'Accommodation Available' as, under Fascist law, all hotel rooms must be listed. This being Naples, I guess I selected the cheapest bed on offer in the Western World and, so, worthy of record.

Passing through a typical entry, sizeable enough to pass on an elephant, howdah and all, I found myself in a paved yard enclosed by a high, rectangular light-well, which echoed with screams, shouts and argument, overlaid by canned opera and children quarrelling. A distant square of blue sky could only be seen through a criss-cross of washing lines. Okay so far.

Up a once-grand stairway, which got steeper and narrower as one climbed, to the fifth floor.

A sad, slow-witted girl at the top eyed my pack suspiciously then, with a dead cigarette hanging from her lower lip, indifferently kicked a loose floor-tile back in place as she led me to where a section of the corridor had been partitioned off with plywood to take a bed. All mine.

The décor was remarkable. Every surface, including the ceiling, had been pasted over with blue and white striped wrapping paper, a cut made around the door with a blunt instrument so it would open. A rectangle of paper had been peeled away to reveal a fly-blown pane of glass to admit light.

Some bright urchin, in the process of sealing in the bugs, had unwittingly produced this smart décor *à la* Cecil Beaton.

The bed would already be occupied by little beasties out for my blood, so I laid the sleeping bag on the floor (a ploy too obvious to deceive Neapolitan fleas), pulled off my boots and told my legs that, at last, they would have a break from foot slogging . . . together we had 'done' Italy!

There is a complex of narrow streets along the waterfront which the *Baedeker* guide advises visitors in carriages to view in passing, but not to enter. Here I located digs rented out by an impoverished family who still clung to their up-market past, the table napkins being heavily embroidered with coronets. What I at first took to be a 'mummy' in the corner, draped in black, I found to my discomfort to be the countess, who followed my every movement with beady little eyes.

This conniving old ancient was convinced I was the son of an English 'milord' and considered me a catch for her anaemic granddaughter who, alas, had a face like looking into the back of a tablespoon but, big deal, blonde hair and so was also considered a great catch. Damn.

A coward when it comes to close contact with the female of the species, I adopted avoidance action and settled in for Christmas.

Huddled in a tattered raincoat stuffed with newspapers against the cold, I sketched the Neapolitan street scene. Once, in the slum quarter a woman screamed at her children who arrived with a charcoal brazier so I could warm my dead fingers. I find people who experience poverty are the most inclined to be kindly.

Later, when I innocently asked for a cup of tea, I was directed to a druggist across town, where the proprietor brewed the herb over a spirit flame in a laboratory beaker. This sip of home must have induced nostalgia, as I then risked what remained of my cash on a can of genuine English marmalade . . . a final Christmas treat.

No cash left, I shouldered my pack and boarded the ferry (steerage class) for Tunis – African territory and very French; but only after a last hurried watercolour sketch of the romantic Castel del Ova.

Years later, when I paid a visit to my old haunt, it wasn't there. Allied bombers had wiped it and, I guess, many of that mix of bent, straight, lively and, on occasion, generous Neapolitans off the map.

Note the trams and horse carriages. Cars had not yet arrived to destroy the atmosphere. In Prout's brown ink, wet washed, on tinted paper.

51

Another continent, and various types of hunger

As I landed with one mildewed five franc coin in my pocket, I risked a night at a three star hotel where they would be unlikely to ask an Englishman for money up front. It worked.

After all, being an ideas man is a risk business. In this case, I knew that a friend in the UK had sold some of my drawings and that a money order was awaiting me at the Tunis Post Office. An exciting moment next morning when I walked up to the grille and claimed it.

"Comment vous appelez-vous encore?" The postmaster shuffled envelopes again, *"Il n'y a rien pour vous ici."*

Roughly translated, "We have nothing here for you." Hell.

After a number of visits, the guy at the Post Office eventually located my envelope where it had been lying for some months covered in dust. By then the money order barely covered my bill at the hotel . . . where I was already suspect and avoiding the eye of the man at reception. So, back to square one.

I was looking moodily at the café over the road, where I had planned to celebrate sudden affluence, when a German student who had overheard my predicament suggested I put up in his apartment until I was solvent . . . that is if I would vacate it while he was entertaining girl-friends. Okay by me; not then knowing the measure of his virility.

Good news. The manager of the local *Bon Marché* store, who I met in a café, agreed to put on a show of my pictures.

Bad news. My room mate warned me that the police were hunting for me. (An alien artist is not permitted to sell his work on French territories.)

I left hurriedly and joined up with an unemployed Belgian engineer who had a camera, to act as his photo retoucher. Apart from taking revolting pornographic close-ups of his wife, he proposed acting as portraitist to the officers of the Foreign Legion. Okay by me. (This was before colour film and, so, one of my jobs would be to colour-tint sepia prints.)

As these officers were a sensitive ethnic mix, it was necessary to view each guy to get the colour of his eyes and colour-match his skin. This meant frantic trips across desert tracks to visit Legion outposts, mounted precariously on the back of a powerful Harley Davidson motorcycle. Four headlamps and open exhausts ensured that anyone within a three-mile radius would know we were coming.

If commissioned portraits were off, he would offer, in desperation, to make enlargements from the troops' passports; my task being, by application of lamp black and a soft stump, to make the resultant blurred images, sometimes with a crack down the middle, acceptable when framed.

Outside the window, blue sky, what else, and palm fronds that stir in the breeze as I flog at retouching the fish-faces of guys, each wishing his unique arrangement of two eyes a snout and mouth to be imprinted for all time on bromide paper: two eyes a snout and mouth, two eyes a snout and mouth.

A break to sort out the next likely face, when an irate, much medalled, and fierily moustached Colonel of the Foreign Legion bursts through the doorway, flourishing one of my better 'full colour' efforts.

He thrusts it at me angrily. I have put two white spots on his eyes. He has no white spots on his eyes.

Of course he has. I turn to the window. "See, there are two reflected highlights in mine." He doesn't trouble to look, not needing a non-military guy to tell him he has no spots on his. Remarkable.

So, with great care, I spot out the highlights.

I aim to earn sufficient cash to cover my fare home and to this end the amused boss at Thomas Cook's Agency, accustomed to serving wealthy travellers, is investigating the cheapest possible way of doing just that. But my photographer friend suddenly loses interest in fish-faces and me, having been offered what he called a "remunerative commission". Guessing that this will be pornography again, I shoulder my pack and make for Sidi Barrani and then along the African coast, seen off by a whirring flight of flamingos.

Not that I have anything against pornography as such, so long as it is elegant. After all, it is already in most peoples' minds, but he had a mind as constricted and basic as the toilet in a Jumbo jet.

I left hurriedly . . .

53

As I tramped, one pace following the other with a rhythmic swing, Kipling's 'I am the cat that walks alone, and all places are alike to me,' was running through my mind; maybe I felt a creepy affinity with that cat.

A month later I was resting on the corner of a disused hen coop at the edge of a run-down Berber village, an open bully beef sandwich in my hand – lunch – when a vicious bundle of feathers, a half starved hen, snatched that last piece of tinned meat and fluttered off with it in a whirl of dust. Taking careful aim I threw a stone and missed; I was never any good at cricket. Dejected, I realised that somehow the spice of adventure had gone out of walking. Time I made for home.

Thin ice – in the heat

Hitching a lift on the back of a limping truck I arrived, bruised, at Tunis, unaware that Nature had laid a snare for me, having decided that, along with copulating frogs and rabbits, it was time I made myself useful.

Nature is experienced at triggering off this sort of thing, be it dancing flowers, a tweak on a spider's web, or the mandrill's blue behind.

Which reminds me – beauty is in the eye of the beholder.

This presentation took the form of the most exotic Mediterranean beauty I could imagine, posing in front of my associate's camera in a ridiculously wide brimmed hat – and very little else. She was perched on a high stool, one slender leg to the fore, as she stroked her foot into a neat little high-arched shoe. She smiled. I fell, heavily. (The human foot, viewed objectively, is something of a deformity, so we style such shoes to conceal this truth.)

Motivated at last, I settled down and attempted chocolate box versions of the lovely, in this pose and that, for the cover of an 'up-market French magazine' which, to be honest, was quite notional.

Those old life classes in Room 13? Don't make me laugh. I used pastels on tinted paper to record the soft modulations of her body, as oils are sticky and take a hell of a time to dry. Not art with a capital A, but something wonderful.

Ghastly thought. What I remember as a flower of perfect beauty is probably an arthritic granny by now.

When the invariable outcome of close proximity reached the point of no return and I hurriedly drew back into the safety of my isolate shell, I guess Benvenuto Cellini must have turned in his grave.

Disgusted with my lack of courage, like an ass, I took a deep breath and made for the desert.

Some time back I had noticed an oasis on the map and calculated that the track to it would be about two days' march. My friend at Thomas Cook shook his head, "Young man, that road is impassable, the post van hasn't used it for months." As I left he held up a finger, like a strict nanny, and reiterated, "No."

Next day, as a swinging string of grunting camels passed me on that same track, I came to the conclusion that Cook's man was installed to advise monied tourists who travelled in soft-topped automobiles with brass headlamps. True, scatters of sand and then dunes had blown across the road here and there, but once over them I was on track again. Some time later, plodding through the sand in a heat induced daze, I realised that I had not seen the track for some time. All in the dazzle was dunes, dunes, and yet more dunes, mound beyond mound, like the swell in a motionless seascape. Not much hope of direction from a sun directly overhead.

I guess I must have found my way back somehow, albeit in the wrong direction, as I was jerked out of my daze by a group of angry Arabs in head cloths, throwing stones and curses. I had stumbled over, and so desecrated, an ancient Islamic burial ground. Civilization at last.

I settled back to the chore of touching up those blurred faces of desperate men, my mind the while going its own way . . . picturing smiling red lips, slender legs . . . and, surely, there was a scent of perfume in the air?

Getting back to square one

I was now faced with the problem of collecting sufficient cash to cover the fare home.

After days of pillion riding behind the Belgian, in a cloud of dust over desert tracks, to Legion outposts to trace the guys who owed us for photo-enlarging their faces, then impatiently sipping syrupy mint tea to placate polite Arabs in their tents, dark to blindness after the dazzle outside, we extracted just sufficient cash to cover 'Slow Class' tickets to the UK . . . if it was still there.

At the last moment, with hard boiled eggs and a chunk of bread in my pack, my long trek terminated at the Tunis docks to the throaty roar of open exhausts and a shrieking skid.

The intercom in the wheelhouse of the ship for Marseilles was already ringing 'slow ahead' as I scrambled up the gangway: last man aboard, much to the disgust of a man on deck who directed me to a grim triangular space under the forepeak where anchor chains are laid to rest and rust.

Classified with unwanted immigrants as a low form of life from the bottom of the heap, I was angrily turned out of the third class lavatory, and a French one at that – but why should I care, I was on my way home.

A violent storm at sea – Marseilles harbour – crisp icicles decorating the rigging. With newspapers stuffed up my jacket, tramping Paris in the snow, (no money for coffee) until in the early hours the Night Mail slowly drew to a halt in the London terminal, with a belch of steam and a sigh.

A loner in limbo.

A sketch while waiting for the city to come to life. Soft felt pen on yellow tint paper.

The platforms were deserted, the terminus yellowed with fog under gas lamps, as I stumbled round piles of mailbags scattered like dead bodies on a battlefield.

Not the glorious moment I had dreamed of, no brass band playing 'Land of Hope and Glory', but when the bar opened at last and the bold buxom beauty behind the counter arched an eyebrow and said, "And what's yours, dearie?"

English!

What had I gained from this interval of wandering and wondering? The top of my silly head, with its mixed input of contrived urban artifice had, at least, 'been to the cleaners'.

57

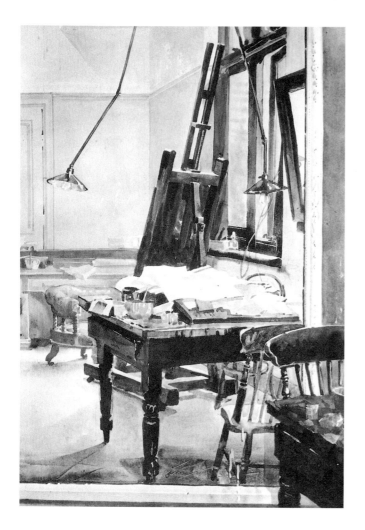

The den, where pristine white paper is converted into a saleable product.

Landed, like a hooked fish

Walking the once familiar London streets I felt as an immigrant must feel – not in on the act. True, I had provisionally made up a tie from a red-spotted duster and a strip of French elastic, but this didn't quite do the trick. The City appeared to be populated with half-dead pedestrians in slow motion . . . or had my perceptions changed?

No. In my absence, believe it or not, the American notion that you could get something for nothing by investing what you hadn't yet got, had proved to be flawed. As a result, mentally retarded tycoons splattered the sidewalks on Wall Street and the whole Western World had gone bankrupt. Three cheers, I suppose, but the crowd in Trafalgar Square, instead of feeding the pigeons, were themselves queuing for free handouts of soup, while Welshmen in miners' helmets were pacing the streets, singing for pennies.

I was refuelling with coffee and a bun – in what you might term a restaurant, as it did sport tablecloths – when the Italian proprietor agreed to hang my sketches on the walls, for sale at a low mark-up as, "Face it, signor, there ain't no cash around for luxury goods." But it was apparent, when after a few sales I was rigged out in an off-the-peg suit, young dreamers with sketches of Italy under their arms were not in great demand. Come to think of it, that is something of an understatement.

After humping my folio up innumerable lino-covered stair-cases, I decided on a desperate last fling. Taking a deep breath, I pushed through the portals of Carlton Studios – then the leading commercial studio in Europe and asked to see 'God', that is, the Director.

Carlton started when two hopeful graphic artists (one who would attempt anything in oils, the other in black and white in the Art Nouveau manner) set themselves up in an attic in the East End; for a low rent, as the London smog drifted thataway. One day, a gaunt young Canadian in a torn raincoat introduced himself and pointed out that they could produce more drawings and so make more money, if someone (a hungry Canadian, for example) visited clients for them.

The number of drawings an artist can produce is limited, but there is no limit to the number an agent can SELL.

When I arrived on the scene, Carlton Studios had a building of its own in the West End and employed forty top artists. The Boss? The Canadian, of course – Archie Martin.

Sitting behind an executive desk under a portrait of himself sitting behind an executive desk, he eyed me gloomily then flipped through my work. Not suitable for advertising, but I could draw, and (he cheered up) I looked sufficiently innocent.

After downing a pill for his peptic ulcer, he went into the story of how, when he was young, he struggled selling newspapers in the bitter winters of Montreal. Then, as though curious, he asked what was the minimum a young man could survive on these days? Always willing to oblige, I made a tentative guess at £3 a week.

So he signed me on at £3 a week – with a three-year contract.

Well, I would eat for three years if nothing else.

I was soon to learn that one was able to get the 'else' by working overtime, twelve to fifteen hours a day instead of the statutory eight. This was in the early days, before bright yuppies in the advertising agencies took over, realising that the real meat on the carcass comes not from artwork, but from selling space; employing esoteric young men for 'think' sessions, consumer research and all that lark.

After all, the stuff these guys come up with now, was obvious to us even then.

In the thirties there was the *heavy brigade* (still romantically termed the 'working class'), who would dodge work whenever possible. Their exploited wives would have for spending what the man of the house hadn't yet squandered in a bar or betting shop. *En masse* a great deal of cash, but very limited outlets.

The *suburban conformers*, who hoped to appear better off than their next-door neighbours. A wide variety of outlets when tempted with the correct bait, if they hadn't already been hooked and were in debt.

The few who had *gotten-rich-quick* and whose wives or girlfriends ensured that they spent to achieve 'class'. Advertisers naturally supported the wives and girlfriends in this happy process. Some slick artwork here.

The *intellectuals* gathered in ghettos, such as Hampstead. A great deal of opinionating, but little spending power.

The traditional *county family* crowd? Only memories. No money at all.

Carlton Studios, where we arty types contributed to the betterment of mankind, had one of those unremarkable brick frontages that might mask a dealer in bric-à-brac or mechanical steam organs. Only an architect or tax official would think of Carlton Studios as a building: Carlton was *us* – if a gaggle of do-it-yourself specialists, who saw the world in terms of line, half-tone, or wash could be considered as having a 'corporate image' (an expression not yet coined).

We were interested in technique, in which we were tested daily, and considered the wets who painted for the galleries as misguided amateurs.

One afternoon, for the fun of it, a few of us played truant to view the Royal Academy Show. Hearing my companions' comments on the work exhibited thrilled me – I realised how lucky I was (even at only £3 a week) to be learning techniques from professionals.

I had no desire to own a car.
Drawing one, as of anything, makes it
an intimate possession – pro tem.

The following year, for a bet, five of us sent in paintings we had in stock. Quite a party when they were all accepted and hung 'on the line'.

In fact we had a 'gallery' of our own where off-the-cuff ideas were put on show, each illustration hoping to be linked to someone's product – when moneyman Martin would, if the sale was discovered, release a percentage to the slave responsible.

One day a company director, who was planning to market a white powder he called 'health salts', happened to admire the distinctive image of a cheerful old gaffer with a shadow under his nose, and decided to identify with it. From that moment his company never looked back. When I arrived on the scene the salts were selling like mad and 'Grandpa Kruschen' was a byword throughout Britain.

Old G — Young G

As an untried apprentice I was dumped on Fred Gardner – one of the original artists in the attic and known to the inmates as 'G'. I became 'Young G', and the initial has stuck with me for the rest of my life.

No *ormolu secretaire* to work on this time, but a sturdy table that had done battle in many kitchens, and had since been so smudged and patinated with paint that its top had the appearance of a well-worn palette.

It could well be hanging in the Guggenheim today, together with other less happy accidents.

When I was shown in, the great man was sitting at a wind-up easel lining in a drawing of Grandpa Kruschen haring along the road on a bicycle. A slip of yellow paper pinned to the top of his board (in the trade, yellow is for creative) carried the scribbled slogan: *'Prompted by that Kruschen feeling, Grandpa raced the train to Ealing.'* Then, *'Five inch double column, half-tone, Monday a.m. And fix it, your last one smudged.'*

Fred Gardner swung lazily round in his leather chair, eyed me appraisingly over horn-rimmed spectacles and, tossing the creation my way, suggested I make a start by drawing-in the wheels; a task which obviously bored him. It frightened me, but he had already turned away to stretch a fresh sheet to sketch in a man's foot. It was a beautifully drawn foot, somewhat marred from an academic point of view by the addition of a broad black arrow pointing to a ripe corn on its little toe.

Come to think of it, the only artwork handled by men of the Renaissance, like Michelangelo, would be of idealised saints and princes. No corns detailed.

When I saw my bicycle wheels reproduced in the morning paper I was thrilled – I was IN.

Italy, and the leisure to dreamily consider this or that, was a thing of the past – now to action.

As the new guy I was, of course, exploited and would creep into the studio with some trepidation – what 'sticky' job will they throw at me today? But in time I became the studio 'stand-in' for any senior artist who was too busy or indifferent to take a job on. Each had a known style and to imitate this was the supreme test – don't talk to me about climbing Mount Everest.

Fortunately I never suffered the ignominy of having my finished artwork turned down. At first, maybe, they were kind, but later, any technique was expected of me – penmanship, the airbrush, starved brush, line and wash, flat colour, scraperboard, pastel; while my first effort in oils was for a magazine cover. Gosh, there it was, first go and on the bookstalls!

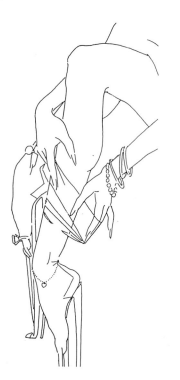

An image in the mind, smarter than meaty reality.

As unexpected tasks came down the conveyor belt non-stop, each labelled with the threat of publication date, we had recourse to a fantastic library of picture references and press cuttings, anything from a crystal chandelier to the underside of a turtle. Cubitt, the guy who acted as librarian, had seen hard times and shared a basement with an old busker, who tore newspapers into patterns for the delectation of theatre queues and for their spare change.

I once discovered Cubitt on his knees outside St Martin's Church, correcting the rigging of a ship incorrectly rendered by a pavement artist who had adventured beyond drawing the customary loaf, "Easy to draw, hard to get." At weekends he would hold the crowd in thrall with quizzical argument at Speakers Corner. A witty cynic with a high IQ who threw it all away – "Pearls before swine," he would say with a twisted grin.

"Hello, G. And what can we do for you? King Edward is it? The King or the potato?" So much for objects.

Figure? We had a male model who had 'failed' at Eton and a female model, second grade, who would turn up late breathing gin – who cared, it was her body we needed. We would pull her leg unmercifully about a top-hatted old gaffer, her boyfriend. The joke was on us when he died leaving her a small fortune, including the *avant garde* Cambridge Theatre, and, wearing a mink coat, she would strut past us in the street like a randy hen.

The camera was just edging in on the act, so the attics had been rigged out as a photo-studio where one would hear the assistant in the dark room timing the development of a print, "Elephant one, elephant two, elephant three," as they do, but he was stone deaf – which, in the dark, posed a communication problem.

For a difficult job I would arrange a photo pose to work from. Once, one of the girl artists turned up to surprise me, under the spot light, stroking the creases out of a nylon stocking way up a hired model's thigh – "Well, caught you at last." In practice, a photograph is non-selective, recording the bits one would avoid drawing anyway. As Fred Gardner, my mentor, said, "Better work from the real thing, however horrible." True enough, seen close-up that model's photogenic leg would have been improved with a closer shave.

As a slave who worked fast (and so paid), I was too excited by the work of American and Continental artists, the effects of offset on reproduction and the exact spacing of a typeface, to give a damn for politics – who cares who votes for whom. As Bernard Shaw pointed out, his charlady had the same power in the ballot box as he.

We were more interested in food. "Say Tovey, did you know you can get a three course lunch at that little restaurant – back of St Martin's Lane – for one and ninepence?"

"No! Three courses?"

"Well, if you count in the coffee. Not bad?"

I still retain the habit of reading a menu backwards, the prices before the dishes. By the end of the month it would be the Express Dairy; a piece of brown bread, pat of butter, portion of honey and a glass of milk. I skipped meals to pay for Wells's *Outline of History.*

Lack of food, however, took its toll and after I had been missing for three days, lying flat in my digs, old G turned up with his arms full of provisions. "Only thing wrong with you, Young G, you need feeding up."

Technique is all

Occasionally I would pop into the office to pick up the next job, to be told there wasn't one.

Oblivious to the non-stop chaos of two verbal clients hitting the telephones at one time, Phipps-the-progress-man impatiently holds two receivers off the hook while he directs a slow-witted messenger boy.

Seeing me, "Nothing for you at the moment, G."

Into left-hand 'phone, "But you asked for it to bleed-off. No, she wasn't insulting you, it's a technical term . . . hold on."

To me, "Do something for the Gallery, G."

Then into the right-hand 'phone, which is barking at him, "Because the bloody blocks got mixed, that's why. Just had to be a Dr Barnardo's baby and White Horse Whisky."

A side comment to me, "Sod's law," then back on the

'phone, " . . . but it only appeared in the first edition . . ."

The while, our up-market but tarty artists' rep., Neamy, ignoring this comic turn, is airing her magenta fingernails until the varnish dries. She glances my way, "What he said, do something useful for the Gallery, G." Hell!

As I drift down the empty corridor that 'not wanted' feeling creeps in on me again.

I find the usually easy-going Hodge, who two days back was giving me a reading of *Le Morte Darthur* while I inked in a cartoon for a Dutch newspaper, in a non-communicative mood. He is attempting to paint a surgical section through the thigh of a pig so it looks appetizing. A smoked ham. Why should I care? He, at least, is busy.

I doodle around, tether a tea cup to the radiator with thread, so it'll jump off its saucer when the tea girl collects it, construct a pretty little aquarium from celluloid to hang my old *meerschaum* pipe in, and paint a robin outside the window. But it's no good; I sit looking gloomily at a blank canvas, dreaming of the day I go freelance.

I wander off to see what the other slaves are up to.

The introspective Trevor Jones. Suitably encouraged, he will scribe a perfect ellipse so you can't see where the end meets its beginning – then another ellipse scribed within it, and then

On-the-spot art
in pastel and 'poster paint'
for full colour reproduction.

another within that. The dexterity of Giotto; necessary if one is to draw a lady's powder compact. "Don't look where the pen is," he would say, "concentrate your mind on where it's going – it's already *there* really, all you have to do is ink it in. Whatever you do, don't hesitate." Years of practice, of course.

Young Biffa. A willing slave. Laying a flat wash, the board dampened and slightly tilted, the paint in the saucer dust-free and exactly the correct mix, he works boldly across and across with a flat hogshair brush, picking up more paint with every third stroke, then, swinging the board round, he starts the other way.

Know where the curve is going – and don't hesitate.

Frosty, his myopic eyes enlarged behind glasses like car headlamps, is holding his breath, putting in the odd accents that make the car he is rendering this year's model, at least to the car buffs. Automobile-mad, he spends his weekends sketching racing cars tearing round the track at Brooklands.

Jock, in a roll-neck sweater, captain of a rowing eight and master of the wandering line, is delineating dainty lace undies with a fine mapping pen.

Cubit-Smith, who would prefix his name with 'The Honourable' given half a chance, is laying in a portrait of a carefully made up starlet – Merle Oberon. She is posed self-consciously, pencilled-in eyebrows raised in permanent surprise, the spotlight aimed to define her cleavage . . . I close the door gently with, "Oh, sorry, old chap. See you later."

At the far end of the corridor in a rag-tag zone we call 'The Zoo', I greet Alex, a good natured Scot who is brushing in a detailed rendering of a ghastly quilted bedspread for a mail order catalogue. Black and white wash, not even the fun of colour. A living, if you work slickly enough and quickly enough. The next subject? A pile of blankets. Poor Alex, and with a wife and two kids.

Down a back stair to the harem, the Fashion Department – girls and more than a whiff of Coty perfume. Eyed as an interloper I drift over to Pearl Faulkner. Slender and angular, posed at her easel as though I'm a camera, wet-brushing a free

Miss Upper Crust market.
Loose starved-brushwork which
looks casual, but is the final
of three trial tracings.

sketch (which is not as 'free' as it looks) for Vogue. The accepted curvaceous creature of unknown species, wearing the aloof expression of a superior model who has inadvertently stepped over an open drain; legs that go on for ever.

Lifting one of her candies, I return to my own room to find Bowmar who feeds the world with smart stiff-necked gents sporting the latest in men's suiting – the exact cut of the lapels and set of the shoulders. He is commenting scathingly on the carelessly drawn jackets in portraits at a recent Gallery show, when a ginger head pops round the door. It is Mr Phipps-the-progress-man (who, by the way, got his job on someone else's specimens).

"I say, Bowmar, pull your finger out. You still have three full-length figures for Moss Bros. promised tomorrow." Bowmar, now busy angling with his pencil to save the life of a house fly struggling in my paint water, mutters menacingly: "You just bugger off."

A certain freedom. Nevertheless, we were professionals and always delivered on time – time being the last minute before going to press.

Beating the clock

In those days, the most sought-after advertising space was the full front page of the *Daily Mail*. This, the only full front page ad. in the world, cost a bomb. One day someone failed to come up with his material and the directors of Hercules bicycles, who had been waiting on the sidelines, gave three rousing cheers and took up the option . . . only one day to go. Over to me.

I made an early start (the most difficult part of any operation) and by the time the rest of the slaves arrived I had a key drawing with five tracings; one for each of the artists concerned.

By tea-time we were huddled round the master drawing, each sticking up his bit of the jigsaw. One stuck on the hand-lettered title, another the cutout bicycle, actually a two-man job, as a meticulous guy had spent half the day putting treads on the tyres. Then Bowmar positioned the hero leaning in a manly attitude, hand on the saddle and smirking hopefully at his pretty girlfriend the while. I had already painted in the setting, with an invitingly soft straw-stack . . . and a village church peeping over the distant hill to indicate a happy outcome. Four sharp cuts with the guillotine, a protective overlay, and a messenger boy ran off with it.

A period of calm as we sat back, legs outstretched, and rubbed rubber solution off our fingers.

Mr Phipps-the-progress-man appeared, frowning at his watch. "That job ready yet? What? Gone? But the client's outside and he hasn't seen it."

"He'll see it like everyone else, breakfast time. We're popping over the road. See you."

"For Christ's sake," wailed Phipps. "At least let me show him the rough."

When the proles are all tucked in bed

We relished the freedom to be ourselves, even taking pleasure in night work when the building and everything in it would be ours.

"A rush job, G. You and young Tovey. It'll be an all-nighter." Sure. At last, the job is completed. Damn, we're locked in. Delicatessen opposite just closing. We signal from the third floor window, haul cheese and apple pie up in a wastepaper basket – captives beleaguered in a castle. Collect cushions from the Fashion Department and bed down. Radiator makes clanking noises. Open weep-valve, a hiss of air and all is quiet.

Later. Sounds like a window is being forced open? Can't be. A bump, from the floor below. I nudge Tovey, "Burglars!"

He grunts, "Go to sleep. It's the cleaners."

"What, at four o'clock in the morning?"

We hold our breath listening. Swing doors give a creek. Shuffles in corridor slowly creeping our way.

In a whisper, "When I count three, we'll jump them, flash the torch and YELL."

"One – two – three!"

Surprise! Three policemen are hugging the wall, more scared than we are. We see them off the premises, wish them the best of luck, then go back to sleep.

Miss Middle Class market. Rendered on dot scraperboard from a photograph, to give crisper reproduction on coarse newsprint.

Come morning, a treat. Bacon, eggs and a brush up at a classy restaurant. No rush. Quiet stroll in Hyde Park, throw stones at squirrels and admire dishy girl secretaries on their way to work.

Back at studio . . . turmoil. Accounts department flooded. Damn. I forgot to close that weep-valve. Mr Bloom, the pompous guy who keeps the books, quivering with anger, sticks up a bold warning sign:

"DO NOT INTERFERE WITH THE RADIATORS."

We quickly change it to "Do not interfere with MR BLOOM" . . . then back to the drawing board to see what this day will bring.

A bosh shot at domesticity

I shifted digs so often that marked on a map it would look like an outbreak of smallpox; Chelsea, Bedford Park, Westbourne Grove, Earls Court, you name it. Then I settled for a while in *fairyland*, a romantic cabin in an old orchard which I shared with young Tovey. We painted it *à la Ballet Russe* (to prove to ourselves that we weren't suburbanites, I guess), the garbage bin cerulean blue, elegantly titled CAVIAR in shocking pink. "Caviar," muttered the dustman as he banged the lid back, "and what the bloody hell is that?"

Chuffed with our arty decor, we invited Phipps-the-progress-man over to admire it, forgetting that most of the furnishings had been purloined from Carlton; trundled eight miles in the dead of night on a hired costermonger's barrow – the hurricane lamp thrown in for good will.

"Damned cheek," he exclaimed, until we pointed to a fish tank with costly curved glazing ('lifted' from a nearby building site) and two chubby Renaissance cupids ('borrowed' from a tomb in a derelict church). This cheered him up somewhat. As we pointed out, with innocent logic, the world did owe us a living.

70

A draught of fresh air

Joysmith, one of the senior (reasonably paid) artists, had purchased a boat. This fact knocked my overtime for six when he commandeered me to be its one-man-crew. No call to purchase a yachtsman's cap. This was not one of those tarted-up weekend affairs that only come out in fine weather, but a tough thirty-five foot, brown-sailed fisherboat, and built to face the North Sea in all weathers, as pictured on calenders, topsail and all. (Thus I learned how to tie proper knots, which later proved to be more significant than a 'doctorate'.)

Come Friday afternoon, tune into the Shipping Forecast –

Fastnet – 3 miles – freshening – gale imminent.
Lundy – fog – lowering – force 8 gale imminent.
North Ireland – 5 miles – deteriorating – gale imminent.

"Hell. And I guess that goes for the Dogger Bank, too."

"There's a loose stay-wire needs splicing and the cabin hatch could do with a coat of varnish?" Carlton and rush jobs can wait. "Right. Pick you up usual time, then."

The pick-up being an old Morris jalopy that juddered when cornering and had lost its bumpers.

February is early for sailing in this latitude. Bitter wind and overcast as we tack down the Thames Estuary, while I peer through the gloom to make for a gap between the derelict landing stage on Brownsea Island to starboard and a bobbing marker-buoy to port.

A sudden gust. Here we go – 'gale imminent' – as sleet streaks by, horizontally. Visibility nil and over she goes – mainsail flat in the water. Being non-amphibious I hang on to a stay, which vibrates in the wind. What price Cape Horn? The knot that matters is already coagulated with ice, so Joysmith cuts the main sheet with his clasp knife and she rights herself, after discarding everything that was loose on deck – bar me.

We appear to be static, but in fact we are haring blindly along with the tide, a bit of foresail (referred to as *foreskin*, by the boating fraternity) giving steerage way. Steer where? "Soundings," gestures Joysmith, so I creep up front dropping the lead then, at last, shout in the teeth of the gale, "Let go!"

Joysmith drops the anchor and, as she swings on the line, reassures me with, "Absolutely cosy, old man, too shallow to be in the shipping lanes," and proceeds to light his pipe. A lazy supper – salt beef followed by fried Dundee Cake and Camp Coffee, and so to our bunks.

Comes the dawn. A line of stockbrokers' yachts are moored just offshore, as though for a regatta. There is one vacant mooring and – what do you know – we are in it, an ugly duckling consorting with swans.

One wondered what all the fuss had been about.

But once, during a crisis, Joysmith's stiff-upper-lip comment was so blissfully inept, it must be recorded.

The case of the minnow and the whale
We had located a cheap mooring at the far end of Portsmouth harbour – a good funkhole for a fortnight's sailing on The Solent.

True, the Navy, shipping and shuttle-boat ferries would look on us as a butterfly intruding in an elephant house, but we soon took the chore of dodging other craft at our ease, like crossing a busy thoroughfare in slow motion.

We would make a rude gesture as we passed the *Nelson*, largest battleship in the fleet, which had been tied up there so long we reckoned that, given another month, she would find herself grounded on her own excrement.

After flogging across the wake of a pushy ferry, we lost what breeze there was in the lee of a rust-bucketed, red-leaded dredger. No fret, all the time in the world.

Joysmith is lounging, feet up, at the tiller and I have just poked my head through the fore-hatch to take the air – while scouring a saucepan – when we slide clear of the dredger's arse and I suddenly go hot all over.

Aiming straight at us is another ruddy great island of a battleship, the *Renown*, home from China Station, her marines all lined up like toy soldiers. Gosh, that explains why the guys on those Admiralty tugs had been signalling us.

In the face of imminent débâcle, Joysmith calmly quotes a traditional navigational ruling . . .

"Steam gives way to sail."

Like hell it does. This heavy grey mass was probing its way along a dredged channel, chary of grounding on the mud, (as the *Nelson* had some months back, when it rubbed its smooth bottom on a sandbank named, believe it or not, the Hamilton).

A naval type, casting the lead from a projecting grid up on the *Renown*'s vertical side, made this only too clear. I looked up from under his gumboots, as he first plunged the lead in front of us, then wetted us as he swung the line, just missing our stern.

We were still bouncing in the *Renown*'s wake when a passing ferry pilot barked through his speaker, "Near thing, what?" Joysmith didn't bat an eyelid, "Every damned bloke in the harbour has his eyes on us, G," he muttered "so ACT COOL."

A month later a contretemps occurred when only a fool would act cool.

The case of the cut-velvet carpet

When Joysmith asked me to join him on an exciting night job I didn't hesitate for a moment, though my fingernails still smelt of plasticine from two weeks' late work modelling a setting for a film – and for which I had not yet been paid.

He was redecorating Romano's, the historic restaurant in The Strand where our proud-bellied grandfathers once primed wasp-waisted chorus girls with oysters and pink champagne.

I was to help him paint a large mural, but as the restaurant was open during the day we had to operate at night; no problem, as Romano's backed onto Covent Garden, the vegetable market which came alive when the rest of London slept.

Two weeks later, as morning light leaks through the fanlight to the sound of road-men hosing the Strand outside, we are balanced on a plank spanning the restaurant's imposing serpentine stairway.

As this is to be our last stint, we call in some workmen (who all go by the generic name of 'Charlie') to remove the protective drugget, so we can judge our work against the sweep of plum velvet carpet below.

Perhaps a touch of white here and there, to bring up the foreground? So, up onto that springing plank again with a fresh kitty of white paint.

We couldn't decide which of us kicked it, but I will never erase from my mind the sight of that bucket as it bounced, splattering the carpet first right and then left, as though it had a malignant purpose of its own.

With the help of a work-force of 'Charlies' we cleaned off the intrusive white splatters with turpentine, but had now added an odour which didn't blend too well with the chef's *haute cuisine.* The bill for the carpet's removal and cleaning

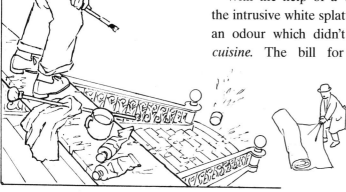

swallowed up most of our fee. Never mind. We had been part of Covent Garden, dodged nose-bagged horses, rattling trolleys and skips. Cockney shouts, the smell of apples, cabbages, horse piss – and violets, if you could find them.

And we had redecorated Romano's, which must make me something of a period piece. No charge.

Stamina

As we made our way home early one morning, I crossed Piccadilly Circus, then swathed in mist, and asked a scruffy street vendor, roasting chestnuts over an old oil drum, for "Two twopenny bags, please."

One of a couple of street girls, who were warming their backsides by his fire, giggled and said, "Does he mean us?"

Hell. I was also on night work, but hadn't the stamina to raise a smile after four hours balancing on a plank.

Bad show; a designer needs a sense of humour if he is to survive snags on sticky jobs and the foibles of clients.

The case of the artist who didn't exist

One slave, a chap named Angrave, had the luck to open the elevator gates when the car wasn't there, fell three floors, broke both legs and was able to set up on his own with the insurance money. I opted for a less dramatic method.

The top artists' agent at that time was Don Candler, a cheerful braggadocio who belted around in a supercharged sports car, had hairs bristling from his ears like antennae, and attracted an unlimited sequence of dishy receptionists that came down a conveyor belt from some delightful Bunny Club in heaven.

He cornered me one day, proposing I join his team part-time and pocket a good fee once in a while. On my reminding him I had a contract with Carlton, he brushed that aside with, "No need to publicise the fact, just use another name."

I developed a free 'scraper-board' style, which the Carlton bosses wouldn't recognise, and called myself 'Leslie James'.

One morning, I'd just finished shaving when I heard Candler's car roar up to my digs, (now an attic, decorated Bauhaus-style), the scream of tyres as he pulled in, then the man himself pounding up the stairs. "I've got you a super job,

A loose scraperboard technique by some guy named Leslie James.

G. A series, home page, four column, and with a top agency – what do you think of that?" But Carlton had so loaded me with work I had to say no. Hell and damnation.

A few days later Neamy, the Carlton rep., said it all again adding, "They wanted that chap Leslie James, but he's too busy – so I've got it for you. Think you can imitate his style in scraper?"

So there I was, carefully producing 'fakes' in my own scraperboard technique . . .

When not doing my arty bit, I would browse through bookshops, still hoping to discover the how and why of the Universe, filling my head with the philosophical gymnastics of Descartes, Kant, Herbert Spencer and the rest.

I was also out of my depth with gregarious human beings and evaded becoming intimate with any, particularly the female of the species. As we were fifty-fifty male and female there were plenty of them around, but up until now they had impinged on my life no more than penguins on the doings of the early explorers. Nevertheless, I had them classified into three categories.

Ordinary: female vulgaris. Essential, I supposed, to undertake the dull jobs and pair up with men to produce babies, which emerged from the womb too soon and had to be house-trained – another dull job.

Ladies: these followed a characteristic behaviour pattern, were hyper-critical of men and, so, were to be avoided. (Probably a different species.)

Goddesses: I had sighted so few, even when at Cartier, that they should be written in the singular, Goddess. An extremely rare exotic. Desirable and rather frightening for that reason.

I was now twenty-five and, I suppose, what Bernard Shaw termed 'the life force' was about to catch up with me.

Ordinary

I join the great majority

Selfridges' West End store had been built on the lines of the Parthenon and housed an assortment of goddesses, as had the original temple. These were selected by Gordon Selfridge to titillate the visitor's eye and give the store a bit of 'class'.

The untouchable girls who posed in perfumed perfection in the cosmetics section were voted, by Carlton's eye men, as the loveliest pick-ups in London. There was one beauty in the theatre booking section that Selfridge himself, a bit of a sugar daddy in top hat and frock coat, singled out as he made his daily circuit of the store. One morning he led her to the centre of the ground floor and held up a finger, indicating 'listen'. All around was the jingle of cash registers ringing as the change went in. "You," he said, "are the most beautiful girl in my store, and you are now listening to the most beautiful sound in the world."

Lady

How do I know? Well, I spotted her too, dared to smile, she responded, and fixation was complete. She had the appearance of cool sophistication, but proved to be as immature as I. Like babes in the wood, we played the 'girl meets boy' theme. I would see her home on top of the bus or, with beating heart, find her waiting for me after work under the clock.

Alas, as we had nothing in common and little to talk about, the lady eventually tired of this scruffy artist and became enamoured with a guy who, to my disgust, ponced around in a

Goddess

tuxedo – floor manager of a Super Cinema. The wound, such as it was, soon healed.

Then a coincidence occurred that makes me wonder if the Fates play games with us, after all.

I was on holiday with two other Archie Martin slaves, drifting down the river poling a punt. One quiet morning Tisdall and his friend wandered down the towpath to buy provisions, while I stayed behind to punch new life into the cushions.

When they returned, I was surprised to see that Tisdall had picked up a newspaper, a thing we never read. Temporarily men of leisure with nothing else to do, we shared its pages and settled back for a quiet interlude. Tisdall's friend had the bad luck to get the advertising pages, so he returned the compliment by reading aloud choice snippets from the Personal Column.

Suddenly he stiffened, stared at me over the sheet goggle-eyed and read, 'G. If you still love me . . .' etcetera, and an address, signed 'Mary'.

I no longer remember the exact phrasing of that neatly worded advertisement, only that it identified my girl from Selfridges. Trapped immediately by a subconscious drive, I was led in triumph to the nearest railway station. The last I saw of my companions was two minute figures jumping up and down with excitement as they and the platform receded rapidly, until the train, taking the curve *en route* to Paddington, hid them from view.

It turned out that the goddess was even less worldly than I had supposed. Bedded by a Spanish salesman who 'had something to do with films', she found herself pregnant and was searching frantically for a husband to make her lower profile respectable. In the thirties unmarried mums were not the 'in' thing, particularly for the 'respectable' class where conformity was the rule of life – a rule that seemed to have passed me by. I was delighted to become normalised in this ready-made way, even to act as sponsor for a hundred babies (so long as none of them were mine) if, by this means, I could dedicate my life – when not producing artwork – to admiring this exquisite example of artwork come to life.

A cartoon of Gordon Selfridge.
When at Cartier I had designed a gold
cigarette case for him, ornamented with an
engraved portrait of one of the notorious
Dolly Sisters . . . a beauty.

There is a picture of the goddess in my memory, sleek legs revealed by a loose cloak as she poses gracefully in the subway, *en route* to the marriage registry, her wide-set grey eyes observing me questioningly from under a cute little straw hat, tilted cheekily forward in the manner of Myrna Loy.

I sign my second contract

The registry office was like the waiting room in a police station, except it was furnished with an imposing roll-top desk, behind which sat a bald-headed little coot with a polished pink face who had obviously handled this mating process many times before – and, by the look of his tum, *before* lunch.

To me it was the antechamber to heaven, glorified by the presence of my elegant goddess, whose beauty defeated the off-stage interference of a garbage truck manoeuvring in the yard outside the window.

Honeymoon? Be realistic. I was due to complete a poster for Esso, so back to Carlton for another late stint . . . I would now need all the overtime pay I could muster.

A new phase . . . a shadow boxing, this time at suburban respectability. We all act a part and, after eight years of going it alone in top floor digs, this seemed to me to be as good a part as any. I would feel quite impressed with myself, the genuine thing, as I climbed the footpath from the railway station to the little house on the hill in its acre of freehold ground, thinking that the Establishment and all it contained was paid for by artwork. True, it took acres of artwork, but nevertheless remarkable.

"How many times must I tell you to wipe your shoes when you come into the kitchen? You're as bad as the boys."

"Sorry."

That epoch making bun-in-the-oven I had committed myself to fostering turned out to be twin boys.

Adventure into Flight

One morning I arrive at the studio to be told Archie Martin wants to see me. But I am not in trouble this time, it is friend Thompson.

Being a Quaker, he had refused the artwork for a beer poster, unprofessional, so he had been fired. I am to take over his work. Martin wastes no time, "You have an appointment, ten o'clock tomorrow, Short Brothers, Rochester."

I refuse to replace Thompson, but he explains it isn't the beer ad., then tempts me, "I understand it's a *big new flying boat*." This was to be a breakthrough, not only in my little world, but in the world of flying machines.

Down at Rochester a great metallic cathedral, the hangar, yawns over a concrete ramp which slides into the muddy river. Thompson and his troubles are forgotten; I have fallen in love with an aircraft. She isn't built yet. It's the *idea* of her. Unfolding blueprint after blueprint I am lost in their complexity – all arcs and curves. Then up comes a print called GA, for 'general arrangement' which the engineers don't trouble to number, but it's the clue to all the others. I find one straight line, the datum line from which all the measurements are taken, and I am away, drawing this line at an angle, then hanging the transverse frames along it like coat hangers in perspective, then

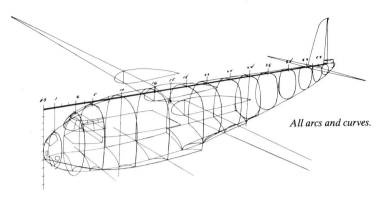

All arcs and curves.

scribing in her contours until she looks like an anatomical drawing of a whale. The chief engineer grunts approval so far, but I dare not line up the wings in his presence, knowing that the laws of perspective won't work for this. One needs to jigger them until they look right. I make my way back humping a load of blueprints and full of excitement.

Three months later, with the poster already up on the hoardings, the chief engineer asked me down to see the flying boat make her maiden flight. I arrived to find everyone on the slipway watching the silver beauty poised over her reflection as she danced lightly on the water. Her Perseus radial engines spluttered into a roar that settled down to a purr as she slowly taxied, to be lost to sight round a bend in the river. The *Canopus*, as she was named, looked like my drawing – what I had seen of her. A tense moment.

The director and design engineers remained standing in a silent group . . . waiting. The flying boat would, of course, be airborne as soon as she gained speed and 'unstuck', but would she *fly*? All these people's hopes and resources were invested in this one thing – a new type of manmade bird. It seemed a long wait.

Straight off the drawing board, the prototype under engine power. Will she fly?

81

A faint drone drifting in on the wind; it gets louder, she roars past, up river, at five hundred feet. A flash in the sun as a wing dips. She is banking steeply, frighteningly, then she makes a tight turn over the town and comes roaring straight at us – a flip of shadow as she clears the hangar roof by a few feet and is gone, back to the open water. The pilot has been showing her off like an errand boy on a new bicycle. The chief engineer brushes away a strand of hair that the wind of her passing has blown across his eyes, grins at the works manager, then fumbles for a cigarette – so moving I want to shout or cry.

On the way back, as the train rocks past derelict warehouses and stock-brick tenements, a period of gloom sets in. Even the best graphic art seems pretty trivial compared with tooling up for an aircraft.

Nevertheless, I am all excitement again when I hear that Jack Beddington wants to see me about a poster. After all, designing an aircraft means being one of three hundred: designing a poster – you're on your own.

Beddington was a director of Shell who had a daring policy on publicity. Anything unorthodox and people would say, "It must be a Shell stunt." His posters brought Modern Impressionism onto the streets of London while the Slade School was still painting peasant style figures in romantic poses.

JB, as he was known, emanated power and, so, was rather frightening to meet – an alarmingly high IQ behind an alarmingly high forehead. He even convinced the oil moguls that they needed John Betjeman, the poet, on the payroll.

To get any place an artist needs a streak of luck and Beddington was mine. He must have seen some potential in my work, which was more than I did. Looking back I now realise that I had a patron. He would ring me unexpectedly, "I want you to meet this client, Gardner, but first you will have a shave, and don't turn up in those arty corduroy trousers. It's the product which makes an artist, not his beard or the clothes he wears."

Feeling rather put upon, I would go straight to the Gentleman's Hairdressing Salon at The Savoy and have the lot (drawing the line only at a manicure) and send the bill to Shell – they would pay. Beddington had a sense of proportion, and of a man's dignity (unless he thought him a fool, then God help him).

When I turned up with the completed poster I found him in an angry mood, glaring at a thick manuscript on his desk, "Do you see this, Gardner? I commission an aeronautical consultant to prepare a script for an exhibition and what do I get?" He flipped the pages testily, "It's textbook material; the man's a fool." He observed me appraisingly. "It's for an exhibition about how aircraft fly. Do you know how they fly?"

I said I thought so.

"Do you know what I mean by the word exhibition?"

I said yes, I'd visited some.

"Well then, see what you can make of it."

Too overwhelmed for words by this bolt from the blue, I nodded as he tossed me the manuscript. Then, apparently regretting his impetuous gesture, he asked how long it would take. It was Thursday, so I said I would deliver the treatment on Monday.

FOR HIGH PERFORMANCE

Flying machines were still considered exciting when I handed this poster to Beddington on that fateful morning.

LUBRICATION BY SHELL

VICKERS WELLESLEYS   JAMES GARDNER

No man alive could prepare a detailed thematic treatment for such a project from scratch in three days. Nevertheless, Beddington shrugged and gestured me away with the back of his hand – not unkindly.

"In every man's life comes a tide which, if taken at the flood . . ."
(Apologies to William S.)

He wasn't to know, but for the past few months I had been swotting-up on that very subject. Since Rochester and the flying boat, I had become curious as to how it was that several tons of dead weight would trundle clumsily along the runway and then, bingo, it's up in the air and climbing steadily. Suction? I had even joined a gliding club – stick, canvas and string in a tent at Tring.

I was proud of my glider pilot's licence, No. 86, which gave entry to the Royal Aeronautical Society's HQ, but I did not have the temerity to enter the place until they advertised a lecture on 'The Aerodynamics of Bird Flight'. As Leonardo da Vinci died before he solved the problem, I went along to see what had been made of it since. After all, I had already bent a rib attempting to soar on a down current and remembered how, when the landscape came spinning up at me, my thoughts were not about the theory of flight, but of the two enthusiasts with whom I shared the sailplane, and here was I about to be intimately involved in smashing it up.

That particular meeting was in the Society's library, where I found three silent members warming their behinds at an imitation log fire. The man who mattered looked me over rather curiously, then commenced a technical dissertation on the

Corrosion of Light Alloys. I surreptitiously eased out my diary – wrong date.

After sitting politely through the lecture I made my way to the Natural History Museum, where I was illustrating insects for a Julian Huxley film on biological SCALE. As I climbed the steps into the Museum, a notion suddenly hit me like a bomb . . . insects fly. Then I fell into the trap and undertook my first bit of 'research'.

Who needs a university degree when practically everything that is known (so far) is stashed away in museum libraries? It was not long before I had drawings of how an earwig folds its wings (I didn't know they had wings), how the brittle wings of a dragonfly have a kink built in, so if it tips an obstruction they spring back unharmed, and how a beetle flips its wings by rapidly clicking its abdomen casing as it flies – click-click-click like an oilcan. Soon I had absorbed so much odd information on flying, from pterodactyls to helicopters, that I could write a book about it. And I had.

When I left Beddington's office that Thursday morning, a much-corrected manuscript of my first book, *How They Fly*, was already in being at my digs – half of it tucked under the breakfast tray and the rest on the floor. I pulled out my old Underwood typewriter and spent the weekend turning two-dimensional book into three-dimensional exhibition.

Preparing visuals for Huxley's film,
I became aware of the intricacies of insects
– Nature's most successful go-getters.

A wing span comparable to that of my sail-plane.

Unaware that I'd spent months on the subject, Beddington seemed quite surprised when I placed my offering in front of him at the appointed hour, all neatly tied up with a pink tape bow. He raised his eyebrows, put on a "What have we here?" expression, then sat back and flipped through it. Even Beddington must have been amazed – all that in three days!

He covered his surprise and informed me, poker faced, that I had the job. By this trick of omission I let him believe me to be something of a genius. Nevertheless, I was not a little frightened at the prospect of filling a large gallery with something worthy of the great man.

Even a genius must give birth to a first off

It didn't occur to me that I could delegate, so I set up shop in Carlton's basement with a jobbing carpenter, three apprentices, an aerograph machine and a glue pot, knowing that I could call on the Photographic Department for blow-ups. Avoiding intellectualising, what the critics would term 'Art', I used techniques I could handle, converting them into 3D, taking care that every exhibit was elegant, ingenious, or in some way out of the ordinary. Exhibitions I had seen so far had been very ordinary.

Remembering my success in the knockabout world of the playground, (boot box settings at two cigarette cards a peep) I painted delicate flying machines on layers of glass, mezzotints with depth, then a new look at the ordinary, comparing an aircraft wing with the Bermuda sail on a yacht – suction again. Nothing of course is *ordinary*. I sprayed all the exhibits, including a Merlin engine, matt white, to be viewed against walls in citrus yellow fading to sky blue – it made one's mouth water.

Not realising that such an exhibition would, in normal circumstances, be handled by a team of researchers, script-writers, a planner and exhibit specialists, I produced it as a one-man show, even finding time to lay out a brochure. This, in the form of a news sheet with invented headlines and bits of copy, dating back to when Leonardo crashed that 'bird machine' at Fiesole.

The only reference to the client was a scallop shell, fresh from the local fishmonger and mounted on a modest white plaque at the exit. Emphasis by understatement.

My reward? Well, Carlton took the fee, but on press night prior to opening, Betjeman, the people's poet, mounted the rostrum and gave an oration in the manner of W. C. Fields.

"My dear friends, and any gentlemen who may be honouring us with their presence – and that dear cleaning lady who is patiently awaiting the termination of my peroration. What we see here is not the expected public relations exercise for our friends Shell who, by the way, paid for it, but (pause) *a prayer to God."*

As it turned out we would soon be cheering 'Those Magnificent Men in Their Flying Machines' as they dropped bombs on Germany.

That's Shell —That was!

The 40's

WAR ON TWO FRONTS

Me join the Army? Don't be an Ass
Oh, to be a civilian, now that peace is here
Give us a chance
Bishops come in all sizes

Meanwhile . . .

London Blitz begins

David Lean: *Brief Encounter*

Hitler attacks USSR

American troops take Iceland

Amy Johnson feared drowned

Girls appear in nylons

USA kicked in pants at Pearl Harbour

Babe Ruth born

T.S. Eliot: *The Cocktail Party*

Hitler commits suicide

'A-Bomb' vaporises Hiroshima

Women's skirts go up, men's turnups down

Lights go on again in Britain

Flying saucers reported over USA

Orwell's *Animal Farm*

"Here's looking at you, kid!" – *Casablanca*

Orwell writes *Nineteen eighty-four*

Me join the Army?
Don't be an Ass

'. . . looked sufficiently innocent.'
Sketch of Young G by Old G.

Then came that Sunday morning when 'Oh, oh, Elizabeth' on the radio was suddenly interrupted by the hesitant, stilted voice of Neville Chamberlain and his hair-raising announcement that from eleven o'clock that day Britain would be at war with Germany. So, the scared rabbits were to fight again. Damn Hitler.

We blacked out our windows and sat waiting for the bombs to drop.

The first bomb came from an unexpected quarter when Archie Martin told us artists that our salaries would be halved for the duration. He gave us the option of looking for other work, the smooth bastard. What can a commercial artist do in wartime?

While the rest of us had been going about our business wearing blinkers, one guy, a whiz-kid from an ad. agency, took action. He sold out and made for a Pacific island to bring up his boys well clear of power drunk politicians. Unfortunately, he hit another lot who needed his island for an air strip and ended up in a Japanese prison camp.

Question: what action could *I* take?

Then I remembered engravings of battle scenes in old copies of *The Illustrated London News.*

The flat black glass front of *The Daily Express* building didn't look any too welcoming, but the half-pint boy who operated the elevator was friendly enough. The editor, or sub-editor, was somewhat taken aback by my proposition. After a pregnant pause, avoiding sarcastic overtones, he pointed out that since the Crimean War a device called the press camera had come into use. As I was leaving, folio unopened, it must have occurred to him that when something newsworthy did happen, the cameraman was seldom on the spot at the time.

Could I picture a modern battle situation accurately and quickly – while sitting at a desk in the editorial office?

Bad news.

Status quo.

*Allied
success.*

"Surely, that is what I've been trying to say, sir." It was as easy as that.

While I waited on events, the daily war map (then more important than the horoscope) must be updated; a sad record of the Allies' retreat across France. After marking-in the Front Line with great care I would, to my chagrin, find that a competing paper had shown the salient flattened out and another road junction in enemy hands. Now I was in the picture. My job was to keep pace with the 'stop press' news – before it happened.

One guy forecast good and bad news right through the war with remarkable accuracy in a cartoon strip, *The Adventures of Jane.* This featured a leggy blonde with precocious boobs, whose adventures continually put her through the tantalising process of dressing and undressing. It would go like this; fully clothed, bad news; partially revealed, status quo; a rare glimpse of her more intimate parts and we would confidently count on an Allied success. Her adventures were followed by everyone in the Forces, from brigadiers down, until we finally entered Berlin, when it was knees up and all over.

I would envy that cartoonist having his fun while I eyed the ticker-tape on my desk as it busily punched out reams of misinformation – then, impersonal as ever, it would chatter out a bit of real news.

SUCCESSFUL OPERATION NARVIC +
TWO ENEMY CRUISERS DESTROYED +
ANOTHER REPORTED DAMAGED +

My 'phone buzzed urgently, "Report Editor's desk, pronto."

The Editor looked quizzically over his glasses, "Narvic. I want a feature picture, five column, four and a half inch. You have two hours before the Irish edition and then another hour before we put the London edition to bed. Can you do it?"

"I think so."

"Look here, chum, we're holding the front page, so you bloody well do so. For your information, Narvic is in Norway – now get cracking."

92

Fear and adrenalin doing its stuff, I chased up to the library. "Map of Narvic. Oh, you've got one. Any pics. of the area?" A cruise leaflet guide to the Norwegian fjords was unearthed. "It'll do."

Back at my desk, I hunt hurriedly through folders of press cuttings; men and equipment, ours and theirs. No German cruisers, except an old one going through the Keil Canal, the details that matter obscured by flags. Some English destroyers. Good. I lay out the map, stretch a piece of damped paper on the board, prop my watch against the water pot, decide on a suitable viewpoint, one eye on the contour map, and sketch the scene. Time stands still. I am in Narvic Fjord. Light coming from the left? Watercolour washes are slow to dry, so I use a starved brush and blotting paper; the crash-artists' best friend. A destroyer belching smoke, its wake curving off in perspective. Plumes of white spray from near misses . . . the drawing board gives a twitch.

"Come along, laddie, she'll do fine and you'll have her back in a brace of shakes." That'll be for the Irish edition. A cup of tea, now cold, then an hour to clean up the smudges and make a finished job of it.

Half an hour later, as I make my way down the concrete exit to the rhythmic clatter-thump of the presses, bundles of papers are sliding down a chute to be caught and manhandled into

Two hours from ticker-tape to the Battle of Narvic. HMS Hunter *going down in the foreground.*

waiting trucks. A top copy is thrown my way. Bloody marvellous. On the front page, under a leaded headline 'Naval Victory at Narvic', is my artwork, reproduced in half-tone, the highlights deep etched. Oh, well, another little victory of sorts.

I continued with this schoolboy game of war on paper; long dull periods punctuated with sudden bouts of frenzied activity until the war got too serious for artwork – however realistic.

I plucked up courage and pulled my one string – Jack Beddington – though I doubted whether his influence extended as far as the War Office.

While I was waiting in limbo, as it were, Noel Carrington, who had published my first attempt at a book, *How They Fly*, showed me a charming children's booklet illustrated in hand lithography and printed on coarse newsprint paper.

A friend had brought it from Russia, where it was issued to their primary schools. Could I produce one like it – on aircraft? I said I'd have a go.

Today, colours are separated for reproduction by a photographic process. As I was about to revive a lost art – rendering each colour on a separate plate – I had to work closely with the printer at his works near an airfield in Kent.

Rendered with a greasy black litho crayon on three metal plates. First for yellow, then red and then for blue. For orange? Solid on the yellow plate and a faint rubbing for red on the next – to overprint. Scary.

I watch the great offset machine as the pages flip round a roller and shoot out at the end – first all in yellow, then oranges, and so on until, finally, the full colour picture. Not bad. Maybe those oranges are a bit strong? "You can't alter a thing," said the printer, "it's a *fait accompli.* You should guess right in the first place, old man."

I was barely tolerated at the works, as hand litho did the photo union-men out of a job.

I soon got the trick of it; a lack of registration here and there giving the 'hand-worked' effect Carrington had admired. As I carefully line in the wing struts on a rendering of the Wright Brothers' first power-glide at Kittyhawk, I lift the crayon from the plate with a jerk as, with a deafening roar, a flight of Spitfires thunders overhead; Merlin engines at full throttle on an intercept course to a life-and-death dog fight over the English Channel.

Twenty minutes later I would listen for their return, one by one. Patrolling power boats would be tossing out to sea hoping to pick up pilots who had bailed out. Aircraft could be replaced, but not trained pilots.

After the war Air Marshal Tedder told me that when the *Luftwaffe* failed and Hitler angrily countermanded the invasion, we had only two incomplete squadrons of fighter planes left with pilots to fly them. This Battle of Britain, he told me, was

THE FIRST SIGHTING
Three Hurricanes on patrol signal,
"Its on! Foxes coming in at 3,000
feet, not a sortie, it's armada!
We are going in, over and out."
Litho illustration for a wartime
Puffin Book, Battle of Britain.

as important to world history as had been the battle of Agincourt in 1415. (That was when conscript yeomen with long-bows, diarrhoea running down their legs, decimated the pride of France; the autocratic sons of nobility mounted on chargers decked out with historic heraldry.)

While these young pilots flew honourably into battle, here was I right under their flight path doodling artwork . . .

Me, join the Army? I guess so

A week later I was climbing a spiral stairway under one of those little domes that pretty the Whitehall skyline, trying to keep pace with a sergeant of the guards who, on reaching the top, saluted smartly and then barked as though the bare attic in front of us were a drill hall, "Sir. A *Mister* Gardner, by appointment, sir."

Observing me balefully from behind a trestle table was a phenomenon that was to dominate my life for some time. A high receding forehead, Neanderthal eyebrow ridges and a moustache that bristled like a swatch of coir matting. Colonel Buckley.

I heard later that a mountain near the South Pole had been named after him – and no wonder. I also discovered that, despite appearances to the contrary, his odd mind had a quixotic grasp of the situation. When ordered to provide the army with an issue of camouflage officers, he had decided to select civilians who had reached the top by using their eyes. This being a rare enough occurrence in Britain, he had collected a mixed bag – Victor Stiebel the couturier, Jasper Maskelyne the magician, Oliver Messel the set designer, Talbot Kelly the bird watcher, a bunch of arty artists, and two honourables (probably included to give the unit 'a touch of class'). Now he was glowering with bloodshot eyes at yet another arty type who looked as though he subsisted on buns and had never ventured beyond the confines of the London subway.

He shot questions at me as though reading lines from a theatrical farce. "Done any huntin'?" Pause. "Done any shootin'?" Pause. Then, in desperation, "Any fishin'?" This game of negative ping-pong went on for some time, but I needn't have worried. I had already been listed as a Second Lieutenant in the Royal Engineers (Camouflage), one of the lowest forms of life in the Army. He was a yachtsman and I knew how to tie knots.

I dashed round to purchase an off-the-peg uniform, unfortunately fixing the badges the wrong way up.

This was pointed out when I arrived at the training centre where, in a high-walled barracks rather like Wormwood Scrubs prison, I was shown how to salute so that I would, at least, look like an officer. I was then decanted, with the rest of the new boys, to Farnham Castle to learn the ploys Buckley had used in the previous war (useless) and the logistics, weaponry and deployment of a modern army in the field (which was less entertaining, but proved to be very useful indeed).

Come the end of the course we gathered, with mounting excitement, to watch as our names and postings were thrown up on a screen. Some to Southern Command, some to HQ York, to Dover Defences, the lucky ones to North Africa. The screen went blank. My name hadn't appeared at all. I had a recurrence of that not wanted feeling in my tum I used to suffer at school when cricket sides were picked.

This situation was far worse. I had been completely overlooked.

The camouflage ploys of a previous war.

A prima donna with a ginger moustache

Later in the mess, Buckley grunted over his whisky that I was to stay on – as an Instructor. I faced this appointment with some trepidation, having been warned that just one slip and I could find myself climbing nets with the Commandos, or spending the war years in a hut on a frozen bog in Iceland.

This dire fate struck Basil Spence, (architect of Coventry Cathedral), but he asked for it. As one of our crowd, Spence had turned up for a refresher course flaunting a typical Fifth Army moustache. We were strolling on the terrace after dinner when Buckley, noticing him mumbled, "Captain Spence, that moustache is too large for your face."

"He can't say that," said Spence striding after him. I asked what response he had made. He grinned, "Sir, isn't that the pot calling the kettle black?"

It hadn't been worth the grin . . . two weeks later he was way up in the wilds of Scotland with tough young Commandos, struggling with a full pack through icy water and barbed wire before breakfast.

When not saluting the Colonel in the broom cupboard, which, with a whole castle at his disposal, he had perversely selected for his office, I would be lecturing to whatever captive khaki audience I was aimed at, from liberated Poles to company commanders – or shooting at cardboard Germans in the comparative safety of the moat.

Nights would find me working in my room, but my fellow officers considered my preoccupation with work quite extraordinary, drifting in in two's and three's to watch me doing it, while discussing such immediate matters as likely postings, the wine list at the Ivy restaurant, or whether old so-and-so was related to the Shropshire so-and-so's.

Among the chores when not lecturing, I devised a demonstration of our latest dummies to impress top tank commanders. On one memorable occasion they were in a group viewing five real tanks and a dummy at a hundred yards.

"Which is the dummy?" I asked. Before they reached for their field glasses I blew a whistle. Four men rose, apparently from nowhere, and lifted a pneumatic dummy high into the air. "Good show, what?"

In wet weather dummies acted as dry cover. On this occasion, when the dummy tank was lifted the top brass were surprised to see a uniformed trooper wobble to his knees while a dolly bird ran off, hurriedly adjusting her skirt. (The culprit was fortunate enough to be in the Canadian Forces and so outside the observers' jurisdiction.) The four invisible men had been lying behind small screens of open rabbit-wire spotted with bows of coloured webbing and local grass. This simple trick had worked against sharp-shooters, in full view, on a dirt road.

Cherchez la femme

Any off-beat item that landed in the Colonel's IN tray would be thrust my way. For example, a 'circus', the Army's name for a training show in a tent. This was to demonstrate concealment in the field, a well-worn subject which I must jolly-up to involve the troops. One item would be Buckley's favourite lecture topic – 'The Net Curtain Effect'. (Here there should be a trumpet fanfare and roll on the drums.) The principle was simple enough and intended to explain why the Army issued *'Camouflage nets, other ranks, for the use of'*.

I devised a dummy window fitted with sections of black and white net curtain on rollers. Turn the handle and view it from outside; first white – see nothing, then black – see all. All what? I devoted long hours to detailing a desirable female, shapely leg poised high as she stroked on a sheer nylon stocking. I was carefully lining in the seam when . . . "Humph!" Buckley was peering over my shoulder.

"You'd better get some clothes on her, don't yer think?" I pointed out that she had a flesh-coloured bra and knickers. "Make them show up then," following which remark the old puritan drifted off to cause trouble elsewhere.

Seeing it was an order, I gave her an open, black-net bra and lacy black knickers, very saucy. I had just popped the finished dollybird on a cupboard to dry when an unexpected Staff Colonel from Southern Command turned up to ask whether I could camouflage Canterbury Cathedral so that, from the air, it

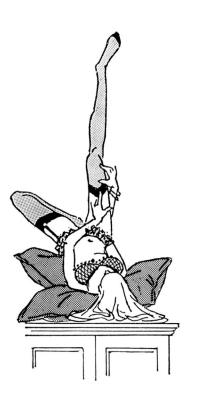

would look as though it had suffered a direct hit. This was to deter the *Luftwaffe* – Hitler's '*Baedeker* raids'. I was explaining that this wasn't our job, when he noticed the cut-out lady and barked, "Did you produce THAT?" Hell. Now I'm in trouble, thought I, when he bent down and muttered, "Could you do one for me?"

What a laugh, but the Canterbury deception was too tempting a project to miss, so I laid on a phoney pattern of bomb damage using scrim, steel wool and a scatter of bric-a-brac.

Southern Command's Camouflage Officer told me later that the prim Montgomery, who lacked a sense of humour and so took himself (and, fortunately, the enemy) seriously, would take visiting VIP's to view the pretty lady, while he turned the handle. What do you know?

A Paper Tiger

During one short interlude, when Buckley had gone off to Chittagong, (after first getting me to practice forging his signature, so I could deal with War Office bumph), a request arrived marked MOST SECRET.

Apparently, as the enemy had been frightening us for eighteen months, someone at the War Office decided that we must do something to frighten them – 'we' being me. This would be done by 'leaking' information about a secret weapon which didn't exist – *proposals requested IMMEDIATE*. Had we been asked to think up a weapon to be actually produced, I would have been at a loss. As they only wanted ideas, the problem was to keep the flood in check.

A giant reel to be launched at the enemy trailing a cable which, at the critical point, would be detonated. Wow!

A ship, its davits slung with tanks in lieu of life-boats.

A flying spinner that sent out a swathe of used razor blades at head height? No, too difficult to control.

One of our bright guys proposed that we parachute call-girls over enemy lines with stainless-steel teeth inserted you know where, and though all is fair in love and war, it was then I decided enough was enough.

I was subsequently instructed to PROCEED – whatever that meant – with an item I had added to the list at the last moment as ballast for the more flighty notions.

A hard-hitting tank

I was not particularly addicted to tanks. True, it was Winston Churchill who got the first produced using Admiralty funds and concealing the purpose of the allocation by entering it in the Navy books as a 'tank'. The name stuck. I preferred to ride ON a tank to riding IN one, and the same goes, I guess, for tigers. When on a tank one must wear a helmet and, as we were at least four hundred miles from the enemy, I would (illegally) appear in a light-weight *papier maché* version which we mass-produced for dummy troops.

On the day in question I was clinging to the turret of a Crusader Tank as it floundered over a blasted heath, blasted enough to be allocated to tank trials, when I observed, between bumps, that the enemy was, in fact, in sight in the form of a gaggle of Staff Officers who were aiming their field glasses my way. Question: does one salute senior officers while straddled on this bucking monster? The problem did not arise as, at the critical moment, my paper helmet was hooked off by the branch of a tree and, caught in the breeze, sailed gaily off to land in a gorse bush.

Fortunately, the high-ups, seeing I was an Engineer, didn't bat an eyelid. Other arms denigrated the Royal Engineers by referring to us as the 3M's. Nothing to do with Scotch Tape, the M's were – "Methodist, Moribund or Mad!" Okay, so let's be mad and design a tank that will frighten the enemy, even if it will never exist.

I pondered. To design a tank must be difficult enough for the specialist, but as this one would never be built it would be easier. Also, once one has decided what an object is to do, it almost designs itself.

What must a tank do? It must move fast, climb obstacles, present a small target, have a thick skin and carry a knock-out punch. I made her low with a smooth duck's belly to breast obstacles and a rotating gun turret at the rear to annoy attacking aircraft. Then my 'most secret' item. Having given the tank an exceptionally low profile, I had added two caterpillar tracks which projected forward to hinge up when climbing, taking the weight of the tank on two great shock absorbers. These were borrowed from the 155mm field gun, one of our best weapons;

a convincing bit of 'committee compromise' which might help to fool the enemy. Then for the real business, a thumping great gun.

One trouble with a high-velocity gun is that it shoots straight, so I 'invented' a breech-loading mortar that would send a canister of TNT sailing over the brow of a hill to hit the chaps on the other side when they were least expecting it.

I wasn't too sure of the next move myself. I checked with the Tank Development buffs. *Ten inches too wide for railway tunnels, air inlet too low for river crossings, and how did I propose they get the engine out for maintenance?*

CO Tanks agreed to have the bits that showed detailed by his technicians. He pointed out that my tank must not only deceive men practised in the deceiving business like Von Roenne, but Krupps whose tanks out-classed anything the Allies could put in the field. "Unfortunately," he remarked, as we examined a slab of German armour-plate, "our tanks are designed by a committee. Can you imagine even the bow and arrow being designed in committee?"

Deceive Krupps? Creepy. I visualised some square headed Prussian with duelling scars on his leathery face. Back to the drawing board.

I soon learned that in the Army, (that is, when there is a war on) ideas were not enough, you had to see them through. Good discipline for a probing mind. I once smugly presented Buckley with an 'appreciation' of a scheme we had been requested to vet, proving it to be unworkable. "Well?" rising blood pressure, "You say it's nonsense? Then make it workable, man, we're not here to sit on our fannies." I left with my tail between my legs. Buckley's patience, like Hitler's, was quickly exhausted.

If the Colonel nailed you on evasion or partial untruth, beware. Life was like riding a fairy cycle on a tight rope, as he was liable to throw his telephone through the window or, after glowering angrily at a wall chart listing officers he had appointed, stab at it violently with a chair and storm out of the room, leaving the chair stuck in the wall like a surrealist offering by Salvador Dali. In addition to designing this bogus tank, I must see the job through . . . devise some means of getting it as a fact to the enemy.

Blue-prints, passed under a café table in the fold of a newspaper? Lisbon would be the place. No. Drawings can be faked too easily, this tank must be shown to exist. A film-take of one on the move? Possible, but difficult, and to get a most secret filmstrip into enemy hands without the operation being suspect? It would have to be a photograph – of a beautiful, perfect, undetectable model made the more convincing by blemishes, like the little mole on the flexing calf of that model I had so admired in the Cartier days.

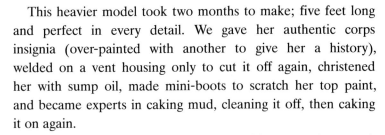

This heavier model took two months to make; five feet long and perfect in every detail. We gave her authentic corps insignia (over-painted with another to give her a history), welded on a vent housing only to cut it off again, christened her with sump oil, made mini-boots to scratch her top paint, and became experts in caking mud, cleaning it off, then caking it on again.

Unfortunately, when I came to think of it, every photograph is taken with a purpose, so I had to concoct an innocent purpose. The War Office laid on a special tank exercise and I

THE G TANK
Identified by the forward tracks and long gun. Experts said tanks were too unstable for such a gun – that was until the Germans introduced a gun of this size on their Tiger tank!

went into the photo-transplant business. The faked picture was planted in a popular 'daily', where the dot screen would defeat anyone using a magnifying glass.

The picture? Jack Benny the entertainer posing with the troops. In a gap between two grinning faces some tanks could be seen throwing up dust in the distance as they plunged across a patch of scrub. If the trick came off as we hoped, a memo would be passed down enemy intelligence channels:

CONFIDENTIAL + TOP PRIORITY + POSSIBLE NEW TYPE BRITISH TANK + UNORTHODOX SUSPENSION + EXTREMELY HEAVY ARMAMENT + NOW UNDERGOING TRIALS + AIR RECONNAISSANCE CONFIRM + IMMEDIATE +

We left it at that, while I considered what form the next offering would take. As every move carried a risk, I decided to give them the lot in one throw; a close-up photograph of the G-tank that would reveal every detail – else what had we made the model for? Problem. The enemy know that visitors don't wander around security areas with cameras slung round their necks.

I arrived one wet morning to case the joint where tanks were born. Easing uncomfortably out of a second floor lavatory window, I took an angled shot of a cobbled yard adjoining the workshops. Two REME craftsmen posed in the centre of the picture, backs to the camera, looking attentively at nothing. One had his knees bent.

The result, an amateur snap-shot marred by two blurred lines made by out of focus telephone wires. Only a fool would attempt to fake these when he could use an uninterrupted view, which was why I had selected that particular window. If I could get away with it, those telephone wires would be as good as a watermark.

We photographed the model at the same angle on another dull wet morning and, after a few bosh shots, managed to get a perfect superimposition. Now the two mechanics were looking intently at the sprocket wheel which drove the G-tank's forward tracks. I then airbrushed-in the blurred cables.

The composite picture was finally photographed with a common Kodak, using stock film. I scribbled on the back of the print: 'Show this Vera. She always liked Jock's backside and all. Fred'. Then crosses for kisses – in blue-black ink, which I had read somewhere can be 'dated'.

I carried it around in my hip pocket for a while and then asked an ATS girl (daughter of an Admiral so quite safe) to keep it in her handbag for a week until it had absorbed that unmistakable 'cosmeticky' smell.

It went off by dispatch rider and I heard no more – until after the war, when an engineer, just returned from a fact-finding mission, told me that the Japanese, of all people, had a 'J' version of the G-tank at prototype stage.

Not a waste of time, as this was a most successful effort at industrial design. Does anyone need a tank?

Tiptoeing through the tulips

All the while, having the notion that a guy who stuck things with a substance called cow gum and put slides in a projector the correct way up could do anything, Buckley threw a non-stop sequence of chores my way. When not designing a rope-making machine (that didn't work) for the workshops, photographing frogs' eyes in infra-red, or cancelling demonstrations owing to the rain, I would secretly be designing pub broadsheets for the Ministry of Information, which purposefully insulted Hitler and his henchmen . . . to augment my pay.

But though I was dressed and drilled to look like a 'gent', born to give orders, (while shooting game birds or Germans in season), I never really slotted in.

The rest of the guys, being much happier at legalised gang warfare than that non-directional personal pastime called peace, took to the life like ducks to water. My sense of not belonging was sharpened by an underlying fear – a wrong foot or word and the hammer of God, in this case the CRE (known familiarly as Shit King), could swat me like a fly. Happy days.

Dynamite before breakfast

On one occasion, four of us 'irregulars' got so bored listening to top brass opinionating in the mess on what ribbons who got, where and why, that we decided to drop a gentle hint. One morning we reported for breakfast wearing battle honours. Mine were quite an eyeful, being strips cut through the word VOGUE, which had been printed on a magazine cover in multi-colours.

"Mornin'," followed by a walrus grunt indicated that the CO had arrived.

Noting our ribbons from beneath lowered lids, he glowered down at his plate, his complexion becoming more and more purple, then thrusting back his chair with a crash he strode from the room. Dynamite.

From that day the Colonel and I were separated by a divide. In the upper echelons of the Army good manners were equated with honour, and I had transgressed. The difference thus exposed was fundamental, the distance between the playing fields of Eton (where the Colonel had been born under a gooseberry bush) and sooty Willesden Junction, (where I had, apparently, crawled out from under a stone).

The Army had obviously hit this problem before, as aspiring officers were handed an instruction manual which started with the startling statement, '*You are now a gentleman and servant of the Queen . . .* ' Then behavioural hints - '*Fellow officers do not wish to converse at breakfast* (how true). *It is customary to pass the wine to the left. No smoking until the Queen has been toasted. Gentlemen do not discuss betting or ladies in the mess.*'

Unfortunately, there were no instructions as to how a 'gentleman' farts. This set me a quandary when, sitting on a plank over a latrine in drizzling rain at a Forward Headquarters, Lord Alexander, Supreme Allied Commander, turned up, let down his trousers and seated himself at my side completely at ease. College education.

Buckley's hidey-hole boasted a side door which opened into the mailing room. The Corporal who was guardian of this door had mounted a knitting needle on the corner of his desk to act as a flag pole, with a little flag that could be pulled up and

Fifth Army Headquarters in Italy.
A wet watercolour in the rain. Latrines?
Follow the duckboard to the left.

down. On the day in question the flag was up at the top, meaning that the colonel was not only in, but in good humour. Good.

Let's mount a dummy war

The great man fumbled in his IN tray – like a pig prodding an indigestible presentation copy of Rossetti's *Sonnets* that had fallen into its swill – and tossed me a TOP SECRET file. It was headed DECEPTION PLAN. We were to report on the feasibility of mounting a 'display' (three cheers, we had got them using the word at last) to lead the enemy into believing that a full-scale invasion of the Continent was imminent. I was pretty sure we would not be prepared to mount the real invasion for at least a year and guessed this deception plan was intended to draw German Forces away from Stalingrad, where the Russians (then our allies) were beleaguered.

"Nonsense of course," Buckley mumbled as he saw me conning it. "Some fairy at the War House who enjoys playing charades."

The Colonel was a 'concealment' man (else why hide in a broom cupboard?). To him, 'display' in any form was bad form.

Facing the risk of being immediately transferred to Iceland, I clicked my heels together and formally requested, "Permission to have a go at it, sir."

Taken aback, Buckley concentrated on his pipe for a while and then muttered, "I'll have to put yer in purdah, yer know." Purdah meant no communication with my fellow men and when the edict was put into force, my 'fellow men' made this an occasion for a new form of indoor sport, assiduously avoiding all contact with me as though I were a carrier of some contagious disease – like swollen head, for instance. Not that I cared – I had a problem to work on.

The deception plan was a logical situation and could be coped with. What made me go prickly all over was how to present it to the top planning committee; bright guys from Sandhurst, West Point and wherever. I decided to set the whole thing up as I would an advertising campaign in peace time (not that I had ever set up an advertising campaign in peace time).

TYPICAL DECOYS. A gun battery pattern.

Some ten weeks later an anonymous, elegantly attired Staff Colonel whisked me off in a staff car with motorcycle escort, the plans in a brown paper parcel on my knees. The escort was there, of course, to make it obvious we were carrying secret information.

At Planning HQ, red tabs lined each side of a long baize-covered table, waiting for me to perform. I laid my offerings before the head man. First a slim folder: "The deception report, sir. This first folder contains Information Received by the Enemy, and these," I laid out some fat files and a pile of folded blueprints, "show how we do it. This last is the Cover Plan, to ensure that those involved are not aware of our intent."

A private army that isn't there

In preparing the report I had first asked myself the stock military question – against what? Obviously, against enemy intelligence. How do they get the information? From little snippets in the press, the radio, informers identifying men on leave, and coastal zones closed to visitors. All this keeps them busy, but more important is the unimpeachable evidence obtained by high-flying aircraft. The ground patterns. I knew how revealing these could be, as I had a collection of photographs developed from the few high-flying snoopers we had brought down.

My first course was to have air mosaics taken of possible assembly areas. Then I faked, on a series of transparent overlays, the telltale marks that are made by a flat-footed and tank-tracked army on the velvety green of England – scars, dumps and tanks, well concealed but leaving the marks of how

False vehicle tracks reveal HQ.   *Activity indicates use of wooded cover.*

they got there for all to see. There were badly draped camouflage nets just to show we were trying, and landing craft – thumping great things that cannot be hidden or mistaken for anything else.

The enemy would plot them on a map, just as we did when they were assembling barges to invade us the year before.

At that time we had few dummies on the stock list and, to help matters along, I concocted detailed drawings of non-existent equipment, giving them authentic-looking stamps and numbers. Hence that pile of blue-prints on the planning table.

I was told later that McNaughton, Head of the Planning Committee, picked up the top folder, read for some time in silence, and then looked up with a tight grin. "Fascinating – it's a *whodunit?*"

He had been reading a bogus post-dated German intelligence report 'for the attention of the Fuhrer'. Part I – Information Received, date; Part II – Sources (air recce, media monitors, informers, interrogation); Part III – Reliability Grading; Part IV – Conclusions Drawn. This *whodunit?* was cross-referenced to the files and blue-prints with cross-bearings that pin-pointed the positions faked on the air-photo mosaics.

Some months later when I entered the Colonel's sanctum and performed the customary ramrod-salute act, he fiddled with his pipe and muttered, "Don't stand there man, park yer fanny." Ominous. True, he had ordered me off the premises some days back for appearing without full kit and gas mask during a 'red alert'. He glowered at me, "Do you think the War House have gone bonkers?" A rhetorical question. He hated saying it

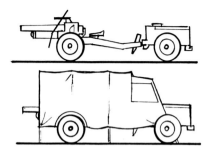

Wolf in sheep's clothing. Concealment was difficult in a desert – but an innocent truck may mask a fieldgun and limber.

"That deception sprat of yours has caught us a whale."

From that moment the concept of 'deception' was accepted at top planning level. Bored Camouflage Officers were suddenly upgraded – and I got a new job, in charge of Army Deception.

"The army hasn't got a name for it," said the Colonel. "You'll have to think one up for yourself." So I called myself Chief Deception Officer, Camouflage. ('Camouflage' was put in for camouflage.)

Crimes before breakfast

With an indefatigable Wally Cole (the only other officer in the crowd who wore an off-the-peg uniform) I scoured the country-side looking for the impossible – a country house that had not been requisitioned by the Canadians. We found it – Pierpoint House, Surrey, a tudorbethan folly complete with minstrels' gallery, a string of courtyards, a park as far as one could see and, beyond, a boggy wasteland churned and tortured by tank tracks and scattered with spent cartridges. A set-piece for Frankenstein's Castle in which to develop our most secret secrets – when we had thought some up, that is.

A designer's dream – sketch out an idea, ring a bell, hand it to a tame specialist with, "Get this put together, will you," then a stroll round the workshops. Think of it – I was Commanding Officer of an RE company made to my own specification. But I drew the line at growing a moustache.

This is the Army. Design? First, I must put on a pie-faced act again; this time as a judge, confidant and marriage counsellor to three hundred and fifty odd-bods. A Chemical Artificer tried to support two wives on one pay book. Another man attempted to forward his dirty washing to a Dowager Lady somewhere in Ireland (then tantamount to enemy territory), another wanted to marry a local bit of skirt, or room-mates objected to some poor bloke's smelly feet.

A stroll round the workshop? First, 'Crimes' before breakfast. The Adjutant marched offenders in one by one.

"Left right, left right, att-e-e-n-shun! Cap off! Textile Refitter Goldberg – sir."

One of the girl clerks, a cheeky piece, has reported an incident. "Written deposition, sir." Apparently this rather

110

unprepossessing Goldberg had made her a handbag from a piece of antelope skin – in return for favours to come? Bag completed, he pinched her bottom for starters. Silly cow – a storm in a teacup. "Three days San and Gen.," (slopping out the latrines). Damn. I must report this to the Queen Bee, the bossy boss of girls in khaki, who had recently called me to book for isolating the females well away from the men in a small farmhouse, forgetting that I had stored explosives there for the same reason. Oh well, you can't win them all. Next.

A quick-tempered extrovert had created a disturbance when parted from his beloved bagpipes. In future he must practice in the bothy at the far end of the estate. It is customary to march up and down while playing? Nonsense. Next.

More serious. A pyrotechnics guy had 'talked' in the local pub. This rates a court martial. I don't know how to run a court martial, so I award him a month's detention in the glasshouse; a prison for military offenders. And so it goes on.
Next.

Thank goodness, breakfast.

After a day playing at Army, I would switch on my desk lamp and lean over the drawing board to the sound of the Adjutant blowing into his trombone and bursts of laughter echoing up from the sergeants' mess. What on earth do they find to laugh about? I must concentrate. How does a platoon of men erect a dummy Bailey Bridge, in range of the enemy, in the dark, so that no man has to cross the river twice?

DUMMY BAILEY BRIDGE

Slack steel-wire ropes, spanning the river, support a series of lightweight metal frames connected with a criss-cross of webbing. During night erection taped sound provides the authentic clang and occasional swear-word of engineers at work.

But every one of this collection of comedians – as varied as the insect specimens in a museum – had the 'know-how'.

Carpenters, photographers, plasterers, fitters, chemical artificers, tinsmiths, pyrotechnic experts, and a concreter (who deputised as cook).

They could cheat when necessary – just as a craftsman cheats when planing over knots (to catch them unawares); or a typefounder casts the 'o' just a little bigger so it looks right. The worker ants had taken over as fighter ants – but it was a devious kind of fighting.

You name it and we'll make it

Together, we could produce anything from explosive camel dung to a high-powered-pneumatic-duralumin-framed-river-craft to be dropped by twin parachutes. Put us on a desert island and we could turn it into a trading estate before you could say, "For Christ's sake, stop!" An assorted lot, culled from those untidy workshops you discover up blind alleys and under derelict railway arches.

This visual deception business now became as much a part of the Allied murder game as the pattern on a cobra.

The German army-pattern bicycle pump I devised to keep the French Resistance chaps happy looked innocent enough, but it blew quite a number of Nazi officers' arms off.

An apparently threatening situation can, on the other hand, be just fireworks.

If one's forces are inferior to those of a well-prepared enemy, you resort to deception, which may hold him off for a time then, when you are ready to attack, your most vital weapon is *surprise*. My job – to make this possible.

I was not unduly shocked to find that the issue of army training manuals was limited to warrant officers and above, so I prepared a little illustrated booklet *Surprise Attack*. An idle Canadian Map Unit (the Army prints maps of the territory ahead as it advances) printed it off for me and to my joy, MT1, the Training Branch, issued it to all ranks. No charge. Amazing what one can get away with – when there's a war on.

Although I was now a Staff Officer, I still found it necessary to augment Army pay by secretly doing commercial work in

Surprise

The first principle of

Attack

A HANDBOOK FOR N.C.O.'s

Prepared under the direction of
The Chief of the Imperial Staff

An airliner of the future. How wrong can one be?

I occasionally produced a press item to supplement Army pay.

my billet. This deviation was only known to my batman, a circumspect 'Jeeves' in battledress who, in his lush days, had been Beverley Nichols's gentleman's gentleman. The indignity of having to press my off-the-peg uniform and clean those Gobi Desert boots must have put his urbane manner to the ultimate test.

Surprise attack

Say you plan to occupy an island – Madagascar – mountainous, no suitable beaches, the one good harbour well defended. You can't surprise the enemy as to time; they will have seen you coming. You can try frontal attack, old style, and you will be at a disadvantage – or you can do the other thing.

One of our fishing boat's chances to ram and sink an enemy submarine.

To do the other thing, you send a flight of bombers in full daylight to drop a parachute division, not on the harbour but way over the mountains on the other side of the island. The defenders in the town see clouds of parachutes drop away in the distance, then a signal flare as it bursts against the sky. Then they hear sporadic rifle fire and the occasional thump, echo, thump of a mortar, then the chatter of a bren gun and so on. Their comrades over the mountain have obviously been

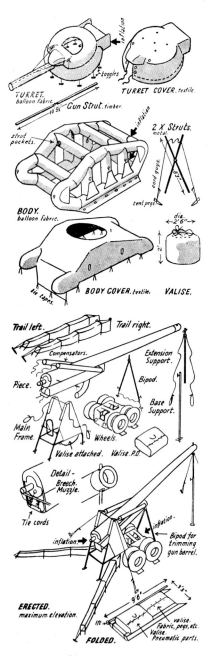

Hours at the drawing board detailing for production, then checking prototypes, next guessing the requirement, then illustrating instructions for their erection, in The Pneumatic Man's Bible.

surprised, are outnumbered and in trouble, so off they go to the rescue – leaving the harbour virtually undefended.

The defenders have, of course, been fooled. The parachutes were one-third scale, and hanging from them were little stuffed puppets we called 'angels'. When certain angels hit the ground, their stuffing would come out and unroll as a neat plastic mat laced with detonators, blanks, signal flares and rounds of 'rapid fire', all linked to an intricate pattern of slow and fast time fuses. They were the 'effects men'.

Detonators can be temperamental, so when laying out an 'angel-mat' (well away from the officers' mess) it would feel like 'tiptoeing through the tulips'. Pilots who flew them must volunteer – I am afraid *must* was the significant word – as one detonator, triggered off by altitude, would activate the rest.

One of our guys, who ran a 'cat circus' in peace time, joined the pilot on a sortie, just for fun. The plane took off from the airstrip at Gibraltar, climbed steadily until it was a speck in the sky . . . then there was a flash.

Pilot, buddy and their dummy angels were now with the heavenly angels.

Double bluff

During the campaign in Egypt the Camouflage Officer was ordered to join a desert reconnaissance. At a particular spot the Commander drew his victim's attention to a group of tanks beleaguered on a slight rise in visual range of Rommel's patrols, or rather to shapes that had once represented tanks but which now, bleached and tattered by sun and wind, had become an abstract in stick and canvas, a sad demonstration of how Nature holds all the trump cards in the long run.

The Commander turned to his ADC, "Lay on a patrol tomorrow so this fellow can clear that stuff away. Wouldn't fool a rabbit." "But sir," the Camouflage chap interjected, "those dummies were put there to replace real tanks, which were moved over to Palestine to liven up a show being staged there to impress the Turks."

"That operation folded a month back," was the gruff response. "But, sir, the Jerry patrols think those are just dummies. The *real* tanks are under them now . . . sir."

Improvisation on-the-spot

On a sticky occasion, when I was due to face an enquiry (some 'unmilitary' activity), the Colonel very sportingly saved my skin by sending me on an 'urgent' reconnaissance of the battle zones with an impressive pass signed by 'He who must be obeyed' – Chief of the Imperial General Staff. This was considered almost indecent by the British Forces, who would take avoiding action, but the Canadians and American units were suitably impressed and treated me like a General.

I was swanning around in Italy at a time when Allied Sherman tanks were easily outgunned by the enemy's heavily armoured Tigers. A Canadian armoured division had, at last, been issued with a few tanks carrying guns of similar range. Snag. Tigers would concentrate fire to first knock these out, then deal with the rest with the six-pounders, at leisure.

I got the Canadians to knock up some little dummy six-pounders from fuel cans on a 'do-it-yourself' basis and mount these on the back of the new tanks' reversed turrets. They could now advance with the gun that mattered out of sight on trail. When well in range, they would rotate turrets and engage the Tigers with a fair chance of catching them unprepared.

The first pneumatic dummies were born when long-promised reinforcements of tanks failed to arrive in Egypt and, so that Rommel would think they had, the Camouflage Officer was ordered to supply a dummy armoured brigade.

Italy. Floods had carried away a vital Bailey bridge. Under the direction of the Engineers, a permanent bridge was quickly built by local masons. Military traffic switchbacking over it when the arches were only one brick thick.

The big gun out of sight.

115

An early pneumatic pretending to be a Sherman tank, on weathering trials at Farnham.

Armour out of the air

Make dummy tanks? Okay. But with what? Supplies were so short that they were already using Worcestershire Sauce as a medium for repainting trucks that had been issued for desert warfare painted dark green.

Searching around, he came upon a large stock of rubberized fabric intended for patching observation balloons. As there weren't any observation balloons, he commandeered it. Air pressure has the habit of turning any container that restrains it into a sphere, so the first pneumatic tanks had a somewhat busty appearance – except in the night chill when they would ease down as though hatching eggs. But pneumatic dummies had one great virtue – the material that made up their bulk, air, was always available on site, while the envelope could be carried around in a grip bag.

Undressed to reveal technique.

A pneumatic anti-tank gun.

With later development such pumped-up equipment was difficult to recognise as bogus from a hundred yards, if seen in the right context, of course. After one windy night a Camouflage Officer was yanked out of his bed to be told that his pneumatic three-tonner was up a tree – bad form.

Dummy equipment designed in my unit was soon being manufactured at locations all over the country. Our production line at Manchester was actually producing a pneumatic tank every three hours and if the enemy had taken to using rubber bullets we could have staged a first-class war. With this in mind, I had put together and illustrated *The Pneumatic Man's Bible* – a comprehensive catalogue of our dummies and how to deploy them. But the War Office refused to print it – said the information was classified. And so it was.

'Lead us not into temptation'

How, I asked myself, could we win this damned war if my stockpile of lovely dummies was rotting in Ordnance Stores? Deciding to print and be damned, I indented for paper (in small batches to allay suspicion), applied for a Craftsman Printer and installed him with a fount of type over the gatehouse, labelling the door 'Caxton' to divert suspicion?

I had noticed a disused printing machine when on a hurried visit to the cloak-and-dagger department of MI5 (to dazzle-paint some motorboats shocking pink and emerald so that they

117

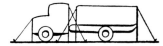

Evening – device fully inflated.

Morning – chilled air contracts.

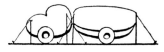

Midday sun – air expands,
device simulates a balloon.

wouldn't be seen in moonlight on an SAS escapade in the Adriatic). I purloined it and we were in business. To cover myself, I inserted the word 'NOT' in front of the customary acknowledgement 'ISSUED BY AUTHORITY OF THE WAR OFFICE'. No one noticed. In fact, the department concerned blindly took on the task of distribution.

Seeing my amateur efforts come out in print induced that smug feeling like a fat cat faced with a saucer of cream. As a youngster I had been given a junior printing outfit – little rubber letters, a pair of tweezers and a pad sticky with purple ink. But a real printing press under one's command? That can prove to be highly dangerous.

Our Company collected rations (even the Royal Family had rations) from the Army NAAFI in Aldershot but, as we were confined to our own territory, we were given a NAAFI branch on the premises and, being opportunists, had formed the questionable habit of drawing rations – both ends.

One day when I had mislaid my coupons the Adjutant, a wily old regular, suggested we print some just for use in our own NAAFI. I was startled, "But that would be forgery!" "No," he replied, "not if we print some *to our own design*." In an aberrant moment I grunted, "Okay, then," and made my way down the corridor.

We were soon accustomed to using these pretty home-made coupons – thus doubling our rations for cigarettes, chocolate, etcetera – until one unforgettable morning a white-faced corporal dashed into the office. "Sir. Trouble, sir. The new NAAFI Inspector, sir, saw your coupons and threw them up in the air, sir. And, sir, he says they aren't coupons at all . . . sir."

A chill hit me . . . horror headlines in the Sunday papers.

COLONEL FORGES COUPONS
Faces Court Martial

An irate crowd at the gates hoping to lynch me as I am taken off in a covered van under police guard. But, as ever, our cheerful Adjutant had the answer. He was walking out with a blonde poppet in Aldershot who had a blonde poppet sister.

It happened that this inspector had solicited intimacy with the seductive sister, but she avoided him, as he suffered from, I hate to say it, halitosis. But she agreed to tolerate the bad breath for a while – for a 'consideration'. God bless whoever invented blondes, even the Aldershot variety. I was saved (at least in this world if not in the next).

Softly softly catchee monkey

I took another risk, spending a large chunk of our development grant on a great three hundred foot rig framework for dummy tank landing craft – these would be key items if the plan did come off. Quite a problem, as the dummy must be assembled easily, quickly and in the dark, if necessary. I gave this LCT the code name Big Bob and then draped it with camouflage nets so it looked like something else; but a visiting high-up saw it, asked on whose instructions I had squandered the money, then buzzed back to make trouble. I needn't have worried.

One morning a dispatch rider swerved to a stop in front of our building and, saluting his space-man helmet, handed the Duty Officer a heavily sealed envelope. TOP PRIORITY.

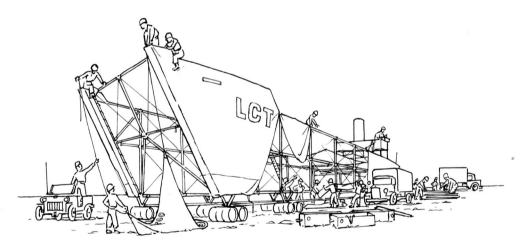

Instructions to organise the supply of near a hundred Big Bobs, as though we got them off the shelf like cans of beans.

Gosh! We must now get them built (in secret), train crews to erect them, locate sites from which to launch them and find 'volunteers' to ride them out to sea.

Erection trial.
Two Spitfires circling overhead to attack any enemy reconnaisance plane approaching the area in daylight.

119

Launching a dream

Old Buckler's Hard, where wooden fighting galleons were once built, is made a security zone and, with a Spitfire circling like a kite overhead to warn off snoopers, our prototype takes form. It is as big as Nelson's flagship, bigger, but there the comparison ends. The duralumin space-frame is so lightweight that a large twelve foot section is a two-man lift and the cross-wires that brace it are exactly measured so the twist of a Spanish windlass will stiffen each section trim. We locate the bolts with pins as used for nappies, only larger, so the crew can work by feel.

The men are wearing blindfolds. I'm not, as I must work out a drill so it can be done by numbers.

The launching wheels are our luxury item; stern wheels of Dornier aircraft brought down in recent raids. (Nice to think the Germans are contributing their bit.)

The oil drums on which this sophisticated framework is mounted look ridiculous, but we will soon see if our calculations are correct and they ride just below the waterline. And that is how she floats, a delicate silver lattice poised on its own reflection, a fairy pier drifting out to sea. Looking down from one of the planks that serve as a bridge, I see a few slender tubes, taut bracing wires, then deep water thirty feet below flowing by quietly as though she isn't there. Perfect.

While she was being dismantled I strolled up river and crouched, lazily watching a few dainty autumn leaves sailing then circling in the eddies as they floated down on the clear stream.

There I was, being paid, watered and quartered to play a crazy *Alice in Wonderland* game – not even a *real* war. Are we all mad?

Mad or not, each move we make triggers off the next, so on to production. Every manufacturer in the UK was already working to full capacity but, with an eye on the future, I had collected a hoard of steel conduit – a more stable currency than cigarettes. With a bit of horse-trading and the supply of a large hangar I enticed a manufacturer to set up a production line.

Big Bobs built, the Navy declined to man them –

Big Bobs assembled around the South Coast in preparation for the planned 'ghost' invasion aimed at Calais. Here, a string are seen moored in an estuary ready to take to sea.

"Unseaworthy". So GI's straight from the States were conned into it before they had properly gauged the alcoholic content of British beer. That settled, I located slipways where they could be launched, with cover nearby for concealing the components during daylight.

One Big Bob discovered in an undressed state and the whole deception operation would be blown.

This may sound pragmatic, but life had its odd moments, like my first reconnaissance flight along the coast to photograph possible launching sites.

Club-class with a camera

The Flight that normally served us was busy committing mayhem over enemy territory, so I rang Major Wills, an old stager who camouflaged coastal defences in peace time and was not yet fully aware that there was a war on.

"Sure," he replied, "pick you up at Odium airfield, 8-pip-emma. Don't forget to have a pee first like a good lad, and immediately I touch down, jump aboard, smart."

I guessed that this indomitable freelancer was not in the habit of notifying Air Command. Highly irregular.

His De Havilland Dove droned out of the mist as planned and I was in her as she taxied for take-off. Visibility low at forty yards. I was watching raindrops chasing each other across the window in the slip-stream, when I saw a vertical cable and

121

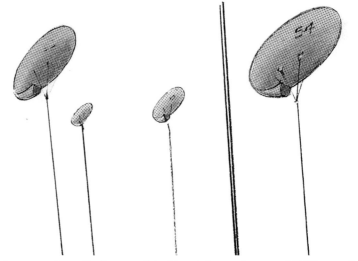

then another, flash past. My blood froze. I tapped Wills on the back, shouting above the sound of the engines, "Balloon Barrage!"

"Not to worry," he replied, "over Southampton," pointing down with his finger to make the point. As dangerous as playing Russian roulette, but we were soon out of it and in glorious sunshine, when an argument broke out between Wills and the pilot. Pilot said he smelt burning. Wills said nonsense. The pilot won and we were soon circling down to land at Old Sarum, an emergency field.

"Oh well, a chance for a pee and a quick drink," said the ever-cheerful Wills as we waddled towards the hangars, parachute packs between our legs. Noticing some mechanics on the tarmac jumping up and down and gesticulating, I looked back to see our pretty little plane enveloped in a tulip of flame. (I might note that Major Wills was an inveterate pipe smoker.) Half an hour later he had breezily conned a local Air Force pilot, over a glass of beer, into flying us the remainder of the reconnaissance. Major Wills was a lovely man.

Some time later I was testing a prototype in the Naval harbour at Westward Ho with Johnston-Marshall, one of the bright boys who had escaped Singapore to join us. The Americans had just introduced the DUKW, a boat with wheels (except that it could also be described as a truck with a propeller). Anyway, it had its uses. I decided to design a pneumatic version to be dropped by parachute for river crossings in the jungle war.

We were having a difference of opinion with the Navy, who insisted that a boat wouldn't steer with the prop. and rudder mounted forward. Seated aft, the guy who operated the craft couldn't see to steer through thirty fully equipped troops. As I innocently pointed out – they put bus drivers in the front. The fact that our craft ran circles round everything else in the estuary settled that argument.

The Four Horsemen of the Apocalypse

Trials over, we were taking in deep breaths of ozone and scanning the horizon, as landsmen do when they sniff wet seaweed. We lazily observed, right along the line of dazzle where sea meets sky, a faint ochrous-grey blur, too continuous for cloud – what could it be? Below it we soon made out dozens, no, hundreds of little smudges - ships! It was the Allied invasion fleet, the largest armada there has ever been, making for the Normandy beaches.

The timing of the invasion, the best kept secret in history, (except did Elizabeth the Virgin Queen bed Sir Walter Raleigh?), was ON.

We leapt into the jeep, JM put his foot on the starter and we made for base.

The ten-mile coastal strip from The Wash to Land's End is closed to all visitors, and it is very quiet on the slipway at Dartmouth. It is almost dark. Our sage-green crates, tucked under hedgerows, are only distinguishable by code numbers in luminous paint which seem to hover like blurred fireflies.

Aerial. ***OPERATIONAL PNEUMATIC DUKW***

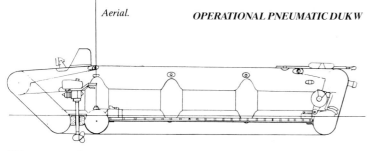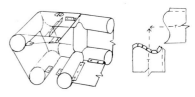

Pithers power unit.   *Duralumin lattice to give rigidity.*   *Inflation pump.*   *Fabrication technique.*

We hear a small convoy of trucks creeping down the hill (no lights), then a hundred or so GI's jump down and make for the field at a run. They have done it all before.

A contented burp and the flicker of a signal lamp indicate the arrival of an Admiralty tug. A grass rope splashes and, to the sound of creaking as bracing wires take up the strain, a newly erected craft moves slowly down the ramp, bending like a lilo for a moment as it breasts the water to send a wave off into the darkness. A spark glows red over the plank bridge as a nervous GI draws on a cigarette, then the thump-thump of the tug's screw grows faint and the waters are still again. Already shadowy figures and an occasional grunt and click indicate that a sister ship is being laid down.

Again that friendly burp, a splash – then sparklets of water fan out in the starlight as the tow rope twists and pings like a violin string under strain. There is an ominous creak, wires snap like rifle shots, the whole structure distorts and a frame falls away. One of the men, with great presence of mind, cuts the rope with an axe. I wonder where he found that axe?

Already there is a greyness in the sky.

"Quick you guys. Dismantle! Clear the site!"

We retreat to the cosy warmth of a blacked-out pub.

"Well," say I, "bet this is the first time a ship's been built round a thumping great bollard."

"In normal practice," says JM, "ships are not constructed in the dark, nor, come to think of it, are they built without bottoms." True.

Back at the mess, some visiting blokes have tuned-in to the German news – Goebbels' frantic counterblast to the BBC.

Disgusting. A bunch of fairies playing at war, like it's amateur theatricals.

Rather sick. The phoney English voice we called Lord Haw Haw (which sank the *Ark Royal* so many times that when she actually was sunk no one believed it) is doing his best to undermine our morale, as usual. After informing us that the clock in the High Street at Guildford is twenty minutes slow – just to show – he continues: "You will be interested to learn that yesterday, at precisely 6.20 a.m. your Greenwich time, intrepid pilots of the *Luftwaffe* bravely penetrated your defences, sank three craft intended for carrying tanks and damaged two others, completely blocking your important harbour of Dover. Heil Hitler."

"Turn that bloody thing off, somebody." So, that's five of our dummies already destroyed. Damn. They're to be looked at, not shot at.

Once we were ordered to send the Big Bobs out to sea powered by their outboard engines. I crossed my fingers. They had not been designed to take rough seas or gale-force winds. In effect, every hour we were instructed to maintain the deception kept Rommel with the main mass of German armour immobile, while the Allies were fighting it out round Caen.

Worth the effort?

An investigator who examined the Pentagon Papers after the war reported:

"Never in the history of warfare has such a decisive effect on battle resulted from the undercover work of a few faceless men."

So, like my schoolboy hero Hannibal, we had used deception as an integral element in battle.

Oh, to be a civilian, now that peace is here

War over, notice that I was no longer needed came in the form of a 'regular' colonel (frightfully polite but not much up top) to take over. Just as I was jumping into a truck for the railway station he had me called back to his (my) office, "I say, old boy, before you ingenious fellas desert me – what do I do about the atom bomb?" I hadn't a clue.

From a stereotype in uniform that returned salutes like a clockwork toy, I faced becoming a civilian again with the same apprehension I had felt five years back when I was shoe-horned into the Army.

A lack of identity when I first essayed into public view in a 'demob' hopsack jacket and pork-pie hat, as self conscious as a young girl must feel when launched in her first party dress.

No design projects to think about, I started thinking about myself, which is dangerous. How was I to make a living when, I guessed, all the good jobs had been nobbled by guys who had not been playing at soldiers?

I need not have worried. Sir Stafford Cripps, Chancellor of the Exchequer and proponent of austerity (who, it was rumoured, subsisted on a diet of one currant a day in a glass of water) had it all worked out. A prod from my pre-war trigger man Jack Beddington got me in on the act.

It takes time to roll the corrugations out of corrugated iron, convert Spitfires back into saucepans and provide women with 'undies' not made from surplus parachute silk. Cripps, deciding he must give the public something to look forward to, laid on an exhibition of 'things to come'. This was to be set up in the galleries of the vast Victoria & Albert Museum – then empty; its treasures having been evacuated (with the children) to the country.

This, the first big post-war show, was to be called, optimistically, 'Britain Can Make It' and I was the guy selected to make it. (Beddington was still under the misconception that I was a genius – no need to disabuse him.)

Cripps pointed out that, as no one had a clue as to what would turn up, I must introduce 'decor' that would give people a lift, even if the exhibits didn't.

What exhibits? I borrowed a pre-war mail order catalogue – the authoritative listing of Twentieth Century Man's survival kit, including many items we had completely forgotten in the last five years – and plotted a floor-plan to cover everything, from machined *broderie anglaise* to electric toasters and double-barrelled sporting guns.

Peace had really broken out.

The Design Council, who were collecting exhibits, realising that an explosion of babies was due – result of troopers making the most of their leave -- informed me that I had omitted perambulators. A pity. The nanny pram was all that remained to us of a long line of horse carriages; most elegantly slung on leaf springs by leather straps. Hyde Park wouldn't be the same without them.

My layout, as complicated as today's printed circuits, left no space for prams but, noticing a vacant building lot across the road, I jokingly replied that, as they felt so strongly about it, I would make arrangements for a special pram park on an adjoining site.

Some months later I was visiting a warehouse (to inspect dolls), idly watching the floors flip by the latticed elevator gate, when I noticed an area half the size of a football pitch given over to prams. Someone had taken that facetious remark seriously.

I was learning about people. Make jokes if you must, but never in writing to a civil servant.

Lesson number two would be obvious to most people but, being accustomed to operating in the little, rectangular world of a drawing board, I had the happy habit of thinking and going it alone. Now, unexpectedly faced with controlling a national project I was still, with Wally Cole, my 'Man Friday' from Camouflage, unconcernedly going it alone.

The female of the species, Army style.

It had not occurred to either of us that we could employ a secretary, or that we even needed one.

Enter Mehitabel

One afternoon at the Design Council offices, we were enlivening a tea break by climbing onto someone's desk and peering over a nine foot partition, (to see who had quietly closed a door on the other side), when we were held by a very engaging sight – a dollybird changing her stockings. The service hat on the table indicated that this girl, who had revealed fifteen inches of delectable white thigh, was a 'Wren'. A superior type. (Most girls who volunteered found themselves in the Army, but the *crème-de-la-crème* were skimmed off first to give the Navy a bit of class – they were termed 'Wrens'.) My contact with females having been limited for some years to category one, 'ordinary', in anonymous khaki, this first peep at a category three, rare 'goddess', well, pretty near goddess, gave me to pause.

Maybe this *Homo sapiens* crowd I was landed with had something after all. Wide-set eyes, tilt-up nose, slender neck and marvellous legs. Sensing me there she caught my eye, arched a neatly pencilled eyebrow and froze, one hand still tensioning a slender suspender. I flushed redder than any Rear Admiral and heard myself say, "I do beg your pardon, we were looking for a secretary . . ." It turned out that she was applying for just such a job, so we now had a secretary – and how, and her name was Mehitabel.

I didn't see the thigh again for some time, but it was reassuring to know it was there.

We set up office in the Victoria & Albert Museum in a little curators' room off the Costume Gallery. As soon as a chair and table arrived and I could settle down to drawing – I hit a problem. How to design a show that would look complete in every detail if we didn't get exhibits? I concocted a new kind of layout plan. Instead of presenting the goods to the eye, as one would in an open market – and that is how exhibitions have evolved – I tucked them round corners, behind screens and in little enclaves, so at first the visitor would see lots of 'decor ⌐ no goods – wouldn't even notice ┐ ⌐ere *were* no goods at all.

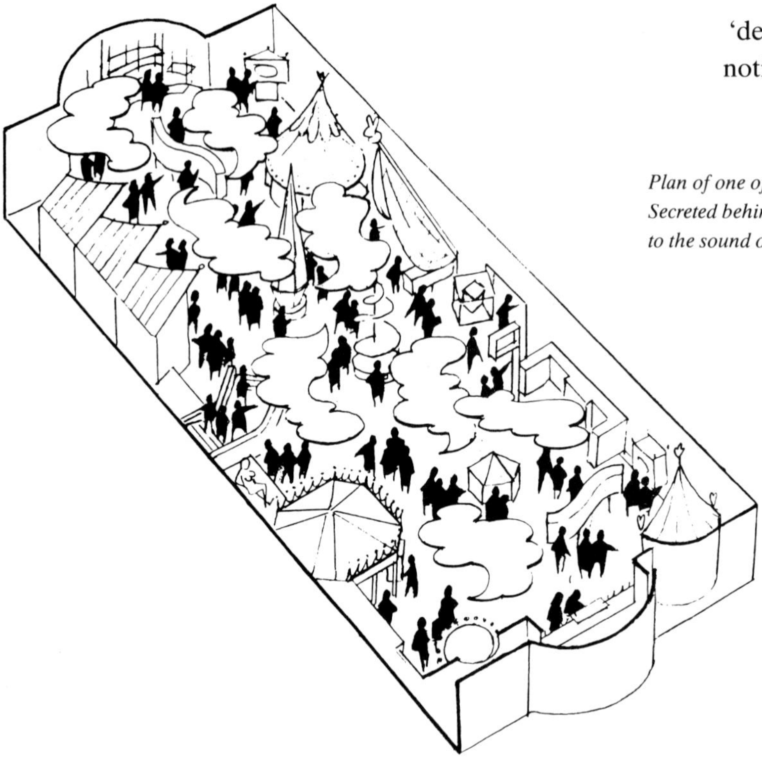

Plan of one of the galleries. Secreted behind the decor and to the sound of soft music.

Cutlery
Ornaments
Tableware
Timepieces
Fancy goods
China
Kitchen ware
Furnishings
Drapes
Bed linen
Jewellery
What a bore . . .

This introduced a surprise element.

After spending the day trouble-shooting, Wally and I would put our feet up and have 'bangers and mash' in a little green hut across the street, where the cab drivers made us honorary members of their club. Then back to the paper work, or what in the trade we call 'chasing'. Nobody moves unless he is pushed. It was my job to get the show open, so I had to push. To me, filing cabinets were for entombing ideas under numbers, so Mehitabel, who had an orderly mind, was left to do the filing while I papered the walls with graph paper and used *that* as a universal check list. Our small room soon looked like the stomach of a computer, but I found this rather homely. As a boy I had used this same method to list the progressive development of what we call Civilization (I believed in progress then). By dropping a line, one could correlate Thomas Arne composing 'Rule Britannia', Joseph Bramah inventing the water closet, and the Montgolfier Brothers going up in a balloon. (It did not occur to me at the time that these could only be related by installing a closet under the balloon, with the navigator sitting on it singing 'Rule Britannia'. Interesting, but unlikely.)

And there I was, in the V & A updating items along the picture rail, against time which flowed downwards: items which varied from a tented valarium in spun fibreglass (then a startling new development) to hairnets for suspending golf balls.

As you may have gathered, Mehitabel had a proper and ladylike background, so we gave her the mornings off (if a morning can stretch to five in the afternoon), when she would arrive as from a garden party, bright and ready to join us in a second eight-hour stint. After dictating orders and listing 'musts' for the next day, Wally and I would unfold our camp beds and pass out – to the happy tappity-tap of the typewriter.

Our plans shocked the Director of the museum. I was converting his dignified marble halls into theatre – marrying the new Mars-Group's 'functional' mode with pageantry; a sort of Camelot, a romantic twilight of tented drapes. Too romantic? Anyway, a change from boarded-up windows, leaking sandbags and weed-covered bomb damage. Yes, and we would perfume the air in the women's fashion section. A fresh start. No inhibitions. Exhilarating. (Trouble: I did not realise that body warmth increases the potency of perfumes, until an irate he-man complained that feminine emanations had caused caustic comment on his bus ride home.)

Meanwhile, I was supposed to be selecting and coordinating a team of designers (who all seemed to have ideas of their own) providing settings for thousands of assorted exhibits, and doing my best to show some semblance of authority over five contractors who knew more about building exhibitions than I did. (A good thing as it turned out.) The 'easy riders' hadn't yet taken over, and we all worked as though we were still at war. Wally and I kept up a routine of working sixteen hours a day until, near the end, the effort of climbing three shallow steps would set my heart racing.

Lesson number three crept in uninvited from under the

A rendering of the designer, who flatters the goods – and the visitor.

131

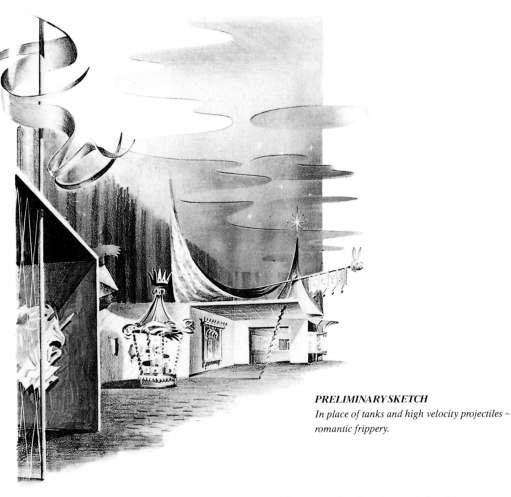

PRELIMINARY SKETCH
In place of tanks and high velocity projectiles –
romantic frippery.

carpet, as it were. In the Army I had become accustomed to taking it for granted that one issued an instruction and something happened. Now, I discovered, I had unwittingly strolled into another battle zone. One shifts the gear-lever into top only to find the whole set-up suddenly going into reverse. Disconcerting.

The first bout started quite innocently. Barbara Jones, a mural painter, was perched on a trestle, when a tubby man in a raincoat twitched at her skirt and muttered something about 'cards'. Now Barbara was an avid collector of interesting postcards, but not *that* kind, so she said, "Go away you nasty little man."

The nasty little man turned out to be the Union District Organizer, so the fat was in the fire.

Battleground

We had a meeting. The artists were told they had to join the Union. But as artists don't get a weekly wage packet, and go to the loo in their own time, they took a poor view of being press-ganged. The Union bloke said they had members who could paint every bit as well as that bunch. He obviously could not differentiate between putting on paint and painting. A portrait artist who painted ladies and gentlemen would, I guessed, be the same to him as a man who lettered those words on the doors of public loo's. Eventually, the artists joined. Had they not done so it was obvious Britain Would Not Make It.

Every morning I would say to myself, "Let's get really organized," then inform anyone who cared to listen that, come what may, we would spend this one day working steadily down the trouble-shooting list. Some mornings I would not even be given time for the small pleasure of the good intention. A hand, for example, would shake me out of my camp bed, "An Air Force officer to see you. He's already waited an hour."

And it all came alive in 3D, to the ominous sound of 'The Nutcracker Suite'.

Now what the devil have I done with my shoes?

The natty pale blue uniform looks annoyingly pimpish, even effeminate. "Your Spitfire, sir." He almost salutes then, seeing my stubbly chin, stops himself just in time and holds out a sheaf of papers for signing. "Brought her in from Biggin Hill this morning, sir."

I pause for a moment wondering where the devil he landed her. "She's outside, sir," he indicates the window. I stand on a stool to look down. Of course, it came by road.

Down below, the commuters' cars are edging round the obstruction, for all the world like a procession of ants crawling round a dead beetle. The Spitfire is on a low trailer; its wings folded as though still emerging from the chrysalis. A Spitfire, brand new and all mine . . . except that I don't need it.

Or do I? Just a moment. Didn't I ask the designer doing a section on wartime inventions to introduce the tail of a crashed plane in his set-piece? That Spitfire stood on its low-loader for days, but the Air Ministry, who had spent thousands to produce her, now treated her as disposable. In desperation we cut off her tail and shoved the rest on the district refuse tip. A case of premeditated murder if ever there was one – worse than drowning a kitten. The Smithsonian would give thousands of dollars for her today – one of the most beautiful devices Man has designed.

That interruption over, I fumbled around for the ashtray, to find it hidden under a swatch of cloth from Morton Sundour – *Chartreuse* green slashed with white stripes, the stripes spotted with dabs of magenta. Not too ghastly – it even started a fashion. I compared the sample print with the colour sketch – okay. It is for a 'nonsense' (something not logical, but likeable): a great swag that is to be slung from a thirty foot pole with a rabbit's head on the end – whiskers and all. The White Rabbit from *Alice in Wonderland*. Groan: "Has anyone seen a rabbit's head around?" No. So off to Fidel Schorr's studio in the Fulham Road. A skilled craftsman, but liable to come up with what the Germans term *kitsch* if left on his own. On the other hand, he clad three elegant mannequins I had purchased in Paris, as bird-women, with feathers individually

Fine textiles.
Previously 'For Export Only',
to pay for armaments.

134

lapped, so their bodies glinted like kingfishers on the wing: if God designed us as his top product, why did he give birds the feathers?

Back in the museum, I make a detour to evade two talkative Czechoslovakian geniuses, Lewitt and Him, who are arranging umbrellas on a stylised cutout tree, and pause to admire two sweet young men from Liberty's, who are garnishing a reclining female plaster nude with trails of black and white lace.

Maybe a bit sexy? Yes, for when I showed the Queen round during the opening, someone had discreetly covered it with a dustsheet. I didn't see the point. If royalty are insulated from sex, how is it they manage to maintain an endless supply of royal children?

Then I came up against Lee Ashton, the Museum Director. As Mark Twain remarked, "A cauliflower is a cabbage that has had a college education," and, in my experience, this applies to the inmates of most museums, but Lee Ashton was a flower of a different kind. He appreciated fine things, had big ideas and, like Mae West, carried them forward with aplomb. At this moment he was looking moodily at a twenty foot bronze

Treatment of the sports equipment area, by Robert Gooden.

The tearoom – service from the 'Caravan'. Designs incorporated in the laminate table top for the first time.

Buddha with SMASH UP chalked boldly across its belly. He had chalked it there himself a few days back when I argued that this Buddha obstructed circulation.

The great man looked it up and down for a while, and then spoke, "This is a very ample Buddha and a great deal of misguided effort must have gone into manoeuvring it to this precise position – but it has no other merit. Nevertheless," he indicated the chalk instruction, "we must consider the Board of Trustees." He flipped a toffee paper off its tummy with a lawn handkerchief then turned away with a shrug, "I suggest you move it into the courtyard."

It is still there today, posturing in the lotus position, a trickle of bird lime over one eye.

The unforeseen = crisis

Back in the main hall I find work at a standstill. 'Flats' are hanging at odd angles and the men on the high rig are having a quiet chat. There is a problem. Wires for suspending lower 'clouds' will have to pass through the upper 'clouds', which are already in position. "It may look okay on the drawing, Mr Gardner, like it always does, but how do you reckon we're supposed to get at them up there?" Here we go again.

Before I can solve it, Basil Spence (whose release from Camouflage had been arranged so he could 'architect' the show) comes up, with his flowing moustache and nervous friendly grin.

"Come on, G, we've got it working at last." He points to some rectangular black holes thirty feet up. "Any minute now, so stand by."

He is referring to the museum's prehistoric ventilation system, which should suck the stale air up and carry it away along a system of ducts. If this does nothing else it will dry off the final coat of paint and keep the more fragile exhibits fresh for the opening. Good show.

There is a steady, distant hum, then it slowly dawns on us – we are about to experience a happening. The ancient ducts, carpeted with a five year deposit of museum dust, don't suck, they blow. Groping through the choking dust, we stumble for

Even the pans and brushes became heraldic devices.

Travel goods, an opportunity for Lewitt and Him to introduce their characteristic artwork.

the stairs and end up in the mezzanine loo, eyes streaming.

"They sure blow," I remark. "Must be powerful fans."

"Yes," says Spence, "it's a Pleinham Extract System, you know. Fans probably started up in reverse. We'll soon get it to rights."

"Of course," I reply as I wrap the corner of a towel round a finger to wipe the dust from my neck. "We'll have to close the building till it settles." A pause. "That'll mean overtime to get the show open." We call yet another contractors' meeting.

With only two days to go, I am doing the rounds with Mehitabel in my wake taking notes – except that she isn't. She has been trotting behind, poised on some sleek, high-heeled shoes that had taken my eye among the exhibits, but deciding enough is enough she is now resting on a plinth and stroking her feet. I stand for a while, looking down as though hypnotized. She changes pose, self-consciously.

"Don't move. I am more interested in what you're *sitting on*. If you can sit there, so can the blooming public. Question is, how to stop them?"

I have it. We'll mount a row of spikes along the edge; the tops off iron railings.

"Make a note – we must chase them in the morning."

New lamps for old

As we enter the next section it looks dull, unless my eyes aren't adapting to the lumen level. We are using fluorescent tubes; an invention so recent that this is their first use in public. They should be giving more light than this.

"Do you think it's dull?" Mehitabel thinks it's dull.

"Right. Let's find the electrician." He is a dour Scot.

"Ay, it's gloomy enough. Have ye no' heard? We're clean out o' tubes. I've tried every stockist from here to John o' Groat's, and the makers. Not a one to be had." He almost seems to relish the fact. We open in two days, and to a half-lit show?

It is only as we are climbing up to our little office where, sad to say, my wall computer was discarded long ago in deference to orthodox files, that I suddenly remember . . . The Design Council's offices in Petty France are fitted out with fluorescent tubes from top to bottom and I – still – have – the – key – to – the – door. Some bottled beer, a truck load of ribald electricians, and as soon as you can say, "Let's pinch the lot," they are balancing on tables and stripping them down.

The day before opening. The security men arrive and kick us tradesmen out, so I put up at the rather pukka Rembrandt Hotel across the street.

Early morning, when the alarm wakes me, I find a cryptic note pinned to the counterpane. "Gentlemen who associate with Royalty clean their finger nails, wear a white shirt, remember to say Sir or Ma'am, and don't get a swollen head." No need for a signature. How the devil did she get in?

After dutifully cleaning fingernails, (using a toothbrush), I lie back and ask the ceiling, "Where, oh, where do I get a nice white shirt at seven o'clock in the morning?" No response. Then it occurs to me that there are some super shirts draped on dummies, just across the road.

I had no difficulty in slipping past the janitor, who knew me. Prowling around the 'Modern Man' section, I eventually decided on sea-island cotton with an almost invisible pinstripe. Arranging a silk handkerchief round the neck of the lay figure, as a cravat to fill the gap, I crept across Brompton Road with the trophy stuffed up my jacket. So, apart from a red tie, (which the Queen remarked on), I was once again in regulation uniform.

Chatting up George VI (the guy to the left). Far right, Clement Atlee, then the Prime Minister.

The opening went well enough, except when the King – that is George VI – got left behind. In an attempt to be all things to all men as we paced pompously along, I noticed that the toes of his shoes tended to turn up, like mine. This made me feel quite friendly and I steered him to a corner and opened a case, so he could take pleasure in handling some sporting guns. This ploy worked and the King even lost his hesitant stutter. Then

I had a prickly feeling that something was wrong. It was too quiet. The entourage, myopically watching the Queen enjoying her professional act in the charade, had forgotten the King and was now out of sight in the next gallery. So, like a porter in the rush hour, it was, "Excuse me. I beg your pardon. (This way, Sir). Make way please . . ." until we caught up with the official party again.

A success? Too tired to care

Next morning, with the public due in, I sat moodily at my desk feeling as virile as a wet sock. The gang had already broken up and left me with myself and my future, neither of which could well be avoided.

Basil Spence, with an eye on *his* future, had treated the Directors of ICI to a posh lunch at Wheelers. Finding he hadn't the wherewithal to pay the bill, he calmly passed the hat round. Spence will survive, thinks I.

Wally Cole had surreptitiously put a deposit on a kiln at Rye and gone off to lead the good life making pots. As for Mehitabel, she would already be in the country and was probably wrapping her thighs round a pony that ought to be put out to grass. She'll be back . . .

The 'phone rang. It was the director of the Design Council.

"Good show, and are you okay, G?"

"I guess."

"We've hit a snag. The man who was to administer the show has taken ill. Can you hold the fort for us for a couple of days?"

I managed to gather sufficient energy to say, "Yes, I suppose so," then replaced the receiver and closed my eyes.

Later, looking down from the window to see if there was

still a world outside, I found the wide street solid with people and traffic in a jam-up. The show must be a success, but surely somebody ought to be controlling that crowd. Then it hit me, I was the temporary somebody – so I rang the Police. In two shakes of a duck's arse mounted police were herding the populace until they formed an orderly queue, which extended from the entrance all the way round to the domed Catholic Church on Brompton Road.

Surely, thought I, if a God who designed the Universe had really been under that dome, the queue would be facing the other way. But Cripps had done it – 'Britain Can Make It' was on.

The world that was

Released at last, I re-introduced myself to my wife and suggested a get-together trip to Stockholm to see what the Scandinavians (who had kept well clear of the war) had been up to while we were dodging Hitler's flying bombs.

There was an amusing side to these doodle-bugs as, unknown to the Germans, the engine would cut out directly a bomb commenced its dive. Pedestrians would be casually going about their affairs, quite unconcerned as the doodle-bugs throbbed overhead, doodle bob – doodle bob – doodle bob . . .!

Suddenly silence, then all within hearing range would dive for cover – and that included old ladies. A sort of Russian roulette in the sky. There was only one serious moment, when a doodle-bug landed smack against our HQ. I was awakened to discover that the bed cover was pressing heavily on me under a load of ceiling plaster. No sign of fire, so I turned over and went back to sleep, to discover next morning that the blast had scattered a month's tobacco ration to the four winds. The Nazi bastards.

Such tribulations were soon forgotten when, stopping at Copenhagen *en route*, we decided to dine expensively at the Vivex, their top restaurant. Someone put a little Union Jack on our table, then a handsome tenor in a smart tuxedo signalled for silence and sang 'Land of Hope and Glory' at my wife and me, to tumultuous applause. Embarrassing, but – gosh, we must have won the war after all!

Arriving at the Swedish fairyland with its well-dressed sanitised people, brightly-lit shop windows and dancing neon signs, I was able to readjust to the civilised world . . . like picking up bruised bananas discarded by a barrow-boy. (We hadn't seen a banana for five years.)

When not picking up bananas I concocted a plan. With what was left of the Design Council fee, I calculated that there would be sufficient to put two month's rent on what had once been servants' bedrooms on the corner of Duke Street in London's West End.

True, the stairs would have collapsed had not each one been supported by the one below it and bombing had left the ceiling with a bulge, as though an elephant was sleeping in the attic but, with odd bits of furniture from Carlton, a drawing board and a T-square 'borrowed' from the polytechnic, a redundant filing cabinet from the Design Council (side door), we were in business.

AN EXPERIMENT
Purchasing a novel invention
– the felt pen – I try it out sketching one
of the world's most beautiful buildings,
Stockholm's Town Hall.

Was it Disney who said,
"Suffer the little children, let them come unto me."?

Black mark in the Doomsday Book

'Britain Can Make It' was followed by an offering in Edinburgh, redesigned with a Scottish flavour. In the process I earned two black marks.

To entertain youngsters, I experimented with mounting a child's view of the show at low level - a chance to uncover the pomposity of 'grown ups'. As compère, I introduced a stylised rendering of the Scottish lion which shocked the pompous *Lord Lyon King of Arms* – top Scottish herald. He informed the press that my, ". . . wee beastie in a kilt was an insult to the honour of the Scots."

I had the fun of replying in the press that recent versions of the Scottish lion, which his office put out, looked more like bits of wet flannel. The London press jumped on the G bandwagon. Dour Scots, their hackles up, responded angrily . . . war was, fortunately, averted.

I received a card informing me that after the Queen had graciously opened the show, I was to attend luncheon at the Usher Hall in her presence. Too busy to read invitations, I tossed it into the IN tray with others, unread. Come the day, there were hurried whispers at the Usher Hall when my place at the top table was seen to be vacant. The police and hospitals were contacted to no avail, with the result that the Queen and her guests impatiently waited twenty minutes for lunch to be served. Meanwhile, I was unconcernedly tucking into eggs and bacon at a bun shop across the road. Back at Duke Street a missal arrived from the Lord Provost of Edinburgh informing me that my behaviour had been "tantamount to *lèse-majesté*". Wow! I'll never get that Knighthood.

 **Give us a chance**

13 Duke Street.

'We' comprised Smithy, an apprentice from Carlton Studios, who had the romantic looks of Robert Louis Stephenson which girls fall for. He also had a well-matched glass eye but, using the good one, he could produce beautiful artwork.

Our 'corporate image' was enhanced by Phelps, a tall guy who dressed well enough for a City bank yet could handle most everything and, to my relief, Mehitabel, who had forsaken her old pony in the greenery for the bright lights of London.

Carlton directors said I couldn't manage a business – they gave me three months, then sat back to watch me go bust.

Run a business? I purchased a pad with carbon interleaves and three rubber stamps, one for INVOICE, one for STATEMENT (in the event of an invoice being ignored) and, optimistically, one for PAID.

Fortunately, a bright girl, secretary to Mary Adams who ran BBC Television, took pity on us and introduced Mehitabel to the mysteries of double-entry bookkeeping. Even so, it was a near thing.

We were playing a game of leapfrog, aiming to get paid for Job A before we had spent it all working on Job B. As Henry Ford said, "Keep on producing something people need and it's bound to come right in the end." Nevertheless, come pay day, Smithy and I would creep onto the landing and pool our loose change to make up Mehitabel's wage packet. Meanwhile, to pay the more immediate bills I would be working at night, which meant the addition of a camp-bed to our office furnishings. The tax bastards – sorry, officials – caught up with this survival ploy twenty years later, when they were working out a vendetta against the few romantic independents who still managed to survive operating as individuals.

But Henry Ford was right. In time the cash-flow caught up with the jobs.

We took it for granted that, if we really tried, we could handle anything.

DIY at Duke Street

Five flights of stairs, one telephone, one secretary, three slaves, a fire extinguisher and a tea kettle. We took anything that came along on the conveyor belt . . . or, rather, up the stairs. No word processor, copier, FAX, or computer in those days. Committees had not yet proliferated; we worked person-to-person, so maintained a certain dignity.

Shell.

A TV play in production.

An international conglomerate.

The Rocket argues with its inventor.

PR for the oil lobby.

A fifteen foot Buddha for Ceylon.

They look better in nylon.

Conversation piece.

Surrealism for high fashion.

Cooker. Not modular, so 'no sale'.

The first updated aircraft interior.

Vinegar bottle.

Mrs Pooter conceals her anatomy.

'Atoms for Peace' at Geneva.

So . . . what next?

'Anything' could be: a new airport at Lydd, a matchbox cover, a stand for Campbell's Soup, an oil dispenser for Shell, or a setting for London's exhibition centre, Olympia. Every job brought its own problems.

A squatting loo for geriatrics? I discovered that the level of water in the trap had to be raised to allow for evaporation during extended holidays.

A three-reel PR film for ICI, the chemical group; the crowd they commissioned had made a mess of it. Looking back, my version, though it cost a bomb, wouldn't rate an Oscar.

Occasionally, I inadvertently made an enemy. I needed twenty budgerigars to go in a wire cage that was formed by the crinoline-shaped skirt of a dressmaker's dummy – Surrealism was the in thing.

The head of the august Budgerigar Society turned up with the birds, but refused to release them. "An insult," he exclaimed.

Later, when I introduced an aviary in a Zoo to take hundreds of these birds, the same guy turned up. Seeing me, he drove off. No loss, as a guy who ran a pet store, awakened at 4 a.m., came down in his night-shirt to loan us three bald-headed vultures.

Occasionally an opportunity for something elegant – packaging for cosmetics. This led to a world shattering idea; lipsticks packed in paired tones so, if applied as per instructions, the soft erotic pout of the lower lip would be emphasised.

One scheme for Olympia was okayed from a model, but when scaled up I found I was committed to produce chandeliers each as high as a three-story building. To save weight I introduced an array of the silver witch-balls we hang on Christmas trees, only four times as large. The local safety bloke said, "No breakable glass over a public walkway" – so Mehitabel was soon scouring the West End for hair-nets to trap them in.

Now that I was responsible for such vital aspects of the way of life in the Western World it became clear that installing a

Ceramics and moulded plastic.
A 'loo' for Guy's Hospital.

Feature for a fashion show at Olympia. Modelled in clay and cast in fibrous plaster. The birds in the skirt cage were for real.

camp bed in the office was not the complete answer. I crossed my fingers and took on a draughtsman (who was jolly), a modelmaker (who was not) and a research assistant (who was educated). She was to apply her high IQ to those elusive items that were coming more and more into my life – facts. This because, apart from producing designs to sell goods (which was easy and paid), I would take on projects dealing with *concepts*, which were complicated and didn't pay. But they are what life is about – maybe.

We hit a snag. If I proposed a charge for research, clients would go pie-faced. This guy can draw – hell even his kids can draw, but a designer *'write'* . . . I must be trying it on?

Exhibition halls were our battle grounds and I could soon sketch the floor plans from memory: Lisbon, Stockholm, Geneva, Milan, and the rest. Here I became aware of a tough internationalism that made our tight little island seem a wistful dreamland.

THE IDEAL HOME EXHIBITION
Dressing the Great Hall at Olympia, after winning the competition four years running. The most popular annual show in Europe.
  Above, 1st year. Drapes in donkey-brown with robin's egg blue trim and white bobbles. The fascias below, in moss green velvet, with sprays of sulphur and white ostrich feathers as accents. The structure at the end was cast in titanium. To the left, the 2nd year. The bandstand was mounted on a slender fifteen foot column.

The most important of these European events was at Hannover; a crossroads for trade since the Middle Ages. Here I put up a prestige exhibit for the Atomic Energy Authority – fuel elements floating in space (on glass) against a background of glowing, orange light. Not bad. At least the German director of the Fair thought so, as he slapped me on the back saying that he had just seen an atomic exhibit in Rome not half as good.

I saw no reason to tell him that I had designed that one, too. He then invited me and two physicists, who were lazing on site, to dine with himself (important) and the *Bürgermeister* of Hannover (even more important).

In a crowded dining-hall, stereotypes of Hitler's henchmen, Goebbels, Goering, etcetera, now civilians, were engulfing sausage and sauerkraut with lashings of beer. Our group had reached the stein of beer stage, when the proud-bellied *Bürgermeister* put a plump arm round my shoulder and said.

"You should know, Gardner, we Hannoverians have always admired the English."

"Yes?" say I.

"Your Royal Family," he continued, "they came from Hannover."

Why bring that up, thinks I, but they are, after all, members of a very old mafia. "And your Prince of Wales. He would stay at the *Schloss* up on the hill every shooting season."

Something snapped inside and I heard myself saying, "Same with my relatives. They came over for the shooting seasons; First World War, Second World War."

A frigid pause, broken by one of our boffins choking into his beer. Almost justified the war, but bad show.

Back in comfortable England and another trade exhibition. Two o'clock in the morning. The great void silent except for an odd sanding machine buzzing away in one of the galleries.

I flop down on a roll of carpet, which looks soft but proves to be unexpectedly hard, straighten my stiff back, slowly lever off a shoe and wriggle my sticky toes. Then someone else lands with a thump alongside me. It's Bev. Pick, a fellow designer.

"How many stands have you got, G?"

"Fourteen."

"Fourteen clients to please at one time? We're mad."

I join the manipulators

A guy I met in the Army who followed the doings of the classy crowd – knew who had married into a stately home and who had been blackballed from the Constitution Club – said, "Why flog yourself, G? Join J Walter Thompson's as a 'consultant' and buy yourself a decent car." At the time I was having an affair with a VW Beetle.

I hesitated. Faced with cash-flow problems, I decided to apply the Mae West factor. *When faced with having to choose between two evils, she always selected the one she hadn't yet tried.* So I joined the rat race.

Nobody knows what the 'J' stands for, but Walter Thompson's on Madison Avenue were the pace-setters who boosted the consumer image. Incisive executives in Ivy League ties chased the dollar to pay alimony to previous wives, until they folded under stress and the incumbent wife would give three cheers and take all. Just a part of 'The American Way of Life'.

JWT's London branch had put on a suitable anglicized veneer of gentlemanly consideration. I must say that, compared with the razzmatazz of Madison Avenue, Berkeley Square had something of the tree-shaded calm which Americans associate with a college campus. Here, every Wednesday, I became a member of an elite, where guys with university degrees (or wealthy uncles) operated in 'product groups' which would gather over coffee to discuss the piddling ploys we associate with 'whiter than white' washing powder, or the 'mint with a hole' in it.

To justify my considerable fee I had to produce at least one winner a week, but I found that the size of the fee inhibited the flow.

Arriving rather bleary-eyed, I would be greeted by a little slip of paper (yellow for creative again).

Problem. An exhibit is required for a conference of professional vets (a cynical lot) that will encourage them to look kindly at yet another new promotion, a dog pill sponsored by a German pharmaceutical group. It is called DIT.

MOTOR SHOW
It looks fine, that is until the ghastly public arrive.

Late-comers to the show, the only space available is an unwanted corner abutting the bar. Hell, it's only the size of a six foot bed. Brilliant answer. A patch of artificial grass. Along the back, a neat white picket fence with rabbit-wire above it; behind the wire, five or six cut-outs of my Scottie dog, McTavish, with their little legs animated to twiddle round like mad as though making for the bar. Then the all important message . . . 'Have a gin and DIT'.

It goes down well with the vets. (The client, who would not appreciate this throw-away attitude is, fortunately, in Düsseldorf.)

By the time the essential picture, plans and a specification are completed the Thompson building is in darkness. I feel a sense of relief as I make my way across Berkeley Square. On Wednesdays I am all theirs, signed up and paid for like any call-girl, and must adjust to whatever turns up. It might be décor for the Grosvenor House Hotel ballroom, charting the intricacies of the tin-plate production-line at Ebbw Vale or a soft option, like next week when I am to judge a competition – some puff-ball PR promotion.

The light touch can make dull advice digestible.

Operation kiss-arse

Come the day, I don a clean white shirt and feel almost ebullient. No brain-teasers this time, I guess; I'm to judge in company with a film starlet.

Thompson's dignified Georgian library is hung with glossy photographs – almost indecent; like hanging a bra on a bishop. Close-up I see they show ghastly window displays made with 'Scottie' tissues.

Why the starlet?

Who cares, as she turns out to be a real stunner. Nevertheless, I decide to give each offering ten seconds of undivided attention, though an occasional brush against the lady's thigh is disturbing. Now she's posing ecstatically in front of her choice. Oh, dear. A ghastly hotch potch of paper-scottie-puppies. Strong little fingers are squeezing my arm. No go. I divert her to a more commendable offering. Okay? Fixed smiles, photo-flashes, then sherry and biscuits in the ante-room.

I am deciding to give the lady full marks for bodywork but, alas, not much up top when a PR pansy drifts over fingering his Haileybury tie. Trouble. The display we selected is disqualified owing to a 'technical hitch'. Would we please pose again in front of the runner-up. Smiles, more photo-flashes. Dollybird has won – game, set and match.

Apparently there has been a three line whip to muster a party; *canapés* and, gosh, champagne. Dollybird cuts the cake (a fair simulation of a dog in sugar icing), then a rather weak rendering of 'For He's a Jolly Good Fellow'. Dollybird is presented with a giant pink chocolate-box with a pink satin bow. Mine is coloured *eau-de-Nil* and, as soon as I can flag down a taxi, I jump in with that oversized chocolate-box well out of view.

A drawing a day keeps the bailiff at bay. Back at the studio, I settled at the drawing board to detail a self-dispensing mustard pot. Fascinating idea. You buy a little can at the supermarket, pop it into a neat 'free gift' plastic pot which punctures its bottom. Press its top and the spout deposits a neat dab of mustard on the edge of your plate.

In the event it went with a bang with the mustard people, but on user trials it was found that children would pop dollops of mustard all over the table cloth. Completing the design (not yet aware that it was to be stillborn), I lit my pipe and relaxed. Fantasies of dining out and remarking, "I designed that little pot, you know." Awed glances from the rather superior guests.

'Lead me not into temptation'

Mehitabel, standing in front of me, a pert expression on her face – says she has accepted an invitation (at twenty guineas a head) to an 'Advertising Creative Circle' dinner. Formal dress, of course.

"You know full well that affair is run for and by the public relations blokes – and hangers-on that want to be IN," I say angrily.

"You must show that you *exist*, occasionally." She pouts. The upshot – I take her with me (at twenty guineas a head) to bolster my morale.

We are well into the second course. Mehitabel seated

154

opposite me with, surprise, a vacant place next to her, when some blundering ass squeezes on all-fours between me and my neighbour, to disappear under the table. As the close-up view of Mehitabel from that vantage point would, in ancient Greece, have launched, well, at least five hundred ships – I was about to take action, when the interloper pops up in the vacant seat beside her. It's old man Benson.

Benson was no ordinary; he built up the successful agency bearing his name from scratch – a cool look at people, plus imagination. His apology takes the form of a ponderous wink then, arming Mehitabel with a slender cigar, he starts propositioning her with images of a feather-bedded future as his PA, at double the wage I give her; the while flicking an eye my way to see how I take it. At the Green Chartreuse stage he pops up at my side and comments, "Lucky chap. Where do you find them?" Then serious, "I'm getting a bit slow old man. Need a body to take over."

With that, he turns away to greet a formidable career woman upholstered in satin. Then, focusing on me again, leans forward to touch my hand, as God does Adam's on the Sistine Chapel ceiling, and says, "YOU, for instance. Not the rat race, G, do as you like,

be *creative*."

If, when at art school, a genie had popped out of a paint pot and said, "Little man, give me your immortal soul and I will make you top man in a top advertising agency," I would have replied, "Lead me to it." (No risk, as I hadn't an immortal soul, anyway.) Now it had happened, I was trying to think up a way to say no . . . without being classed as a fool.

Bishops come in all sizes

Happy to design anything that came along, I occasionally found myself in cahoots with the most unexpected characters. Fair enough. Come to think of it, I didn't select myself. The same must go for journalists, but for them it's just an interview. A designer, on the other hand, needs to work with a guy and end up on polite terms so his bill gets paid.

Bishops are quite rare.

I did once meet one of the fraternity who operated before this trade was dignified by the name of *profession*, a witch-doctor in the Upper Volta. This ancient guy was sitting in state on a lion's skin, a little child squatting at his side to prevent outsiders stepping on his shadow. Our discussion was like communicating via international satellite, as he must not be spoken to directly, only through his *interpreter*, an attendant in a pop-art loincloth holding a six foot staff topped with what looked uncommonly like a phallic symbol.

Anglican bishops I can take in my stride, having once been invited to His Grace The Bishop of Winchester's family Christmas party where we played musical chairs. He won every time, of course, as who could bum-thrust a bishop in gaiters off the last chair? This grand old boy still lived under the delusion that the world had been especially created for the pleasure of bishops; the ground rules having been laid down when they were top and their god was an avid reader of the Court Circular in *The Times*.

Today His attention is obviously elsewhere, as I discovered when I followed up a surprising invitation to visit, of all people, the Bishop of Coventry.

My only previous visit to Coventry had been during the thrilling days of the Second World War, when the Nazi battle machine was poised only twenty odd miles away across the Channel, ready to invade. I was in uniform at the time and on my way to inspect an armaments plant at Sheffield, where the

156

enemy had already taken advantage of the fact that the blast-furnaces and rolling-mills extended along a narrow valley – the ideal target for line-bombing.

I arrived on a bitter winter night, under the swinging beams of searchlights picked out by gusts of driving sleet. Broken walls and twisted girders that once supported a roof while, under the stars, on the debris-littered plant floor the sad shapes of damaged machine tools stood idle in the snow. A narrow rail track, trodden snow-free, led like a black snake from the glowing blast-furnace to a small isolated brick block. There were two such blocks, built over the *only steam-hammers that could shape crankshafts for Spitfire Merlin engines*.

Shapeless silhouettes of men in cloth caps, wrapped in flapping shawls and leaning against the blizzard as they trundled skips of molten metal along the open track to the forge. The thud of drop-hammers almost knocked me over, as craftsmen handled the red hot metal with waste-wrapped tongs. They ignored the drone of bombers overhead, and when their shelter shook with concussion as a string of bombs detonated . . . another bit of the plant . . . maybe some other guys had copped it?

These two vital drop-forges, though hot-spot targets, were too small to pin-point, or so the men hoped.

"Picked out by gusts of driving sleet."

After the war pompous administrators and intellectualising architects patronised these same steel-workers, treating them as solids down a waste pipe; while friend Basil Spence won the competition for a new cathedral (and became 'converted' by association – to be referred to in the profession as Saint Basil).

THE CITY OF LONDON
Lord Mayor's Show backdrop, borrowed
from Ancient Greece . . . but somewhat
marred by soot and rain.

On that same journey I visited Coventry and accepted the hospitality of Gibson, the City Architect. Discovered his young children in the firelight playing a pre-war board game I had invented – 'Zoo Zag'. (For *that* moment, I thought of designing as worthwhile.)

Supper, then bed to the wail of air-raid sirens, the occasional crump of a bomb followed by the usual urgent clanging of fire bells. Not to worry. The, "It'll never happen to me," syndrome of a born survivor. Next morning Gibson is jubilant, the *Luftwaffe* had flattened the largest store in town and so cleared an area for his post-war dream – a two-level shopping concourse. In old Coventry? God forbid.

The bishop in purple

On this visit I was met by a man-of-the-world cleric who first introduced me to Gibson's new shopping centre and to a buxom barmaid in an up-market pub, where I was fortified with double whiskies against my impending introduction to His Grace. The decor of this hostelry, the walls of which were mounted with synthetic leopard skin, soon induced us to call, "Same again, please."

This bishop would not be caught playing 'musical chairs'. He proved to be as up-market as the pub, but not to the extent of wearing synthetic leopard skin (what a nice idea).

Lunch at the manse; starched white tablecloth and napkins, chilled white wine and two acolytes in black who sit like observant crows with never a word. The handsome prelate, hair photogenically tonsured (or is it a toupee?), the orthodox dog-collar over a purple silk front which sets off a large crucifix suspended from a slender gold chain. Obviously one of God's top guys . . . but why the free lunch or even be polite to me? "As you know, Gardner, there are thousands of workers from up north assembling cars and tractors in the area, but none of them show the slightest interest in my cathedral . . . and, by implication, in God."

Had I any suggestions? I was somewhat taken aback at the Church's anointed PR man so casually passing the buck – nevertheless, interesting.

He then mooted, "What about a medieval pageant?"

I must avoid that one, having organised and designed fifty or more floats for London's annual Lord Mayor's Show.

Military bands, clowns, acrobats on stilts and a circus elephant that ran into the crowd when startled by fire-crackers.

As I stood on the terrace of the Mansion House to see it all pass by to the sound of a steel band, giant bulldozers and the largest earth-mover in the world given eye-appeal by lashings of leggy girls in hard hats, short donkey-jackets and open mesh net tights, the Remembrancer of the City of London muttered in my ear, "Not quite the right thing for the City, Gardner." Black mark. A minimal fee – and a bronze medal of 'no commercial value'.

Back to the Bishop. I pointed out that a pageant would involve him in a great deal of organising and all for a one-day show . . . and 10-1 it would rain. Let's attack this problem with army-style logic. What are these workers you are interested in, interested in? Take-home pay, pubs, football, TV and bingo. Girls dolling themselves up and dating leather-jacketed youths at discos.

Belief (and the Bish.) had been left by the roadside.

In a pause, while His Grace concentrated on dissecting an almond trout – under the watchful eye of the little figure on his crucifix, I gave the problem some thought. Most of the world's troubles have been triggered off by theorising intellectuals, sectarian religious leaders and the like. (Whoops! Delete that last item.) Now, what can a non-intellectual do for this concerned Bishop?

Pretty posers on massive bulldozers, at some expense, to dig city gents.

Driving into town, I spotted a bevy of brand new bulldozers in aggressive spectrum yellow, queuing up to push our ancient heritage into the ground. The ancient Celts, using muscle, scrapers and baskets, had created Avebury; a mounded and ditched fortification that is still a wonder of the world. It would be simple to bulldoze a great amphitheatre – to remain for all time – and surround it with a tented circus-cum-festival. Get the workers organised and involved . . .

The Bish. fell for it. One of his crows, who had been secretively taking notes suddenly stopped, his stump of a pencil poised in time and space: I had mentioned fee. Upshot – Bish. agreed to pay for plans and pretty pictures to tempt industrialists to sponsor the affair.

I was well ahead with the scheme when Britain dived into another recession. As a result, Coventry workers were lining-up for the dole, those potential sponsors went back to their golf course, and the Bish. wondered if he was in the wrong business after all.

I tossed the visuals to join other stillborn babies in a plan chest labelled MISC PROJECTS . . . and cleared the drawing board for the next problem.

In this marginal trade one soon becomes immune to the unexpected.

An exciting happening . . . which remained in my head.

Reasons I have experienced for a scheme to be stillborn

An exciting job in the offing? It can go like this.

Love at first sight:

> Possible client is impressed by our credentials, and by Mehitabel when she brings in the coffee.

Getting intimate:

> We delve into research and soon know more about it than client does. He is impressed and so are we.

Pregnancy:

> I go into *purdah* then, bingo, we produce a unique, fully-developed concept.

a   The sponsor gets cold feet.

b   The committee prove to be a bunch of wets.

c   There never were any sponsors.

d   Client was over-optimistic.

e   We are over-optimistic.

f   Damn. The client's budget was in $ not £.

g   No go – we discover the project is political.

h   The price of oil drops out of the bottom of the barrel.

i   The treasury of the host country puts a hold on sterling.

j   An architect eats up the available funds.

k   Client is moved to another department.

l   The job is killed by a lawyer's contract.

m   Client steals the idea and goes off into the blue.

n   Someone else gets there first.

In spite of these and other hazards, one out of three design projects survives to see the light of day, so back to the drawing board.

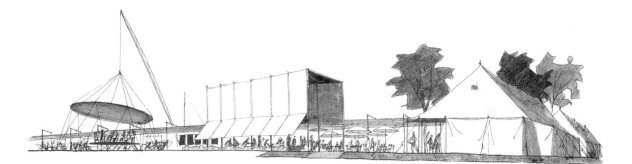

The 50's

Meanwhile . . .

Marilyn Monroe in *The Seven Year Itch*

Dr R.G. Bunge freezes human sperm

Berlin blockade lifted

Festival of Britain

Betrand Russell awarded Nobel Prize

Alec Issigonis designs Mini car

My Fair Lady

McCarthy witch-hunt

Washing powder becomes "whiter than white"

'Comet', first passenger jet, takes off

Hovercraft invented

Watson-Crick plot DNA Helix

Women take to stiletto heels

Hillary climbs Everest

Elvis Presley: 'Blue Suede Shoes'

Monkeys survive space flight

Disneyland arrives on scene

Part of Festival Gardens, Battersea. Follows . . . how it became my baby.

Blue mood in the loo

Settled in the only sanctuary at Thompson's available for meditation, the loo, I observe the distorted image of my face in the brass door-knob and have doubts. Why the hell am I here?

Guess I am comparable to a busy little dung beetle navigating its load in the path of an unstoppable juggernaut: industry, retailers, priests, politicians, and now . . . admen. and the uncritical breed who follow their lead.

It will be apparent to any observer that we are born to conform. *Homo sapiens* is one of the classes of animal that live in packs, so Nature has jigged us thataway. A pack needs to follow a leader and, occasionally, one brat in approximately thirty is tooled up by Nature to ignore the opinions of others. A potential leader or an opportunist that needs swatting (read history).

The conditions for survival change, so Nature takes the precaution of dropping the occasional odd-bod; a prophet, poet or visualiser who can imagine other worlds; what the City gents term 'futures'.

There are scientists, of course. Interfering guys who have put their finger in and knocked Nature off course but, having all purchased one of their own products (a computer), they now give us the theory of CHAOS . . . meaning, chance is a fine thing; that anything can affect everything else.

The flutter of a butterfly's wings or an elephant farting can contribute to the greenhouse effect. True, Nature sometimes has a hiccup, resulting in a marginal type like the guy reflected in that door knob who, by the way, is still waiting for something significant to happen. Wouldn't it be exciting if artists ran things, thinks I, rising from the seat to wipe my behind.

In 1951, it happened. The Socialist Party, unexpectedly voted into power, decided to celebrate the coming millennium with a great

FESTIVAL OF BRITAIN

when the lucky voters would all view themselves in a rose-tinted mirror and give three rousing cheers . . . not realising they were paying for the show. Lampposts are painted in gay colours, floral clocks appear on village greens, the people who turn bunting into flags have a heyday and there are pageants galore, while a stately aircraft-carrier jettisons its armaments and slowly circles the island to the sound of a Marine Band playing – not 'Land of Hope and Glory', but jazz.

Very un-English.

Even district nurses buzz around in shiny new cars, while shocked civil servants are informed that artists and designers not only exist (officially), but that they will be paid by the Treasury.

This is where I came in.

Pie in the sky makes a landing on South Bank

Londoners going about their daily business had for years looked with a blind eye at the southern bank of the Thames, where brick warehouses and an ancient brewery were fronted by derelict wharves slowly rotting into the muddy foreshore.

This was to be the site of a great exhibition.

"Not in our backyard," said the Opposition, "Spend the money rebuilding St Thomas's Hospital," knocked sideways by a direct hit from a flying bomb.

Gerald Barry, one time news editor and dilettante of some culture, provided the face-saving answer. He pointed out that it would be just one hundred years since Prince Albert inaugurated the historic Crystal Palace Exhibition.

This glass structure, a wonder of the world, was so vast that it enclosed mature forest trees and ate up a whole year's supply

Glazing the Crystal Palace.
The nineteenth century craft workers were
faced with Paxton's advanced technology.

166

of glass. In those days flat glass was still hand-blown into cylinders, then cut and flattened – one hell of a job – probably why the building, planned for completion in 1850, opened a year late.

No forest trees this time and that gave us three years to go – to open in 1951.

The direction of such an affair would normally be passed to some time-serving politician, but the job was given to Gerald Barry, the guy who had triggered-off the show. This proved to be a stroke of luck for all concerned, not least us designers, who were by now panting on the sidelines . . . just hoping.

Some top-talkers settle in

Self-acknowledged experts gathered like moths round a candle to form a happy bureaucracy of Theme Convenors and Scientific Advisors, who met to play one-upmanship round committee tables and then bury a paper-chain of words under numbers. *(Giving notions numbers is an old trick – it makes one feel organised.)*

After sitting through a number of meetings, it occurred to Barry that he had better find someone who could visualise in 3D what the public would actually see, and get the bloody stuff made. He appointed a team of four designers to do just that.

To check the way these unpredictable types checked costs, the Treasury put in a watchdog, named Campbell; a Scot with the essential probing nose and, I discovered later, a quizzical

The 1851 Crystal Palace.
The first system-engineered building in the world.

167

Air tent at Gothenburg.

A wisp of smoke from the mannequin's cigarette . . . for a moment the lounging figures appear to be live.

sense of the ridiculous which, I suppose, prevented him from going mad.

Barry, who lived in the clubby West End world, didn't include me on the team. When I should have been sipping cocktails and pulling strings, I was crouched over the drawing board in my Duke Street hide-out designing an air-tent for a fashion show at Gothenburg and interior treatments for the latest Trident aircraft – when I introduced sleek plastic window surrounds for the first time in place of dolls' house curtains, which the public kindly referred to as lavatory seats – and an *actual* lavatory seat for Guys Hospital, so the inmates would squat when doing their thing.

Gordon Russell, head of the Design Council, remembering 'Britain Can Make It', insisted that I be included on the team. Once again, by happenstance, I was IN.

We all had our own businesses to run, excepting Hugh Casson, a buddy of Barry's, and had perforce to meet, after everyone else had gone home, in a small room off the Strand where we would attempt to grab ideas out of the smoke-filled air.

Where do we go from here?

After a full day's work elsewhere, we would slump round a table littered with paper and coffee cups to shoot down each others' bright ideas, knowing that before the evening was out we must decide which artists, designers or architects were favourite to produce the notions we had not shot down – to the steady thump of pile-drivers and cockney cranes across the river, knocking down walls with swinging balls.

This was no ordinary piece of land. When the dust had, at last, settled, the silence was almost disturbing and that patch of naked clay, in full view of Big Ben and those classical monuments to Inigo Jones, Pugin and Christopher Wren, screamed to be brought alive.

We must, at least, have a vision. Depressed by the obscene post-war blocks spawned by the Bauhaus ethic – which treated people as identical components to be neatly boxed out of the way, making the occupants bitter enough to daub the words 'SHIT CITY' on a block near our studio – we must create a

168

townscape for tomorrow, not for the gratification of developers or those guys who call themselves architects – but to please the people (meaning us, of course).

The three orthodox members of the team – Misha Black, Jimmy Holland and Ralph Tubbs, the architect – were to set out the orderly world of 'science'. This left Casson and I, who were less predictable, to unravel the unprogrammable peculiarities of these Anglo-Saxons with a Celtic streak, now balanced on a tightrope between a glorious (so the anthem says) past, and a dubious future. As hopeless as attempting to swat a gnat.

First, Casson and I contrived a trip to the Milan Fair to see what our neighbours were up to. Finding it a bore, we decided to play truant and hopped on a train to Zürich with the idea that any city we had not seen must contain the unexpected – it turned out we were right. The unexpected came strolling down the main street in the form of Robin Darwin, recognizable two blocks away by his flat-brimmed black hat and air of pompous unconcern.

An air of pompous unconcern.

Grandson of Charles Darwin he had, to his credit, made monkeys of the Establishment and thereby procured funds and prestige for The Royal College of Art, of which he was the Head, (much of it spent on crystal glassware and full-bodied wine for the Senior Common Room).

Over lunch we asked what was he doing in Zürich? He was *en route* home following a successful lecture tour in Greece sponsored by the British Council, of course. *(Mental note: they can jolly well pay for our lunch.)*

Lecturing on what? "The organisation of The Royal College of Art."

"But surely the Greeks don't give a hoot for the College, or how it's organised?"

"My dear compatriots, you miss the point. The Greeks who attended didn't care what I lectured about. They came to hear English as spoken by an educated Englishman. It's culture."

Robin's distinguished grandfather would have used that word to describe bacteria isolated on a Petri dish. Anyway, after that, he jolly well did pay for our lunch.

Which is the reflection? No glass.

'O wad some Pow'r the giftie gie us to see oursels as others see us!'

To our consternation we concluded that the British way of life appeared to be made up from a discarded jigsaw, the pieces of which no longer made a picture; so Casson and I took refuge in the quixotic.

We introduced a fountain that gave the sound of waves breaking on a beach; a royal coat of arms made from black buttons and straw; and an Alice in 3D looking at a reversed Alice in 3D through a mirror that wasn't there. Elegant idea. We had an equestrian statue of Tenniel's mad White Knight cluttered with useless bric-a-brac, on his white horse, galloping like a Foreign Office Under-Secretary down the corridors of power, and a sad guy in a shabby raincoat perched on the end of a punt out on the river, eternally watching his fishing line while the festivities crackerjacked all around him.

After handing a lot of super jobs to other designers, a streak of meanness took over and I kept one of the plums for myself.

'The Origins of the British People'

In Milan I had explained this to Castiglioni, a leading Italian designer, but he burst out laughing at the idea of us British making a display of our dubious origins. When Imperial Rome was at its height, we were flogging in the mud behind a wooden plough, snaring rabbits, or looking for lost sheep in the Welsh hills.

It took quite a bit of research sorting the wheat from the chaff.

"Surely, these Saxons have fair hair?" I would ask the expert.

"Well, not all. That's a recessive gene, so you'd better play safe, keep it neutral."

My next try. "Were Neolithic dwellings infested with mice?" (I was aiming to avoid words and to identify a shape as cheese,

170

I proposed introducing a stuffed mouse nibbling at it).

"Well, we have no record of mice."

"But they did have domestic cats."

"Well, yes."

"Then they must have had mice."

That settled it as far as I was concerned. Then, to my relief, Jacquetta Hawkes was appointed. I remember her sitting through the Scientific Co-ordinator's lecture on 'The British People' in silence.

Observing the faces of the guys round the table, she had decided that they were all greedy except Casson and I. Since then I have found this unorthodox classification useful.

As we were leaving, she turned to me, "I've never heard such nonsense in my life!" Jacquetta was not there to impress a committee, but to pass her exceptional know-how on to the guys who were producing the exhibits. The Saxons had fair hair, mice nibbled cheese and I heaved a sigh of relief. The matronly Boudicca was not driving a bronze chariot; apparently she stood in a vehicle more like a dog-cart, made from withies bound with leather thongs, drawn by two plump ponies.

The 'Brits' a hundred and twenty generations ago.

Boudicca on the war-path, on her DIY chariot.

The delicate bridge between the talkers and the doers finally collapsed when the Chief Co-ordinator – a Cambridge man who knew how to chivvy huskies to pull a sledge in the Arctic, and so had an answer for everything but was not interested in the Theatre or the Arts – turned down some paintings of notables. Then it occurred to him that paintings can be analyzed by X-ray so, discredited as *Art*, they became specimens for *Science.*

Barry was angry, "What would that man exhibit then, an X-ray of Sybil Thorndike's skull?"

He turned up late next morning, straight from the Garrick Club, to wave an old mezzotint in front of our eyes. It depicted the Georgian elegances of the old Vauxhall Gardens. Bewigged bucks strolled under pleached lime trees, sporting their silk-clad calves and taking snuff for the edification of females in even higher wigs, whose wasp-waisted tops sprouted from mounds of ruched drapery.

An announcement.

"We will design an elegant pleasure garden, and it will be upstream, well away from the South Bank." He slumped into a chair with a satisfied grin and added, "And we will keep its treatment strictly to ourselves . . . no committees." A conspiracy, and it was obvious that Casson and I, with Barry, were to be the "ourselves".

There was no roll of drums but – WOW!

Even the Garden of Eden harboured a snake

I had read that the old Vauxhall Gardens were closed down when it became apparent that the billowing skirts of the pretty ladies masked an intriguing item which they hired out by the hour.

Modes and manners at the Regency Pleasure Gardens, Vauxhall.

Today? I pictured tired mums and dads in flapping raincoats dragging ghastly children, sucking candyfloss, in their wake. And, they would be decanted on the site by the bus-load. Who cares? Only having four or five jobs at Duke Street, co-ordination of half the South Bank, not forgetting the origins of the above-mentioned British People, to handle – I plunged into the experience of a lifetime.

I envied Casson his inborn charm. That man could even convince a hardened politician that the Arts were vote-catching (being England this was no mean achievement). This gift was making his presence at the South Bank so essential that I was left to go it alone. True, we ended up with a group of four – Barry, a guy who had been running the Shakespeare Theatre at Stratford-upon-Avon, a watchdog from the Ministry (government, not church) and, finally, myself to pump in ideas, prepare plans, write the minutes and, unfortunately, the costs.

The small back room

To discover what it was all about, I flew (at my own expense) to see how people behaved in pleasure gardens on the Continent. As the plane buzzed over Battersea Park, the site we had been allocated, I noticed a brilliant, rectangular green near its centre, little realising that this innocent patch of turf was to be the centre of a battle. In Britain, even the Prime Minister dare not dig up an established cricket pitch.

Unaware of this impending threat, we four conspirators would meet in a hired room off Sloane Street to plan the 'happy happenings'. "Keep it elegant," says Barry, concerned that there was no Casson to guide me along the narrow path of 'good taste'.

I passed a miserable morning wandering round the 140 acre site in the rain, wondering how to start.

First, I reckoned that everyone would need two square yards of ground to walk on if they were to keep moving, and so arrived at the minimum paved area. As the site was not a sphere, but flat with a boundary, and people moving at random were bound to hit the fence, I provided an outside loop-way for them to drift onto, with paths leading from it into the centre. In the event it worked quite well.

Treatment. We must avoid nostalgia – outdated. Modern abstract? Too advanced for our visitors. This left me groping in a visual vacuum, as I observed rectangles of deeper colour on the walls of our little HQ where a previous tenant had hung pictures. No good dreaming, we must get moving. I offered up ideas . . .

An avenue of slowly revolving flower beds? NO. (Hell. A lovely colour drawing thrown away.) A toadstool maze? NO. A Punch and Judy theatre? YES. A ping-pong ball fountain? YES. Alas, it only worked on the drawing board – too much wind.

A small riverside music hall. YES. (Compéred by the articulate Leonard Sachs, this proved to be one of the most popular events in the show.) Giant tortoises creeping around with exotic plants on their backs? NO. An underground grotto, the Four Winds. YES. An aviary filled with budgerigars. A mouse village? AGREED. (Every item agreed at these meetings would bring some unforeseen side effect.) In this case the mice began to eat their village, so I added a little timber-yard where they could sharpen their incisors when not running in and out of the houses. A petrified forest. NO. Heads, bodies and tails, as revolves where people queue? NO.

A pause for coffee, then a deep breath ready for the next round.

Remembering the pneumatic devices we developed during the war, "Why not a pneumatic giant – storybook version – who slowly inflates till he's thirty feet high?" YES. A clock

A petrified forest? NO.

that, on the hour, goes mechanically mad? YES, if I can find a sponsor for it. (This became known as The Guinness Clock.) Pretty girls dressed Nell Gwyn-style, to sell oranges? YES – but the right kind of girl, mind you. (Oh, dear, I thought, not Nell Gwyn in tortoise-shell specs. reading Evelyn Waugh.)

We must cater for all tastes. As a boy I would frequent the British Empire Exhibition at Wembley (having found a way in at the back). Once in the grounds I would bypass the helter-skelter and gravitate to the Palace of Beauty to gaze wistfully at those objects of Man's desire: Helen of Troy, Salome, Cleopatra, Josephine and Lady Hamilton . . . not in wax but in real, soft, powdered flesh and made desperately desirable being behind plate glass – and by Pears' Soap, of course. I could already see myself interviewing a queue of likely call-girls for the job. What about a Palace of Beauty? NO.

The mini-committee would then decamp, leaving me with my assistants at Duke Street to make it happen.

To work. We coopted a Welsh architect to supervise the contractor, who had two virtues: one, he sent in the lowest bid, two, he had laid out airfields during the war under enemy fire. (As it turned out he would be repeating this experience.) Meanwhile, I groped around for unorthodox artists who, touch wood, would think up exciting treatments with style. The group included John Piper *(romantic architectural paintings)*, Osbert Lancaster *(intellectual cartoonist)*, Guy Shepherd *(theatre settings)*, Hans Tisdal *(graphics for textiles)*, Roland Emmet *(crazy cartoons)*, Gordon Him *(charming children's books)*, and the rest.

Too good to be true

Then the news broke. The cricket pitch had won the battle and the pleasure gardens idea was dead as a dodo.

"Oh well," as Stan Laurel remarked to Hardy when the gold-dust they had gleaned after two years panning in the mountains had leaked through a hole in his saddle-bag, "Easy come, easy go."

Back to the South Bank where, having put ideas for a symbol to dominate the site out to competition, we now had the problem not only of keeping our eyes open, but of choosing between a blob with a hole in it, three triangles having an

The pneumatic giant.

175

The Skylon.

argument in space, or a slender needle poised on nothing. We selected the last, an exercise in precision engineering, after assurances that it would stay upright at 150 feet as it did in the little model. This feature which, like Britain, had no visible means of support became known as the *Skylon* and was safe so long as no one stood under it in an electric storm.

An electric storm of another kind was only just avoided. Barry called a meeting. The renowned sculptors Jacob Epstein and Henry Moore were to select sites for their offerings. Both grand guys, but agree sites together? They were as compatible as oil and water. There was an uncomfortable pause until Moore, in his down-to-earth way, suggested we have separate sessions. Moore and I went down to the Savoy Brasserie where he bent over a plan, held flat by pepper-pots on the marble-topped table, as he cogitated over direction of light, the viewer's eye level, background, and height of plinth, while I sipped coffee.

One of my dreams, working while relaxing at a café table – Continental style.

Returning to the conference room, we discovered that Epstein had been less fussy. He did not care where his piece was placed so long as it was, "Here," pressing his thumb on the centre of the concourse, the site reserved for the *Skylon.*

That meeting with Moore stood me in good stead a few years later when I wished to mount one of his finest pieces in front of the UK pavilion at the Brussels World Fair – his

South Bank art by Epstein.

famous reclining woman, sculpted knees up so her garment fell away like so much weather-eroded rock. When the Arts Council asked for it, Moore refused, saying he did not sculpt to sell Britain (meaning the Arts Council).

I went out to his country work-place and talked him into it, but he insisted that this was to be just between him and me: I would be responsible for it and design the plinth.

Alas, the professional firm of shippers I employed broke her arm off. We patched it up on site, but it was months before Mehitabel was, at last, able to shame me into facing Moore with the fact that we had amputated his masterpiece. He must have been more than upset, but a generous man, at least to anyone he thought was a doer and not an intellectualizer.

"Understood," he said. "Should have put an armature in that arm. What about a glass of wine?"

South Bank art by Henry Moore.

10 Downing Street wins the day

After some hectic months, I was clattering down the stairs when Campbell, accosting me with a firm Treasury finger, said, "Remember Battersea? Well, could we do it, starting from now, with . . ." (he mentioned a figure less than two-thirds of the original budget). "Must have your answer by ten o'clock tomorrow. Meeting at the Home Office. Ring me." A sly grin, "We've lost nine months, G. Think you can do it?"

"No problem," I gaily replied.

Half the cost of such a project is soon swallowed up by mundane items such as drains, power lines, paving, pumps, piers and planting. Not much left for FUN.

Hairy moment. Describing my intentions to Herbert Morrison, the deputy PM, standing in the mud to my left.

Turnstiles at the Chelsea entrance. Not the Vauxhall Gardens, but a certain elegance.

I balanced the reduced budget by listing half the effects as 'sponsored', signed and sealed the ghastly thing and went to bed . . . not realising that fostering this reborn baby would eventually turn my hair white.

We must tread daintily, as the boys from the press are watching from the side lines aiming to crucify Herbert Morrison – the Deputy Prime Minister who is fathering the show – on the cross of the Pleasure Gardens.

To please him, I placate local councillors with soft visuals showing verdant trees. To tempt hesitant sponsors, hard visuals of lively crowds looking for some place to spend their money.

"Keep it *elegant*," said Barry. I have a notion he plans to wear Georgian knee breeches and a wig for the splendiferous Royal Opening – and the feeling that my lack of background and occasional slips from grace (synonym for corny ideas) troubled him. When the layout was already making its mark on the ground, he decided there would be a competition between myself and Oliver Messel, the theatre designer who came from Barry's world. We would present our proposals to the Committee and let the best man (Messel) win.

Two weeks before submission date I was busy designing a costume for Aer Lingus' air hostesses (green for Irish), when Mehitabel put her head round the door and ushered Oliver Messel into the office.

178

He smiled at me with those big brown eyes, pet dog begging a titbit. "G, darling," he hesitantly stuttered, "You are so *clever* at visualising. Could you be a *dear* and prepare a perspective of *my* settings for the presentation?" He opened a folio, pretty Rococo pastiche – wedding cake, but beautifully done from cribs and just Barry's cup of tea. My fingers itched to make an aerial perspective of it all, so I did.

The first time a competitor has prepared a presentation for his opponent, I guess . . . let's just accept the fact that I'm an ass.

Come the day, Messel and I wait in uncomfortable silence in an office as bleak as a police interview-room, even down to the brown lino. A long-faced gentleman peeps round the door and beckons Messel (I begin to wonder if I am there). He goes off with the visuals I had produced for him; white grottoesque pavilions peeping through a tapestry of trees, Canaletto-style figures grouped in sun-dappled glades. Even a gondola on a pretty lake. Just Barry's cup of tea.

The Inquisition

For forty minutes I watch the hand creep inch by inch on the flyblown clock, then a buoyant Messel bustles back. "G, *darling*, your turn now. They'll simply *adore* your scheme. I'll be so *thrilled* if they choose yours and I'm sure they will."

In I go and address Sir John French at the head of the table. Knowing Messel only too well, I decide to counter his appealing pose by acting severely 'practical' – covering items such as car-parks, turnstiles, the contractors and timing, then point out that after a late start on the site . . . They sit round a table discussing a re-plan without any idea of the cost. With that I win the day, much to the chagrin, I suspect, of Gerald Barry who is sitting next to Sir John.

Messel has a lawyer who sends me a letter stating that if any of my designs are influenced by what I have seen of Messel's sketches, he will sue me.

Here we go again.

Four restaurants, three pubs, an outdoor theatre, a dance pavilion, kiosks, turnstiles, two lakes; one for boating and another to reflect fireworks. Planting, a complete fun-fair and,

The pineapple tower, which had golden balls continually cascading down its sides.

179

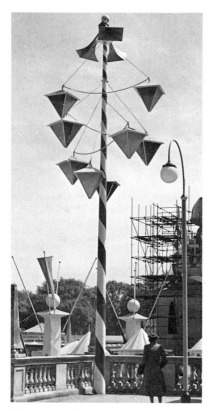

Piazza lighting.

Main vista reflections.

Cockerels; a wall painting.

The Guinness Clock.

A stylish kiosk.

180

as we were on the Thames, a landing-stage for river-craft – everything designed to look pleasurable, even the litter bins.

Soon, timing became so critical I would deal with the 'rest' on my own drawing board, with two out-of-work film-set designers and a young engineer to convert sketches into structures that would stand up . . . including tents, which we introduced just to make life difficult.

An up-market fun-fair

I position the fun-fair strip – hopefully a controlled version of Coney Island, with its big dipper, steam organs, booths and barkers as far away from the distinguished (and vocal) local residents as the site permits. To tempt the public into it I introduce a piazza; a fairy-tale ballet setting. Once visitors enter it they are trapped – to spend all their ready cash on dizzy rides before they find their way out at the end.

The Piazza, as developed on site.
Setting, as for a Russian Ballet? It must also satisfy the regular showmen.

Touch one of those trees and I'll shoot

I have a go at anything that comes my way, but planting is another thing. I inveigled Russell Page (who was so often commissioned by the wealthy elite on the Continent that I thought of him as French) to come to my aid.

Standing at six-foot-six, autocratic, wearing Cossack headgear and flowing cloak, he had a way of looking coolly down his nose at anyone who was not *au fait* with the established gardens of France and Italy.

I admired him greatly. He wasn't a book man: Page had *been* there. When I proposed a one foot curb to edge the large, formal lake, as I had seen it at Tivoli Gardens in Copenhagen, he tut-tutted and referred me to the original Tivoli, in Italy, where the slab is four-feet wide and laid only two inches above the surface of the water. How right those early Italian designers (and Page) were. And he knew plants, but referred to them by their Latin names. "Doesn't mean a thing to me," I would say. "Surely you must mean those giant rhubarbs round the lake at Kew?" "No." He would then patiently sketch the leaf pattern for me, so I felt like a blind person being instructed in braille.

There were many majestic trees on the site, but I obtained permission from the official park keeper to cut down a few. Anyone who reads this without trembling with anger is not British. Trees are sacred. To prevent a public outcry I would quickly mask the great stumps with a hexagonal seat and cover the cut with potted plants. Fine, until early one morning the straight-laced career lady responsible for National Parks, walking her dog, heard a shout, "Timberrrr . . ." then the crash as a giant tree fell.

Question in Parliament, but it came to nothing. After all, those same guys were sponsoring the show.

By now my hair was one tone whiter.

I was so busy trying to keep thirty or more balls in the air without dropping one, I invited a number of artists, journalists and the like to a sumptuous dinner (paid for by Campbell, but he didn't know it yet) at the Café Royal, hoping they would contribute some notions. We were so importuned by waiters pushing dishes and refilling glasses, it was not until my guests were urbanely fingering their brandy goblets that I mooted the idea.

Too late. It takes all of a bucket of blood to digest a rich meal, so there was little left for cerebration.

Nevertheless, one guy came up with a quixotic idea. Brooding and in a rumbling, subterranean voice he said, "Climbing trees, don't we all dream about climbing trees? Something of a monkey – or is it the Arcadian – in us?" A startling idea from a guy who appeared to weigh every bit of fifteen stones. I thought about it. We couldn't have grannies climbing, but we could have a spiral stairway leading to slender walkways, bridging branches from tree to tree and have fun up there; an owl with a revolving head, a great grinning cat on a swing, a toy-town mounted along a bough with an under-ground railway hanging under it.

The fun-fair boss warned me that no one would pay to climb a spiral stair, but Barry said, "Yes." It was in.

And I thought the war was over

The concerned surveyor, who had not been asked to triangulate the spaces between the boughs of trees before, discovered that even on a still day the great trees were moving, slowly swaying this way then that, so our bridges must flex. When we had, at last, positioned the delicate steel catwalks, who should I see striding towards me but 'Shit King', the Chief of Engineers, who, during the war, had viewed my Deception devices with a bilious eye.

One of the locomotive designs by Emmet for the 'Oyster Creek Railway'.

Now disguised as a *consultant* for the Ministry, he was viewing one of the spans with that same bilious eye – then said it didn't look secure (he must, after all, justify his fee). I must test it immediately with double the calculated load.

"Right?"

"Right . . . sir!" Damn, I had almost saluted.

Next morning the longest span was piled with bricks until its deflection reached the limit. A last brick and we just made it when . . . down came the rain.

Hell. Bricks are porous and absorb quite a weight of water! They were immediately covered with a sheet of polythene; thank goodness my engineer friend had foreseen rain when he looked up at the threatening sky that morning. Saved.

Back to the drawing board, where I was designing a kiosk a night to keep on schedule. Decorations borrowed from the reference book I had most recently flipped through – it might be Swedish embroidery, Strawberry Hill Gothic, French chinoiserie, Crusader tents from The Cloth of Gold, or a Dublin pub.

We ordered marine-quality paints specially mixed to seventy-five colours. No primary colours, leaving showy effects to the flowers who do it best.

Those little, slatted park seats would come out with banana slats and ginger frames; every sign was treated as 'art' and the litter receptacles (cane panniers) were mounted under a green-tinted lamp that made discarded banana skins and ice cream cartons look 'pretty'. FUN. We had those hooded cane seats seen on continental beaches specially produced for loving couples, and a Battersea seat made up from thin rods which gave the hundreds required a spidery elegance.

Then a real problem caught me with my trousers down, as it were . . . lighting.

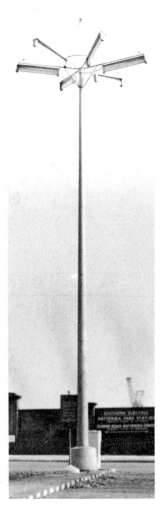

WORKING AGAINST TIME
The local administration were so slow making a decision, I designed these standards and had them installed on the main road leading to the entrances - connecting them to the mains on a DIY basis. No one queried the operation.

Main Vista illuminations.

Excuse me, your light-source is showing

Unlike the theatre, with its static audience, this audience will be strolling around on stage, so we must not be caught with a light-source showing. As complicated and interesting as a game of chess. No expert in Britain was experienced in outdoor illumination on this scale, but the South Bank organizers had appointed a Dr Lo Kalff, from Philips in Holland, to act as their consultant. I decided to pump him for know-how.

Kalff proved to be a slow-moving mountain of a man who spoke like God from on high, logical phrases rumbling down his well-formed front like an unstoppable landslide.

He took me on a quick flight to Arnhem, in Holland, to view illuminations he had installed for a local festival. Dusk found us seated at a restaurant table by a window that gave a wide view of Arnhem's main centre. "Any minute now and the lights will come on," said Kalff in the manner of God saying, "Let there be light." Sipping soup, he glanced repeatedly out at the blackness. Then the great man frowned and beckoned the waiter, who raised his eyebrows in surprise. The festival had terminated days ago. No illuminations.

Kalff crushed an innocent table napkin in his fist, carefully deposited it by his plate and strode with great dignity towards

the swing doors, I guessed to the 'phone. Pompous ass, I thought, but a few minutes after he returned – hey presto – the whole town came alive with light. Through the window I saw fountains rising like delicate translucent flowers above their reflections in illuminated pools against a curtain of luminous trees. I had misjudged him.

As we strolled around the town, Kalff pointed out this trick and then that. To illuminate a fountain the light must be directed up the spout. If you direct floodlights at trees they will appear flat like cardboard cut-outs; the light must be inside them. How to conceal light-sources in troughs in the ground, in the forks of trees, on the tops of walls, in recesses provided for them in roof structures? (But he had no trick for illuminating beds of flowers. I decided they were for daylight viewing only.)

When I got down to work there were thousands of lamps, but this essay in illumination brought with it an unexpected bonus. I discovered that the best effects were not foreseen – an accidental reflection on water, moving leaf-shadows across a path, a spill of sodium light producing a scatter of gold-dust on a lawn.

Fortunately, working for the Government, I was able to skip regulations like any well-trained bureaucrat. Instead of armoured cable for power lines, I would bury plastic-covered cables two feet down, touching wood that the gardeners would not prod that deep. For underwater lighting, instead of the regulation cast-iron box with a sealed glass cover, (as expensive as a box at the opera), I dunked naked bulbs, the joints sealed with rubber sheaths (available at drug stores in packets of three).

Concealing the light source.

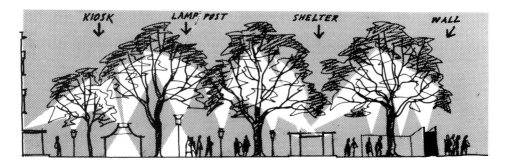

Where angels fear to tread

Late one night, wishing to observe the effect of some new fluorescent lamps which, when programmed, would flood the great banks of trees so they would fade from copper to gold and then blue-green . . . I found the site deserted and the power switched off.

No problem. Squeezing into the NO ENTRY transformer block, I pulled the heavy switches down to ON – sufficient power, I had been told, to illuminate the city of Birmingham.

Terrific, the effect was delightful, and so to bed.

Next morning my sin was found out – result, a confrontation with the militant Electricians' Trade Union. I had to apologise for pulling their switch, or the men would be called off. Hell. I felt rather put upon, as King John must have felt when forced to sign the Magna Carter at Runnymede a few miles up river.

Back at Duke Street Mehitabel composed an abject letter of apology for me to sign, but even my pen refused to cooperate. I tossed it angrily into the litter basket. "Wish I still had that old Parker pen," I complained. "Fat, lacquered red and with a bladder in its belly; always worked."

"They don't make them any more," she told me.

A month later one arrived in a neat padded box. Mehitabel had fluttered her eyelashes over the transatlantic 'phone and the makers had sent an original specimen from their Pen Museum. What a girl.

The inevitable crisis

Just about then I had a creepy feeling that the budgetary aspect of the operation was beginning to drift. There is a weakness in the committee system and this applied to our mini-committee, who would agree a proposal and, with a cosy feeling, move on to the next item. It was no one's job to calculate the cumulative cost of decisions taken over a series of meetings.

As I was still writing up monthly reports, I humped a stack of files to Duke Street and, with the help of Mehitabel (who I did not see enough of these days) and the adding machine (which I wished never to see again), I spent the weekend ploughing through figures which totalled hundreds of thousands of pounds – such a lovely spring day outside, it was like being

GARDEN EXTERIOR ART

Every surface was given a special treatment, but always in a style that would appeal to the public.

188

kept in at school.

My worst fears were realized. Sponsors had proved hesitant, but we had gone ahead. How else would we complete on time? A mistake. When I tabled the figures at the next meeting no one appeared to be unduly concerned.

I was, so I asked our Shakespeare Theatre guy to sign the monthly accounts from then on. "But we're not overspent," he complained. I then showed him how we had become *over-committed*. Come the day when we had to submit the final the bill, we would be way over the top of the Treasury Vote. "Advisable to inform the Minister concerned . . . don't you think?"

As a result the opposition in Parliament had a rare old time. Question: "Would the Minister please inform us who this person is, James Gardner, who signed the statements?" Answer: "I am informed that he is the designer of the project." "Oh, a *designer*." (Laughter.) Obviously a long-haired type. Not worth a reprimand.

Next morning my car, accustomed to the route, was making its own way down Baker Street, while I ticked off in my mind items which needed chasing: little cast-iron hands for the signposts; woven basket panniers to be mounted as litter receptacles, and thirty-five Queen Anne lampposts, which Islington Council was to pass on to us. As it turned out, they all fell to bits when dunked in 'pickle' to remove the paint – just another straw to break the camel's back.

As I climbed up to the office an excited Mehitabel rushed at me pointing dramatically at the centre-front-page of *The Daily Express*. A photograph of me (looking a bit of an idiot, as usual) and under it in leaded type:

FESTIVAL MAN No. 2
OUT

It was like being hit with a rubber bullet. Reading on, I found that the blurb referred to our Theatre friend who, having signed that last statement, had been made the scapegoat. (I guess they didn't sack me as half the job was still stored in my head; the next best thing, in those days, to a computer.)

Some exciting attractions were unplanned.

In no time at all a concerned editor, followed by his legal advisor, came thumping up our stair. I guess he had his fingers crossed.

When I said I was too busy to worry about the error he raised his eyebrows and retreated, a doubtful expression on his florid face. "Really, G, you're absolutely hopeless," wailed Mehitabel. "He has millions, and expected you to sue." Why take advantage of some poor photo-researcher's error when I have better things to do?

Funfair =150 obstinate individuals

Mondays were set aside in my diary for Amusement Area, and I would approach the site warily.

These fun-fair boys were a tight clan who operated by their own rules, cheerfully surviving on the public's loose change. They were sensitive to the weather and omens. (You never see green in a fun-fair – bad luck.) They look on us lot as a herd of cattle to be milked when the going is good. Fair enough, erecting a fun-fair is hard work.

Standing in the driving rain I have just given the Mirror Maze man his taped ribald laughter (in exchange for a more restrained façade) and am attempting to master the machinery that operates the Ladies Tumble out of Bed, while I explain to the owner that he may get away with 'topless' in Germany, but this is to be a family outing affair, when a six-foot Irishman with a chest like a doormat, grabs me by the arm.

He is erecting the Big Dipper and tells me three of the concrete base blocks are out of alignment. Serious. The cross-braced structure of a switchback only rests on these blocks so it can move on them as it extends and compresses under the thrust of the hurtling cars carrying screaming passengers to apparent catastrophe. If they were aware of this they would probably scream all the louder.

When I laid out the Tree Walk, the money in the till aspect had not occurred to me. An eccentric Irishman, the uncrowned king of the fun-fair world, warned me that my Tree Walk had as much chance of romping home as a horse with three legs. When, in the event, it proved to be a money-spinner, he buttonholed me in the Ghosthouse Bar to tell me why. "You see Gardner, me boy, it's a matter of timing. A ride only pays

190

if the crowd see the riders having their money's worth, and it can only take money while it's stopped. Now, that Tree Walk of yours; people are queuing to go up it *all the time*."

An octopus named Oscar

True to form, I was now expected to fill gaps when sponsors failed us. It started with a small pier I had erected out on the river to take a pavilion. I was rather proud of that pier, designed by hunch straight off the drawing board.

When a peak-capped naval type (from the Port of London Authority) arrived to check it, he opined that my structure – a lattice of steel scaffold poles resting on a mat of similar poles laid on the foreshore – would not last a month. "It's nothing but mud, man, just mud. The river will scour it away in no time, and then where will you be? I'm warning you. And you must place a dolphin off each end or it'll be smashed by barges in no time at all."

As the whole event was bankrupt, and we could not afford to take the pier down let alone build dolphins, I asked him whether he was authorized to instruct me, or was he just giving advice.

As he came under the heading of advice, I wished him good morning and left it at that.

In the event, the river current just flowed calmly by the slender tubes and the pier stood for a good fifteen years. The question of the moment was, what do we do with it? I suggested a Mississippi river-boat and the team agreed. It was a nostalgic little affair taken straight off a record sleeve for *Showboat*, a paddle-wheel thumping around at her stern and smoke belching from two tall smoke-stacks to the sound of 'Old Kentucky' on a mechanical organ we got from Belgium. It even had fairy lights at night – but still no sponsor.

"You've had the money for the boat," said Campbell. "It's about time you put your thinking cap on and put something inside the thing to make it *pay*." So that's what triggered off Oscar the Octopus. He was beautifully modelled in off-white rubber and pneumatically operated to move a tentacle now and again, suckers sticking to the tank while he observed you through the murky water with two sad glassy eyes. Late one

I little realised that years later I would design a real stern-wheeler, to ply on the Mississippi.

191

Experiment with tents

Tent in process of erection. Hoods attached to the perimeter frames link the cantaloup tentage with the zigzag glazed screen.

The sprung dance-floor. Band platform and bar to the right. The window recesses to hold seats and tables as rest areas.

Exterior treatment of the Crescent Restaurant by Patrick Gwynne. Note flower planters to mask the guy wires.

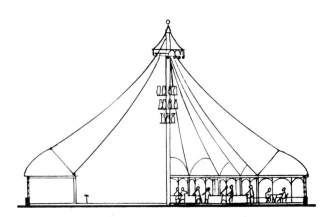

Section through the Dance Pavilion showing inner and outer tent.

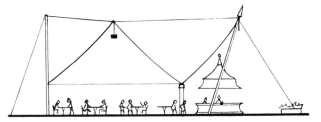

Cantilever system to eliminate poles within the Crescent Restaurant.

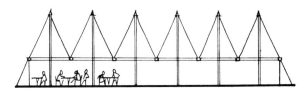

The pattern of fabric pyramids is kept taut by suspended guttering.

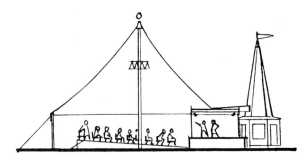

A two-way stage, which can operate to a tented audience if it rains.

night I concocted a history to make him authentic.

> "First sighted from HMS Teviot
> in the English Channel,
> OSCAR,
> the largest octopus in captivity,
> was later discovered in the swimming-pool
> on the Duke of Westminster's yacht and now
> lives happily on a diet of tinned spinach."

Some months later the RSPCA forwarded a letter sent in by three concerned ladies, bringing the Society's attention to the fact that a creature named Oscar was restricted in a cruelly small fish tank at Battersea and was being fed on a diet of spinach which they were sure was quite unsuitable. Good for them.

Let's dance

When I flew over to visit that pleasure park in Sweden, the most popular feature had been a fine dance pavilion – so we would have a dance pavilion. Having erected canvas structures in the Army, I decided it would be tented, the largest single-poled tent ever erected, (except the great tent of Kubla Khan, if one is to believe Marco Polo), and sited it to act as a focal point in the garden layout.

It was circular, so the fabric swept up to the apex as a series of tapering segments, cantaloup-style. Okay on the drawing, but the top tent-makers said it couldn't be done. Not to be defeated, I asked a competing branch of the family to have a go, just to show. My responsibility? Sure. The tent fabric alone weighed fifteen tons, so I made the central post a cruciform of two intersecting steel joists, crossed my fingers, and set about laying the foundations.

When the day came for hauling it up, not having the traditional circus elephants available, we used four heavy bulldozers. At a signal, each slowly backed away from the centre pulling its heavy steel cable, while I held my breath, until she was up . . . but dangerously near the firework platform. To prevent a catastrophe, I had mounted sprinklers at the peak so the fabric could be wetted before the pyrotechnics began. A good thought, as later I would see glowing incendiaries bouncing down her sides.

Nevertheless, I had miscalculated about *people*. The British, unlike the Scandinavians, are too shy to take to a dance floor in public during the daytime, so we hired 'call-girls' with partners as starters. No loss.

The river takes over

It was not possible to shelve all my other work and, occasionally, I would sneak away. On one occasion I returned from working on a new aircraft to discover that the elements were about to destroy all our work.

The tide is at the full and the river, higher than the footpath, is only held back by a fragile footing designed to support

THE RIVERSIDE THEATRE
The chinoiserie cupola projecting over the stage was devised to avoid the proscenium looking like a giant outdoor fireplace.

railings. A cluster of barges floats by almost at eye-level. My mind freezes as I see the waves in their wake chasing each other along the wall towards me, here and there toppling over it to wet the pavement. But there was worse to come. Battersea Park had at one time been a wide bend in the river, and the river was about to take the area back. Dig a pit to drain a patch and mud soup wells up to add to the débacle. Giant bulldozers and scrapers built for airfield construction are half submerged in the swamp, tilting helplessly at odd angles – as are the foundation blocks we had so carefully centred.

The experts – and there are even experts in mud – said the silt would never dry out, so it would have to be pumped into tanker-trucks and ditched down river. This was a slow laborious process, as was getting around the site in gumboots until, slowly, it began to take shape again; but it was obvious now that we would not complete on time.

With a sinking heart, I drew up a revised time schedule.

Making for the admin. meeting I passed the now completed Open Air Theatre, packed with excited workers – not working. A Cabinet Minister who, attempting to placate the natives –

now in their fourth strike – was retreating to his limousine followed by jeers and catcalls.

A patch of spring sunshine swept across the lake as two happy ducks quacked and waggled their tails at me . . . and well they might, had they viewed the new administrator appointed to replace our Shakespeare Theatre friend. The picture of a provincial linen-draper, obviously pleased with himself, as he parked his cigar and pointed me to a seat. How did he get the job? He was reputed to have an IN with the fun-fair clan, having run a pleasure-beach in some out of the way resort in Wales. I explained that, with the late start, repeated strikes, the wettest winter in history and the river flooding, it would not be possible to complete on time.

After a meaningful glance round the table he pronounced, "The show will open on the agreed date," under the impression, like any politician, that saying the words would make it happen.

Litter baskets illuminated at night with shaded green light.

Beware the Ides of March

I suppose I was the Caesar of Battersea but, alas, there was no Cassius to warn me that this pompous little belly on legs was planning to stab me in the back.

So, over to the South Bank to paint an on-the-spot mural, (the Viking Ship from Sutton Hoo), as the artist commissioned to do it had gone off holidaying with the fee. Terrific! This gave me the excuse to do some practical painting – while people commiserated, saying, "poor old G."

Waiting for paint to dry, it occurred to me that there we all were, busy as ants on a hot day, putting up the show, completely forgetting that it was intended to commemorate the 1851 Crystal Palace, *and there was no exhibit to mark the fact.*

That night, after turning in, the image of a miniature pavilion haunted me – but what was the point? It was not in the plans and the moment when moneymen tighten the purse-

A friendly signpost – but not quite Barry's cup of tea.

strings had long passed. To hell with it. I threw off the sheets, found a sketch pad and produced a pretty, tinted visual of the idea. Small but significant. I mounted it on a high platform constructed from old Victorian ironwork which I had seen in a catalogue; a coffee table book intended for nostalgia rather than use. Inside, little maquettes of Queen Victoria greeting

An off-the-cuff South Bank item I enjoyed more than others, as it was not officially planned or budgeted for.

foreign notables to Handel's ceremonial music on tape, plum velvet, a draped canopy, potted palms . . .

Next morning, Barry, as might be expected, fell in love with it, and money-man Campbell, giving a conspiratorial wink, found the money.

Feeling chuffed, I returned to Battersea to face a débâcle. It looked for all the world as though some vindictive monster had staggered round the site vomiting tarmac.

The new administrator (with one eye on the Honours List) had decided to have a Royal Opening as planned, and had instructed the contractor to lay tarmac wherever a 'hard' area was indicated on the plan – *and to get it done before I returned.*

The flights of shallow steps leading onto the main concourse, a classical fantasy designed to give visitors a sense of precision and authority, looked like a cascade of black treacle creeping over a pudding.

196

The depths of despond

Sitting on the only bit of friendly territory left, the running-board of my converted London taxi, I looked around at the work of the artists and designers about to be rubbished. No point in crying out, "Help." Barry was an Establishment man if there ever was one. The guy from the Ministry wouldn't risk his pension. Casson? Not fair at this late stage to pull him onto a sinking ship.

As a last resort I would go to the top, the President of the Royal Institute of British Architects.

I gave the starter a kick – the tired old engine coughed – gave a lopsided thump – then hesitantly started. A good omen as I made for the RIBA's dignified HQ in the West End.

"A Mister Gardner?" Receptionist is aloof. "The President, and no appointment?" A doubtful pause, "*Urgent*, you say?" Intercom rings. "Take a seat. I'll see . . . when he's free."

An interminable wait in the travertine lobby as I moodily watch bright young architects drift in, then leave *'by the same door as in they went,'* (Omar Khayyam).

At last I am through the polished mahogany doors as the President looks up from clearing detritus from a heavy talk session. I describe the *blitzkrieg* at Battersea, its causes and the piddling little guy who ordered it. The great man expresses concern: after all it is a national project. He agrees that the RIBA is instituted to support an architect faced with such a situation, but – he plays with an onyx paperweight – "You must understand, Gardner, there's little I can do. One: you are not an accredited architect. Two: when the client who runs amok is acting for the Government, there's little anyone can do." I pointed out that *we* were both aware of this, but the guys I was dealing with were not.

Believe it. Next morning the sun peeped out from a cloud as the President stepped down from his Daimler limousine and, after carefully avoiding puddles and a tipped-up wheelbarrow, laid his expensive-looking briefcase with combination lock on the Committee table, gave those present a cool nod, then authoritatively laid down the law – manipulator Moses just down from the mountain. Completion date was postponed and we were once again on schedule.

The Pleasure Garden chair, designed not to intrude visually on the planting. So popular, it almost defined the fifties after the show.

Happy youngsters, some of whom would grow up to act as assistants on projects I am involved in today.

I was blamed, of course, but who cares when friendly bulldozers are already backing and thrusting around the site, scooping up tons of glistening black tar, while surveyors with their levels and striped poles are busy marking out the paved promenades. My hair had gone a little whiter, but the battle was WON.

No Royal Opening. Instead, the first person to pass the turnstiles would be one of the millions of ordinaries for whose pleasure the gardens were designed – and they arrived by the million.

Money up in smoke

The opening night? There must be fireworks, no half measures, biggest show ever, blockbusters, as they do in Italy. I leaf through a *Pyrotechnics Catalogue*. (Warned that it is a cheat, like most sales talk for consumer desirables, as rockets are measured by *circumference*, so reduce expectations by three.) Right. There are Whirling Dervishes, Thunder Devils, Triple Scatter-flashes, Whistling Dragons, Howling . . .

I give up and decide we will ask the two top suppliers to each put on a show – and let the best man win.

Two glorious starry flash-bang nights, sheer bliss, crowd open-mouthed, a final corporate sigh, "Ahhh . . ." as the final stars trailed to earth. Drifting smoke, ominous smell of gunpowder, and I wonder where the casings fell?

The cost? My hat! Even a government squandering a loan from the European Bank won't cover the cost of more than two such extravaganzas a week, so I place that contract before they have second thoughts and design the largest illuminated sign in the world to animate the show on other nights.

Months later, the ongoing Festival with its millions of gaping visitors forgotten, I am concentrating on other work, but decide I can no longer ignore a dreaded buff envelope in the pending tray. A tax demand? No, it is a handwritten note from that meticulous Treasury watch-dog, Campbell. He wrote that many consultants, architects and the like, had pocketed good fees from the Festival. In spite of my major contribution I hadn't so he had contrived, unofficially, to scrape the enclosed from the bottom of the barrel. Out fell a very useful Treasury cheque.

In return I sent him the best visual of the Pleasure Gardens I could find. It probably hangs in his study today, a reminder of our conspiracies and tactics in the Battle of Battersea.

My hair had turned white, but who cares.

I will never forget the very last night when, after a farewell dinner in the Riverside Restaurant, we essayed out into the crowd to see the great firework finale.

Foreseeing this, I mounted water sprinklers at the apex of the tent, to operate when fireworks were on the menu.

199

The whole of London seemed to be there and we soon lost contact in the press of bodies which ebbed and flowed wherever there was standing ground. It was amazing so few had to be pulled out of the lake. Near me a party had made space to do a 'Knees Up Mother Brown', as waves of singing swept the crowd.

Then, as the last sparkling trail met its mirror image in the lake, *". . . there was such cheering as had not been heard in Britain since Mafeking night."*

"Without vision the people perish"

It became apparent that the South Bank show had not been put on for the people but for politics when, Festival over, the new party in power demolished the lot. For some reason, probably in error, the little Crystal Palace pavilion was left standing for some time, a cheeky reminder of what had been.

Unfortunately, responsibility for maintaining the Festival Gardens fell to the London County Council, as it was on their patch. Not interested, they passed it down to be run by the admin. guy and an ex barrow-boy who promoted a fast-food chain. Not wishing to be in at the death, I resigned.

Today the area is a desolation where lonely spinsters walk their pets of a morning. Dogs at least appreciate the few lamp-posts that remain.

So THAT'S where the rainbow ends.

I was self-indulgently proud of this clock, designed for the Chelsea entrance.

A traditional Bath

Russell Page, who had advised me on planting at the Pleasure Gardens, 'phoned, "I've given your name to the Marquis of Bath. He has a design project in the offing. Ring him."

This notoriously erratic nobleman proposed installing *son-et-lumière* (illuminations with sound effects) at Longleat, the greatest of Elizabethan stately homes, set in twenty thousand odd acres of man-made landscape.

The house was large enough to satisfy Solomon and all his wives three times over, but Bath had opened it to the public to cover the cost of upkeep and camped out in the modest Mill House. Well, not exactly 'camped out', as he had recently acquired an extremely young wife who was not only easy on the eye, but – at no extra charge – had applied 'penthouse' décor to the Mill House with impeccable *picture-book* taste. The white piano, pasted over with playing cards, complemented the swans that occasionally peeked through the sitting room windows. Very nice.

The Marquis was leading me on a safari through some of the hundred or so rooms in the great house, when we surprised his son and heir. More than quixotic enough to follow his father's lead; hair awry, draped in a silk dressing-gown, he was painting at a large canvas with oils, tippling whisky the while.

Painting completed, (with erotic overtones), he would hang it alongside others (with erotic overtones) in his own gallery. An art dream-world. No critics. Very nice.

Fortified by a stiff whisky, Bath and I climbed interminable back stairs (no elevators) to the attics, as he muttered about a leak – difficult to locate under that acreage of slate and leaded roof – when, turning a dusty corner, we came upon an old portable hip-bath which retainers would, I guess, fill from buckets of warm water when an ancestral Bath needed a clean up.

The original Bath? Apparently not. That would be the City of Bath, where the Ancient Romans slipped off their togas to dip in the healing waters welling up from a mineral spring. A pity.

That evening we gravitated to Bath's study to savour vintage wine (just the one glass, thank you) and talk, disappointingly, about *everything* but *son-et-lumière*. Leaning against the mantle, he opened the session by asking my advice – could he afford a colour TV? I told him I already had one, but turned the knob to get rid of the colour. I was unaware that he was quietly topping up my glass, as he changed the subject from vindictive death duties, high blood pressure, the expanding universe, the pros and cons of four-wheel drive, the best season for planting deciduous trees, to (naughty) how much I would reduce my fee if he paid it in cash.

In the early hours and many top up's later, Bath apologised for sleeping me in a dainty bedroom; a setting intended for spoiled society dames. Padded bed-head, pink-draped with tasselled fringes and, on the marble mantle, two sweet little china shoes, each garnished with a live orchid selected to match the *décor*.

Feeling rather like a wart-hog in fairyland, and bending down to remove muddy shoes, I suddenly felt sick. Diving into the diminutive powder-room, I threw up into the sweet little onyx basin with its purpose-made gilt faucets . . .

Nothing like the guilt I felt as, cleaning the fittings with my underpants, I observed a close up of my too well-known face in the dainty bevelled mirror.

Upshot. I enjoyed a tour of the chateaux of the Loire, viewing *son-et-lumière* with a lighting guy, at Bath's expense, only to inform him on my return that, as Longleat park was so extensive, income would never cover the cost of the miles of electric cable to it. It was *not on.*

The bailiff, who ran the estate, heaved a sigh of relief; he had expected me, as a commercial bloke, to take on the job for the fee – whether it made his boss a loss or not.

Groping in the dark

No *son-et-lumière* but, by mid-winter, I was having lunch with the Marquis of Bath at an inn named The Marquis of Bath. After finishing off with cheddar cheese, we drove up into the Cheddar Gorge where he wanted me to devise illuminations for a cave the locals had just discovered. We stopped at a fault that zigzagged up the rock face; being slim, I was just able to squeeze through.

Bath put a torch in my outstretched hand and said he'd wait outside. I soon discovered why.

I am no potholer. Unexplored caves can be pitch dark, wet with slime, icy cold and, in winter, may be two feet deep in ice-water, which sneakily laps over the top of one's gumboots. Excitingly beautiful . . . reflections of the limestone patternings above mirrored in flat metallic pools. A drip, and the reflected abstracts animate into grotesque forms. Stalactites – brittle needles that ping to the touch, or spirals – like that elegant verdigris steeple in Copenhagen, but the other way up – and peeps, through odd-shaped apertures, at secret worlds no one will ever visit.

My damp survey plan, drawn with a wet pencil and numbed fingers, could well be taken for an anatomical drawing of the ulcerated stomach of an ostrich. I was proud of it.

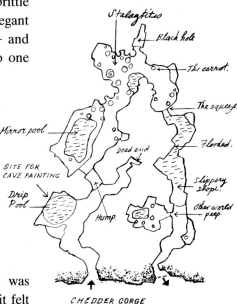

CHEDDER GORGE

Though I hadn't felt my gumboots for some time, I saw they were still there as, angling my upper half to navigate a twisted cleft, I heard Bath's distant voice hollowly echoing my name, then again and again until, suddenly, I squeezed into the open air through another fault down the road.

It had been so bitterly cold inside that, though it was freezing enough outside to see my breath, by comparison it felt pleasantly warm.

As I empty gumboots and insert dead feet into shoes, the Marquis and his bailiff watch me, frowning. Bailiff peers at his watch, "Yes, sir, he's missed the train." Bath isn't interested in my remarkable plan, "Didn't you hear me calling, Gardner? You've missed your train." Echoed by the bailiff, "Yes, sir, he's missed the last train." Like two turns in a comic opera.

I make a suggestion, "We might just make it in the car?" The bailiff purses his lips, then shakes his head in negative warning. He was trying to save my life, but how was I to know that Bath, when put to it in his Bentley Continental, was considered a crazy man at the wheel, even by his friends.

He made it, flattening curves by cutting across verges, attacking blind corners at full throttle and treating the straights as a race track until, at last, we dived into the town at a considerable lick. I stiffened in my seat and shouted, "Traffic!" He took the station corner like New York cops in a film and pulled up with a jerk. "It's all right, Gardner, they know me round here." What an inconsequential remark.

He just had time to shout at me as I closed the carriage door, "Gardner! Go ahead with that mastodon." He referred to a crazy notion I had of faking Stone Age paintings on one of the cave walls – on the far side of a pool, which would prevent close inspection. I enjoy producing fakes. Bath's response, when I reminded him that this cave had never been occupied by Man, had been pragmatic. The *hoi polloi* from the nearby city wouldn't know that. And the archaeologists?

"It won't fool the boffins," he grunted. "They know it hasn't been occupied, so why worry?" Okay, but then I'm not a Marquis.

Back home and a hot bath, while I meditated on how to get concealed leads to concealed illuminations in that slimy world of stalagmites – or is it stalactites? I shuddered. Then, how to feed water to drip from the cave roof to produce widening rings of ripples on the surface of the still pool below?

I lay back and, purely as a technicality, meditated on whether the cave paintings at Lascaux, in France, were faked by some local joker? Surely not – best change the subject.

Unexpectedly, I will be catapulted to the Far East.

Compete with the Taj Mahal?

India arrived at Duke Street in a taxi while I was arguing with a policeman; one of those flat-hat types who float around in long black cars like the Queen. He objected to a large animated sign for Hennessy brandy which I had just erected on a bomb-site in Piccadilly.

A cut-out audience is viewing a theatre proscenium. On stage, a classical villain with fierce moustache, top hat, black cloak, is holding a swooning blonde in his arms. She flops. Villain says (balloon caption): "Is there a Hennessy in the house?" Cut-out audience hold up bottles of brandy. Idea corny, but the artwork top line.

The police were not objecting to its vulgarity, but to the fact that cars and buses were slowing up so people could look at it, resulting in a glorious traffic jam. I must 'unanimate' it *immediately.* I'd already (very cleverly) circumvented a crisis. On discovering there was no power-main on site, I enticed a dedicated cycling club, the London Harriers, to animate it by pedalling like mad on bicycles fixed behind the hoarding. I was now faced with the diplomatic problem of unanimating *them.*

I'm about to dash down the stairs when Mehitabel ushers in a little man from Bombay.

He tells me he has just finished interviewing a number of designers for his boss, R.D. Tata, when, by chance, he heard my name mentioned. Can I spare fifteen minutes of my time before he catches the plane to India? Reckoning that the traffic block in Piccadilly can wait for another fifteen minutes, I toss my hat at the peg, miss it, then politely offer him a chair. He tells me that his boss, Tata, is sponsoring an 'important' pavilion for the first international fair to be held in India.

Seeing my 'never heard of him' look, he patiently points out that R.D. Tata owns India's cotton and steel mills, chemical plants, builds locomotives, assembles cars, runs Air India, owns the top hotels and the newspapers. Wash your hands with soap, or wipe your behind anywhere on the sub-continent and you acknowledge Tata's empire.

Farouk Mullah, for that is his name, then tells me this project is to stimulate young Indians (who have the habit of lying in the shade chewing betel-nut) into hitching up their loin-cloths and, by the application of *private enterprise*, hitch India up out of the Third World.

Let's play with the problem. Mehitabel brings in tea while I talk. "First, you must capture an audience until you have indoctrinated it. That means a *controlled* circulation. Sugar? Good. Well, we'll need an inviting front to pull them in, then plan the pavilion like an Edwardian mousetrap – except we don't drown them at the end; maybe have a gimmick on the lines of one we introduced at a conservation exhibit in Dublin."

"Two ways out, one for those INTERESTED and the other signed NOT MY AFFAIR. People leaving by the latter have a lapel badge pinned on them reading I DON'T CARE." A pause. "Subliminal," I add. "Makes them care." Farouk looks bewildered. I guess Ireland ain't India. This calls for a diagram.

I sketch a plan for the 'mousetrap' (a question mark with the entrance at the dot) and hand it to Mullah, who smiles gratefully and scrambles down to a waiting taxi, followed by a breathless Mehitabel with his umbrella.

Gosh – the traffic jam in Piccadilly!

207

The Raj – now under new management

Two months later I am flying to Bombay by Tata's Air India, drawing pad resting against a seat back to complete the last visuals while in flight . . . but I hadn't calculated that, travelling eastward, I would lose six hours.

The prospect of finishing the job in a hotel bedroom makes me feel sorry for myself. I am booked in at the Taj which, as one would expect, is owned by Tata – who holes up in a penthouse on the roof with his beautiful Canadian mistress. Its main elevation disappoints me, until I hear that the architect (an Englishman) failed to turn up at an essential site meeting, with the result that it was built back to front.

It is said that when the architect discovered this he penned a letter of apology, then committed suicide in his bath. Out of character. Far more likely, he issued a revised site layout, sent it in with a report rationalizing his error, then followed up with a fee for *supplementary work*. Maybe I'm biased about architects; anyway, I'm no longer feeling sorry for myself.

Next morning, viewed from a taxi window, I find Bombay to be disappointingly homely; a heated-up version of older London buildings in heavy-handed Edwardian vernacular and with the same cast iron railings.

Sad how British Imperialists lacked the magic touch (except when they designed follies or seaside piers for home consumption, acknowledging the romantic East, with all the curlicues).

The man who runs an empire

My appointment is with R.D. Tata. With pounding heart, past bowing attendants, I ascend in a padded elevator escorted by a poker-faced eunuch. Room one, expensive carpet, smiling second secretary; room two, even more expensive carpet, smiling first secretary; room three, behind a littered desk sits Tata himself in shirt sleeves. He looks up sharply, eyes flicking to his watch *en route*, puts on a polite smile and points to a chair.

Sensing that I am facing a man who counts seconds (in rupees), I hurriedly slide the delicate perspex model out of its box, place it at the best angle, press the button and – thank goodness – the lights come on. Tata is aloof and a bit frightening. Now he's practical and to the point. In other words, he likes the pavilion, adding, "The design is *excellent*. I approve. But, alas, we no longer have people who can produce such craftsmanship."

And that was that. The rest was for his economic adviser, Minoo Masani, to clarify.

The void between Duke Street and Bombay

In the cool of evening, overlooking the Bay of Bengal, Masani taught me quite a bit about Asian economics (and my habit of underestimating a situation). He was not the local-college-boy-makes-good I had anticipated, but an Oxford scholar and Chairman of the UNESCO committee concerned with underprivileged peoples – and I was beginning to think I might be one of them. Nevertheless, we got on well enough. He talked and I listened; anyone who knows me will consider this sufficiently remarkable.

Interview over, a flight to Delhi to check the site (occupied by flea-bitten monkeys) and engage a Sikh contractor, a tile-maker and a nurseryman who, as it turned out, gave me the wrong advice on planting.

Four months later I'm back at Delhi airport, smuggling paint. At that time everything in India was either red ochre, dog-shit buff or white, so I had treated the pavilion front as a complicated fret in cerulean blue and magenta, not knowing that there was an absolute bar on pigments crossing the frontier (friend Masani's 'practical economics').

As one must never allow an initial concept to be watered down, I must smuggle the pigment in. I telex Mullah to meet me at the customs' barrier carrying a raincoat – how English – to screen the act of passing the stuff over.

The cans proved to be larger and heavier than I had expected, but I managed to stroll up to the barrier pressing them to my body while clutching a heavy suitcase. Mullah was so excited at greeting me he forgot the ploy, and there we were in full view of the official's eye and me breaking out in a hot sweat. As the customs' bloke turned to have an altercation with a porter, I pushed the cans across. Poor Mullah, I guess police cells are rather uncomfortable at 120 °F in the shade.

I find Nat, my assistant, in the excise shed, sitting in a patch of sweat on our pile of crates. Apparently they have been there five days, and so has Nat, while petty officials 'mislay' the documents, find a discrepancy, or pass them on to another petty official, who hands them to a plump man in a Gandhi cap, who goes off and doesn't come back. A real comic turn.

A new face doesn't do any good either. In desperation I ring Tata's agent.

He arrives in a smooth, black Mercedes; not one speck of dust. Out of the sky? Introductions, all smiles. He goes off to negotiate, while I join a bunch of layabouts admiring the car.

The smooth man at the top

But he is back already – no smiles. Flinging open the offside door, the agent gestures me in and we are off. He drives to a lush part of New Delhi: well kept avenues which the Mercedes acknowledges with an even gentler purr. Dignified, stucco mansions in the Regency-style, like one sees peeping through the trees round Primrose Hill, each set in a veritable Garden of Eden; silent, rotating sprinklers emitting holy water. Political top-types' perks.

The door of one of the most distinguished is opened to us by a bearded butler in a turban, who ushers us through a cool tiled hall to a dining-room where we intrude on a sizeable family at lunch.

It looks for all the world like a Victorian family gathering but, a sepia print, in reverse – the clothes are white, the faces are brown. They are all smiling. The head of the family greets Tata's agent as an old friend, the children are admonished for staring at the funny Englishman and conversation proceeds in Hindi. After clearing space on the table our host signs the forms with a flourish, and we are bowed out to settle back in the car. All over.

"An occasion for you to meet our Minister of Foreign Affairs," says the agent then, at my vacant look, "Surely you recognized him – he is our version of your Mr Anthony Eden." I try to imagine the reaction of one of our top ministers if a commercial agent knocked him up at his home to sign a release for some odd crates lying in the docks.

210

Anyway, it works like a dose-of-salts and, as the customs' guy releases the crates, I make a crack about Indian bureaucracy. "One of the things you taught us, Sahib . . ." he grins.

At the site the heat hits me like a blowlamp. In the dazzle and dust I wade through groups of squatting untouchables – who have replaced the monkeys – and, squinting up at the high fretted front of the pavilion, am relieved to see that it is exactly as detailed and *the right way round.* Then I see the planting.

Quick answers a long way from home

It will take two years before those wilting sprigs are worth looking at, and we open in a week. Getting a lift to the Delhi Government Nursery I discover a quiet, cool world; the whole area roofed with slatted screens for shade, each row fed by a sprinkler pipe so the plants look privileged and happy. That's more than the labour force on site does.

There's no sign of activity except a plump lady in a pink sari negotiating with an old Hindu in a dhoti. She picks out a little potted plant, then another, compares, does a switch, then reverts to the first one. More discussion. Why fret? All the time in the world.

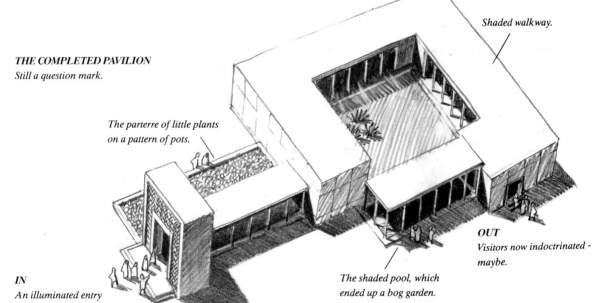

Shaded walkway.

THE COMPLETED PAVILION
Still a question mark.

The parterre of little plants on a pattern of pots.

OUT
Visitors now indoctrinated - maybe.

IN
An illuminated entry entices people to enter.

The shaded pool, which ended up a bog garden.

211

Meanwhile, I observe that a large area has been given over to this same plant. The greyish leaves nestling on the terracotta tops of the tightly-packed pots make a delightful pattern.

As soon as the old man has sold the plump lady her individual plant, I beckon him over and pace out a block eighty feet by ten, "How much?" The laconic English. He takes an interminable time counting, but it isn't wasted as, in a corner, I discover five mature yucca specimens that will make bomb-bursts on the lawn which fills the centre of the question mark layout . . . or should: I haven't seen it yet.

Back on site, I am happy to note that the lawn is there, only to be faced with a problem that almost defeats us. True, the lake bordering this lawn is as planned, shaded by a high canopy supported by rows of slender columns. The tiles lining it were to be glazed in diagonal blue and white, as I had demonstrated to the potter on my last visit. (He didn't take kindly to straight lines – and I wasn't surprised after trying it with his cow-hair brush.) But I can't see the tiles for cement sludge and sand.

To distract my attention the Sikh contractor is popping offbeat questions at me concerning our Jesus Christ.

True, this is a change from the usual questions about first division football but, not to be diverted, I tell him he must clean the pool out and refill it. He says, "Impossible." I say, "Why?" He tells me, in his clipped English, that there isn't a drain. I point to the wire grille clearly visible over the outlet. "Yes, yes," he explains, "there is an outlet and a pipe, but may I respectfully point out that there is no sewer, so we have taken the pipe as far as indicated on your drawing to fulfil the contract, and plugged it." He's having me on? But no sewer.

So . . . what? That explains the squatting workmen and flies. No pool and only five days to go. A flower bed? Not under a canopy. Wire the lot in as an aviary? Maybe the Indians don't cage birds. Then an idea gelled. When flying into Delhi airport, I had noticed a wide river winding its way across the plain, bristling with rushes and almost paved with lilies. That's it. We'll convert the lake into a bog-garden.

The Sikh is surprised. "What river?" After some argument over a map it is located, but some distance away. Jets travel fast.

At first light next morning, Nat, a tall, rangy, white-clad product of New Zealand, drives off in a cloud of dust with five underfed labourers who, leaning miserably on the shafts of their hoes, sway with the lurching of the erratically-sprung truck.

I wait all that day. The sun touches the horizon, flattens like an orange, then goes out. Patches of scrub are now silhouetted against an indigo sky, the tzz-tzz of insects, bats flitter by, then the workers' campfires are extinguished one by one. The Sikh foreman gives an apologetic smile, shrugs, and goes off to wherever he goes leaving me, perched on a dented oil drum, to wait it out.

It's getting chilly, it's smelly and I've run out of tobacco. Low level moment. At last a flickering light, then it has gone, then I see it again through swathes of ground-mist. It grows steadily brighter – the vehicle's solitary headlamp. The decrepit truck lurches over a cement-worker's bucket and then creaks to an abrupt halt; draped with sodden weeds and dripping water like an ice-truck. (There's the stench peculiar to rotting vegetation.) Nat climbs down and, ignoring me, helps two zombie labourers lift down what appears to be a dripping corpse. The zombies amble off in the darkness with the moaning bundle sagging between them.

"How did you get on?" Nat, who prides himself on sartorial perfection, slowly peels a tangle of dank weed off his wet trousers, then gestures to the back of the truck. "That's what you wanted, isn't it? Well, you've bloody well got it!" He slopes off.

Nat is usually the friendliest of men; even has a dry sense of humour on occasion.

The bog-garden turned out to be a success though, in the process, I discovered that lilies have ten foot stems which tangle like live spaghetti; but at nightfall there's a bonus – the croaking of frogs that had come along for the ride. A bit

213

incongruous, perhaps, against the pavilion's precisely detailed front, softly illuminated in the twilight by hundreds of miniature coloured lamps. Even Nat, who is now rather proud of yesterday's exploit, agrees it's better than on the model. Tata will be pleased, that is – *if he doesn't go inside.*

Babies delivered, but to the wrong address

Morning, a telegram. The key exhibits, which we had shipped by P & O express liner to Bombay under captain's orders, had been carried on to Colombo. Gosh, that's in Ceylon – another country.

Delayed by bad weather, the captain had dropped the mail into a bumboat at Bombay to keep the ship on schedule. Reading the small print on the back of the lading list, I find that's how it goes. So, Tata's agent again. This time to get the stuff trucked up the length of India and in a *hurry* – a word little used in India.

A few days later, when I had almost lost hope, a great mud-caked Scammel truck lumbered up, to stop with a gentle hiss of steam from its spurting radiator. An admiring circle of untouchables crowded the driver as he narrated an epic story of diversions across dry river beds, getting bogged down and then hauled out by buffalo. A detour round Bangalore – barricaded because of language riots – to find himself back-tracking dirt roads that ended no place; which could be the name of any of a thousand villages. Lost in space and time.

ELIZABETH

was daubed across the truck's dusty bonnet. "Why Elizabeth?" I asked. The driver gave a wide grin. "We name her after your English sacred cow, Sahib. She bring us luck."

Nat and I proceeded to manhandle the exhibits into position – to the amazement of the Hindus who had never seen an Englishman carrying anything heavier than a polo stick.

The largest crate contains a precise, geometric pyramid built up of neat, white blocks. On closer observation, each layer is seen to represent a level in the hierarchy of authority. On even closer examination, each block is seen to represent a desk and,

Throughout the show, young India is seen pedalling into the future. Simple to animate, as the rotating wheels carry the legs around with them.

behind it, a figure wearing the official Gandhi cap and white jacket. These are named District Commissioner, Area Supervisor, Tax Collector and so on down to the bottom level, the Village Boss. Not quite the bottom; the pyramid is resting on something dark. Peep under and you see it is supported by hundreds of little men in loincloths, wire men bending under the pyramid of bureaucracy. Fun planning it in London, but here and now?

Come opening day, when that great statesman Nehru looked me in the eye as though I was a *real person*, I registered it as a top moment. But when he questioned, "Do you think your exhibit will have the intended effect on the young generation?" I was at a loss. More concerned with the client's motivation, I had thought of the theme as no more than the usual public-relations ploy, so my response was a weak, "Yes, sir."

A memorable moment thrown away.

Look assured and one may even convince oneself.

After handing over to the wallah who is to act as manager, we have two whole days to see India. (Journalists have written books on it in less time.) Our train to Agra is not only full, but has a layer of passengers on the roof. I spend four hours sweating in a stuffy guard's van, one buttock on the edge of a much worn tool-chest, between an aged guru and a female Parsee who smells of baby – so Nat can photograph me standing in front of the Taj Mahal.

"I must say it makes our pavilion seem a bit trivial," comments Nat. He clicks the camera. The Taj Mahal may be a visual cliché, but it is reborn with every dawn; an image of refined proportions so precisely poised and exactly delineated that a stray cloud, drifting across the sky like a powder-puff, intrudes on its symmetry.

Tomb for a princess, as exquisitely feminine as a model coolly posed on the cover of *Vogue* – to be admired from a distance, but not to enter.

I resist the flesh pots

And the same can be said for the exquisite partner Tata provides for me when I dine with him at a posh Bombay club. While I am captivated by the cluster of gems on her pink-tinted toes and the diamond set in her straight little nose, she is on the carpet at my knee, in the attitude we see dancing-girls take in Mogul miniatures.

Tata, with no warning preamble, then offers me a top job – designer to the Tata Consortium and for a staggeringly high fee. Being something of a coward in such matters, I opt for the world I know; the dampness of Nordic Britain. No dancing-girls.

As I escort the oriental beauty home, she reveals that she has performed on TV in Paris and London, knows the top stores for women's clothes in Knightsbridge and spends much of her life exercising, on a diet of vitamins. So much for the mystery of the Orient.

En route home on the plane an American businessman, seated next to me, disgruntled in spite of three large bourbons on-the-rocks, turned and remarked in an aggrieved voice, that here he was on a crusade to sell the American Way of Life to those natives and they just didn't want to know. And there was I, one of the British Raj lot they had kicked out, treated like a buddy and called Sahib.

"I guess," I replied, "that's how the cookie crumbles."

I was not to forget the Delhi exhibit, as a month later a letter arrived from the dedicated wallah I had left in charge.

Dear Mr Gardner, With respect I am sure you will be pleasured that the plants are watered green and the mechanics are operating as your instructions. With apology I am writing you this time of concern at an unfortunate circumstance. A week after opening and very successful, the Foreign Minister makes a visit. At first he is very happy and all smiles. Then he comes to the pyramid exhibit and there is strong discussion. He asks me, am I responsible? I say, yes, for the care of the pavilion, but not for the exhibits.

He asks who is responsible and I say Mr Pootbaba, so he tells me to bring him up quickly. I ring, but Mr Pootbaba is just leaving so I try Mr . . . (a list of five gentlemen who were on Tata's committee) *. . . but they are all 'unavailable'. The Minister is hot with anger and instructs me to close the pavilion. Next morning shocking to see two armed soldiers barring the entry. Mr Tata's agent visits, and with his assistance I arrange for the pyramid to be removed.*

I did not think it necessary to mention your name to the Minister in this regard. I remain your humble servant.

A name which translated means 'bottle-seller'. What a man.

Back on track

Only at the odd depressed moment did I regret refusing Tata's tempting offer. Not troubling to be selective, I had plenty of work and ideas came easily enough; the problem was – *how to make it pay*? I would get so interested in each job that I tended to spend more and more time on it . . . anything one does can be done better, but that doesn't increase the fee.

Guessing that two big projects had used up my quota of good luck, I settled down to *'the mixture as before'* – visualising whatever came my way.

I little realised that Campbell and an Under-Secretary from the Foreign Office were conspiring in the corridors of power.

All was revealed when three of the Festival design team met on neutral ground – a café – to sign off a backlog of costings. Casson and I were kept waiting so long in the help-yourself queue, I ate my bun. On my asking the cashier to take for it she said, "No. Only what you have on the tray."

"But I've eaten one!"

Shocked, "You can't do that."

"But I just have."

Impasse. I had crossed the line of normality and entered a frightening zone where the rules no longer applied. Confused, she fumbled at the till with trembling hands, then rang up the wrong amount. Poor girl.

That contretemps (and the Festival accounts) settled, Casson and Misha swapped rumours – who was doing what in the design world. These two were the natural choice for any important project that might come up. Casson knew all the right people. And Misha? He ran a well advertised design research unit, comprising four floors of departmental assistants, only a few doors down the street from my converted servants' bedrooms.

As the odd-man-out, I sat back, sipped tea and thought about nothing.

Misha was probing. A sideways glance at Casson, "You know, there's a Brussels World Fair in the offing . . . ?" Their eyes met, duellists assessing each others' ploys before the handkerchief is dropped.

I tipped up my empty cup to read what the tea-leaves made of it – a shape vaguely resembling a split infinitive.

"An interesting job." Casson looked questioningly at Misha, "I wonder who will be involved? The news should break soon . . ."

Placing my cup carefully on its saucer, I coughed to remind them that I was still there and interposed apologetically, "I was given the job two days back." Brotherly but cool termination of tea party.

Not a bit part – the whole shinazzle

Having to commit themselves to open view at a World Fair causes a flutter in the bureaucratic hen-house.

First, some literary old bird goes broody and hatches a theme proposal. This is pecked at, with some scattering of feathers. Meanwhile, an architect – the cock who crows loudest – goes off with a pavilion to design under his wing. The hens go into committee and, with much clucking, select designers, artists, writers and the like, while free-range lobbyists peck around to ensure that the result can be offered up for international consumption. No sex: it will be opened by the Queen.

This time the guy from the Ministry had risked his neck and, perhaps, his pension by simply passing the whole baby over to me with, "Get on with it, G, and be sure we open on time."

I guess his experience in dealing with the Festival had taught him that a group of four, in a small back room with their eye on the ball, or even a taxi driver, is likely to come up with a more coherent result than a hierarchy of place-men.

But the Foreign Office wouldn't let go, of course. The 'status quo' man in his plushy, Whitehall office eyed me suspiciously and then, in a plummy drawl, aired the idea that the French should be impressed with a, "Panoply of pageantry." He had a point. The French envied us our Royalty, but detested

UK PAVILION, BRUSSELS
Preliminary sketch for the
processional entry hall.

CRAFTSMANSHIP
As installed. Hand-embroidered banners,
specially woven carpet and drapes.
Attention to detail – the royal crowns
topping the rope barrier posts were gilded,
each little inner cap being in red velvet.

everything else British – except our habit of losing at international football. Frogs -v- Perfidious Albion.

Eventually my scheme was approved by a bogus committee I had devised with the Ministry chap; names so high up in the Establishment that they wouldn't trouble to question anything, so long as they were treated with infinite respect and given a good lunch. I must have been on form at the presentation, (thank goodness I was talking and not listening), for they all clapped when I had finished. The flunky who ushered me out remarked that this was the first time he had heard anyone in the Foreign Office show enthusiasm for *anything*.

Chuffed, I sent a considered estimate of cost to the Treasury.

One can think up an idea for such a pavilion with good intentions, but something somewhat more solid is needed to build it with. The Treasury halved the budget and instructed me to go ahead as planned.

I let fly with a great cathedral-like entry-hall. Deep purple, lit by narrow shafts of light admitted through navette-shaped apertures filled with stained glass. A thick, carpeted walkway flanked by heraldic banners; a childhood memory of St George's Chapel at Windsor. To the right, a sort of 'Camelot' buffet mounted with gold and silver trophies from strong-rooms at the Tower of London. The City Guilds' specimens of fine craftsmanship in gold are rare, as the treasures have invariably been melted down by improvident kings to pay for warring and whoring. Nevertheless, the Goldsmiths' lent me the one Elizabethan solid gold plate left to us; heavily embossed, nearly three feet in diameter and a sumptuous meal for anyone's eye. It was displayed unprotected, almost within reach, but put a finger to it and warning bells would ring – or so I hoped.

To the left, a stage half masked by the fall of a swagged drape – which Mehitabel hung one night while I nervously steadied the tower-ladder; the Belgian workmen refused to rig it, *"très dangereuse,"* as they drifted off to the local brasserie. On the stage, a costumed group of the guys we romantically think of as Great Men, watched by a sweet young Bluecoat boy, blue gown and yellow stockings, with some books under his arm . . . sentiment.

To terminate the 'cathedral', in place of the altar, there must be a portrait of the Queen. Those they offered me were no more regal than bread-and-butter pudding. I guess the lady's position at the peak of Burke's *Peerage* had inhibited the portraitists – all except one, Annigoni. He hadn't batted an eyelid, but painted her as a Queen in all the brave dignity of the Garter robes. A bit 'chocolate-box', perhaps? Sir Philip Hendy, then Director of The National Gallery, thought so.

Outraged, he decided this man Gardner needed a salutary lesson on what is and what is not Art. I turned up at his office for the showdown, to find that he already had Annigoni's portrait mounted on an easel. In the cold light from a high window, the technique did look a bit thin; more turpentine than oil.

Hendy then whisked the drape off a painting positioned alongside – a Rembrandt self-portrait. Not really fair. Like engaging a full orchestra playing Beethoven's 'Fifth' to put down a trio fluting a Viennese waltz. I dug my heels in and kept the Annigoni.

General layout. Our pavilion was so popular, the director at the adjoining site complained our queue was obstructing his way in.

Geometric crystal forms were then suddenly in vogue and hexagons, first used at Brussels, remain an off-the-shelf answer for architects who are groping for a rationale.

Periodically, the blare of a trumpeted fanfare would cause prickles of excitement to go up anyone's spine; but not the architectural critics, who shuddered. When visitors entered they would doff their hats and stand for a moment, then make their way circumspectly along the deep-pile carpet.

It was then I realised why the Vatican invests so much in gilt and gingerbread.

I preferred the reaction of a lady journalist from *Le Monde*, who viewed the setting for a while, in silence, then clung to my shoulder, tears in her eyes, and said, *"C'est magnifique, c'est trop."*

Fun, later, when the leading art critic and I were lined up to be unavoidably 'honoured' by the Queen; he the OBE, the CBE for me. "Rather a joke," I whispered as the stiff-jointed old battle-horse knelt awkwardly to be touched with the sword, "I'm getting mine for designing the Brussels show and you get yours for condemning it!" I don't think he saw the point.

Haste to the gods

Do it all myself? Okay, but I needed updating on Science and the Arts, so asked Andrew Miller-Jones, who mastered the intellectual programmes on the BBC, for help. He suggested we invite Jacob Bronowski (Science) and Marghanita Laski (Literature and the Arts) to join us for dinner at his house (I to pay for the wine). We could then broach the subject. A bit scary. Bronowski practically invented the universe, while Marghanita was an aloof critic who knew it all; liable to be unforgiving when faced with 'don't know's'.

One evening I was lying on a rug in front of the fire, deep in a paperback, when the 'phone rang. It was Miller-Jones, speaking with his mouth full. "What's happened, G?" Then in a stage whisper. "Couldn't delay dinner any longer. B and M are at the table now."

"Gosh. Sorry, old man, forgot all about it. Too late. It'll take me an hour to get into town." The 'phone gave a click and that was that.

Bronowski, already a god, proved to be a benevolent one. He rang me next day. "Had a blackout? You missed a good dinner. When shall we meet?"

Scene painters enlarging artwork by Smithy; backcloth for the stage settings based on old church brass-rubbings.

Guessing that the female of the species is less forgiving than the male, I gave up the attempt to enter Marghanita's sophisticated orbit, but years later she gave a friendly and objective critique of a book of mine, so perhaps I was wrong in my sexist assessment.

Jacob Bronowski represented science when Britain was still in the lead; the first jet passenger aircraft, the discovery of the DNA helix, systemic weedkillers, sonic underwater exploration, genetics, the first radio telescope.

We were also in the lead with animated devices – every exhibit being active – so behind the scenes it looked as though a mad mechanic was having a nightmare. At one point thirty-five film projectors were all shooting at a cluster of screens.

This concentration of animation techniques proved to be a breakthrough in what the media now terms 'communication'. It also left me with half the site to fill and very little left in the kitty. Co-opting Hugh Casson and his Royal College of Art students, we treated it as a quixotic exhibition garden, fortunately shaded by fine trees. "An exhibition in a garden – how English!" visitors would say, little realising how English we were in not having sufficient money to pay for a roof.

There was an outdoor library, paved with stones and lit by lampposts; a fountain of water-cans painted 'bargee' style; two mermaids holding up an umbrella which showered rain on them with the phrase 'It always rains in England' (I tend to undersell, but the official Tourist Board had me change it to 'It *sometimes* rains in Britain', so no point). Tiles set in an occasional wall gave interesting facts like – 'We have a Society for the Protection of Old Goats'.

As we expected, this quixotic minutiae impressed the foreigners. Popular?

The Swiss, whose pavilion was on a nearby site, complained that the queue for the UK pavilion was blocking their entrance.

The serious Germans, whose pavilion was an elegant, intellectual exercise in steel and glass, objected to my bingo-hall affair and erected a wall to mask it from their site. We had a meeting. Germans refused to remove it. We said, okay, but you must plant our side of it with English roses. Germans went into a huddle, and then said, "We will plant it with roses, *but they will be GERMAN roses."*

Even as the roses were lining up under national flags, national characteristics were creeping out of the cupboard like spiders.

This could sometimes be amusing. One of my early visits to the site happened to coincide with a general strike, but I guessed that, in spite of it, our 'individualists' would be working. Short of cash, we had contracted the steelwork to a small non-union set-up comprising four enterprising young welders.

On arrival, I found the whole area deserted except for a dense crowd of onlookers, who were bunched round one end of the UK plot.

Pressing through, I discovered that they were all gazing myopically at the only sign of activity – our four welders sipping tea. Completely indifferent to the crowd, they were coolly enjoying their 'tea break' protected by a cordon of Belgian police.

Up the British. Our showpiece would be a world-beating energy machine named Zeta.

Integral night illumination. The walls were shipped over, ready-wired and lamped.

We produced this replica of Zeta and installed it as a key exhibit in the Science Section, before it was discovered that what they thought was fusion had been a malfunction . . .So we had to add a notice stating that it didn't work. Hot flushes in the Atomic Energy hen-house.

Alas poor Zeta, I knew him well

Early one morning the Duke Street telephone rang. The Atomic Energy Authority wanted me to visit their (Most Secret) Research Centre at Harwell to take details of Zeta. Urgent.

"Zeta?"

"Well, it's strictly off the record. I hope this 'phone isn't bugged." And, in a whisper, "We've actually achieved fusion."

Gosh! Splitting the atom's nucleus as a controlled reaction can be highly dangerous, but fusion, the *building-up* of atoms, which demands temperatures comparable to those on the surface of the sun (if we could do it), would be safe. A twentieth century version of the alchemists' dream.

Having an official pass, off I go to Harwell to be led by Security to a small hush-hush room, where a hesitant PR type showed me a photograph of the device; untrustingly holding onto a corner of it with finger and thumb. Somewhat annoying but, having a photographic memory, I concentrated on it.

PR was then called away, soon to be replaced by a '*Dr Who*' character in a white coat, sent in to explain the photograph, I guessed. He shrugged, "So, then you would wish me to show you Zeta?" Would I not!

In the research lab. I was introduced to a large metal doughnut, mounted in a complex rig of gadgets and wires. With some pride, White Coat then made it work . . . a buzzing sound, a loud thump, a flicker and that was it.

Or was it? Yes, it was. Fusion!

226

PR then bounced back. Shaking with anger, he frowned angrily at White Coat and bundled me out. Okay, okay.

I had been instructed to illustrate the device as it would look in operation in a power hall of the future. Fun. As I was off to the airport next morning, I passed the night preparing the visual, three happy Zeta's mounted one above the other, a gantry over them, little controllers in a glass cage – an H.G. Wells's vision of the future.

After proudly showing it off round the studio (a habit I can't resist), I tell Mehitabel she must seal it in a double cover, the inner one marked 'MOST SECRET, FOR THE ATTENTION OF . . .', take a taxi and deliver it soonest to the boss guy, in person, and get him to sign for it. Which she does.

On her return the telephone is ringing. I am not available? Please identify yourself. She is then sworn to secrecy. When this game of blind-man's buff is completed, she is instructed to search for any scribbles or tracings on my desk and in the litter bin, and BURN THEM IMMEDIATELY. She must then ring back to confirm that she has done so.

Mehitabel is curious, "Wasn't Mr Gardner's picture satisfactory?"

Response, "It has been *incarcerated.*"

The detail of its fabrication must have been too revealing for the pic. to be seen by the CBI, the KGB, or a shop steward of the Boiler Makers' Union.

Alas, some months later it was discovered that the key exhibit in the pavilion was no miracle after all. What they had thought of as 'fusion' was only an inconsequential side-effect.

In each aperture an animated exhibit; deep sea exploration by remote TV, growing plants, a ship navigating by radar, a jet engine in full blast, beating heart. Popular?

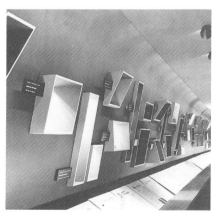

Excuse me, but I'm the designer

In England, along with scientists, engineers and odd-balls related to the arts, designers are considered to be marginal types – they sometimes work with their *hands.* This will be apparent if one glances at the table plan for the Grand Luncheon held to mark the opening of the British Pavilion.

A modest guy seated opposite me at the end of the last table volunteered, as he spread some *paté* on a piece of toast, that he was a reporter from *The Barbados Post* – then asked, "And what is your connection?"

"Oh, I designed the affair they're all celebrating." He obviously thought I was having him on. "But, surely, the designer should be seated at the head table?"

I then explained my G theory as to the origins of the pecking order in England. It is still based on who, in the past, would enter a gentleman's stately home by the front entrance: the lawyer, architect, doctor, vicar . . . and, maybe, the odd artist who painted portraits in oils to picture the gentleman's favourite horse – or his female, who would probably look like a horse.

These 'front door' guys, you will note, are now considered to be members of the 'professions'. The rest, who used the tradesmen's entrance, are considered to be in 'trade', like the plumber, motor mechanic, craftsman, or scientific buff. When Madame Curie – who discovered radium – visited the UK, she observed an excited crowd on the station platform. Adjusting her hat, she leaned out of the carriage window to discover that they were welcoming a cricket team in the adjoining carriage.

This is England. A designer? He will be given a place at a corner of the last table.

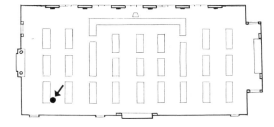

Table layout for the Grand Luncheon.
Establishment were served at the long
table in pecking order.
To find the designer, see arrow.

Nothing is forever

My regular evening climb up the footpath to play male lead in a TV-style sitcom – which, as one might expect, turned out to be more situation than comedy – was abruptly terminated by the death of the essential female lead, Mary.

I did not reveal this stroke of fate to my collaborators at the studio for some time, but disposed of the little white house on the hill, passing the proceeds to the boys. I offered Mary's wardrobe to Oxfam and, after ferrying the household chattels to a local jumble sale, made a sacrificial bonfire of what remained. Lighting up the whole hillside, it attracted the attention of a fire-float and a breathless policeman wheeling a bicycle. Oh well, thought I, wiping motes of floating ash from my smarting eyes, the locals will soon be made aware that suburban dream number 5,700,083 is now kaput.

Back to the drawing board

"It may be a distinguished studio, north light and all, but I can't live with all that *arty* furniture," I complain.

"You're lucky to find a place in Hampstead," says Mehitabel, "Take it and you can get rid of the arty stuff later."

So I did.

"Back at the studio I was emanating gloom.

"There's no pleasing you," Mehitabel interjects. "Surely you haven't forgotten Monday. It was a scream."

Coronation Pomp

True. I had spent that morning with the august Mayor of the Royal Borough of Kensington, plump pink face and whiff of aftershave, inspecting my efforts at Coronation decoration. These included an imposing triumphal arch straddling the main road in front of the Albert Hall and wild tea-roses romping over the porch of the Gothic Parish Church.

All went as planned until the chauffeur slid our long, black limousine into a gap between a line of similar cars slowly making their way down the High Street.

We were stuck in that funeral *cortège* for half a mile, like a replay from one of the old Ealing comedies.

The preliminary visual . . . erectable?

Yes. The triumphal arch as erected.

230

In addition to other work, a sudden rush of decorous *décor*. A maypole in the Strand and viewing stands on the processional route (none of which, fortunately, collapsed). A setting at Olympia and, key item, a sizeable exhibition, The Two Queens – with only three weeks to produce it.

This included a Tudor setting of the 'Virgin Queen', approached by a canopied walkway. There were two steps at one point where, prior to opening, an old girl in a fur coat stumbled, then lay on the floor in a fit of hysterics. She happened to be my client's mother-in-law.

You can't win them all.

Viewing stand: the Travellers' Club.

The Two Queens

ELIZABETH I
The quite convincing gemstones on her
elaborate costume were – lollipops.

ELIZABETH II
She is set well away from the viewer,
as we used a cut-out photo – touched up
- which deceived the public.

The trick is in the detailing

In Olympia's Grand Hall, a fully detailed replica of the Coronation Coach, with horsemen, outriders and all the trappings – even to the correct medals on the officers' breasts.

Over it, the highest draped canopy I have ever designed. Later this was shipped to New York for setting up in Madison Gardens.

Modellers, mural artists for the coach panels, upholsterers, costumiers, leather and metal workers and, of course, gilders. It cost a bomb.

Top show – no Oscars

There were no satellites as yet for transmitting TV overseas. I prepared thirty or more deceptively realistic illustrations of the forthcoming event. These were filmed, edited, canned and sent overseas for local transmission during the ceremony to actual sound. Hours at the drawing board, as my record-player blared out 'Zadok The Priest', while I visualised the affair, step-by-step.

First trumpeters, then pan up the organ pipes to the Gothic vault.

Angles taken to sync. with the actual sound.

Sketches from the storyboard.

The 60's

MAKING HAY IN THE USA

'Tweedledum and Tweedledee agreed to have a battle'
Museum – handle with care
The birth of a white elephant
'The French Connection'

Meanwhile . . .

President Kennedy assassinated

Contraception pills introduced

USSR invades Czechoslovakia

West Side Story

'Pop Art' takes over

Jackie Kennedy marries Onassis

Massacre at Sharpeville

British 'Rock' sweeps world

The Great Train Robbery

Berlin Wall erected

7,000th performance of the *The Mousetrap*

TV competes with cinema

Saturday Evening Post folds

First 'Concorde' space flight

Film – *2001: A Space Odyssey*

Spacecraft lands on moon

Tweedledum and Tweedledee agreed to have a battle

The 'Commies' (in the sixties, that is, when they were Communists) put up a trade show on Broadway. The New Yorkers were impressed.

When the FBI – not the Washington lot but the Federation of British Industries – heard about it, they decided they must do bigger and better. But on Broadway? "Isn't that where they have theatres, cinemas, pansy actors and film stars . . . ?"

"Surely not, old man, that's Hollywood. Way over on the other side yer know – California."

To play safe, it was agreed they would engage an artistic type to impress the New Yorkers; give the show a proper Broadway image, whatever that is!

The Government then nervously poked little horns from the security of its shell and decided to back the industrialists by sponsoring a nostalgic introduction to the show – not about goods, but about 'This England, this sceptred isle set in a silver sea . . . ' After all, the Russians may be 'Big Brother' and have a lead in satellites . . . but they don't have dog roses growing in hedgerows and they are not, and never will be, a sceptred isle.

They also decided to employ this same arty type. So now I had two masters, both addicted to holding meetings, but there was a building to fill – the Coliseum – and I got them to cover a three day visit to case the site.

Having successfully manoeuvred through the stampede at arrivals, I drifted out into the comparative calm of buses and taxis where I was accosted by a natty Englishman with a neatly-knotted Etonian tie, who offered me a limp, manicured hand, "James Gardner?" He is from the Embassy.

Driving to my down-town hotel, he tells me he has arranged dinner at the Green Room Club, table booked, time for a shower, he'll pick me up in – expensive watch – twenty minutes?

Damn. It's four o'clock in the morning UK time. This Embassy guy must have anticipated meeting one of those cool socialites one sees pictured in *The Tatler* fraternising with gushing débutantes and coining clichés about avant-garde art.

The club dining room turned out to be pleasant enough, softly lit, and crowded with *habitués*; all very fond of themselves and dropping names. Our table had been laid for three and I was still battling with the menu when an exotic female seated herself, with some ceremony and a whiff of . . . Dior, in the vacant chair.

There, only three feet away, was the most startlingly desirable, set-on-fireable female our species had served up, to date. An artist at make-up, her every gesture beautifully poised. When the loose drape of her low-cut dress dropped, as she leaned forward, I had that same sense of anticipation I experienced at school when we successfully manoeuvred the well-developed (but short-sighted) maths mistress to bend over and correct a copy-book.

When this theatrical dame extended a powdered arm to crush a cigarette, I observed that her wrist was hung with – gosh, like the old days – thirty-carat baton diamonds. Viewing this, dream-like, as though in a stalls seat, I was startled to discover that *I* was on stage and expected to *perform*.

Leaning dangerously forward, she said she simply adored Englishmen.

"Tell me," the lady asked, "what's going on in London? Have you seen any good shows recently?"

By the time I blundered to a pause, with no help from the Embassy chap, her velvety eyes filling my whole horizon, as she murmured, "I do love listening to true theatre-English." So I did my best, hoping that my suburban diction wouldn't spoil the party.

On the drive back I put my excitement into words, "I must say, I thought that a most remarkable lady – the one who sat at our table." The Embassy guy stared at me for a moment in a state of shock. "My dear fellow, you didn't recognize her? That lady, for your information, was Zsa Zsa Gabor." And, I guess, he had been to no end of trouble to entice her there. But why turn up to dine with me? Surely not for the meal-ticket with all those lovely diamonds.

Next morning all I saw of Manhattan was a glimpse down Seventh Avenue while I waited for the pedestrian sign to switch from 'DON'T WALK' to 'WALK'. The Coliseum proved to be a disappointing brick-faced block at the Park end of Broadway. Leaning against the wind, I sized it up. It had no windows, there was a factory on the roof where it manufactured its own climate and, once inside, one heard the stuff coming through nozzles in the ceiling with a low nasal hum.

My job was to check the architect's plans. To a designer measurement is all. Even in New York *measurement* is the yardstick of profit indices, diners' card ratings and icy-faced banks, where real estate is measured in height and a man in dollars – or inches. Like when I got stuck at an interminable rye-on-the-rocks session, while a contractor and his agent calculated how many yards of prick they had put up their wives. "Now let's take an average week . . ." (Their women, of course, are obsessed with weight.)

No snow in June

Weight. When I first sighted the main hall of the Coliseum, I was dismayed. High up, a lattice of girders straddled the span and, above them, a writhing tangle of ducts which, I supposed, was the stomach of the climate factory on the roof. The best way to mask this would be to sling up a great tented drape, a valarium (as the Romans did in *their* Coliseum). Even with the lightest, fire-proofed fabric it would weigh a bit. Then there would be scaffold hung from the girders from which the drapes, in turn, would be slung. But I had done it often enough in London's Olympia.

However, the Coliseum engineer would have none of it. The roof wouldn't take any additional load; in fact, it was in the conditions – IN PRINT.

I meditated over this impasse while dealing with a portion

of deep apple-pie and glass of milk at Schrafts (why do all American waitresses wear white Minnie Mouse shoes?). I hazarded a guess at the dead-weight involved, paid for my apple-pie, and put the figures in front of the engineer.

"Like I told you," he said. "It's not on."

"Do you have snow in New York?" I asked, having seen press pictures of the stuff piled high along the sidewalks.

"Sure. You bet we have snow." He seemed rather proud of it. "But I don't see what that's got to do with your problem?"

"Well, our show takes place in June. You don't have snow in June, so we can use the built-in allowance for snow-load."

He tapped his teeth with a slide rule for a while, suspiciously eyeing my figures on the back of the Schrafts menu, then gave the go-ahead. Saved. I was bucked – it justified the trip to New York. Eight flying hours and I was back at the studio, well ahead of the picture postcards. Though stubble-chinned and limp as a wet sock, I just had time to turn up at a meeting with my masters, the FBI.

Jet-lag dims judgement

As I eased my way through the mahogany doors, Edwards, as Chairman, was reading the minutes of the last meeting and putting no end of charm into the performance. Good committee man. I found an empty chair, tipped it back out of the line of fire and concentrated on keeping my eyes open. Balfour, my Government boss, wasn't present; a good thing, as he had sent me a *Theme Proposal* that was so inept I hoped he'd forget it.

Suddenly Edwards arched an eyebrow in my direction, saying, "I see that Jimmy Gardner," (no one calls me Jimmy) "has this moment arrived back from New York. He will now give us a report on the suitability of the building and any preliminary ideas he may have for its treatment."

I have no difficulty in talking, even without thinking, if it's about a job, so I described the Coliseum. I should then have sat down to modest applause, but I heard myself going on to give an oration on the American Way of Life in general and (though it had nothing to do with the FBI guys round the table) Balfour's tired *'Theme'* in particular. I pointed out that apart from a few Anglophiles in Connecticut (I only knew four

240

Americans and that was where three of them lived) and Virginia (that's where the other one lived), the people in the USA didn't give a hoot for Britain – or Europe for that matter.

Response. Twenty blank faces. Damn, and I'm supposed to be the ideas man – something constructive? So I improvised. "To impress New Yorkers, we must do something they think only they can do, but do it *better.*" An uncomfortable silence broken by Billy Rootes, the bluff millionaire car manufacturer. "*Sounds* all right, young man, but how exactly do you propose to do it?"

Then I made an error of judgement (not advisable in my profession) and described visual images just as they came up in my mind.

"Let's have a guards' band – one thing we've got, bar Royalty, they haven't – but put it across on the largest cinema screen in the world: back projection, so the guards will be marching right alongside the visitors as they come in, with multiple sound sources, so the sound marches along with them. We can get the chap who did the theme tune for 'The Bridge on the River Kwai' to compose a march, and sell the records all over New York."

Damn. I was already designing the record sleeve. Better think of some way to put science across.

"Say we pick four or five examples where Britain leads. The radio-telescope, the hovercraft, float-glass, the diesel-electric locomotive."

The model Hovercraft I designed for this exhibit, when the prototype was shaped like a doughnut and skidding over the water just off the Isle of Wight.

"Wide stage, a neat young scientist, in a white coat, at a glass desk – he talks, things happen behind him – a starry sky, a heaving sea – sound effects jumping around – a live show."

I could see it; theatrical 'tricks', projections, animations, all pulsed electronically.

But the bright young scientist idea hadn't gone down at all well (business men don't like scientists). I explained that 'canned' sound was impersonal, but a serious young man, wearing glasses, speaking his lines with a genuine Oxford accent? That might impress the New Yorkers.

"Even if what he's saying doesn't." A cynical comment stopped me in full flow. Edwards, like a sleek hostess smoothing out a crease in an otherwise unsullied table cloth, covered the unexpected situation with professional tact, "I am sure we would all like to thank Mr Gardner for giving us this preview," he smiles my way, oh, so friendly, "of the Ministry's intentions . . ."

I relaxed . . . then it hit me. I had casually committed the Government to a scheme they knew nothing about. Balfour, the bureaucrat in charge, had to hear my version before it was relayed to him with sarcastic overtones.

Next morning, in a standard, bleak *eau-de-Nil* Ministry office, Balfour, who had something of the appearance of a desiccated ostrich, was leaning back in his swivel chair, hairy hands clasped as though in prayer, examining the ceiling. Obviously a more circumspect rendering of yesterday's notions was called for. It is difficult to sound convincing when the audience appears to be in some other place. Eventually I dried up. Balfour scratched his Adam's apple thoughtfully, then asked what it would cost.

I grabbed a frightening figure out of thin air. He now focused on me, instead of the ceiling, and spacing his words so the message would sink home, "You go ahead, b u t - t h a t - i s - t h e - w h o l e - o f - t h e - T r e a s u r y - v o t e. Not a penny more, it isn't there to get."

Then, offering up my coat like a cloakroom attendant, he added in doubtful voice, "We're putting all our eggs in one basket."

"No. In two baskets," I replied as he shook my hand . . . personal, more committing than a signed contract.

Strange guy – eggs – an ostrich after all.

As the elevator took me back to earth and the indicator lamps flickered down through the numbers, my spirits sank with them. Having 'sold' the idea, it had become a job. Now I had to make it work.

Back at the office, Mehitabel is on the 'phone. "But I've already been on to their Plastics Division – somewhere in Wales. No. No good at all. It was the gentleman *there* who said try Arthur Rank. You don't? Then who supplies the big screens for TV? Oh – but not big enough. Right, we'll try *them*. Oh, no, you've been *more* than kind. *Thank* you."

She unwinds her legs, wrinkles her nose at me and says, "Hollywood."

"Okay, book a call for four o'clock, that will make it nine in the morning over there." She glances at the clock, "No, I'll make it five o'clock. Coffee?"

In the studio I find my partner, Simon, with his mouth full of plum cake, browsing through an official leaflet. Tall, prim and pallid, he has the looks of the stereotype civil servant. This reassures doubtful clients.

I ask if he has laid on for the filming – his mind is someplace else. "We can't use astro-turf on that Nestlé job. Not cleared for fire. Any other ideas?" Then, "By the way, for your information, seat belts are soon to be made obligatory for stiffs in coffins."

I rise to the bait. "Ridiculous. How can one know once the lid has been screwed down?"

"Malcolm Arnold," Mehitabel chips in. "You asked for the name of the man who arranged the theme tune for 'Bridge on the River Kwai'?" "He'll be expensive," mumbled Simon, "and, by the way, you've a date at Elstree Studios, eleven tomorrow." And I guess they'll be expensive, too.

Come next morning I am driving down the motorway in a downpour, periodically braking as lumbering lorries mud-spray the windscreen. At my side is a mute little mole hugging a briefcase. He is from the Treasury – *they don't trust me.*

Stalled by the clever guys

At the studios we are given the full Martini treatment, then steered politely into a committee room; cosy atmosphere of big business. "Cigars?" Mr Mole, sensing this is a bribe, retreats, even smaller, behind his briefcase (I wonder what he keeps in it).

The technicians assembled round the table, though quixotically dressed, have taken up proper boardroom attitudes and appear to be waiting. I explain how they are to film a guards' band, close up, sideways-on, marching in sharp focus across a sixty-three foot wide projection screen.

"It'll be the widest in the world."

"Maybe, but you won't get a screen that big."

"I've got one."

"Oh?" in doubtful intonation. Hell. They *are* a cool lot.

A hatchet-faced bloke in a deceptively jolly T-shirt tells me you can't take a close up that wide and, even if you could, Studio One, the largest in Europe, is not big enough to shoot it. I wish him dead. A technician, behind dark sun-glasses, is sliding angles around on a planning board. The two black discs turn my way.

"Not enough *depth*," the mouth says.

"With a wide-angled lens?" hopefully.

"No," says the mouth, kindly enough, "not even with a wide-angled lens."

I make a desperate try, "What about using two cameras side by side, angled so each takes *half* the picture?"

The lips again. "Even then, the line of marchers farthest from the camera would be way out of focus. No go, I'm afraid."

He sounds quite human. Hatchet-face, who doesn't, chips in with a final knock-out punch, "Military bands march four abreast."

I hadn't considered that. Maybe, as depth is the problem, I can get them to march three abreast. "Suppose I get them to march three abreast and we use the *same* camera in two different positions?"

By now it is clear that the whole operation has become one of academic interest, but he replies, just for the record: "Sure. But the band would have to march by *twice* for two separate takes. Project the two films side-by-side and you'd have one hell of a mix-up in the middle where the two pictures meet."

The boss at the end of the table, deciding we are getting nowhere, moves his chair back and stands in pot-bellied profile, fingering his cigar in demonstration of a bandsman playing a clarinet.

"Forty-eight bandsmen marching over a centre line *twice*, each man in *exactly* the same attitude," he lifts a plump knee, "and tooting *exactly* the same note? Not even your bloody guards' band can do that, old boy." The technicians grin and move towards the door. My hackles are up. Now or never.

"I'll deal with that end of it. We'll book the studio." I sign the contract, then get Mr Mole to sign the contract. Hell. What a start.

A guards' band had already agreed to lay on the march past. Their job, after all. Next day, when I at last got the Bandmaster on the 'phone, the instrument all but exploded in my ear.

"What! March *three* abreast. Never. Won't do at all. Training not right, marching order not right. A military band *never* marches three in line." A pause. "Take my advice, old man, try those Scottish girl pipers. They'll do it standing on their heads if you act kindly to them."

I am floundering in the bog of despair when he rings me back, after what must have been a good lunch. "I've been mulling it over, old man. Put you in a bit of a quandary, eh? Tell you what, I'll put 'em through the paces for a few days, see how it works. Out of *order*, yer know. Have to fit it in with other duties, but we'll make it. Don't fret yourself." Another hurdle cleared. That angel on the cloud must be watching over me again.

I had not yet informed the Major that his men would need to march past the camera twice, with *split second timing*. I would ease that one in when he was fully committed.

Okay to sit in a corner jotting bright ideas on paper, but the business of steering them through, by and around *people* can be as tricky as fly-fishing.

People!

Two weeks later I joined a bunch of tourists peering through the railings at Waterloo Barracks. A rectilinear block of guardsmen, in denims, was moving across the parade-ground, step-stop, step-stop, like a mechanical toy; a drill sergeant checking the length of each pace with a measuring stick. The unerring precision, individuals moving as one, made my spine tingle. The Major barked: "Right!" Then to me: "It'll do, with a bit of polishing. Calls for a celebration, eh? Where's your friend Arnold?"

Malcolm Arnold was in on the act. "No problem." He even agreed to compose the march with instruments sequenced to enhance our sound effect. I had joined him in a second floor, back-street practice room to hear it run through. Out of my depth. What I know about music – real music – could be written on a flea's kneecap.

I had once attempted a musical conversation when seated next to Malcolm Sargent at a dinner (after he had just conducted 'Zadok the Priest' with the full Halle orchestra and choir). I was properly snubbed. A friend told me later I should have chosen the great conductor's hobby – chrysanthemums. But, I don't know much about chrysanthemums either.

Arriving at the hired practice room, I found it furnished with a piano, wind-up stool, two spindle-backed chairs and a cracked water jug. Arnold, seated at the piano: "I'm not much good at playing this thing, you know," he remarked, (liar), then proceeded to finger military band sounds, thump-boom-boom, thump-boom-boom – "That's the drums," then higher up the scale (with voice-over) twiddle-twiddle-burp – "That'll be the wind," . . . and so on. Performance completed, he swung round, inquiringly, on the stool – the moment I dreaded.

I tried to look professional as I said, "Smack on!"

It had sounded okay to me, so off he went to prepare the score.

"This is *concert pitch*, old man," says the Major, "We use *band pitch* . . . but we'll sort it out." This job is getting too complicated, thinks I, as we go off for more *gin* than *it* in the snuggery at Wheeler's. This was followed by lunch – if an afternoon devoted to fish-food and pink champagne (and two girls who appeared from nowhere) until the evening diners began to trickle in, can be termed lunch.

But, between courses, I did hit the germ of an idea – how to mask the mix where the two pictures would meet in the centre of the screen.

The backcloth could show Piccadilly Circus decked out with streamers and flags, so contrived that a banner and streamer meet at the centre to mask where the two images meet. Snag. The films were projected from *behind* a translucent screen, so anything painted on it would come out in silhouette. Now for it. If those streamers were painted with fluorescent paint and lit by ultra-violet light from the *front* they might, just might, have the same brilliance as the film. The whole show depended on this trick, so it had better come out right. I ordered up a sample of translucent screen and one night, when the drawing office was empty, I experimented, with Mehitabel as unbiased observer.

I directed an ultra-violet lamp onto the front of the screen, then ran a few feet of film through the projector behind the screen to check focus and we were all set to go. Mixing the magic powders, I identified each tint by holding a filled brush in the UV beam so it glowed like a firefly, gave it a twiddle and little droplets scattered like stars, to suddenly disappear as

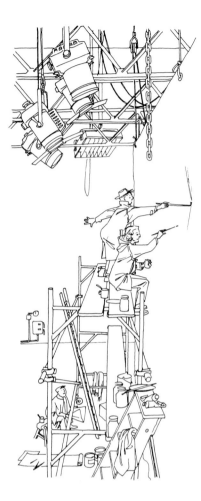

they passed out of the beam into blackness. I painted the UV streamers on the screen, switched on the projector, closed my eyes then opened them again and took a cool look.

The film only showed London traffic, but the fluorescing flags had the right intensity, red against the side of a bus – *the trick worked*. Exciting, and so was the torso that floated under the lamp. Mehitabel's sweater, given a life of its own, had traces of the fluorescing agent that make clothes 'whiter than white'.

Up on the scaffold, but no death at dawn

One more hurdle to go. The artist I commissioned to paint the setting for the backdrop made a sad job of it and had already swallowed the fee, so I produced a design myself. This would be enlarged by specialists onto a vast canvas, in a scene-painter's tower. Quite an operation.

Was the technique I used too stylized? When I saw it full-size in the Elstree studio, I was nearly sick on the floor. At Romano's Restaurant I had sworn that I would never balance on a springy plank again, but I had not foreseen such a crisis as this.

Making sure the side door of Studio 1 would be open over the weekend (I had no union card, so we must avoid the shop steward), I rang Barbara Jones, an experienced mural painter, and suggested she join me – 'for the fun of it'. She knew it wouldn't be but, as a professional, she would do her damnedest to help me fight through all one hundred and fifty feet of canvas with only three days to go before shooting.

In November Studio 1 was so near arctic we could see our breath, (but not as bad as that winter in Gothenburg when the painter had said, "Can't get it any smoover, Mr Gardner, the bloody paint's froze,"). We were saved by frequent mugs of sweet tea, offered up the scaffolding by the cosy watchman who, when not making tea, spent the weekend reading up on the sporting news – unknown territory.

I found it unnerving when the wall of canvas moved away under the pressure of a brush. Near dawn, back aching, too deflated to even stand back and view our work, we decamped for home past dreary rows of lookalike houses with dead

248

windows. "Morning, sir," said a startled milkman.

Hell. The things we do for clients.

I'm awakened, with more tea, by Derek Stuart, my film consultant: his new drape jacket, Arrow shirt and florid tie simply *screaming*, "Just back from New York," – and at my expense, come to think of it. He reports, "Projectors laid on, okay. As we guessed, the Embassy was too upstage to help when it came to the crunch. New York Union rules and rates, of course."

"How much?"

"More than you think." He continues with the story, while I pull on my socks.

"Blokes over there don't want to know about xenon lamps - think they'll *explode*. Still using the old carbon arcs. Archaic. That means we'll have to double up on projectors for 'standbys', while Auntie Annie changes carbons. With that we'll have to double up on crews."

A long thoughtful pause while the penny drops.

"But that will double our crew costs." Bang goes our reserve against the unforseen.

"After all," says Derek, "this was unforeseen." We look into each other's eyes for a moment – then Derek is his bright self again. "See you at the Astoria, lunchtime," and he's off.

The film screen is to be mounted so visitors will be only eight feet away as they walk alongside it. Will it be a blur? We lay on a trial.

The auditorium of the Astoria cinema is empty between shows, except for a squad of Mrs Mop's bobbing up and down across a landscape of tipped-up seats. Behind the little projection window, a head is silhouetted for a moment, then the proscenium curtains drift apart with a whisper, to reveal a wide, blank screen. By the time we have scrambled onto the stage and positioned ourselves eight feet from it, the house-lights are imperceptibly dimming and the Mrs Mop's have taken seats for an unexpected free show. We are about to experience a run-through from a recent release, *Colonel Blimp* – the part where the military band does its march past. There is a crackle behind the screen, then the blare of a brass band hits us and we are bathed in a 'pop' pattern of moving coloured light. Dramatic.

Should use the effect some time. But, when I look at the screen, my worst fears are realized – it is a blur. Derek yells something to the projectionist. He can't hear, but is already adjusting the image to correct focus.

"Okay now?" shouts Derek.

I hesitate, then, "Good enough, I suppose."

"Ours will be much *crisper*." He holds two fingers up in a 'V' sign, "Don't forget, we have *two* projectors."

He is left shouting in silence, as the sound suddenly cuts out. Another hurdle out of the way. But, on our way up to the exit, I realize our screen will be twice as wide.

Tiptoeing through the tulips

In the Coliseum's main hall I had laid on a grand vista – a wide expanse of carpet, sweeping drapes overhead, clusters of mini-lamps like stars, and planting. But this treatment stopped short of a blank brick wall. I had provided a stage below it: the question now was, what to put on the stage – climax of the show, to be pictured in the press and all that lark?

At one of the FBI's interminable meetings, I suggested that I had done enough and why not give the design for this to someone with a *name*, like Cecil Beaton? He had just completed fabulous costumes and settings for the New York production of *My Fair Lady* – give the show a bit of class.

Tough, bluff Billy Rootes agreed. "Met this Beaton fellow once. On the *Queen Mary*. We got on well. Good man." I tried to picture a tough bull-terrier enjoying a sniffing session with a well-groomed poodle – but strange things happen at sea.

Sipping Jasmine tea, observed by two (plaster) Nubian slaves, I managed to sell Beaton the idea but, some weeks later, when I viewed his sketch design, I thought it rather tentative and pastiche in character, and not constructible (my job). When I explained this, Beaton went cold, shrugged, said he'd think about it.

Time passed and the money allocated for the setting was being whittled away. I couldn't reach Beaton, who had gone off on a photo-safari to Japan. More time passed and to nail what money remained, I sketched out a stop-gap scheme of my own. The visual was accepted, and that was that.

But it wasn't. Some months later, Mehitabel covers the mouthpiece of the 'phone and hisses, "It's Cecil Beaton, just back from Japan. How's *his setting* getting along, *and* is it constructed yet?" I use a four letter word.

"I'm terribly sorry, Mr Gardner is at a meeting. I'll ask him to ring you as soon as he's *free*. Good. The same number? Thank you." We look at each other, "What'll you do now?"

I shrug. "You'd better ring up Edwards and Rootes. Ask for a meeting – say it's bloody urgent – sorry – a vital matter that requires an immediate committee decision."

That afternoon, when the well-lunched money-men took their places round the table, I had that momentary sense of power which, I suppose, motivates union officials to call meetings. I might just as well have joined Alice at the Mad Hatter's tea-party and dunked the Dormouse.

I explained the situation, which seemed to me to be quite tricky. Apparently I was wrong. It was simple: they liked my scheme and would carry on with it, they liked Beaton's name and wanted that, too.

Rootes saw no problem. I am to trot round to Beaton and ask him to put his name to my scheme, "For a consideration, of course." Then Edwards, who sensed that some airy-fairy types take a quixotic view of a simple business deal, smoothly added, ". . . and as a personal contribution to the furtherance of Anglo-American relations."

"But he won't *bite* you," said my secretary when I reported the great decision, and which explained the sticky state of my mind when I asked the taxi driver to take me to Pelham Crescent. My heart sank as I knocked on his door. No Jasmine tea. Hesitant, unfinished sentences and prickly pauses. But she was right, he didn't bite. In fact, (out of curiosity, I suppose), he asked to see my visual and disappeared with it.

A long pause. Then a charming young man came tiptoeing into the room, with my visual under his arm, to inform me that the proposal was accepted.

Unbelievable – I had done a Beaton!

Organised chaos

I am awakened by the buzz of the hotel's bedside intercom. Damn. It's one a.m. and men will already be 'marking out' on the Coliseum's concrete floors. Norman Riske, the foreman, modest but quite a guy, with better judgement than any politician I have met, is waiting for me in a dimly lit lobby. Gosh, it's cold.

"Hello, Mr Gardner."

We have two weeks to get the whole show up. Not possible, but we will bloody well have to, even with a leavening of Bowery bums employed by order of a Mayor's office that takes a poor view of Britishers.

The limits of the hall are lost in darkness. A young surveyor, crouching over his shadow, is frog-walking a wide circle at the end of a tape held at centre by another shadowy figure. He is chalking a twist of the compass into actuality on the concrete floor. After hours of this 'marking out' we are joined by teams from the other floors and squat like a band of monkeys for a hand-out of canned beer. It's gassy and called 'Budweiser'. We argue discrepancies as, come morning, when our crates are trucked in, the complex jig-saw must come together – to an inch.

From now on the only indication that night still follows day is the number of men on site; event following event like cuts from a speeded up film sequence – let's hope it has a happy ending.

Some time in time a George Raft figure, slick as a cat in a black gangster hat, taps me on the arm, "Are you Gees?" It is Abe Schechter, the labour lawyer and 'fixer'. We are on the platform from which the public will view the Science Stage I had described (it seems years ago) to the FBI. There's no stage as yet, only a gaping hole. I explain the set-up, "We've had it running in the UK, no problem."

We pass through a group of men positioning a maze of ten foot high white cylinders.

"For what?" asks Abe.

"Oh, they'll revolve and each one carries a message."

"Such as?"

"Could be, *We generate so many kilowatts of nuclear energy – but it still takes three minutes to boil an egg*." I point to the little egg in the egg-cup, "English joke."

Abe grunts, screws his heel on a cigar stub and lights another.

The escalator carries us up to the main hall and a wide expanse of polished floor swings into view, ripple-reflecting light from the working lamps.

Up in the gloom an erector is creeping along a girder like a spider that has fallen once and isn't going to risk it again. He is paying out a thirty-foot wire rope. I turn to Abe, "Drapes to be hung up there." I am trying to convey a sense of *urgency*, but he just grunts, deadpan again.

I lead him to our treatment for the end of the hall, where trucks are manoeuvring as though it were some damned goods yard. "When all that stuff is in," I have to shout, "and we're clear of them, there's a wide stage. It goes right across to where we plan to build a stair-tower to each side. Then there's a set to be dressed on the staging. All takes *time*."

Abe wonders what this 'limey' is fussing about.

A Britannia to rule us slaves

Going up the slow elevator, my mind is far away calculating our chances of erecting my 'Cecil Beaton' setting in time for the opening. The day that approaches as inexorably as, well, death, come to think of it.

Centred, a fifteen foot Britannia will dominate the hall. Not that buxom dame holding a toasting fork, but a haughty Diana the Huntress, slim legs braced back as she holds a lion on a golden leash – a hound based on *The Beast of Henry Duke of Saxony*, which had impressed me on a museum prowl. From under her guardsman's helmet a swag of fair nylon hair (now wound on bobbins) will sweep twenty feet to the ground. Super. But how to make her NEWSWORTHY?

In the States at that time, the desirable female was depicted with upthrust breasts the size of watermelons, but s-m-o-o-t-h, definitely no nipples. Also, by puritanical federal law, the national flag must not be used to clothe the human body.

253

The artwork cubes were in fluorescent paint on two black gauzes hung forward of others painted on the backcloth. This gave an effect of depth behind the figures, which were poised on metal rod cubes in the foreground.

So, our Diana will be dressed, if one can use that term, with a scanty square of silk, dye-daubed with a trace of the Union Jack, casually draped to reveal her proud left nipple.

I am hoping that this nicely modelled item will make the news (even if our scientific exhibits don't).

But it will take more than a bare nipple to disturb this Abe guy, now staring impassively at some muscular electricians who are walking step-ladders around like acrobats on stilts – relaxed at sixteen dollars an hour, doubled for overtime.

Up to the top floor where, under spotlights, students from The Royal College of Art are painting a maze of stage flats with renderings of pub interiors – five bars, each with a different character, to be dolled-up later with warming pans, pewter mugs, stuffed fish, and a honky-tonk pianola which, I am told, still operates.

An elevator named desire

Designers are not supposed to be literate or require a secretary on site but, having a backlog of 'variation orders' to write up, I ring Lamb who represents the FBI. Getting the expected unhelpful response, I take a ride up in the executive elevator to see what they have on the first-class deck. (All-American territory and definitely out of bounds.)

I am circumspectly trespassing along a heavily-carpeted corridor on the softly-softly-catchee-monkey principle, (all very Park Avenue and definitely not my scene), when my heart gives a sudden leap. Through an open door and looking blankly my way from behind a typist's desk, is Venus. A slim symphony in white and gold, as elegantly defined as a painting by Botticelli. She removes her sun-glasses and observes me questioningly from under extremely long, individually-trained, eyelashes.

"Help you with dictation? Sure. Would you like me here or in your room?" What a ridiculous question.

Good intelligence work, she already knows the room I have allocated myself. She floats before me to the soft swish of nylon and I convince myself that even a Brooklyn accent can have a certain charm, as I greedily inhale the faint whiff of musk in her slipstream. (Gosh, it's like living in an up-market TV commercial.)

An hour or more later and I am inventing correspondence, my whole attention centred on an intimate closeup of the gossamer-clad knee on which the goddess has poised her note pad . . . "I beg your pardon?"

"A word you used, have I gotten it right as *soffet?*"

I am startled, as a very English voice from across the room spells it out, "S-o-f-f-i-t, a door lintel, if I am not mistaken." Then, apologetically, "Berkshire, London Clearing Banks. Been here some time, old chap. Don't wish to intrude. Quite happy."

I come to earth and we both watch in silence – two rabbits hypnotised by the captivating sway of a beautiful cobra. The goddess lowers her eyelids, closes the pad, smiles sweetly, straightens her neat skirt and then drifts out of our world, placing each foot before the other like a model on a catwalk. A pregnant pause as the image fades, then to business.

"You say you require a rack for a hundred and fifty brochures? Okay, but it's an 'extra'."

Who said "No problem"?

The people contracted to erect the platform and stair-tower in the Main Hall have ratted on us. Looking for Abe, I pull back just in time to avoid a redneck-driven forklift truck as, with raised prongs, it skewers a crate. A crunch and the splintering of timbers. The delicate cylindrical shades for the pendant lamps are now classified as garbage. I set up a lamp-making factory on the roof, using canteen chairs as templates.

"Abe, know anyone in Manhattan who can take on the platform towers?" Motionless for a full minute, Abe gives a barely perceptible nod, sticks the cigar back in his face and drifts off like a matron out for an afternoon stroll. Are we paying him enough?

Maybe the Romans used sky hooks?

Way up in the vault, I see two figures in dungarees fumbling with a bolt of fabric while another, clinging to the roof girders, attempts to unhook a drape from the end of a slowly swinging scaffold pole. Hang the valarium?

I decide to dodge five vice-presidents and ring the man at the top. A deep, throaty, "Howdy," tells me he exists. I dive straight in and tell him his people are letting us down four days before opening. "It's a simple job," I add. Not true, but maybe it will motivate some action.

Tempted by the executive elevator, I play truant for a moment and, as it ascends, wonder whether that ingenuous appeal will pay off. Tomorrow will tell.

The doors open with a whisper onto the plushy precinct of Miss America's temple. Ten minutes later, when I touch the indicator for down, it is surprising that the elevator doesn't go up-up-and-away. The goddess had said, "Yes."

After a trouble-shooting safari around the upper floors, I return to find our man Grealy, standing in a dim gallery, looking pensive. Then I see why.

Some months back I had persuaded a carpet manufacturer to produce the largest one-piece carpet in the world. An inert mass, it now lay completely blocking the in-out gangway. I give it a prod with my foot.

"No good doing that," says Grealy. "I've had twenty men heaving at it for an hour and we've only moved it a few inches – sideways." He glances at me, sideways.

"When you planned for that carpet, G, did you have any idea how to lay it?"

I shake my head and feel guilty. As we edge our way round the monster I comment, "The ancient Egyptians moved heavier objects than this with manpower."

Grealy isn't impressed, "Slaves and, more important, no sense of time."

Time. Gosh, I have a date.

Waiting under the entrance canopy, I wonder how I will locate her in the press of pedestrians sheltering from the rain. There appear to be at least three million unnecessary females in Manhattan. I needn't have worried. Moving through the dun-coloured crowd, as though it is some irrelevant form of pollution, is a slender figure, straight off the cover of *Harper's Bazaar* (only too true, I am to discover later).

"Be your age, G"

Transport. Yellow cabs sizzle by, spraying swathes of warm water in their wake, but the goddess is unconcerned. Opening a miniature umbrella, as delightful as Chippendale chinoiserie (and as useful), she manoeuvres with practised poise, carefully avoiding those ill-fitting Manhattan manhole covers that breathe steam . . . and I fear for her gossamer nylons as though I have omitted to spray-fix a pastel drawing.

By the time we reach the Plaza Hotel, on the other side of Central Park, her ankles, each as exquisite as the stem of a Venetian goblet, are blemished with speckles of mud.

The Mayor of New York, whoever he is, ought to be shot. (Come to think of it, he probably has been by now.)

As I balance on a little gilt chair in that historic foyer and watch the goddess expertly remove droplets of rain that tremble on the tips of her mascara'd eyelashes, I realise that the Coliseum, and everything we are putting in it, compared with this living work of art, is dead.

An obtrusive violinist, scenting synthetic romance, eases our way to play her favourite tune – from *West Side Story* – which gives me time to relax and think (a no-go area for types like me).

I am brought back to earth, as the goddess – eighty per cent by the grace of Nature and twenty per cent *couturier* art –

turns to drape her damp jacket over the back of her chair (I should have done that). As she eases back, the soft muscle clinging to one shin moves smoothly under the skin, like a sleek slug, to slide caressingly up against its partner – two slinky white molluscs having sex? I am trapped.

Next morning I am trapped again. Grealy, who has never been beaten, is laying that carpet with a bulldozer lured from a nearby building site. He sees me, "Get a barrier up, G, before I shoot someone. Get that damned great truck out of it. This isn't a right-of-way."

A heavy smell of exhaust from the thundering diesel, a seemingly impossible backing manoeuvre, and the driver and his cab are lost in silhouette against a dazzle of light as the vehicle backs out onto Broadway. A sad strip of fabric hanging from the ripped valarium records its passage.

Abe appears with news. It's okay with the platform and stair-towers. He has laid on the best team of erectors in Manhattan; yellow-helmeted acrobats, who balance on steel joists, riveting spaceframes for sky-scrapers.

"They'll be working nights," says Abe. "Double pay – it'll be worth it."

They can't start that night – St Patrick's Day. Gosh, that leaves only two nights. Let's hope they are as good as he says.

Now for those drapes up in the Main Hall. At the head of the escalator I am pulled aside by friend Priddy, who copes with impossible situations without batting an eyelid. He points to a stooping, loose-limbed figure in the centre of the hall.

"There he is, G, old man Weisburg himself. Isn't that

258

something? Hasn't been seen in New York outside a Lincoln limousine for twenty years. How on earth did you get him here?"

My ploy had worked. An old guy with a stoop is directing operations, shirtsleeves held up by those silver expanding bands men wore in billiard saloons. He must be eighty, if a day.

When I make myself known, he drops a bony arm over my shoulder as though we'd been buddies for years.

"So, you're G." A knuckly hand, its back patinated with age-freckles, grips mine. "We'll get it up."

He squints into the void. At least twenty men on the job, and a rangy youth swinging in a bosun's chair. "Grandson," says the old man proudly.

Another all-nighter

As the day workers made for home, Abe's thirty helmeted erectors arrived, riding high on truck-loads of timber, which they proceeded to off-load with the precision of gun crews. Timber, heavy enough to support a tank, was cut like cheese and bolted with compressed air tools, and I began to wonder why I was hanging around.

Their foreman came over for, "The other drawing."

"What other drawing?" I asked.

"For the right hand stair."

I pointed out that it was handed; the right a mirror image of the left. I flattened out the drawing.

"Handed?" His expression made it clear he thought I was having him on. Then it hit me, they had a blind spot. All things to all men, I set out the other stair with them step-by-step.

Obviously not clubable

Next day, come noon, I am irresistibly drawn down the carpeted aisle by a faint whisper of sound. There is a story from archaic times; how the Priest King of Nemi (the sacred lake) deserted his post guarding the Golden Bough (not a pub, a sacred tree) to track Aphrodite as she tiptoed through the sacred grove. Here we go again.

The whisper of sound that beckons me is the soft swish-

swish of nylon against silk as the goddess's thighs brush together. We make our way to the down escalator, about to have a memorable lunch at the Athletic Club – a guy had presented us with a membership card, so no problem.

After all, did I not once give a lunchtime lecture to Ivy League guys at the Rackets Club on The History of American Football – the Four Horsemen, Rockney and all that jazz, and still live to tell the tale.

A heavy-faced building on Central Park. A titled canopy. An insolent grin from the doorman. A hall like a public swimming baths, but in real marble. UP elevator – pressed against pot-bellied money-men and their over-dressed wives. Tight lips painted with Lillian Gish kisses. The last table we would choose, dead centre. A circle of jealous eyes probe. A heavy hush. My mistake, escorting a bird of paradise into the hens' backyard.

Sensing that Venus's defences are all but overwhelmed, I grin – for the audience – and suggest that next time we will try the Brooklyn Zoo. She smiles, like a well-trained débutante under the eye of an ambitious mother, but her hand trembles a little as she sips her wine. When, show over, she stoops to retrieve her handbag, I envy it as being an intimate part of her, then wonder whether these overfed New Yorkers leave a tip at the trough. Guess not.

Next morning I am awakened from a heavy sleep, in the canteen, by the burping of the coffee machine and the rattling of chairs. They want me out.

An excited Priddy is ready for me. Unable to contain himself he exclaims, "G, they're UP!" Of course, the backcloths for the 'Cecil Beaton' setting.

Standing motionless in the centre of the main aisle, I hated to say it, "Terribly sorry, but you've hung them upside-down." He turned abruptly and silently walked away. Another 'all-nighter' ahead.

Two of our resistors are missing

The night before opening, I drift down to hear the tame scientist expounding on British inventions, but the stage is deserted. I check. Stars, sky and shadow effects okay, Hovercraft model running well, cathode tubes not on the blink. Then someone tells me the black box that synchronizes all this is *kaput*. I don't believe it. The whiz-kid, who made it do its thing when we set it up in London, assured me it was "solid state printed circuit" and could not possibly fail.

I hunt up our electrician, who tells me that two small *resistors* are missing. Hell, and tomorrow is the day. Eventually I find the New York electrician calmly wiring up a fan in the boss's office. He says he knows all about black box bugs, but the suppliers closed hours ago.

"You live in Brooklyn. You must know some local dealers, personally?"

A laconic, "Sure."

"Good. Then knock one up right away. Doesn't matter what it costs." He shrugs, still fiddling with the fan.

"Maybe that's how you limeys play it, but not this baby."

Tension released, I grab him by the shoulders, "Then get off the site."

Goreman, our own electrician, eyed me quizzically. "You know, G, you shouldn't have done that. He's the local union bloke. Pop up to the café – you need a bit of shut-eye." My hands were trembling.

When I returned, five hours later, the set-up was working like clockwork; a prissy white-coated student mouthing his lines in the expected BBC manner. Saved.

Goreman, happy as a disc jockey, beckoned me saying some bloke wanted to meet me. It was the New York electrician. He held out a hand.

"You're G, aren't you? Good to know you. I'm Hank."

Calm before the storm

Our custom-made assortment of interlocking items is at last screwed, stuck, bolted or suspended in position. Soon the people who matter will be piling in for the performance of 'opening', but now a period of hush.

How quiet and elegant it is without *people*. A pity about people – just one of those things. Another of those things is a last minute complaint from Lamb. Some cypresses plants I had installed will obstruct camera angles when Prince Philip makes his opening speech.

Watch it. The last time I was lined up to be inspected by the Queen's bedfellow, he had paused in his slow walk, looked me in the eye and said, "Oh, so it's you again," emphasis on the 'you'. I avoid 'openings'.

Borrowing a fancy pair of shears from the Design Council exhibit – "For fifteen minutes only, mind you," – I am soon clipping the shrubs, hat on back of head like a suburban gardener, much to the amusement of some visiting New Yorkers, and Edwards of the FBI, who is doing the rounds with Lamb in his wake.

Edwards comes to a halt at the foot of Britannia, who now dominates the hall – a haughty, *haute couture* Diana. He steps back, considers, then flips the scanty silk drape so it covers the naughty nipple. Good deed for the day accomplished, he pops down the carpeted stairs, readjusting his shirt cuffs like a happy draper. Lamb, who has been standing back watching this performance, unhooks the drape with a flip, turns to give me a quick 'V' for victory, and hustles off to catch Edwards.

All over? Cornered by an over-enthusiastic PR lady, "You *are* James Gardner? Come over and meet the press." What, with Venus in close orbit? Those specimen hedge clippers are now sticky with sap, but my lady comes to the rescue with a bottle of nail varnish remover and, for use as polishing cloths, a pair of used nylons.

Desecration, as uncouth and insensitive as polishing shoes with the *Turin Shroud*. I preserve one stocking, fold it with care and secrete it in my pocket.

 Thus armed, I avoid the press gang and make for Grand Central Station, as I aim to spend two days in Connecticut with Bob Fawcett, an illustrator – one of the gods I worshipped in the old Carlton days – double-spreads in *Colliers* and the *Saturday Evening Post*. As it turns out, I make a memorable fool of myself.

In at the deep end

Quite unaware that I am about to contribute to local folklore, I pay the taxi off and stroll up the drive to Fawcetts' glass-box house poised on the edge of a cliff. Nice view. No one at home. Message pinned to side door:

G
WE ARE AT THE JOLLEYS'
USE THE JEEP

Smart Jeep, white chassis, black hood – locate reverse – escape backing over cliff – hell, no address – driven there once – here we are – narrow lane. Remember – keep to the right – eye open for Colonial-style house – on the left? No. It turns up on the right – right.

Stroll down grass slope – small natural lake – group of bronzed Madison Avenue types reclining – sipping rye-on-rocks – don't recognise any of them, as eight pairs of dark sun-glasses slowly turn my way.

"Say, see that guy. He sure is English. Pork pie hat and a *pipe*. What a honey . . ."

A voice from the pool, "Hi yer, G, have a dip."

Bob Fawcett is wallowing in the lake, observed by some morose bullfrogs.

Now it happens that I am non-amphibious, not having gills like a fish. I keep my nose well above water even when having a bath. A lake? Sink like a stone.

To show willing, I trot out onto the diving board. A neat little dinghy is moored alongside. (I wouldn't know, but this boat was put together from a do-it-yourself kit by the Jolley's children. It isn't stable.)

I step in. It turns turtle. My hat floats, I don't. Can't shout help, superior types watching. Drown with dignity. Can't hold breath much longer . . .

Even laid-back New Yorkers expect the English to be odd, but surely not to step into deep water fully clothed. One leaps for the diving board and yanks me out.

Stripped, a white troglodyte. Clothes laid out to dry. Ink has run on passport. Wet dollars. Tobacco-stained jacket. Shoes ooze water. Am driven back squatting like a bleached Ghandi with towel for loincloth.

Glad you weren't there.

Months later, a London acquaintance visiting in the area was asked, "Do you know a crazy guy from Hampstead — he's called, G?" Local folklore has it that when pulled out I muttered, "Damn it, my pipe has gone out."

So, they're tough guys

Instead of making for the airport, I gravitated to the Coliseum for one last peep. A queue was blocking the sidewalk under a canopy of dripping umbrellas, waiting for the doors to open.

A glimpse of the Main Hall viewed from the platform end, showing suspended drapes designed to mask the grim upper structure.

I sneaked in to find the Government section looking well-tailored and assured in its guardsmen's blue and red, with just a glint of brass. The frustrations of the last ten days seemed, in retrospect, to have been so much unnecessary flip-flap.

Standing alone in the silence, I felt for a moment quite proud of the show, when Lamb, who was becoming more of a Napoleon every day, came striding down the aisle.

"You still here, G?" He seemed preoccupied. "It's pouring outside, so I'm letting the public in. Get them started, old man." "Old man," from Lamb. The show must be a success. By "them" he must be referring to the projectors. Glancing behind the projection screen, I was relieved to see the arcs burning, the films laced, and three crews standing by at the ready.

"Get them rolling," I sang out. "The public will be coming in any minute."

Standing in insolent pose, one hand on the controls, the chief projectionist gave me a glance, then, slowly raising a hairy arm, scrutinized his watch.

"We're under contract to start at one o'clock." He peered intently at the watch. "I don't as yet make it ten minutes to."

Six bovine faces turned my way to see what I made of it. He only had to press a switch.

Farewell to Venus

A corner drug store. The goddess had settled momentarily on a high stool, a dragonfly among toads. I would happily have netted her as a specimen. Instead I dunked a doughnut I didn't want. Lost at my obsessive adoration, she discreetly wiped away tears that welled up in her eyes with a minute square of scented tissue, then, true to her art, flicked her eyelashes up with a little finger; 'cover girl' to the last.

Standing on the crowded sidewalk, waiting for a taxi to be released by the lights, I memorised a last look as Venus drifted out of picture. Head held high, the thrust of a hip as delicate calf muscles, shadowed by a web of nylon, flexed and tensioned, as each neat ankle adjusted to the moment of movement.

She was soon lost in the shadows of another artfully contrived artefact, the Seagram building, whose architect, Mies van de Rohe, said, "God is in the little details."

265

Pressurised but still ticking over

As soon as the plane lifts off the runway, I flip out a note pad and, under a list of 'extras' agreed with the contractor, concoct a jingle to get New York and all that out of my system . . .

When circling around. Flying in from a height
Or looking down-town, as an abstract at night,
The brittle boxes of Manhattan
Make a pretty prismic pattern.
In the street,
Manholes steaming,
Humid heat, cop-cars screaming.
Towering slums,
Lots to rent,
Dolled up Mums, and alcs. who're bent.
A 'nip' between crunches,
The usual white lies,
Businessmen's lunches in Ivy League ties.
Erotic undies –

I am interrupted by the female in the next seat, chummily informing me that she is a journalist.

"You're a writer?" she asks.

I say, "No, a designer."

"An interior decorator?" It is almost a statement but, as this is one thing I don't do, she gets a short answer, "No."

Now where was I? Ah I have it . . .

Erotic undies,
Granny's tight,
Church on Sundays, sex tonight.

Damn. She's at it again. "Just give me one example of something you have designed and I'll be a good girl and leave you to your writing."

Fair enough. I look around for a moment.

"As it happens, I designed the seat you are sitting on, that folding table in front of you and these," – I flick the translucent window blind up and down. "Remember? We once had dolls' house curtains, which passengers used to wipe condensation off the windows." I hopefully repositioned my pad, then, "Oh – and the Dry Fly Sherry trade mark on that 'miniature' label."

Damn. Now she thinks I'm showing off, but someone has to devise these things, just as someone has to bring up babies. More *people*. Complicated, all different and all illogical and, in fact, bloody aimless. In this cheerful mood I complete the jingle

> *Admen clichés,*
> *Gays and pimps,*
> *Girls who're dishes, bums and gimps.*

Then, refusing a plastic tray of airline edibles . . .

> *Strawberry cheesecake,*
> *'Folksy' feeding,*
> *Corn-fed beefsteak, rare and bleeding.*
> *The Whitney Museum,*
> *Like a tart, legs apart,*
> *An exotic display of status, called ART.*

Then, remembering a jumble of bric-a-brac I had glimpsed by the railway track in New Jersey, with a bold sign over it framing a long shot view of the towers of Manhattan . . .

> *By the tattered old Penn line,*
> *Tangled bridges, tanks and dumps,*
> *Some guy's hung a fearful sign*
> *On the city's oily rumps.*

Having got rid of the trauma of handing one's baby over to the enemy, I take a last sad look at my still-damp passport and wait impatiently as the rotating planet brings Europe ever nearer, but swings Venus more and more distant in space and time . . .

Keeping in orbit with goddess cost me plenty in transatlantic telephone calls – my last link with a lifestyle that dated from the contrived elegances of the Cartier days.

When I last met Miss America I did not at first recognise her as she drifted across the hotel lobby. Sandals, long draped hair, a moss green velvet cape like a bishop's cope, pewter chains hanging almost to the ground. Botticelli's *Venus* with the pale consumptive look was now IN.

And I was sure her eyes had grown closer together.

The excitement of collecting

As we must deal with glass, a visit to Venice. Mehitabel
insists on a drawing so, no Canaletto, I have a go.
From the hotel terrace, 2B pencil on a notepad,
just as dusk is falling in the haze.

Evening, Venezia. 91. G.

Museum – handle with care

Back in friendly old UK, where men are more interested in whether barmaids eat their young than Diners Club ratings, I arrived at the Studio to find Max Fry chatting up Mehitabel. Max (echoes of Le Corbusier and Mies van der Rohe) was about to click us into a new groove labelled 'Museums'.

He had just completed a new office block for Pilkington, the glass people at St Helens, where the first steam locomotives puffed sparks and smoke. His building was conceived as a rectilinear exercise *à la* Modigliani, but, unfortunately, the site overlooked factories where they actually made glass; those brick and slate 'happenings' that Lowry loved to paint. A lake had been created as a barrier.

Our clients were so interested in items that affected their way of life – a lunch canteen for middle management, separate from the lunch room allocated to upper management, and a drive in, without ramps, for directors' cars – that they failed to notice a little building at the end of the lake on Max's model, which bore the modest label 'museum'.

Before they could make a decision, the pile drivers were already thumping away; so museum it was.

Pilkington now found themselves faced with a problem. What to put in it? Max Fry kindly brought me into the picture as a bloke who – like a universal undertaker – undertook.

They had no preconceived idea for a museum, so (concept-wise) it was up for grabs.

Fry, top in his profession as an architect, had rather unreal ideas about people. He suggested exhibits that would make the workers thrill at the idea of producing glass, when they were, of course, more interested in what they did with themselves when *not* producing glass. (This cynical view was found to be true when the museum was opened – they never went inside.)

It was a small museum, so I proposed we should concentrate on the *technique* of making glass objects, from the early Syrian beginnings to today.

Small is beautiful

As our collection would be small, compared with the national collections, we would purchase only one example of each technique; the best we could get. Later, as really unique specimens came up, we would purchase them (whatever the cost) and sell the old ones. The collection wouldn't get bigger but, perhaps, end up the finest in its class.

This worked – our initial specimens increased in value the longer they were retained, and paid for the replacements.

I was given two and a half years for research, to locate exhibits, and put the show up . . . *and five days to guess what it would all cost.* Knowing no more than the next man, my guess was, at least, objective and it was accepted. Mehitabel asked if she could do the research, as she knew even less about glass than I did? I guess she was bored with licking PAYE stamps.

In accepting the timetable, I had not considered that museums don't appear overnight; they slowly . . . oh, so slowly . . . grow. A collection of objects is assembled, conserved, labelled and displayed to provide the curators with a way of life. Occasionally these moles would dust themselves and visit other curators at exotic overseas seminars, make enemies, enjoy vitriolic correspondence in technical periodicals, or brood over a paper behind locked doors until such time as they became museum specimens themselves. Another world.

We hadn't much to work on but, hearing that the Corning glass people had such a museum, I made a quick diversion from a trip to New York, and wandered hopefully round it with the rest of the week-enders.

I spent an hour browsing over the captioning – nothing I hadn't read in reference books – yet they had a university research team at it for a number of years. I wondered what they did with their time?

Working on a do-it-yourself, need to know basis, I can only afford to follow lines pretty sure to give results (what the

exotic planning consultants term the 'critical path' method).

Though I was riding an unaccustomed groove, I could see that many of their specimens were out of this world, having been donated by money-men with household names. My clients, who marketed window glass, were gents.

Museum? When not producing glass, their chief interest was in the game of cricket, so no monied sponsors, but we'd beat Corning yet.

One wall a continuous run of window. Visitors didn't come here to view the lake, so I introduced a fibre glass curtain to soften, and structural panels to cut the direct light.

An obstacle race chasing facts

Mehitabel flicks another cigarette stub in the ashtray as, curled up on the sofa, she flags pages in a pile of books, selecting interesting titbits and noting down leads to people. There is a tab of pink paper tucked in one book – Italian – which refers to a Dr Harden. Apparently this guy knows how the Romans made flat window glass. (We have their size from apertures left in walls, but the glass? Only a few little chips.)

Dr Harden, a comfortable man, Director of the London Museum, doesn't sit on his discoveries hoping one day to hatch a book. When asked about his subject, he opens up. The first thing he opens up is a cough-drop tin and tips out some glass chips, the actual specimens we had seen greatly enlarged in the Italian book. He makes us a present of them (exhibit No. 23 – we'll beat Corning yet) and then spoils it all by explaining that his theory is already outdated.

"There's an archaeologist fellow in Wales . . ." Off we go . . . *again.*

Rely on the printed word? I remember an excited Mehitabel finding references to a petrified forest made of glass somewhere in South America. It didn't exist. As with the Indian rope-trick, one never comes face to face with anyone who has seen it with their own eyes. But we did get a glass rod formed by lightning, an ignimbrite, from the King of Sweden's collection (exhibit No. 54 – we're getting on).

One of the earliest known engravings of a glass-maker's kiln, in Bohemia, had obviously been sketched on the spot by a medieval artist, who was (unusual at that time) dedicated to realism. He had recorded one glass-blower with a trouser leg torn to tatters and, up in the roof, two suspended objects that looked like sea-shells, or wasps' nests. What were they?

The British Museum didn't know or seem to care; then someone said, "Try Howard Phillips," who had a glass showroom just round the corner from Wimpole Street. He didn't know either.

INTRODUCTORY SEQUENCE
Examples of basic techniques mounted in screened recesses to give the viewer the pleasures of the unexpected – with mini film projections.

Exhibits play hard to get

When I showed him our shopping list, 'Exhibits to get', he pursed his lips, tut-tutted, then told me some of the items didn't exist at all and as for thirty per cent of the remainder – well, a matter of luck. As likely as coming across a thirty-carat diamond in Green Park, for instance.

How did he know? He was a dealer – *the* dealer. Would he act for us? And that is how we got most of the early vessel glass.

Howard Phillips would call us over and we would stand, bated breath, while he went through the initiation ritual, like a mandarin. It never varied. A finger up, very solemn. "I have picked up something that will interest you." Out of a drawer would come a small specimen swaddled in tissue. Unwrapping it with his back to us, he would quietly step aside to reveal the treasure poised dangerously near the edge of an already overcrowded table. "Unique," he would say. "None other like it." Long silence, eyebrows raised; then, just before I said the wrong thing, he would tell us he knew of something the owner valued even more, and effected an exchange. If our client, Mr Pilkington, didn't want it (veiled threat), it would go to the Melbourne Museum.

He would then relax, give its date, provenance, and maybe tell us it was blown by a left-handed Syrian, or that it had been ground out of a solid block in Alexandria long before the trick of blowing glass was discovered – only he wouldn't call it glass, but 'metal'. We had a whole new vocabulary to learn: *gaffer, footman, prunts* and *trails, broad* and *crown.*

It became clear to me that to enjoy glass one must appreciate the trick of how it is worked. How a gob on the end of a metal rod is blown, moulded, nipped and turned while still in the hot, sticky-toffee state – the craftsman, called a gaffer, manipulating the bubble like a conjurer. I had decided that our museum would show just this and must now see how they do it in Sweden, the Netherlands, Bohemia and gosh, yes, we must go to Venice.

Contrary to the guide books

Midwinter. Canaletto's vision of the Grand Canal is blurred by driving sleet. Details of brickwork and stone loom through the mist. We dive into a narrow alley. Mehitabel holds back. "It's okay," I tell her as we arrive at the hotel – if it can be given that name, "In Venice alleys are as important as high streets." It had seen better days, but was the only cheap place listed 'out-of-season'. Porter, behind a rather scrappy counter, smiled a greeting, grabbed our bags and led us along a dimly lit corridor – round a corner – an even narrower corridor – up three steps – and more corridor – then, with a polite smile, thrust open a door at the end.

Warm scented air, soft carpet, and we float down wide steps to a marble-paved, high-ceilinged hall – three obsequious attendants in grey tailored uniforms smiled from behind a counter, richly carved out of real stone. As I signed a gilt-edged visitors' book, which reminded me of a family Bible, Mehitabel turned aside to adjust her make-up to the décor reflected in a bevelled wall mirror. All rather like a well-researched film set – but in limbo there are no performers. It turned out that the owners of this most elite palace, a landing stage of its own with clusters of striped posts on the Grand Canal, also ran a students' annexe at the back. As the only visitors, we were given the full treatment and deferential service at no extra charge.

"I said it would be okay," I remarked casually. Mehitabel just gave me a sideways look.

Next day, a bleak still morning. The water of the lagoon slides by the boat, flat, dead and matted with sleet. We pass a funeral cortége. Draped figures, huddled under black umbrellas, in black barges weighed down with piles of frozen white flowers. We slip on into the blur, eventually to feel our way up a narrow canal. We are at the small island of Murano, where glass-blowers were isolated in the old days so they could not escape to reveal their secrets; in return, a master blower would be given the daughter of a nobleman in marriage. Status.

Feeling our way down an old stone stair, we find ourselves in the abrasive heat of a great cobbled glasshouse. I nod to the master blower, but his eyes are on Mehitabel, as she places what remains of my damp drawing pad on the end of a glass-blower's 'chair' to protect her miniskirt from the dirt of ages.

Employing the universal language of talking-by-sketching, I draw a vessel, then explain that he is to carry on forming it in the usual way until I call out, "Stop."

A SETTING

A nineteenth century glasshouse showing the conical structure, designed to force a draught, drawing oxygen through the kiln. A technique also adopted in the potteries.

274

"*Arresti*," interjects Mehitabel.

"Right, when I say '*arresti*' you put that piece aside, half-formed, and start the process all over again – that is until I again call out, 'stop'."

"*Arresti*," says Mehitabel.

"Until I call out '*arresti*'. Then you put *that* bit aside and start again."

He thinks I am a little mad, but we aim to produce a series of specimens to illustrate stages in the making of a traditional filigree vessel – the kind with delicate milk-white lines spiralling and twisting up inside the thin wall of its glass bowl. How on earth do they do it?

A secret is revealed

Rolling a thin cigarette, he peers at my sketch, signals his assistants, thrusts his blowpipe into the furnace and collects a gob from the white-hot crucible – we're off. First he holds the blob, now a transparent treacle colour, as an offering to Mehitabel, and indicates with a gesture. She touches it with the tip of her cigarette, which immediately bursts into a puff of flame. He nods approval, then cartwheels the sticky gob along the ends of a row of little glass rods, which have white spirals inside them and have been neatly lined up on a bench.

How did they get those delicate white spirals into the rods?

After embedding a dab of white glass in a gob, when it is still hot and soft – like jam in a doughnut – it is stretched as it cools, being twisted the while, and . . . hey presto, we have a fifteen-foot rod of cold, clear glass with a white spiral inside. One of the oldest of glass-makers' secrets.

Our gaffer, having collected the already prepared little rods on the end of his blowpipe like the petals of a flower that is about to open, holds them in the mouth of the furnace, nips their ends together and injects a puff of breath. The heat expands this and soon, rotating it the while, he has a bubble – which is manipulated to form the vessel. A demonstration of hand and eye co-ordination that makes bat hitting baseball look pretty meaningless.

Glasshouse and kitchen practices compared. When in the hot, malleable state, glass can be blown as a bubble, drawn up as a sheet, rolled flat, and pressed or moulded to the required shape.

For three hours we were trapped by his dexterity, shading our faces from the dazzle-heat, to leave only when fifteen samples were slowly cooling in the annealing oven.

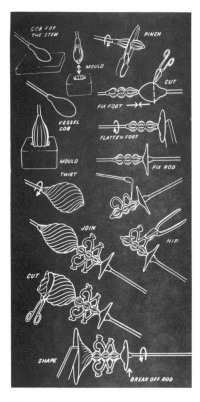

I first produced a sketch for a Venetian goblet. In less than three minutes of manipulation, the gaffer and his team at Ferre Lazzarini had developed it. Providing a progressive sequence of samples took somewhat longer.

Out in the cold again – it seems much colder – we set off for the shabbier end of the Grand Canal. After groping along angled alleys linked with narrow humpbacked bridges, we take shelter in a corner to examine a criminally inaccurate map.

"Offer to draw them a proper one," suggests Mehitabel. At last we are rapping at the shutters of a poor-looking workshop (but don't let that fool you).

"It'll be exhibit number one hundred and seventeen," she whispers.

"If he's got one," is my sour comment. (I guess it's the cold.)

For hundreds of years all imaginable shapes of vessel had been produced by blowing glass, yet it is amazing that no one had come up with a trick for producing flat glass. I was seeking a specimen of the very first attempt, the small discs one sees in windows in the old Dürer engravings.

The treasure already exists in my mind. A modest five-inch disc of brittle, slightly greenish glass, thin, a bead thickening the edge to give it a fragile strength. In the centre, a scar where the craftsmen knocked it off the *punti* – the rod on which he had spun the open-mouthed bubble of flowing glass, ever faster and faster until it suddenly flattened out with a *plick*.

"A medieval rondel?" queries the ancient gaffer. "Not in Venice. All fakes, except a few in the upper windows of the Ducal Palace. All the others are replacements, fakes. To possess an original . . . ?" He holds up his hands. Oh, well, at least we tried. Now we have to trace our way back – but the gaffer gives us a ride in his gondola. A grand old man in a shabby gondola from the shabby end of the Grand Canal.

We have been back in the studio a month when I sign for a boot-box. It is gay with Italian stamps, registered post: at first, nothing but cotton wool, but cosseted deep inside we find a delicate Venetian rondel, with the old boy's compliments. No bill – he *'had occasion to repair one of the upper windows of the Ducal Palace'.*

Right place, wrong time

For specimens of Bohemian glass we will need to probe behind the 'Iron Curtain', to the area where that old fifteenth century engraving originated. 'Intourist' fail to reply to our request but, having visas, we go anyway on a do-it-yourself basis. Surprised on arrival at Prague to see a great Russian tank draped with scruffy armed troops grinding along the main street, the locals going about their business blindly, as though it isn't there – just as the penguins in Antarctica ignore the intrusion of explorers.

Guess we had been too occupied to keep up with the news. *Lesson: avoid being any place at any time when 'history is in the making'.*

The hotel (located by our travel agent in an out-dated guide-book) is in a back street. They have never heard of tourism. Entry is by a sleazy bar, where layabouts slump on fake cowhide seats; splatters on the worn lino floor where locals have missed the spittoon. Oh, well, you can't win them all.

Mehitabel's twelve inches of white thigh, revealed between high boots and mini-skirt, may be okay for Chelsea – but here?

All a bit creepy, the police HQ next door, (shudder to think what is going on in its basement), and young Jan Palac setting fire to himself in Wenceslas Square only three days before.

The front of the National Museum, which contains the treasures of the Hapsburg Empire, now pock-marked with the scars from high-velocity tank guns, explains well enough why men can't be trusted with weapons.

The bloody Communists have taken over.

On with the job. Book tickets for rail journey, change currency with a secretive guy (we pee at stalls in the gents' loo to mask this illegal deal) then discover Mehitabel chatting with a blowsy, but kindly, matron who is in charge of the bar and

277

who has some 'Brooklyn' English. Mehitabel is having fun. "Vodka, G? It's a scream. The old dear says that every other male that comes in asks her how much I charge – they think I'm a hooker!" I am not surprised at that. She continues in a conspiratorial whisper, "Oh, and she says two plain-clothed officials were looking for my boss – that's you. She says they are 'political'." Hell. That puts paid to Bohemian glass. I yank her upstairs, pack bags, pay our bill, prickling with impatience and before they can say, *"Let's pull this capitalist scum in for interrogation,"* we are in a taxi *en route* to the airport. We pass the monumental Gothic cathedral, now in mourning and draped in drab black, and on to the recently completed Western-style airport, plastic tiles and glass, the great concourse empty but echoing with the Beatles' 'All You Need is Love' on tape. Obviously, the Commies haven't got round to this airport . . . as yet.

We have a whole BA jumbo jet to ourselves; more crew than passengers. Mehitabel is worried. Offering a light for her cigarette as a peace gesture and to show how homely things can be, I point out that the cork cigarette-end pattern on the plastic tabletop is from one of the floor tiles in our studio . . . I designed this cabin, so theoretically she is already at home.

At the studio, "You're back soon, G. Did you get those Bohemian beakers with the trails?" Like hell we did. Not to be phased, Mehitabel passes round some glass earrings she managed to purchase while the Russian bully-boys weren't looking.

AN EXHIBIT LAYOUT

Left, pots. Above, animated kiln, a view of old glass-works. Centre, flat glass from blown cylinder. Right, a 'forest' kiln.

'You dare not go a hunting, for fear of little men'

On a job for the Duke of Northumberland, at Syon, I find myself lost in high-hedged Surrey lanes, shaded by untended woods, the kind of woods that might harbour *'little men'*. I come to a slow stop at a mossy signpost. The paint is weather-worn, but I can just make out 'Chiddingfold'. My mind does a quick back-somersault. In the Vatican, in a gallery hung with medieval tapestry maps, I remember having seen a blobby rendering of Britain with a few place names in woven lettering – surprise – one was 'Chiddingfold'. Why so important? Then it clicked; Wealden glass, a drawer full of it in the Haslemere Museum – a medieval glasshouse in the woods. Chiddingfold is where fifteenth century 'forest' glass was blown. The *'little men'* after all.

Excited at this discovery, my interest switches from Syon to glass museum. I backtrack and eventually find the local archaeologist. He has news for me. Another chap has just stumbled on traces of a medieval glass furnace in nearby Blundens Wood, and made a plan of it – exciting, as up till now we have had to guess. Where is he? Oh, I won't find him here. He works (of all places) in a City bank. Back in London, I ring him and he agrees to come round and show me the drawing.

A precisely dressed Mr Wood parks his brief-case then, proudly but possessively, shows me a little plan of the dig. Disappointing. It looks more like a dentist's chart for an outsize set of molars with, at an angle, a smaller set of molars.

"A smaller kiln," says Wood. "Maybe it was used for *fretting* and *annealing*."

"Looks older and more primitive to me," says I. "Perhaps it was the original kiln – then someone arrived from the Continent with more know-how and they built the bigger one?"

"We wouldn't know," says Wood.

We must not use the plan until he publishes his 'paper', and I don't blame him. It was his find. But all is fair in love and war (and research), so I engage our visitor's attention by asking him the sixty-four thousand dollar question for glassmen.

"How did those guys get melting temperatures without a

chimney to force the draught?" (Meanwhile elbowing his little drawing in Simon's direction, with a muttered, "Photocopy, quick!") To keep Wood's attention I suggest, "Maybe they used bellows – as did the local metal smelters?" No use, he's looking around for his plan. Simon deftly picks up a periodical and there it is, back on the table. (Good, we'll beat Corning yet.)

Using the plan and quite a bit of intuition, I reconstructed the scene of the crime, as it were. A timber-framed glasshouse in the woods, with the tools, pots and all the etceteras it had in it, or we *think* it had in it. Then my model-maker produced a meticulously detailed model. The archaeologists (who dislike hunches, however logical they may be) tut-tutted when they saw it – suspect.

Rather nice to see it, a year later, illustrated in scientific journals. The model had been exhibited in a museum and so was now deemed authentic.

I become an expert in a lost art

Our last streak of unbelievable luck came up just as unexpectedly. Our client had brought up the hoary subject of stained glass more than once, but specimens would be as difficult to locate as, well, kidney transplants. More difficult. People with happy kidneys are popping off every day, but the fifteenth century windows of Canterbury already contained transplants – bits used as fillers. Even those bits are hard to come by. Under that puritanical Calvinist, Oliver Cromwell, yokels had been given a pretty free hand, ". . . they shall take away, utterly extinct and destroy all shrines, tables, candlesticks, paintings, and so no memory remains in the same walls, glass windows . . ." That was in 1647 but, even today, there is a common expression, "Let's have a smashing time." It makes one's spine prickle. So it was with an easy conscience that I got agreement to bypass the whole subject. To be truthful, I never did care for stained glass.

Nevertheless, driving back from Scotland down the eastern route, (to avoid the motorway), I found Gothic cathedrals continually popping up on the horizon, and had no option but to take time off and seek out the Sacristan. "Interesting pieces of medieval glass . . . to take away?" York, Ely and Lincoln looked at me pityingly. The request almost verged on indecency, but Lincoln passed me off with a name, Dennis King. He worked at Norwich. Snag with research – having a name I must now follow it up . . .

The little toad in the vestry, when he at last answered the bell, informed me that Dennis King would be somewhere up the west face of the tower. Then he closed the door and returned to his private world.

The tower of Norwich Cathedral floated giddily against the moving sky, one face wrapped in scaffolding. The first ladder was quite manageable and terminated in a steeply pitched roof clad in ancient lead, powdering white and soft in places. A plankway along a flat gutter led to a ladder that was near vertical. I hesitated, but it wouldn't do to lose face now. The rungs sprang back at my feet as I climbed. I hung on to the next ladder, step by step like a mechanical toy until, at last, I was over the top.

Now I saw why it had been impossible to get Dennis King on the 'phone – he had an aerial workshop. Flapping canvas provided three walls, the fourth was the crumbling stone of the cathedral, splattered with bird lime. Looking down, between it and the platform, a giddy perspective of upside-down Gothic.

Squatting in a litter of windblown newspaper wrappings and lead strip, was a man who lived medieval glass. A master glazier to the medieval pattern, he must know what they knew.

King steers me down the ladder (down is worse than up) and we drive off through the mix of old-and-new City, where young mums in high heels and tight trousers are wheeling the population explosion in collapsible go-carts to the unit – constructed supermarket (giving me to wonder . . . maybe we are wasting our twentieth century time). King's workshop put me in focus again. When the town planners turned him out, to widen a road, they provided him with a new workshop overlooking a park. Unfortunately, it proved to be a car-park. Never mind.

Much of the available space is taken up with racks of old and ailing leaded windows awaiting doctoring. King slides out a small *lancet*, "One of the oldest in Britain; belongs to Lincoln College, Oxford." Horny, greenish glass and soft leading which

Mirrors, shown with mirrors in paintings of their period, give provenance without recourse to wordy captions.

gives to the pressure of a finger; small segments, brilliantly coloured and inset to form a geometric border – six hundred years back artisans had put a lot of know-how into fabricating this and, when completed, it must have looked very much as it does today. But it had, of course, been a thing to wonder at.

King leads me down to his den – a litter of books and unanswered correspondence. Digging out an old cardboard box, he blows off the dust and produces some fragments wrapped in yellowing newspaper. Holding a piece up to the light, he rubs its surface lovingly with his thumb. "There you are. That's thirteenth century ruby-red." With a few gay brush-strokes someone had drawn a sun on it so it's alive – someone who has been dead as mud for a long, long time. I sort around the scraps with spatula fingers, the nails of which are already dead, and come on one bit that has a film of translucent yellow wiped over the clear areas. "*Silverstain*," says King.

This piece is black, but with a witty little lion shining out of the darkness – not the stiff symbol the College of Arms puts out these days, but a pet lion making a pretence of being angry. Lovely. Some happy artist had popped it in 'with his eyebrows raised', as we used to say at Carlton. It is golden yellow with neatly permed ringlets, a plump tail coming up from between its paws. It has horribly observant human eyes and a mad grin the artist had wiped onto its face with a flick, then a few sharp scratches for teeth.

"Abraded," says King, then tells me that colouring pot-glass in the oven is very like home cooking, a pinch of this and a trace of that. But, tricky – the correct temperature may not do it, even the amount of oxygen in the furnace can change the colour. Then about that glowing ruby-red. How the thirteenth century glassmen knew the secret. The red was so dense it looked black, so they flashed a thin film of it onto clear glass. The trick was lost for hundreds of years and, I guess, it will be lost again, as flashed glass doesn't bring in a high enough percentage for the accountants. Nowadays, we must use plexiglass, a synthetic substitute.

King is now in full flood. He tells me how the ancients made their own paint (or rather enamel), laid it on with a cow-hair brush, then fused each fragment in a kiln. This pigment was brownish, a mix of rust with powdered glass and a wee piddle of pee. Fused into the surface it became a part of it – permanent. That's not a technique that lends itself to free artwork, but there were some delicate touches and sometimes the quick smudge of a thumb, (a trick used by potters to indicate rose petals on delicate china), or a 'crow's-feet' of lines to emphasize points of tension.

King then laid out his most treasured specimens, not more than twenty in all, some of which I had seen illustrated in those glossy books. Not being aware of the money value men set on 'assets' these days, King gave me them all, "For the museum." I only hoped I could present them in a way people would understand.

Driving home through the moist mist of the Newmarket Downs – where they now gallop horses – a traffic light suddenly appeared, switching from green to red. Pulling up gently, so the unbelievably brittle treasure on the rear seat wouldn't slide off, it came to me that I had never before considered how they got the colour in those moulded glass lenses?

Sir Kenneth Clark, Director of the National Gallery and up-market art critic, honoured us by opening the show. He terminated his well-tailored speech with . . . "If I were given a wish at this moment, it would be to show Leonardo da Vinci, who did not differentiate between the arts and the sciences, round this museum."

Good show, but my mind was no longer on glass, I was worrying about . . .

The birth of a white elephant

The national press were attacking the Government with sarcastic headlines. Apparently, these guys had gone mad, proposing to throw millions in public money at a useless 'white elephant'. The elephant in question was to be a great new passenger liner to replace the old *Queen Mary*, now as redundant as the distinguished upper-crust she had served. That was before the advent of passenger aircraft.

The press realised, of course, that no one in the Government gave a damn for the ship; their interest was to provide employment in a politically sensitive area. In announcing this, they had bared a sensitive area which the press was happily stabbing.

Cunard, who would be landed with the baby, didn't question the notion. Since Isambard Kingdom Brunel's steamship *Great Britain* crossed the Atlantic, there had been a transatlantic liner in Cunard's family. That the press should attack the tradition dismayed them.

James Fitton, an artist friend of mine – velvet jacket and flowing bow tie – who happened to have an IN with the Cunard directors, suggested that if, in place of words, they offered the press an exciting visualisation of the ship, it might turn the heat off.

"Nice idea, Fitton, but you're too previous. She isn't designed yet."

"No problem. I know a guy, Gardner, who can visualise anything from a mushroom farm on the moon to an atomic dirigible."

"This isn't a mushroom farm or that other thing you said, Fitton, but a *Cunarder*." A pregnant pause. "No harm in him having a crack at it – if he isn't too expensive."

I had never before designed a white elephant – interesting.

The 'red funnel' syndrome.

One dull morning some weeks later, I find my way between those stone monuments to Liverpool's maritime insurance, once the moneymaking heart of the City. As ruins drawn by Piranese, they would be dramatic; as it is, they are just dead – a death so slow they don't know it yet. Sad. And I don't feel exactly ebullient myself. If someone asks, "What do you know about ships, Mr Gardner?" My reply, "Well, I once designed a showboat for an Amusement Park at Battersea," wouldn't do at all.

Liverpool's Pier Head looks as desolate and grass-grown as an untended grave. But the Cunard building, its plump classical dome standing four-square, looks as though it is still in business. A snub-nosed tug, breasting a bow wave and wearing a necklace of old car tyre fenders, gives a friendly burp as I push through the swing doors and go up in a slow-but-sure mahogany elevator, to be decanted into a world of brass doorknobs and polished lino.

I fill the interval between Sir John Brocklebank being made aware of my presence, and the important moment when he is prepared to receive me, admiring a beautiful model of the *Mauritania*, hermetically sealed in its case like Snow White in her glass coffin.

To relieve the ennui of being kept waiting, I get out my pad and doodle a quite reasonable sketch of the Cunard building. Too reasonable, so I reposition the dome onto the side of the building, over the palatial entry, so it projects across the street like a motherly tit. Very nice, but not for Brocklebank's eye.

Ensconced behind a vast desk in a high classical hall under that same dome, chilly as a mortuary, he complains of the draughts. Then he comes to the point, "Whatever you do with the rest of her, the ship must have the traditional Cunard funnels. It's the insignia of the line, yer know, Cunard red."

Of course I know. Brocklebank must be wondering why I had been called in at all. Why can't they leave it to the yard?

He has a point there. After generations of constructing ships, the yard-men have built up a massive backlog of know-how. Once the underwater form has been defined by trials in a tank, the rest follows on the lines of the original clinker-built whale-boat, with upswept bow and stern to take the seas – called

286

sheer. This, even when refined and attenuated, still gave the great iron ships some grace and a sense of riding the sea. Then the walls of the superstructure slope inwards very slightly – like the battered walls of old Paris apartments – to give strength: shipbuilders call it *tumble-home*. Even the decks are cambered, so they clear quickly when she takes the seas. All fine curves. A ship's lines are defined on sheets of numbers; so far along, so far in and so far up. The result can be a cobby, bluff-bowed coaster, or a long, slender ocean liner: this is the way the *Mauritania* 'happened' – just as the elegant railway locomotives 'happened' in the early days of steam.

Indoctrinated about red funnels, I climb up the narrow stair to the Cunard drawing office to find oak plan chests, high wooden stools and pale-faced draughtsmen with a problem. This ship will have no sweeping curves: she is a block of utility flats dumped in the sea, and must ride uncomfortably high to pack in the essential accommodation – a piece of floating real estate.

A clumsy model, bits borrowed from the old *Queen Mary* in an attempt to make her look like a ship. No longer on the defensive, and sure she can be shaped to look designed for the sea, as well as for townees, I am itching to have a go.

I parcel a stack of blueprints in brown paper and make for Lime Street Station feeling jubilant – or as near as I ever get to feeling jubilant. Something exciting is about to happen.

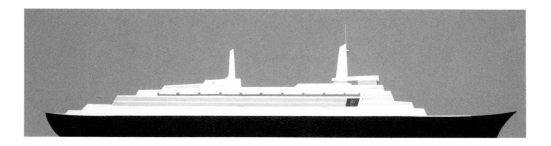

Cunard approved my stately, romantic (but quite unreal) visualization, ship surveyors made inspired guesses and the Treasury gave a go-ahead on the lowest tender (if such an astronomical figure could be categorized as 'lowest'). Then the moment came when Brocklebank had to sign the contract.

FIRST SHOT
Profile of an abortive liner devised to impress the press.

He was aware that once launched, it would be 'over to you' and Cunard could be landed with a fate worse than death – a ten figure debt to be repaid to the Treasury. He picked up the pen, hesitated, then put it down again. The project was off.

I had just taken part in the greatest non-event in shipbuilding history. The *Q3*, as my mythical monster had been named, was dead as a duck and a chance to follow in the footsteps of Brunel was lost.

'Play it again' boys

Cunard didn't give in. Not to have such an important relative in the family was, well, almost indecent, so a bunch of eggheads was brought in to find some way to make the monster PAY.

To cover the cost of her upkeep this ship must be two things at once; in summer a fast Atlantic liner and in winter a leisurely cruise ship. A bow to cut thirty foot waves like a knife, at speeds comparable to a warship going into battle, made her fast for cruising – and gave her range. The South Pacific! She must be narrow enough to pass through the Panama Canal, but this would make her high in the water – top heavy. "Ah," said a brave engineer, "not if *all her upper structure is in aluminium.*"

Tricky, as a ship is a flexing box-beam bridging the waves; the top half of this beam will be aluminium and the bottom half steel. With no other option, they go ahead. All previous ships of her size required four propellers, four turbines and four sets of boilers – taking up space better used for accommodation, which pays.

She was given two large, six-bladed propellers driven by two of the most powerful marine turbines ever built and, to prevent drag, a hull so beautifully streamlined that she wouldn't even throw up a bow wave.

Fine, but someone had to be brought into the picture to turn this block of computerised calculations into a *ship*. To be a success, a ship must have personality – we call a ship *she*, an aircraft is just *it*.

"What about that guy who styled the *Q3* project for the press?"

The biggest toy in the world

One afternoon I climbed wearily up to the office – after inspecting some medieval stained glass in a damp City crypt – to be told that a Sir Basil Smallpiece had invited me to tea at the Athenæum. A comic opera name, an unreal place, and why me?

Mehitabel told me I should read the news. In the shuffling of the *'jobs for the boys'* cards, this noble knight (who, I discover, got it for helping the *real* Queen balance her spending money) had come up as Chief Executive for Cunard. I about-turn and make for the Athenæum Club – a marble mausoleum of a watering hole where Establishment dinosaurs gather to sip port and fart gently after lunch.

Smallpiece beckons a waiter, who offers us tea and muffins with the circumspection of a defrocked bishop.

In the manner he might use when instructing a casual labourer to clip the garden hedge, Smallpiece asks me if I will take on the design of the above water-lines and interiors of the new ship.

All this must be shadow-boxing in dreamland, and I hear myself agree as casually as I might had I been asked to clip a hedge. Maybe *too* casually. He then asks, "Won't you find a task of this scale a heavy responsibility?" I reply that the problem will be one of convincing, or steering round, thirty or so ships' engineers. Scale is no problem. After all, there are many fine ships at sea, but not one effective cigarette-extinguishing ashtray in the air.

After Smallpiece (who, as it happened, once ran an airline) had digested that spurious bit of logic, he asked me to report on the existing Cunard set-up, and propose a course of action . . . He had a point there.

These gents, behind their City desks, had been caught playing with a national project as casually as one might lay out the stalls for a village fête. To Sir John Brocklebank, interior décor was a woman's affair, so he had passed that aspect of the project to his lady who, given the slightest hint of encouragement, would have happily taken on the décor of the arrivals lounge in Heaven.

Lady Brocklebank and two friends.

I asked for a week – to think.

Back at the office, I couldn't resist exclaiming, "Put the flags out. The biggest ship in the world is in the bag!"

Mehitabel beckoned me into the rear studio, closing the door behind her, "Be a darling and show me the contract."

I pointed out that Smallpiece and I had been discussing a ship.

"You haven't got one? Well," (all anticipation) "you must have agreed a fee?" Pregnant pause. "Really, G, I sometimes think you need a nurse. You must take me with you next time."

Needless to say, I didn't take Mehitabel with me on my next visit to that distinguished watering-hole, when I proposed getting rid of much of the dead wood, putting it, military-style, on one sheet of paper. I had been pretty drastic: quite a queue of starry-eyed amateurs would walk the plank.

Smallpiece lit a cigar, leaned back, conned it through at leisure and then pronounced . . .

"Understood, Gardner. I guessed as much, reading between the lines." He waved my explanations aside with, "Don't concern yourself. When an executive reads of his retirement in *The Times*, it's a *fait accompli*." So that's how they do it!

Back at Duke Street, I came to my senses: I had committed myself to taming a monster! Shape a ship, okay. Devise the décor for hundreds of cabins, companion-ways, cocktail bars, restaurants, a theatre and – hell, there was even a synagogue. How to locate and brief twenty or more interior designers?

To shed some of the load, I enticed Dennis Lennon (who had an architectural practice round the corner and could design a smart hotel before the real-estater could nail the site) to help co-ordinate showers, linen cupboards, furnishings and lounges. If he slipped, it would be towards 'International Hilton'. After all, most passengers would be spoiled, monied and used to breathing conditioned air. In practice he didn't slip, so one will never know.

Hunting for a duct outlet on the promenade deck. Later, to my relief, I discovered that shipyard plans were folded like a Japanese fan, to be opened out at the desired area.

Looking over my draughting board, I measure the IBM building across the street with my eye. An opportunity to impress Mehitabel.

291

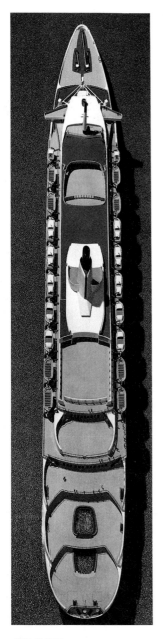

SLIMLINE
Designed to take the seas at speed.
Note the areas of open deck aft,
for sun worshippers.

"See that roof line? That will be the height of the lifeboat deck and there are two more above that." I open the window, "Imagine her bow to be at James Street. She will take in that whole block, while her stern will rest away on the other side of Portman Square. Big, and for real this time." Mehitabel thinks I'm pulling her leg.

A nice idea, but I am about to scribe the ship's bow, a great ploughshare to cleave through a force nine gale.

Fortunately my model-maker had spent his formative years in the mercantile marine and could name any sizeable ship at sea on sight – which is more than the men who build them could, as I was to discover later. To those pragmatic engineers, a ship is a construction job which goes screaming down the slipway to make room for the next. Except that this time there probably wouldn't be a next – so she'd better be good.

For a start we make a club sandwich of balsa wood, each slice a deck, and place a pepper-pot on top where the funnel will be. It's too far forward, but we can't do anything about that. Creeping around with our heads on the floor we check sight-lines; cardboard models of sections, where curved plates meet sloping decks; and stiffening-webs to prevent vibration – the horror of shipmen. The completed model looks well enough, but it is still a preliminary. We can cut back here and build up there to give her the smooth authoritative look of a thorough-bred Cunarder.

Small is beautiful

My model-maker is at his bench punching shaped portholes in the four-foot final model. He slides a vertical spacer step by step along a calibrated rod which runs the length of the ship. So far along, a turn of the bezel, and so far up, to give each its exact alignment. Meanwhile, I am attempting to line up nine rectangular windows on the curved face below the wheel-house; tricky, as it is conical in section.

A real 'shippery' job, so I invite the top Clydebank engineers to show them they haven't a corner in ship architecture. Four types of lifeboat are being cast in little piece-moulds. It looks like hard work. "Why don't you buy some off the shelf from Bassett Lowke?" they ask. "Who do you think

292

makes them for Bassett Lowke?" I reply. "This here model-maker."

The life boats will be finished in white, but two small ones, which rest just behind the bridge, will be in scarlet – a saucy flick of lipstick against her white superstructure. Why? The lives of three thousand and more people sealed in this ship, a floating air-conditioned metal container, may depend on them in an emergency. Say, armed hijackers attack by helicopter. The First Officer will immediately launch one of these to observe and control the situation with radio satellite communication, well away from the ship.

The model is so exact, I tactlessly pointed out, that if they detail the final ship as exactly, she will be a winner. The response – a dismissive grunt.

The day came when the Cunard directors crowded the studio to approve the design. Mehitabel passing round tea while I demonstrate my light switches: a pair of beautifully modelled boobs, soft to the touch; left nipple – the overhead fluorescent, right nipple – the table downlighter. Philip dims the lights and we click away with the slide show – photographs of the model shot close-in (as from the dockside) and distant shots at sea. Quite smoothly put across (for us). Lecture over, general grunts of approval, then the senior director turns to me, "Very interesting, Gardner, but there is one point I must quarrel with." (Wait for it, thinks I, the red funnel syndrome again.) But it isn't that. He continues, "We are building a *ship*. Why do you repeatedly refer to her as a *boat*?"

Completed model. The apparent sheer of her hull lines forward is contrived – to mask decks that angle up from a point just below the wheel-house.

293

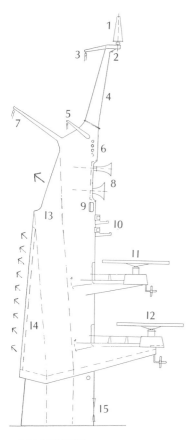

NOT SO SIMPLE

1 Isolated satellite aerial, for registering
   ship's exact location.
2 Sheath for cantline.
3 Signal halyards.
4 Three of the eight aerials.
5 Six halyards for 'dressing' ship.
6 'Panama Christmas Tree'
   signalling code lamps.
7 Main halyard for national flag.
8 Two deep note sirens: compressed
   air and electric.
9 Sensors to automatically control
   illumination of public rooms.
10 Navigation lights.
11 Long-range radar.
12 Short-range steady state radar.
13 Vent for kitchen and laundry.
14 Vent for used foredeck
   accommodation air.
15 Hatch for maintenance.

Rattling up to Glasgow on the night express, I moodily watch a thimbleful of whisky, a British Rail single, as it trembles along the plastic-topped counter – Formica (Baltic Blue No. 1390). Bar tops once glowed with rich mahogany. There's still plenty of hardwood, but extracting it doesn't bring as quick a profit as feeding trees into a maw of a mechanical masher to produce uniform acres of blockboard.

There'll be no timber in our ship . . . FIRE. We are reduced to an unsympathetic composite called 'Maronite' and cover our sin with a thin plastic skin. No brass either. It's getting as rare as gold. So is goodwill. When the crew has done its day's stint it'll be feet up to watch guys kicking a ball around on TV, or to play cards. Polish brass? Not bloody likely.

I guess I am in a brown mood. But Warwick, who is to captain the SHIP, looks cheerful enough – an old salt to the life. When the time comes he'll back her out of Southampton Dock like a Mini.

The discussion moves to radar. Warwick, his back to me, is exchanging technicalities, *sotto voce,* with a guy from Decca. Hell. Unless he puts me in the picture, how am I to mount the antennae and radar scanners? A mast aft? It'll be over my dead body. I can be exclusive, too. Nobbling the man from Decca, I remind him how I once simulated their steady field scanner device for an exhibit at Brussels. He remembers (their 'experts' had said it couldn't be done). After that, Warwick and I got along like shipmates.

Through the spiked shipyard gates – another world.

Where men are men – God help us

Teams of tough Geordies, who treat *the game of workers -v-bosses* as they would knock-out football and where a man who becomes worn out is replaced by his son, do not pass the lunch-break reading Keats's poems. Visitors who are not 'shipmen' are considered twerps and discouraged – and that goes for pale-faced intruders from down south. Okay, I can take it.

As for women, the place for them is at the kitchen sink, or knees up on the bed after darts and eight pints of beer. True, Lady Tweedsmuir, being a director, couldn't be refused. After

I aimed for the 'mast' forward to give character and relate to the mass of the funnel, as a foresail does to the mainsail on a Bermuda-rig yacht.

John Brown's tea, (neat whisky poured into a cup from a white china teapot), her ladyship was ushered up a companionway into the cliff-like side of the ship, to be faced with iron walls and floor enlivened by violet flashes and showers of sparks from oxyacetylene arcs. In front of her, daubed large on a bulkhead:

FUCK THE POPE

When I arrived, Rennie, the bluff six-foot-six bowler-hatted boss put me straight right away, "Directly we lay yon keel, there's money draining awa' like sand in an hourglass, and there'll be no stopping it, not till she's wet her backside. I'll no say you're no welcome, but anything you do to hold back that day costs in brass. You understand, mon?" But I was there to serve the ship, not John Brown's, so I would press just as hard as the game would take.

The effectiveness of my obstinacy could be measured by lunch-breaks. At first, following desultory talk over sherry, I would be ushered into the directors' dining room to find myself sitting next to the boss. Ominous – had I become one of them? Most designers do – in time. I needn't have worried. Before long I was queuing with a tray in the staff canteen, to eat between a man from the tank-room and a Naval doctor. Later it was the works canteen (where you don't need to be invited), or on my own ground – the ship, which towers over Clydebank like a giant metallic whale stranded on Lilliput.

Here I was happier, sitting on the wet steel deck peeling cellophane off a soft sandwich (from the airport) and asking a pre-Neolithic fitter if he could please remove the cap on a beer bottle. Not a man of words, he smashes its neck against a stanchion.

While the smooth-sided hull was slowly growing on the slipway, it was startling to see a chunk of superstructure, larger than a house, swing from a giant crane, to be wielded neatly into place. Delicate lines drawn with a 2H pencil became muscular men fighting the stiff resistance of steel.

At one point, where the observation deck swept in forward of the bridge, there was, what John Brown's chief draughtsman termed, a 'discrepancy'. A tapered section of steel plate sailed two feet outboard when it should have met another plate in an uninterrupted curve.

"What the hell are you going to do about *that*?" I asked. Then I forgot about it. Why? The tough gang had sprung that heavy plate inboard and then welded it for good. Not a kink, yet sufficient tension there to knock a bus over.

Over she goes

Dan Wallace is worried. A ship at sea is an inverted pendulum, so the higher she gets the wider she swings. I am getting her too heavy up top. To drive the point home he takes me in a hoist, up and out onto a flat, windy deck.

Wallace points up at the sky with his umbrella, "Two more decks to come, then the fan-house . . . "

"And the dog kennels?" I interject, but the wind blows it away.

296

"And then that eighty foot funnel of yours." Point taken.

I aimed to make the smoke stack as high as possible, to dominate the great mass of the ship. Getting the clearance under Sydney Harbour Bridge at Spring tide, I gave her five feet.

That night, instead of cutting her nose off, as it were, I decided to cut weight by remodelling the wheel-house and finding a piece of Cheddar cheese, I pared at it with a knife. Job done, the radii were transferred to the draughting board next morning.

Some weeks later, Mehitabel answered the doorbell to discover some long-haired character in a duffle-coat, slung with cameras and with a big cheese under his arm. Could he please photograph Mr Gardner carving the cheese? Some idiot must have talked to the press.

In the days of the old *Queen Mary*, white-faced passengers – even red-faced colonels – would relax on deck-chairs along shaded promenades, well sheltered from the sun.

In the shade on the Queen Mary.

(To wear a tan equated one with the working classes.)

Today a tan is a must, so we eliminated the side promenades and provided acres of open deck aft, where passengers could grill themselves to their hearts' content.

"Sit in the shade? You must be joking."

Funnel in wind-tunnel

The snag was – how to keep the decks free from smuts? To control smoke coming out of funnel must be a pretty simple operation, thinks I, but, at the Physical Research Laboratory at Teddington, I find the orthodox shape doesn't work. The Ministry boffins pass round a number of pictures of funnels in wind-tunnels. Their *pièce de résistance* is a model of an obese smokestack topped with a streamlined dome (so the wind will slide smoothly across the hole where the smuts come out, I guess). This contrasts with the slim yacht-like vent on my (beautiful) profile drawing. Hell. Who is supposed to be designing this ship, anyway?

Back at the studio, I have a model of my funnel sweated up in brass to fit the steam pipes (I had measured them).

A week later, their fat funnel (Exhibit A) is mounted on a

turntable in the tunnel. The blades of the great fan rotate, and a steady stream of steam, representing exhaust gases, drifts out of the funnel to float up and away. Then the turntable is swung so the model is at an angle to the wind. The 'smoke' climbs down the back of the funnel and across the deck. That orthodox, smut-preventing doodah didn't work after all.

Lunch-break. I sneak out to the car-park and struggle back humping my model (Exhibit B). Surprise, surprise, it fits the pipes, and me not an engineer! Exhibit B is set up, the steam is turned on and (gosh) it works, even when angled to the wind at forty degrees. We try it in the worst possible conditions and the smoke flicks, flicks again, then climbs down and across the deck. Why does this have to happen to us?

Then I remember pictures of those ungainly projections on the funnels of the *France*, and the flat mortar-board tops on the *Michelangelo*. "Do they work?" I ask. No one seems to know, or care; foreign ships. We retreat to a table in the small back room. I had been thinking. "What about those 'jacks' the Edwardians devised to top chimney pots; all sorts of patterns? Must be some know-how there." No response – designed by 'tradesmen', not Ph.D. research engineers.

"Let's define the problem," says Glen, the shipyard's research man. "In certain winds the afflux velocity of the exhaust gases is insufficient. They don't get high enough into the enveloping airstream to be carried away."

He looks moodily at Exhibit A, "We must make the funnel as slender as is humanly possible."

"My duct was as thin as that," I interject. But he has a gleam in his eye.

Back to the studio, leaving Glen to play in the wind-tunnel. He strips everything, leaving only three naked boiler tubes rearing up to the heavens . . . the smoke climbs down the back of them.

It won't do that if we can fill the vacuum with something else, so we pass used accommodation air through slots in the funnel. No go. All right, change the conditions – it'll have to be more 'afflux velocity'. Eventually Glen gets agreement for high-speed fans, at the base of the stack, to drive all the used air out of the ship (and there's a hell of a lot of used air), so it

SMUTS TEST
Sir Basil Smallpiece, two hour exposure, promenade deck wind on starboard quarter.

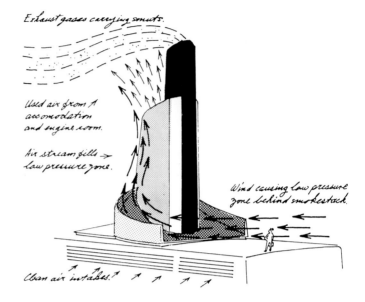

A FUNCTIONAL FUNNEL
Engine room vents, black.
Used accommodation air vent, white.
Below, air intake for the whole ship.
At two hundred and ten feet above sea
level, the highest structure on the seas.

Exhaust gases carrying smuts.

Used air from A
accomodation
and engine room.

Air stream fills →
low pressure zone.

Wind causing low pressure
zone behind smokestack.

Clean air intakes.↑

carries the smuts away with it. This means I'll have to find space for vast sound absorbers, but now we are beyond caring.

I re-think the funnel as two-in-one, with an additional capacious white duct to carry the great mass of air up behind a thin black one. And it works, except the new duct causes a vacuum of its own in *another* set of wind conditions.

"You know, Gardner, half our trouble comes from your profile – it's too clean. There are no obstructions to kick the air-flow up, so the gases are pulled down to fill the partial vacuum your wind causes behind the funnel." So it's *my* wind now.

"Not ready yet? What the devil does that chap Gardner think he's doing?" says an irate director. "You would think this was the first funnel anyone had ever built." I am beginning to think it is.

Glen says, as the ship is too 'clean lined', we ought to try screens. We play with scissors, sticky tape and cardboard until, at last, after checking every possible angle and wind force, we make it work. But the resultant shape is so ugly that, as a delaying action, I refer to it as the 'boot'.

(Psychological warfare – surely even Cunard directors won't accept an object called a *boot*.)

Having, by now, an idea of how wind and smoke behave, I develop a modified form, reshaping the screens into a scoop that will take the wind smoothly up and round to the back of the funnel; an ever-narrowing space so it is speeded up.

This (called the *venturi* effect) was first observed by Leonardo: the flat depression made on the surface of water as it speeds up when restricted by a narrow bridge (an effect which, in fact, lifts aircraft off the ground).

I rushed my new model through to Glen with only four days to go to meet the approvals date. If we didn't come up with an answer by then, we'd be landed with the old Exhibit A. I shuddered and crossed my fingers. Glen said he'd ring. Three days went by. The evening before the board meeting, he called to explain they'd had trouble with the steam-pipes that make 'smoke', and it was two days before they could get any at all. "Did the damn thing work?" I asked. "Oh, yes," said Glen.

THE MODEL
Contrived so her surfaces flow together to produce a unity.

One can't advise the money-men to go for a funnel one hasn't seen operating. Early next morning I drive down to Teddington to check. We stand looking critically at the curved air scoop, while the lab. men get up steam, then a plume flutters out, clears for a moment, then circles down and licks the air vent casing. "Hell," says Glen. "I tell you – it worked yesterday."

I don't say a thing.

A worried tunnel operator dives out of sight and, to our relief, locates a water blockage in one of the feed pipes. Whichever way we swing the turntable, a neat plume of smoke drifts up and away like in a picture . . . so Ship No. 736 (she isn't named yet) has a funnel.

Cunard red had gone to his head

The first sight the Cunard directors had of the model was when they gathered – from the City, or wherever – to be photographed around it for the Sunday press.

One senior director irritably points out that the smokestack is painted white instead of Cunard red. To pacify him, Sir Basil Smallpiece asks me to prepare an alternative funnel in the Cunard colour, so they can be compared. And I thought he was on my side.

A week later he rang. As a buddy of the Queen, he had arranged to show her the model: after all, it would be named after her. I was to meet him at the side door to the palace, and, "Oh, bring both funnels, please. Yours and the one in the Cunard house colours."

He would ask the Queen. To anyone not practised at objective visual design, it would look as expected . . . she would plump for the red one.

At the appointed hour, my model-maker and I were gingerly steering the fragile model into the hands of a flunkey, when Smallpiece asked, "Where's the red funnel?"

"Awfully sorry," I said. "It fell off this morning – and someone trod on it." Smallpiece just gave me a look.

It is launching day.

Five white coaches are feeling their way through the hard, cobbled streets of Clydebank. They are filled with privileged persons on their way to experience the moment when thousands of tons of steel will be given a name and then slide into the Clyde. Ladies are wearing hats, and such hats, to honour the presence of the Queen. Not the ship, *the* Queen.

Queen Elizabeth gives an inaudible speech, presses a button, the bottle drops, Rennie waves his bowler hat in a winding motion, as though to entice the ship to wake up and lumber down the slipway.

Can that massive chunk of landscape move? No.

After an interminable period of suspense (I am wondering whether we had better just go home and forget the whole thing) there is a sharp crack, a gathering roar and, through a cloud of rust-dust from the drag chains, she sends a wave down the Clyde as though a glacier has calved an iceberg. And there we are, looking at an empty space.

Once at sea, this great 'white elephant' proved to be a success – she even paid her way – so the bilious eyes of the press soon turned to reveal other scandals for the delectation of the *hoi polloi*.

I just heaved a sigh of relief and added a portrait of Isambard Kingdom Brunel to my pinboard.

The QE2 *at full speed ahead on her initial trials off the West coast of Scotland. The perfectly streamlined hull leaves scarcely a ripple in her passing.*

The cruel sea

Years later I experienced Wallace's 'pendulum effect', when Mehitabel and I ventured a return trip from Boston (first-class at half-price, nice). The great ship had to plough through exceptionally heavy seas all the way across: the First Officer reporting it to be the most violent gale he had experienced in seventeen years. I became anchored in a corner of the card room by a landslide of tables, while Mehitabel found herself performing acrobatics in the empty gymnasium, as a sixty foot rogue wave knocked a hole way up in the ship's prow. To my relief, the funnel stayed upright. Mehitabel actually enjoyed the trip. What a ship – what a girl!

Launching a hull stern first into Rotterdam harbour,
one can see she is wide in the beam.

Ugly duckling to swan

Having made a redundant steam coastguard-cutter look like a
yacht, a sticky problem put to me by a Texan tycoon, I was
asked to play the same trick with liberty-ship style hulls,
knocked out for ferries at a Rotterdam shipyard, again for an
American client. After working on the *QE2*, this was
comparable to switching from cutting Savile Row suits for the
nobs, to running up off-the-peg togs for weekenders.

These hulls, like many Dutch women, tended to be rather
broad in the beam, so (like many Dutch women) I applied
artifice, and made it a virtue.

First, I gave her a schooner-style prow, and the
superstructure a sculptural form. Radar mounted over the
wheel-house and outriggers on the dignified funnel, made
masts, which went out with sailing ships, unnecessary. Horns
for air vents, projecting port and starboard, gave her character,
if nothing else. I was rather chuffed. I also gave the peak of her
foredeck a slight downward curve to echo the lines of the
wheel-house, but the shipyard boss, a 'gent' of the old school,
was shocked. He had me up in his (grand) office, and gave me
a tiny-tot's lecture on what is and what is not, shipshape. He
told me the sheer on ships' hulls originated with clinker-built
whaling-boats designed to take heavy seas.

304

I pointed out that torpedo boats once had 'turtle-deck' prows, yet took heavy seas. Stalemate. One doesn't argue with an opinionated Dutchman – in his own shipyard.

Nevertheless, while he was stuck behind his mahogany desk, I did my thing down in the yard and faked her lines to give her that sneaky dropped-prow effect.

On the day of launching someone had given her the name *Peyton Place*, after a current American TV soap-opera. The Dutch do have a sense of humour, after all.

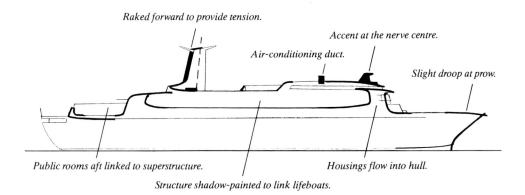

Raked forward to provide tension.

Accent at the nerve centre.

Air-conditioning duct.

Slight droop at prow.

Public rooms aft linked to superstructure.

Housings flow into hull.

Structure shadow-painted to link lifeboats.

CONTROLLED CURVES MASK HER UTILITARIAN ORIGINS.

Months later, enjoying a mobile breakfast passing through Rotterdam on the wagon-lit *en route* for Eindhoven, I glimpsed a very slick modern structure with 'spaceship' probes at its peak, towering over the rooftops. Then it dawned on me: I admired it because it was my own baby – the funnel of one of the ugly ducklings, or was she a swan?

'The French Connection'

Some years back the Paris branch of Shell, impressed by a permanent exhibit I had designed for their London HQ, invited me over to comment on their own efforts; an excuse, of course, for a lush go at the trough.

I admire the French their Frenchness but, being an inbred Britisher who skips lunch, I took a poor view of crossing the Channel to be officially lunched in Paris, where the two hour midday interlude is what life is all about . . . to a Frenchman.

Flight delayed, I arrived late to discover my neatly-tailored hosts lounging contentedly around the debris of an elaborate meal; lipping grape pips and fingering their brandy glasses. *"Ah, Monsieur Gardinier."* They are desolate. Head waiter tut-tuts, clears a place and makes up a plate for the inconsiderate guest. Eventually I am ushered off to view Shell's Paris 'temple'; flight of shallow steps, wide classical portal, cool marble hall.

To the left: shapely lady receptionist, in clinging black silk, smiles from behind an Empire-style marquetry table, set off by a single rosebud poised in a slender glass vase.

To the right: an even more shapely female, swathed in black, smiles politely at this baggy-trousered islander from behind her rosebud.

Carefully contrived symmetry. A whiff of perfume. I already envy the French directors their good tailoring and style (and elegant mistresses) as I am led on to view their exhibit. This proves to be the expected commercial display, albeit rather arty, but spoiled by a sound commentary which rebounds from the polished terrazzo floor. I venture to remark that, with ambient sound, a carpet is essential. *"Oui, oui!"* exclaims my host, but the cost of such a luxury needs to be authorised and the man who should do this is the architect responsible for the terrazzo floor, so *pas de chance.* Even the logical French suffer from architects.

Beau Geste

Some months later, installing a show for the UK Atomic Energy Authority in Geneva, it occurred to me that the wide expanse of soft grey carpet we had just laid would look very well in Shell's Paris HQ. Hunting out the designer of the nearby French atomic exhibit, I asked if he would do me the signal service, when the show was dismantled, of delivering our carpet to Shell on his return to Paris? He enjoyed the idea. Only too easy in a returning container. *D'accord.*

I squat on the floor, using the only telephone as yet connected to pass on the good tidings. A free gift being unheard of in today's rat race, convincing the Paris *directeur* that there will be no strings attached takes some explaining. "No," I say, "There are no customs' forms to complete. It's all arranged . . . You won't be asked to sign anything. It's a personal GIFT." A cough. My UK client, who is leaning against an incomplete doorway, has heard all. "Maybe I'm mistaken, Gardner, or did I just hear YOU giving OUR carpet away?"

I drop the 'phone and with a smug grin, "It's practical public relations, old chap – *entente cordiale* between the 'Brits.' and the 'Frogs'. Good notion?"

Not the end of the story. Some weeks later, Shell London ring the studio. Apparently this Paris *directeur* wishes to return the compliment personally. He is asking what form I would wish his gift to take.

A short interval for cognition then, "I have it! A pretty Parisian *midinette* to serve coffee in our studio for, say, a week, and add, she will be returned in good order, Club Class, Air France."

"You really expect me to signal that?"

"Well, they asked. Nice idea, don't you think?"

A doubtful, "Will do."

One morning a heavy package arrives from Paris. Too small for a midinette, in fact it contains three volumes, *Ancient Monuments Destroyed During the Nazi Occupation of France.* The French may have style and shapely receptionists, but no sense of FUN.

The 70's

THE MIXTURE AS BEFORE

I brush the dust off the word 'museum'
The Statesman and The Nabob
It just isn't done
Margaret Thatcher – milk snatcher
A peek under the carpet
The Mississippi Queen
Three days that shook the world
A stranger? Throw a rock at him

Meanwhile . . .

Patty Hearst joins kidnappers

Margaret Thatcher takes control

Princes Margaret and Snowden split

Film: *The French Connection*

Benjamin Britten's *Death in Venice*

Piggot's seventh Derby win

The 'Watergate' affair

Worldwide inflation

Genetic engineering a reality

Space Shuttle: maiden flight

Film: *Star Wars* takes $185 million

Japanese buy up much of USA

'Yorkshire Ripper' at large

KALFF'S DREAM

*"Unreasonable," said the engineer, "to expect concrete
to float up in space, supported by a devious theoretic
geometry and be bedded in sand. The thrust of that
flat dome and the balcony floors will be held by kilo-
meters of stressed steel cable. Once up, it should be
stable, but getting it up? That's a nightmare."
Remarkable. Once up, it all looked so simple.*

310

I brush the dust off the word 'museum'

The strident wail of a fire-float roaring up Haverstock Hill. Dedicated Muslims busy hanging dedicated Muslims – the population explosion in Bangladesh drowning in floods – in the USA the bitter war between Pepsi- and Coca-Cola is reaching its climax – thousands of old ladies are having their bags snatched and even that timid cat next door is having kittens. One good mark – I have never had kittens. This particular genetic pattern is best not repeated. I only exist when I am producing something . . . the question is, what?

Sniffing at a collection of corn-cob pipes to check if one was still smokable, I was reminded by Mehitabel that I should be preparing a booklet on, of all things, nylon spinning. A subject I knew only too well from my time in Camouflage, when I set up an experimental plant to spin yarn from alginate (that is, seaweed). No sooner were we able to knit ties with the stuff, a German bomb flattened the factory. Maybe the subject of spinning carried that ghost with it. Whatever the reason, I felt fidgety and decided I would concentrate better in some quiet spot – that pretty domed pavilion on the end of Brighton's West Pier?

Anyone can become engrossed in any subject if it is examined with a purpose and I rather flattered myself as a copywriter, but the lonely geriatrics who prowl seaside piers in winter were putting me off my stroke, so I packed up and made it back to Hampstead. If I hadn't I would have missed that old guru, Dr Lo Kalff, the Festival lighting guy, who was "just passing through."

The West Pier, Brighton.

311

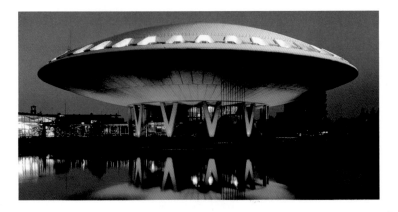

A technological salad dished up in space

At lunch, after objecting to the British habit of smothering our puddings with a lubricant called custard, Kalff tells me that Philips is building a great flying saucer, poised in space, over a lake at Eindhoven. He sketches it on the back of a dinner-plate, then tells me that it is designed, ". . . to shoehorn the people of the Netherlands into the twentieth century," and to show how technology motivates modern society, just as what's under the lid motivates a car. I am wondering why the philosophising, when he comes to the point. He will be retiring soon and would like me to take over planning the theme and exhibits for this project, to be called the Evoluon – meaning *evolution*, I guess. "Fine," I said, concealing my excitement. After fishing around all the designers at the Festival of Britain, he had hooked me.

Then nothing.

A month later Shell, for whom I was preparing a museum, sent me to Rotterdam to be lectured on the intricacies of the hydrodesulphurization of oil (using water to get rid of the sulphur). Sitting alone in a lecture theatre, while three white-coated chemists chalked carbon chains and catalysts on the blackboard, I thought – why not pop over to Eindhoven and pay a return visit to Kalff?

I cringe at even appearing to be soliciting for work, so flourished the bulky Shell file as the reason for "just passing through." I got the job. There is no greater talent than being in the right place at the right time.

So started a period of cross-Channel commuting, when the dining car attendant would lean over deferentially and murmur, "The usual, sir?" Very executive.

I was already doodling visuals for the interior when the building was no more than a pit in the sand. As I saw the great flying saucer slowly take form, like something from a Wellsian space odyssey, my pretty sketches seemed somewhat trivial.

Ascending from the level of the lake in a glass elevator, I would tiptoe round the upper gallery as though on treacherously thin ice. Custom soon normalized the situation – as a fly must find when walking on the ceiling.

Not being a neat little high-speed, mini-mechanism like a fly, but a slow-moving quadruped on its hind legs with a lump of jelly up top that concocted mental worlds of its own, I had problems. How to connect with visitors who, quite properly, expect a museum to comprise silent, echoing halls; sanctuary for artifacts from the past, hermetically sealed in glass cases?

Bateman said it all in a poignant cartoon sequence . . .

Untidy youth, bored, breathes on a glass case.
Janitor drags him off by the scruff of the neck.
There follow long years languishing in prison.
He is, at last, released, now a bearded old guy with a stoop.
Undefeated, he staggers up the museum steps, breathes heavily on the glass case – then falls flat on his face, dead.

I decided I would not have any glass cases, or anything I had so far seen in museums . . . not that I had visited many except, when a student, to take details of a bit of art, or to peek around wistfully for a pretty girl pick-up.

My own groping to discover the *how* and *why* of things gave me a base to work from, and experience of exhibiting in World Fairs provided the technique.

I little realised then, that the way I dealt with these problems would open the door to a new perception of museums, world-wide.

Sitting in my corner, surrounded by reference books, I had laid out a circulation route like a herbaceous border of ideas and was well away writing the storyline – when I was stopped in my tracks.

A SANCTUARY FOR ARTIFACTS

313

An avalanche of experts

I had been commissioned by a multi-national consortium and each department had formed a committee of experts to advise me. Frustrating, as technicians are programmed to think along one line, while I tend to think intuitively – across the board. I had previously been briefed on atomics by John Cockcroft, on radio-astronomy by Ryle, and had been responsible for untangling exhibits on DNA, fluid-bed furnaces, chemical plants and the breeding of plants. I would casually throw in such titbits of experience until Van Puffelen, who had been deputed to be my assistant, (the sort of guy who enters a revolving door behind you, but comes out in front), said, "So that is your strategy. You use one-upmanship to retain control."

One-upmanship? I only knew that a concept could be destroyed by just one misconceived proposal minuted by a committee. We were deep in one of these meetings when a Professor Schouton strode into the room. The chairman (one of Philips' hatchet men) was outraged. "What do you want?" he rudely asked. The Dutch are nothing if not direct.

With a twinkle in his eye, Schouton replied, "I belong to the RSPCG."

"And what the hell does that mean?"

"The Royal Society for the Prevention of Cruelty to Gardner," he replied. "Come on, G. Time for lunch."

In the car he quietly pointed out that the human brain can be destroyed by a massive contradictory input. In attempting to defend my mental integrity in the face of such overwhelming numbers, I would lose coherence and motivation. There were no more technical meetings.

Schouton had founded the first Laboratory of Human Perception in the world. To know that he was truly concerned with what, for want of a better name, I call my brain, helped to bolster my fragile self esteem.

A logical, balanced design is invariably a one-man concept and, given the chance, opinionators and office-holders will rape it. Solution? Develop another idea, or walk out. These technicians dealt with words and even Schouton, when in committee, must always win. He had a trick of letting you say your piece and, when you had finished, fixed you with a penetrating stare, saying, "And . . .?" Of course, you had nothing to add and looked a fool. Later he would pat me on the back and say he agreed with me, in principle. Thank goodness he was on my side.

A lucky dip of visual images

How can one make particle physics, wave theory, electronics, hairy angles like genetics, and human perception *user-friendly* to the ordinary visitor? If I visualise them as I – an 'ordinary' like the visitor – understand them, we will at least avoid boring them with lectures on science.

I will use well understood images as they come up in my mind, but arrange them in unexpected contexts . . . surprise focuses the mind. It may even focus mine.

As visitors step from the glass lift, they will be faced with a giant photo blow-up of the disordered and creepy imaginings of Hieronymus Bosch (the anarchy of a mind not harnessed by logic).

Creepy images of myth and mystery, before the logical patterns of reality were explored.

In contrast, below the geometric facets of a quartz crystal, the modular pattern of a honeycomb drips, producing expanding ripples on a pool of mercury. For the mystery of time, the regular blink of an atomic clock (the order which underlies reality).

Okay for a side exhibit. Something more dramatic as curtain-raiser? A wide primeval rockscape setting, pouring lava, rumbling, flashes of lightning . . . only possible because I have Kempster on hand to paint it elegantly, and Philips to provide the rumbling and lightning. Dramatic, but it lacks a point.

In the foreground, rock outcrops will reveal a sequence of fossils, first plant forms, trilobites, sea urchins, skulls of amphibians and a jawbone of a mammal until, finally, cuneiform script scratched on a rockface signals the presence of Man.

All very proper, but we need a shock to excite the viewers – something biological?

A little stone figurine I once saw in the Louvre, but greatly enlarged to life-size. A pregnant earth mother with ballooning breasts and elephantine backside.

(So that's Mum, birth and rebirth. Memorable.)

For the opening setting, a bit of 'theatre'.

When one of Philips' directors viewed the completed figure, he stiffened. "If that indecent object goes into the museum, I can assure you I will never take my wife there."

"Then that's too bad for your wife," said Professor Schouton. Good man.

Later, I proposed exciting young people with notions for the future – oceanic ice-islands, linear cities, and nuclear-powered dirigibles that, once launched, need never touch the earth again, forever poised on the air like an albatross. However, the 'Think Tank', a group of top scientists who would meet occasionally to sieve through our plans, all came to the conclusion (with no apparent sign of regret) that civilised man would not survive on this planet for more than fifty years at most . . . so *futures* were out and I came to earth.

One member of the 'Think Tank', a sociologist from Utrecht, had a gloriously simple notion:

THE ACCELERATION OF HISTORY

Primitive men would behave to the same repeat pattern for generations before any change in life-style became apparent. As they made tools and organised, (in the interludes when they were not perpetrating a genocide), the tempo speeded up more and more quickly until, today, the living environment changes dramatically before a person comes of age . . .

Then he went back to Utrecht and left me with the baby.

Fine, but how to devise an exhibit to put this *concept* across?

316

An idea that looks at you

Doodling, I boiled three million years down to five distinct periods. Simple to animate on film, but one doesn't visit a museum to look at films; maybe the key is how one presents them? (This was before video-players were available, even at Philips.)

I asked their technical men to develop a compact film-strip projector with a wide-angled lens and exceptionally short throw. I needed five of these and mounted each in a sleek housing like the head of an insect-man from outer space, its single Cyclops eye containing an animated image. The first of the five changes so slowly that one must wait to detect any movement at all, the next quicker, then quicker again, until the last flicks by so fast that one has difficulty in capturing the images at all.

Each of these one-eyed creatures has two arms. One holds a characteristic object – arrowhead, chronometer, electronic valve. Then I had a brainwave – the other arms would support large white discs, each rotating faster than the one before.

Many of my early ideas came from a memory of my Victorian granddad's collection of parlour tricks. There was a stereoscopic viewer which showed, in 3D, my aunts wearing flat hats and standing by their bicycles; a magic lantern with a slide that, when a handle was turned, showed Vesuvius erupting; an early gramophone, with a tin horn that travelled along a wax cylinder to announce in a nasal accent, "This is an Edison Bell Record," (one cylinder had actually been 'sung at' by Caruso). And – the Zoetrope. This was a slotted cylinder. If I rotated it and squinted through slots in its face as they flicked past my eye, I would see frogs jumping over a log; a sequence of cartoons inside the drum giving an impression of motion. The first moving pictures.

I cut slots in these revolving discs through which the modern viewer would see pin men. The first creeping slowly along, the next walking, the next running, until finally there would be the blurred image of a pin man leaping to catch up with himself. I positioned the completed space figures as though coming over the brow of an unreal hill of deep purple carpet.

So far so good.

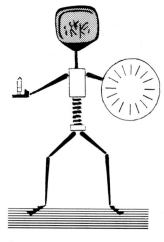

Spaceman.

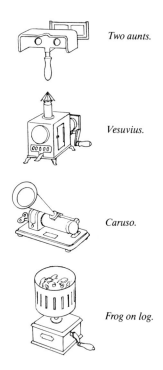

Two aunts.

Vesuvius.

Caruso.

Frog on log.

Revolving globe in spoon shows cultivatable areas. In sphere to the right, egg-heads ponder.

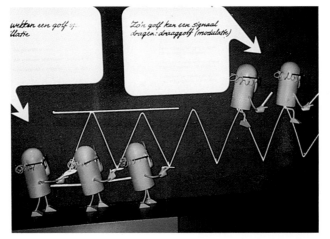

Electrons under control. Here two are riding along on a carrier wave.

Stonehenge a sundial? Professor Hoyle's theory that it was used to compute the seasons.

Quiz units on the upper gallery, mounted to the right, relate to the exhibits opposite.

A day's indestructible waste from New York, bulldozed across the gangway.

The end of a sewage pipe introduces Effluent and Pollution. Title over the loo, 'PROBLEM'. Dutch visitors, who are at least versed in lavatory humour, would wait eagerly to hear the loo flushing again – on tape.

GENERAL VIEW. TOP SCIENCE ON DISPLAY

I watch Mehitabel as she gazes raptly at the word processor silently feeding its floppy disc. Above her are five clock-faces, each giving the time in major cities around the world and, behind her, the FAX which transmits to them via satellite. She has a pocket-calculator, (I count on my fingers), reproduces with a photo-copier, cooks by microwave and decorates her apartment with non-stop sound (in place of wallpaper). She walks elegantly, but never more than a hundred yards, except when her loved one, a minicar, has been sequestered by the enemy for parking on a yellow line. Though we accept these electronic devices, even our own brains, how many people care to discover what makes electrons tick?

Who cares, anyway? Let's dream of an arcadian world; crystal clear streams, floating rose petals, poets playing the lute to the chant of 'Greensleeves'. Not on. I make the point with an illuminated title:

THE INGENUITY OF MAN IS UNSTOPPABLE

The word *ingenuity* is in motion, stretching, turning inside-out, then righting itself (all done with flexible mirrors).

Then *ingenuity* in 3D. A little kid has been playing with nursery bricks. First, he can just balance one over the other, then more and more bricks are added, until the final pile is an abstract in geometry so complex that one wonders how it remains stable. (And so do I, as I place on the last few blocks with a trembling hand.) Projected behind it, scaffolding structures, as in a modern city, in writhing motion.

I cross my fingers and press on to the next exhibit . . . half a mile to go.

There should be a flashing red light over my desk. Warning – don't design anything unless you know how it is made and someone who can make it. Someone to make it? Soon the studio is as busy as a street bazaar in Cairo.

No imagination

A sculptor, who is enlarging the little Stone Age Venus, offers up his clay before casting.

"Gosh. Voluptuous, I must say, but her fanny looks a bit odd?"

"It was missing on the original figurine, so I improvised," says the sculptor.

I doodle on a sketch pad. "More like this, surely?" He exits with a grin.

A breathless Phil, our chaser, arrives with what looks like a

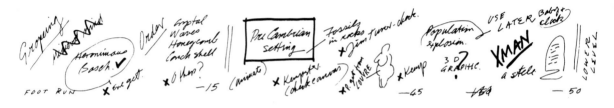

worm-eaten turnip. "This is the most complete wasps' nest I could find. It's a hornets', actually. One can't just get them off the shelf, you know."

"Not geometric. It won't make the point. Try for a bee honeycomb."

"Okay, but after I've collected the bells and bobs from the pin-table people at Balham."

We are foolishly attempting to construct a pin-table exhibit. Complicated. Moon-shot electronics couldn't be more resistant to tinkering.

Mehitabel butts in with a wide grin, waving a note from *The Times* newspaper. They write, 'We regretfully return your advertisement asking for a mandrake. We have to inform you that *The Times*' editorial policy does not permit the insertion of advertisements relating to witchcraft'.

"Would you believe it?" I ask Mehitabel to ring a craftsman I know, "Can he fake one for us? Tell him it doesn't have to scream in the moonlight."

I carefully place the last few blocks.

My desk 'phone is ringing. It's Chapman, the taxidermist, whose workshop was used on location by Hitchcock in *The Man Who Knew Too Much.*

"Hello. Chapman here. That tiger skin you asked me to set up. It stinks to high heaven . . . Ah, you knew. Well, what am I supposed to do about the eyelashes?"

"Hasn't it got eyelashes?" I innocently ask.

Impatient response, "They never do." He takes a deep breath and explains, "The natives always cut them off. They fetch more rupees than the skin."

Then, as to one who doesn't know.

"To slide on their pricks as an aphrodisiac."

A long pause . . .

"You can stick some fake eyelashes on, surely."

A grunt. He slams his 'phone back on the hook.

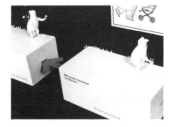

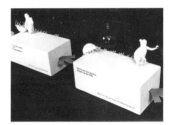

Blame it on the dog?

The dog is barking hysterically at the ankles of some truck-men who are collecting crated exhibits for shipping to Eindhoven.

Some days later, a 'phone call from the Evoluon.

"A grey metal container arrived with your stuff, G. Inside there's some tricky technical affair covered in gold foil. Our expert says it looks like a satellite component. Nonsense, of course, but what is it?"

Hell. Wrong box. Are we in trouble!

It's an actual satellite nose-cone on loan from the Space Centre at Daresbury!

Sneak it back to the UK? That'll mean mounting a 'James Bond' operation.

I appointed one of my assistants, an honest, wide-eyed guy, to pop over with a pick-up truck, collect the satellite and sneak it back past first the Dutch and then the UK customs officials.

"No need to act," I told him. "Just be yourself."

The ploy.

He would first show innocent items, some wine and Dutch cheese, then, before they discovered it, say, "Oh, and there's this."

'This' would be a realistic replica of the human brain, which the museum owed me, nested on a mattress against jolting. He

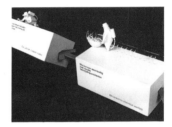

This to amuse the visitor.
Top: man planting – he sees a bug – sprays it with insecticide – bug falls off block, which goes out of balance. Man nearly falls, too.
Finally, man tiptoes along the tilted block – balancing his, and Nature's, needs.

would point out to the officials that the two little button-like blobs on stalks represented the bits of brain located behind our eyes. Creepy?

The officials would be so interested, it wouldn't occur to them to look *under* the mattress, or would it?

Misdirection! It worked with the Dutch but, alas, when the innocent John was faced with UK customs, courage failed him and he told all. No clearance papers? Tut-tut . . . .

He waited for some hours, under guard, until at last the chief beckoned him, gave a dismissive gesture and said, "Off you go. We haven't seen you, or it." A weekend ahead, they couldn't face the aggro, questions and paperwork involved. It's probably taken a year off John's life, but we had our satellite in time for The Royal Society meeting.

For a quiet weekend, a drive into the country, where many artists hang out, to check a painting, some crazy mechanism, or a giant glass eye in the making.

Maybe you are impatient to get on to the final episode. If so, turn to 'Blow the trumpets and bang the big drum' in the manner of a museum visitor who will study one effect, bypass another, then be attracted by light or animation to another. But you will miss a great breakthrough, the start of what museologists (some call themselves that) term 'Visitor Participation'.

Demonstrating the measurement of a 'lumen' of light as a metric constant may have a specialist interest, but the exhibit can be a delight to anyone's eye.

324

Why the pin-table?

That was for 'The Decision Makers'.

A charming figurine of a pregnant woman, mothering a clutch of young children, is looking hopefully up at a planning committee in session. They all have smooth, featureless egg-heads.

The visitor is given three desirable projects to choose from. Selecting one, the player shoots the ball which, as it bounces down the table, triggers not only bells, but the results of his decision on synchronised back-lit pictures and voice-over.

In each case, side effects are seen to negate any good that might arise from the project.

This to put across my pet theory – that unforeseen *side effects* restrict our lives far more than the actual laws.

From then on I introduced a QUIZ with a twist whenever we could think one up.

The angry slot-machine

Having completed do-it-yourself surgery on the pin-table, we took a deep breath and attacked the entrails of a slot-machine, *à la* Las Vegas.

Aiming to take advantage of the Dutchman's obsession with food, we replaced the customary fruit and bell symbols with appetizing pictures of meals set out ready to eat, inviting players to select, "What would you like to eat tomorrow?" When the discs are lined up and the player pulls down the lever, a digital counter tells how many calories they will be ingesting in excess of need.

The serious visitor, taking this in good part, rises from the seat . . . this operates the trick. Two slender brown hands pop out from the device and a voice says, "Thirty four percent of the world population will have only this to eat tomorrow." Cupped in the hands is a pitiful little heap of unpolished rice.

No one kicked the device in anger.

With my habit of pumping in any useful notion that comes into my head I introduced, on a panel below the slot-machine, cross-sections through a pig, a giraffe and a boa constrictor. Polarised animation traced the path taken by the last meal through their entrails.

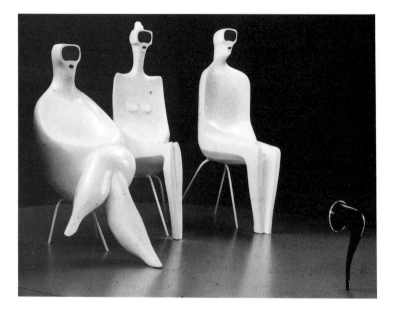

No videos yet, even at Philips. In the heads were specially-made slide projectors, pulsed to the commentary.

People as word processors?

Communication, that over-used word, meant a lot to my clients, who bounced digital messages off satellites.

Let's think – it starts when we mouth sounds. We modelled a group of baboons, beautifully posed and squatting around on some rocks, chattering. We then located a professor who – so he believed – understood their language. "Hi there, that's my banana," or, "Stop grooming my mate, you baboon."

Okay for baboons, but I had found, to my cost, that it is impossible to convey a visual image to another person using words, unless a similar image is already buried somewhere in the other person's head. How to get this across?

I had three smoothly-styled figures modelled, each with a small projection screen mounted in its forehead. One figure represented an academic, one a spinster (rather flat chest) and the last had a lower profile that indicated much time spent at the trough.

An early-type loudspeaker, mounted in front of the group, opened the conversation thus:

"I once had a pretty little bird as a companion . . ." Three images appear in the figures' heads. The academic sees a pigeon on a window-ledge, the spinster a canary in its cage, the businessman a pretty blonde poppet he once propositioned. But

326

already the loudspeaker has narrowed the definition ". . . a blackbird." The three characters immediately correct their mental images – the academic to a blackbird on his lawn, the spinster to a blackbird on her lawn. The businessman? His bird switches from a blonde white to a shapely girl from the Caribbean.

Each character develops different mental images as the conversation proceeds, blissfully unaware of the confusion. In fact, the academic terminates the talk session by remarking (with animated lips), "How gratifying it is to converse with people of like mind."

It was necessary to link speech in both English and Dutch with the picture programme. This led to a biting of fingernails as Dutch, a Germanic language, does not lend itself to the flexibility we have with English; the habit of saying what we really mean between the lines.

Having had fun, I must now deal with electronics. No language problem, as electrons are universal . . . if dull.

We show how a wave-trace of word sounds on a cathode tube is put into digital form – 001, 101, 110, 001, 011, and so on, then how this is sent as pulses riding on a carrier wave into space, at the speed of light, with twenty or more messages slotted together, to be sorted out and memorised by a satellite. When a path is clear they are directed to a specified receptor, maybe on another continent. There, the digital pulses are converted back into a wave pattern sent along a wire, to eventually activate the little diaphragm in someone's telephone.

"Hello. Is that Aunt Mabel? Happy birthday and, by the way, was Granddad's brain transplant a success?" All thanks to computerised men in white coats.

Asked to indicate the function of each light bulb, I had fun. Lamps were pirouetting in a frou-frou, piglets at a trough, or, as above, an internally silvered flood lamp dolling up her opalescent face.

Napoleon Bonaparte's mistress?

No laughing in church, please

There is no intentional wit in the Bible, yet God must have had a sense of humour. After all, did he not kid Man, a little cosmic blip, to believe he was the crown of creation? Professor Schouton once remarked that one reason why I had been given the job was that I had the 'English sense of humour'. Taking him at his word, I occasionally salted the sequence with a G'ism . . . a sense of the ridiculous acts as a release when the didactic take themselves seriously.

Example: to introduce electronics, we displayed portraits of the *name givers*, individuals immortalized by having their names linked to discoveries – Mr Volta for VOLT, Mr Watt for WATT, and Mr Bell for DECIBEL and so on. A bit of a bore, so I added one of my own.

This took the form of a portrait of a coy, high-breasted poppet of the Empire period. I named her *Madame Milly Meter*, the caption explaining, 'When Napoleon inaugurated the metric system, he was so enamoured of this lady's vital statistics he named the new code after her'. Philips' PR men would introduce her to visiting VIP's for a laugh – men of the world and all that.

One day we received a letter from a professor in Munich. Where, he asked, had we obtained the portrait? He had searched the records of Napoleon's mistresses, but could not trace one of that name. To this academic, museums, like churches, are devoted to serious thoughts – jokes are for cabaret and the simple-minded. The reverse is more true.

Having the freedom of the Evoluon, as it were, I was tempted to venture into unexplored territory.

An exhibit named Narcissus

Excitement at the arrival of television! Death to literature? But so much safer. Imagine the chaos that would result if those millions of individuals spent the long hours actually THINKING.

I wondered, do electrons, with their elaborate square-dancing . . . think?

I mounted two TV cameras so that each was aimed at the screen of the other and they could do their thing together electronically. We gave one camera a slight knock and a bright spot appeared on its screen. It drifted, leaving a trail, then both cameras began echoing each other's convoluted patterning without repeats, non-stop.

What was happening? Even the boffins were floored.

THE EXHIBITS. Many demonstrated topics quite NEW to the visitor.

Purely functional, it ended up with a head like an insect. The radar dishes were spaced well apart to give accurate range-finding, focused on moving targets by two acoustic 'eyes'.

Can we create a monster?

This idea was triggered off following a visit to an art show, which the catalogue described, quite seriously, as an exhibition of 'Cybernetics and Serendipity in Art'. One exhibit was remarkable enough to almost justify the hype.

A spine made of stainless steel vertebrae was delicately articulated to manoeuvre a head – and the head was a microphone. It would 'look' your way when you spoke to it. Each vertebrae of the spine was beautifully machined, with inbuilt valves and little polythene pipes feeding in compressed air (instead of blood), impulsed electrically by nerve wires from a little black box under it; the CONTROL.

It had been designed by some guy named Ihnatovicz, so I went to see Ihnatovicz.

When, at last, I located his workshop, a small mail order garage squeezed between two anonymous houses, the miracle-man turned out to be an artist with a mind that, like Leonardo da Vinci's, investigated. An obsessive perfectionist, he made the stainless steel spine segments himself, drilling and honing the valves to one hundredth of a thou'.

He explained cybernetics, playing with a discarded lobster claw from last night's supper. The lobster's limb has only five hinged joints but, by moving each one, just so, the lobster can position its claw anywhere within the limb's radius. (Actually it doesn't, any more than men use the full potential of their brains; like men, lobsters are lazy. But Nature has evolved it so it can do so if it decides to practice aerobics.)

"Could you make a mechanical lobster limb operate like the spine?" I asked.

"How about senses?"

"Why not use radar or an infra-red device to detect the warmth of bodies?"

He looked at the claw moodily, "Everything is *possible*, but it would mean a lot of experiment . . . and cost a bomb."

"Say I get the money. Can you devise a claw, say, (I thought big) five feet long?" He guessed so, and I left it at that.

Back at the studio, I sketched late into the night, designing a wide base to keep public (the destroyers) at bay. Result: more base than exhibit – we'd have to think bigger. I 'phoned Ihnatovicz, "Could you make that claw fifteen feet?" I could almost hear his mind ticking over the 'phone.

"No problem, in *theory*. It's all that dead weight accelerating at high speed, then stopping dead. Pressure up to five hundred pounds a square inch – could be a danger to itself." Doubtfully, "It would need built-in safeguards." He'd investigate.

I was turning his personal concept into an *operation*.

Never mind.

We dive in at the deep end

Back at Eindhoven, I launched the idea to the director who mattered. He grunted and asked what it would cost, so I essayed a figure sufficient to launch a moon rocket. A long, pregnant pause while he studied the ceiling. Hell. Why on earth did I decide to take up designing? "Agreed," he said, coming back to earth, "You must give me a costing breakdown." (I guess that's what is meant by the phrase 'creative accounting'.)

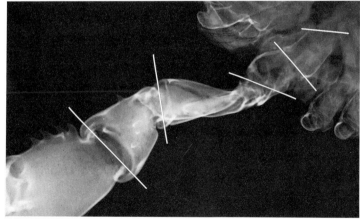

X-ray of a lobster's claw showing five angled hinge joints.

The SENSTER, as I later christened it, had a voracious appetite. We would spend more to justify the money already invested and I had a sudden sympathy with the guys at the Pentagon, who do just that.

I asked the director to fly over to see Ihnatovicz's test model;

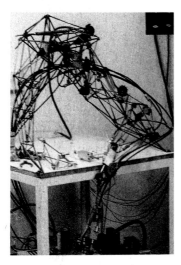

The five foot trial model,
which got us our production budget.

took him for a walk, round Hyde Park in the dusk, to soften him up, and told him the short-range radar developed by Mullard worked well, but what we now needed was a device . . . He stepped aside to pee against a tree.

. . . A device to flick its uncanny eyes instantly and accurately . . .

He then asked whether I could give him the 'phone number of a suitable call-girl.

. . . No, afraid not, but we had our eyes on a failproof micromechanism developed for the USA space programme . . .

He zipped up his fly.

. . . Miniature golden valves that directed the jets of the first moon module, so it could land itself – onto the soft moon dust.

"Good," he said, "You'll pick me up in the morning?"

Arriving at the genius's workshop, I dragged the flimsy side gate open and ushered the great man through a belt of sooty, spotty laurels to where the *Frankenstein* monster was being born. Once our visitor had disentangled his foot from a skein of wire, edged his backless chair away from the steaming kettle, "Is instant coffee okay?" and adapted his eyes to the low lumen level . . . he was 'sold'.

Against the welter of unfinished accidents accumulated in the struggle to give it birth, an abstract construction of steel rods was poised questioningly in space. Ihnatovicz fiddled with some loose wires in its home-made electronic brain (which filled a third of the available area) and the Senster started to move. It was like a thing alive, holding the antennae that were its head *level* – just like an ostrich when peeking round for a bun. Uncanny.

"That was a taped programme," said Ihnatovicz. Then he whispered, "See the red lamp? That means it will now make its own decisions. Say something." "Good," said the director, then jumped as the Senster's head swung swiftly round and peered closely at him with its listening eyes.

Ihnatovicz pointed to one of a hundred graphs that juddered out of a printer.

"Signals will be arriving non-stop and the arm must be reprogrammed instantly. That means *feedback*."

"Feedback?"

"Its 'brain' must know the position and intention of every joint, all the time."

Our visitor seemed a bit out of his depth, so I reminded him that when traffic lights suddenly switch to red, the instant unconscious calculation of how much to decelerate to STOP is far more important than the routine business of propelling a car from A to B.

Over coffee, I told the story of a civil engineer I was working with whose right arm had been crushed in an accident. In the hospital the nurses thought him a very quiet patient but, thinking harder than he had ever thought in his life, he was designing himself a mechanical limb. In fact, he regained the use of his arm but, having designed the limb, he constructed one for a thalidomide victim, a little girl of eight with no arms.

He made a left arm to hold the power unit, then strapped the mechanical right arm in position and instructed her how, by flexing her shoulder muscles, she could direct it – and, far more important, stop it. Imagine her excitement as the arm raised a fork to her mouth. But, what if the power of the gas cylinder propelled the fork on through her mouth to pierce her brain? Horror. But this little girl was properly instructed. After two hours' trial and error she was able to balance a cup of tea and comb her hair.

Our client agreed the essential golden valves.

The fifteen foot Senster eventually took pride of place in the Evoluon – linked to the 'hospital' emergency lines, so if it lost power it wouldn't collapse and do damage to itself.

By now the monster and its maker were one, so Ihnatovicz was shipped with it to huddle over sheets of printouts and brief the programmers, who would be its future custodians.

The erratic movements of the public were more complex than we had envisaged and controlling the Senster's reactions was more frustrating than bringing up a baby. A baby has been tooled up, tested and programmed over a period of four or more million years. Our baby was a first off.

Eventually Ihnatovicz departed (to recover his identity), leaving the computer programmers with their fingers still in its brain. One morning the monster was found shuddering in a corner of its den – it had had a nervous breakdown. I put this

Ihnatovicz working on the full-scale structure. He programmed its responses in a lab. at London University before permitting it to face human beings en masse.

The Senster in its den, focusing on the most active and vocal visitors.

down to a sense of rejection; there was no Ihnatovicz to care, only three part-time programmers on the verge of defeat. An electronic transplant or two cured the shivers and it would still take some interest in the public's antics; but its great days as the Loved One, when it appeared nightly on BBC television, were over.

Alas, the Senster went through its expense account like an adman. in a Bunny Club and so, as medics would put it, its life support system was, regretfully, switched to *off.*

Blow the trumpets and bang the big drum

Came the great day of opening, but Philips' PR, dynamic as mashed potato, omitted to include my name on the list. Designer gives a wry shrug and goes back to the drawing board.

The top brass, concerned at designer's absence, arrange for him (G) to have a VIP lunch with Fritz Philips (God) in his penthouse.

This penthouse proves to be so high up in the pecking order that the elevator cannot reach it. I arrive panting after climbing a sacred spiral stair.

Fritz (not God, after all) presents designer with a silver tablet incised with the customary complimentary message, terminating with words to the effect that *'Nederlands Philips Bedrijven BV will for ever be indebted to said designer'*.

Secretly hoping that this doesn't refer to his fee, G joins Fritz for lunch, over which the great man says he has . . . a problem. Philips have the facility to produce most anything the consumer may need. Snag, the other large consortiums are producing exactly the same things. G remarks brightly that he has noticed that. Fritz then comes to the point, "You're an ideas man. Then can you think of something *new* that everyone needs?"

True, I dreamed of owning a personal airship, quite a small one with a flag carrying the letter 'G' fluttering astern, so I could arrive at overseas meetings gently, on time and with some dignity.

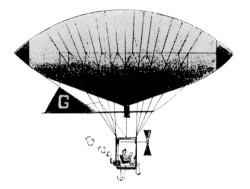

But a new *consumer* product? My mind went blank.

Fritz didn't switch off my 'life support' – refreshing to pick up that monthly cheque like a remittance man, with the difference, of course, that we had to work for it. At Eindhoven they were corporation men, trained to operate in rectilinear buildings furnished with modular filing cabinets, lined up as at a military parade under numbers. They asked would we please make all future drawings fit their module. I took pleasure in replying with the one word – "NO." A useless rearguard action – one can't defeat.

THE SYSTEM

My happy-go-lucky freelance 'need to know' method was now bogged down in group discussions and copies of everything to everyone; an impressive non-stop output of paper to be interred in box files.

This, at least, explained what was going on in those secretive tower blocks that were now taking over London. While the streets were already occupied by the enemy, a mass of almost identical cars, juddering and glaring balefully through modular headlamps, and as unstoppable as a column of Amazonian ants – except ants don't hoot.

Instead of wailing and gnashing my teeth, I left Duke Street to the enemy and risked oblivion by moving lock, stock and Mehitabel to Hampstead; now infested with bookish immigrants, which stirred a cockney bus conductor to sing out, as they once again broke the queue, "Passports, please."

Updating the Evoluon story. To keep pace with the population explosion in an electronically orientated world, the studio completed more than 3,000 drawings; meanwhile . . .

The Statesman and the Nabob

Clients didn't exactly queue up at Hampstead for design services, but fate flicked occasional odd-balls our way.

First a sultan. Embroidered robes, jewelled sword, scent of sandalwood? No. I found the wealthiest man in the world lounging in a bland Savile Row suit in a grand suite at the Grosvenor House Hotel. A buddy of Winston Churchill (polo and square-bashing at Sandhurst Military Academy), he wanted me to design a museum on the great man's life, not the statesman and wartime leader, but as a character – and he was some character.

Where? In Brunei, of all places, on a site which I later discovered overlooked a Taj-type temple and prayer barge, reflected in a still lake scattered with wooden dwellings on stilts. Backdrop, lush jungle where happy head-hunters lurked, carrying blowpipes. Here we go, *Alice in Wonderland* again, and what will the lackadaisical Malays make of an eccentric British statesman given to quoting Latin because he failed the subject at school?

Churchill had no head for business. I have a letter he wrote to me on Chartwell writing paper that I could well have used to float a bogus company.

My dear Gardner, (I had never met him)
I approve your proposal. By all means proceed as described, may I say at unnecessary length, in your letter of (date)

Churchill

This was in response to a request for permission to produce a figure of him in the costume of an officer of the Cinque Ports. Churchill loved dressing up.

The dunce, at Harrow School.
(Rendered as a translucent glass painting.)

Off to Chartwell to discover what was concealed beneath that bulldog image, and thrill to sit in *his* chair at *his* desk – a little bust of Napoleon as a paperweight.

More emotive than at the New York Yankee Stadium, where I was offered a seat and told, "Man, you're now sitting on Babe Ruth's bench, what do you say to that?" Little one could politely say.

Churchill's personal secretary was only too happy to reminisce, while I stroked the friendly old cat who had outlived him. (I refer to a purring tabby puss, not the lady secretary.) When I remarked on the fine Persian carpet in his study, she told me it was gifted by an oriental admirer, but one morning, when not in the best of moods, Churchill tripped on its fringe. Angrily asking for a pair of scissors, he spent an hour cutting it off. He was to regret this later, when a knowledgeable visitor, admiring his most valuable carpet, followed with . . . "Oh, no. What a pity. It's lost its fringe." The abortive operation at Gallipoli was not his only mistake.

It is common knowledge that, as a child, he played nursery games with a great army of lead soldiers and, I guess, that is why his father (Prime Minister at the time), disgusted with his poor showing at school, packed him off to a top cavalry regiment with barely sufficient money to purchase a horse.

But – the Nobel Prize for Literature?

She explained how, sweltering in the heat in his tent on the North-West Frontier, bored with the other officers playing cards and discussing women, he wrote home for some books. Lady Churchill (who took little interest in him) troubled to send *Caesar's War Commentaries.* Then it clicked. He set to and wrote his own commentary on the ineptly managed military skirmishes on the Frontier and forwarded it to the *Morning Post.* They published the article, sent a much needed cheque for £35, and asked for more. Thirty-five pounds for two hours work! It was obvious that the pen was not only mightier than the sword . . . it paid better! So he took up journalism, where he could deploy a fine turn of phrase instead of deploying a bunch of extroverts on fly-infested horses.

I have a sense of inadequacy when in company with other

Playing with lead soldiers.
Detail from a nursery setting.

males, (probably a carry-over from the abrasive world of the
school playground), yet I felt at ease with Churchill or, rather,
with my idea of Churchill. No Goody-Two-Shoes, he had his
detractors. Hilaire Belloc, the comfortable critic, referred to him
as 'that Yankee careerist' and it is true that he boasted an
American-Indian grandmother, charged around on horseback
waving a revolver at Sudanese tribesmen, contrived a hairy
escape from captivity in Africa and ordered the North Sea Fleet
to sea before war had been declared. Alas, in my view, he
cheapened his image by putting himself up as a candidate for
Parliament. Excusable, perhaps, in a man who was convinced
he would die young and must make his mark as bearer of the
family name.

He was a loner. At times of crisis he might disappear, to be
discovered sitting alone at his easel painting a bit of landscape
in oils. What a relief. A clean, blank canvas and the urge to
produce something wonderful for himself but never, of course,
quite succeeding.

"When I die," he said, "I will paint with colours more
brilliant than can be imagined in this world." Guess how I felt
when Lady Churchill presented me with his little palette knife,
still smudged with spectrum yellow and a dab of vivid
vermilion.

He was probably the first notable to order the processional arrangements for his own State funeral, which was followed to the letter. The end of an era. In his pocket, before they laid him under the flag, was found a photograph, not of family or notables, but his childhood nurse.

On the Day of Judgement, if necessary

After a year developing a storyline, preparing drawings and chasing exhibits, we crossed our fingers and shipped it all to Brunei.

No deep-water harbour in that lost world, so we off-loaded at Singapore and, in a tropical rain-storm, beached the crates from a still-operable Second World War landing craft.

I later discovered we lacked one item, a hat. Churchill would always don the correct hat for the occasion, so I punctuated his life story with a sequence of 'titfers' – the flat straw boater worn at Harrow School, the black trilby, the square-sided bowler, the plumed headgear of an Admiral of the Fleet, and even the stetson he sported on the Mediterranean.

When I purchased this on Madison Avenue and told the man behind the counter it was not for my head, but to top a replica of Winston, he exclaimed excitedly, "Oh, boy, believe it! Churchill purchased his stetson from me, personally. You'll have its twin." Stetson, okay, but I had omitted to include the grey 'topper' he would wear in the Royal Enclosure at Ascot.

Now where, oh, where does one locate such a hat in the wilds of Brunei? Ah, I had it, the British Resident. The smug, grey Rolls Royce parked outside the Embassy – a good omen – I signed the visitors' book, ignored the saluting sentry and asked for the gent himself. "James Gardner?" I heard him mutter impatiently to his secretary, "Never heard of him." True to Diplomatic Corps form he was shocked at my suggestion that a Resident would lend even his second best top hat to a commoner. An error. Only an innocent would request help from an inbred Foreign Office type – pointless as barking at the moon. As I left, I couldn't resist remarking, "I hadn't heard of YOU until twenty minutes ago."

Snowy, the English foreman, who ordered the installation as one would an army operation, had sent me charmingly phrased letters before I arrived; how he had arranged an account at the bank, engaged so many Chinese at such and such a rate, and, for eating, recommended 'The Lucky Lady' in Chinatown. Now, in the humid heat, he told me we had two new workers – for free.

Two lithe Dyak head-hunters, naked but for a minimal G-string, grinned up at us from the dugout canoe they had paddled (illegally) from a long-house somewhere in the Sarawak rain forest. They peered at us curiously, as we might at the odd behaviour of our monkey cousins at London Zoo.

Snowy soon had them housed in the loft over a nearby (illegal) cock-fighting pit and in no time had shown them, by gesture, how to lay plastic tiles. The acute observation of these young forest-dwellers had not been dulled by enforced schooling, as had that of the domesticated Malay students who solemnly passed our site on their way to college; sedate in identical white uniforms, with books under their arms.

We have too many *book* people – give me *the visualisers*, as when one of our Dyaks indicated that a silk flag which hung over an exhibit would look interesting stirred by the draught from an electric fan. Gosh, I hadn't thought of that, so we installed a fan.

The Sultan was pleased enough with the show and, after a sequence of reminders, his equerry paid us for the job . . . but were the locals interested? True, the museum is invariably crowded, but *then* it was the only public place available with air-conditioning; a cool rendezvous for a quiet gossip or boy-meets-girl. No doubt a number of Malay babies were named Winston.

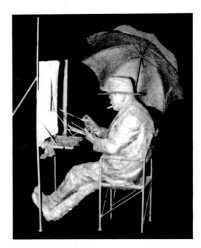

The final item.
A life-size figure, which was
replicated at Madame Tussauds.

In the story treatment I had considered Churchill's public image as a side-effect, focusing on his idiosyncratic indifference to the accepted norm. Very soon I was quixotically evading the accepted 'norm' myself, and it happened this way.

It just isn't done

We were busy working on a national exhibit for the 'Atoms for Peace' conference at Geneva, where Communist Russia was supposed to come clean (laughter in the next room), when a meticulous man from the Ministry arrived in a taxi, a sure sign of seniority, and asked if I would handle an exhibit depicting 'Britain Today' at the forthcoming Montreal World Fair?

In the sixties, the ad-manipulated 'yuppie' sub-culture had not yet invaded the corridors of power and this motivated man from the Ministry had troubled to look up the 'Festival of Britain' file, knew I was house trained and, from a design point of view, had a habit of coming up with the right answer. As bait, he presented me with a script that had been prepared by a Professor of English Studies at Oxford. This innocent don was happily airing all the old clichés: we have the Mother of Parliaments, cricket on village greens, Shakespeare at Stratford-upon-Avon, and bagpipes in the Highlands. He had added, for good measure, that we love children when, as every foreigner knows, the English love dogs.

Not wishing to be involved in a romantic stereotype exercise, I suggested (no charge), with a grin, that a more accurate rendering of 'Britain Today' would be a bucket of diarrhoea under a spotlight. This didn't go down at all well. The guy fled in his taxi and we went back to sorting out 'Atoms for Peace'.

To our surprise he turned up a week later. "Would you take on the project if we forgot all about the don's script?" Having passed a miserable week being castigated by my assistants for that misplaced wisecrack, I was relieved to agree . . . but only if I was given a completely free hand? He agreed.

"No interference with the theme?"

"No."

"Or a prissy editor playing with the script?"

"No."

Quite a party after he left.

Here we go again. I am to meet Basil Spence, who would be architecting the pavilion. A good choice. Spence's answer to a problem was never run-of-the-mill. On the other hand, our mode of parting on the last job we handled together had been somewhat theatrical.

I had remonstrated at his showing the pompous Mayor of Glasgow round the exhibits (a Town Hall in the offing?) and pointed out that, while the rest of us were still working after a night-long stint, here he was, "strutting around with the VIPs like a conceited cock robin." (He was then sporting a bright scarlet waistcoat.) Spence took a pace back, made a karate gesture and then pronounced, "G. We were as David and Jonathan, but the umbilical cord is forever . . . CUT."

The Scots are sensitive blokes, but *umbilical cord* at nine-thirty in the morning. Ye gods, he must have been serious. But we collaborated (perhaps over-politely) at Montreal.

There is an open conspiracy in the preparation of what goes into an international world fair, as the participants must avoid airing their dirty washing in public. Each government appoints a committee of politicians incapable of anything but bland generalisations. No decisions, as this might put one of them behind the tee ball.

Being firmly behind the tee ball, I decided to apply a litmus test to each exhibit – would it meet with the approval of a government committee? If the answer was 'Yes' – I threw it out. In practice this worked very well.

Seriously, you can't be serious

Where the mainline tracks at Waterloo slide into the terminal there is a narrow, cobbled canyon giving onto boarded-up railway arches. Stumbling against dented garbage bins, a huddle of sleeping winos and bruising my shin against a stolen railway trolley, I came on a weathered door boldly daubed with the letter 'G'.

Under the dim arch behind it, lit by temporary flood-lamps, stood a larger than life rendering of an English 'county family', posing self-consciously. Astrid Zydower, a young sculptress,

343

*Astrid's team in full swing
underneath the railway arch.*

whose work was on a par with that of Rodin, but I doubt Rodin
could have produced a sweet little girl in school uniform, a
'Twiggy', all angles and legs, a timorous country parson, or a
frustrated mum, with Astrid's sensitivity. She was wearing a
face-mask against asbestos dust and, balancing on a ladder,
touching up himself's left ear.

This archetypal image would introduce the world to 'Britain
Today' at Montreal. Why adopt this corny stereotype?
Experience. Viewing a national presentation, people feel rather
superior when you give them what they expect to see. For
Russia it was then a great figure of Lenin gazing authoritatively into the future (or a ventilator on the wall). For the USA
– Miss America; mass-produced, shapely girls in sun-glasses
and not much else, parading down a catwalk. All I ever saw
was the empty catwalk, but the American designer informed me
with some pride, ". . . and they wear fur bikinis."

344

After this, surely my stuffy English 'county family' will be no great shakes? Visitors will gleefully remark, "There's the English for you, still living in the eighteenth century." But then they are trapped by a running sign which reads:

> The English, are they . . .
>
> HYPOCRITES
>
> POMPOUS ASSES
>
> DEVIOUS EXPLOITERS
>
> STIFF NECKS
>
> STUFFED SHIRTS
>
> OR JUST SHY?

The notion of depicting actual people throughout the show could well have been a fiasco, had I not discovered Astrid. In the event, I came up with the ideas and Astrid, the figures.

Maquettes for the 'stiff-upper-lipped' county family. Parents and elder son, to the right, are already being distanced from the younger generation by a culture gap.

Ideas that passed the litmus test

I introduced the notion of the moment as it occurred to me – rather amusing, to think of all the other nationals beavering away in committee seeking the safe image. It went like this.

ROYALTY. People envy us our Queen (except the Dutch, who have one that smiles, but rides a bicycle). A replica of the Royal Crown suspended in space, diamonds glinting under a spotlight. Suspended alongside it, also spotlit, a portion of railway buffet cake priced at fourpence. Democratic.

NOBILITY. A dignified old boy in earl's coronet and full Garter robes. On his knees, garden trowel in hand, planting a standard rose-bush. Roses, of course, as in *Alice in Wonderland*, painted red, white and blue.

THE CHURCH. Round the corner, a mild country vicar is discovered balancing on a stepladder, as he attempts to hang a banner for a garden fête. Below, a concerned 'Miss Marple', her hands up, cupping his arse in case he falls.

What next – Parliament, the City?

"No, Mary Quant is for today," said Mehitabel. So off I go to her store in King's Road and to the now notorious Biba, where I grope in the dark for that brave new look, jostling with a gaggle of leggy girls with dolls' faces and heavily made-up eyes, seeking colourful tights, matching tops, sun-glasses, and kinky boots.

Some months later, in Montreal, a local window dresser and I battled all night with slick mannequins, purchased in France; aloof beauties with detachable arms and legs. We fixed tights to those idealised limbs with a staple-gun – to the sound of the Beatles' 'Penny Lane' on tape.

From miniskirt to minicar, enamelled with the Union Jack, its round-eyed headlamps observing the visitor from under sweeping eyelashes. The makers at first resisted this treatment, but after the show there was a queue of contenders to purchase the cheeky little car.

In North America, at that time, the Calvinist male ethic of short-back-and-sides (usually achieved with mechanical clippers, like sheep-shearing) was still current. Long-haired males were derided as *fags*.

First love.

346

THE BEAUTIFUL PEOPLE. Hilliard's classic miniature of Will Shakespeare's boyfriend posing dreamily in white doublet and hose. Alongside, in similar pose, a long-haired Carnaby Street youth in a flamboyant scarlet-lined cloak. He reclines against a phone booth, caressing the instrument. Title: Peacocks again.

BEAUTIFUL. A dainty dressing-table, cosmetics and lacy undies. Looking in the oval mirror the visitor saw, not his own reflection but that of a gorgeous, unattainable blonde going through the private business of making-up. She grimaced as she examined a spot, plucked an eyebrow, then pouted as she offered up her hair in different configurations. These intimate moments were, of course, on film and back-projected. I had trouble locating a goddess willing to show the ideal face 'in process', as it were. This exhibit attracted macho males like moths to a candle.

In contrast we had:

CITY GENT. Beautifully modelled, standing at a bus stop with bowler hat, briefcase and tightly-rolled umbrella. For the rest he wore 'long johns' (a body-clinging woollen vest and long underpants) which all true Englishmen subscribe to. By his side is his dog . . . no, it's a sheep. Title: There is no substitute for wool.

This was too much for the guy at the Ministry (who probably wore long johns) and he asked me to please remove it. I carefully mislaid his instruction – successfully, as it was knocked down for a high price at a Dutch auction after the show.

SUBURBIA. A builder's barrow on its side, with a scatter of white bricks. Follow the bricks round other exhibits to find that they have been laid out by a town-planner to represent an aerial view of a housing estate. One group of bricks, standing end on, looks for all the world like a cluster of tower blocks with, beyond them, a typical industrial estate – all modelled in white. Look closer and see it is made up of a hair drier, a kitchen mixer, a transistor set, an electric toaster, etc. Matchbox or office block – it's just a matter of scale.

The guy who inspired Shakespeare to write sonnets.

IN CONVERSATION
A scholarship student converses with a girl
'of good family' and her adoring girlfriend.
Posing below them, a modern version of
young Steerforth, from David Copperfield.

The experiment of introducing more than twenty different sounds in an area at one time proved to be quite acceptable; church bells ringing, birds twittering, kittens sipping afternoon tea to 'Tea for Two' and students airing ideas about themselves and the cosmos. The guy from the Cultural Office would walk through the show as it went up, to report on progress . . . with never a word; even when he stumbled against a figure of Mum with, in her shopping trolley, a packet titled 'Clean Air, 9*d*.'

I decided to terminate the show with . . .

ART GALLERY ART. Sacred ground. Only after the show had opened to the public was it realised that this innocent exhibit contained a time bomb.

Bypassing the Arts Council, I made a selection from the more adventurous art schools. These looked convincing enough when hung, and viewed by Astrid's version of a quizzical art critic.

More interested in the playing field.

The Sting

One painting, an abstract in greys and red was, in fact, a still back-projected on film. This would unexpectedly dissolve to a sequence of red images, a London bus, guardsmen, a pillar box, Chelsea pensioners, and so on, and then . . . the climax.

England had recently (to everyone's surprise) won the World Cup, so a still of our team, a frantic clutch in mid-air at the

goal mouth, in their red shirts. Then, on sound, a recording of the crowd's victory roar – "England . . . England . . . England."

The footballers slowly faded to that well known painting of General Woolfe, in his red uniform, dying under the flag after the capture of Quebec – and still the crowd roared, "England . . . England . . ."

At that time the people of Montreal were aggressively pro-French and, so, anti-British. It was obvious that this notion had passed my litmus test with flying colours. One of the local newspapers reported they 'admired our nerve'.

When the Montreal Expo. was in full swing a local newspaper ran a competition:

NAME YOUR FAVOURITE
WORLD FAIR EXHIBIT

The winner? When my landlady's cat conveniently died, I had her stuffed and set up as an exhibit, lapping cream from a saucer. Her picture on the front page – fame at last.

As for fame, I don't trouble to put my name on jobs, but once, when designing an exhibit for the *Daily Mail* newspaper, I was surprised to see my name on posters around Olympia.

I rang the editor, to be informed that the paper did not wish to take responsibility for some of my way-out ideas.

Par for the course

One morning my rather French hotel in Montreal, which closed early, discovered my bed had not been slept in. I was leaving the site late at night, when the lights and power were suddenly cut off, to leave me suspended in the dark in an open cable gondola, way up over a frozen lake, in a blizzard. After yelling for help, I was eventually retrieved, to be defrosted in a 'house of convenience', where local businessmen and politicians bedded their mistresses.

All good fun but, as a result, I was a day late picking up a fat envelope which contained a script from the Ministry of Education – for a show I was putting on at the prestigious Milan *Triennale*. A cover note from Mehitabel, 'You will probably decide to re-write this'. Terse, but how right she was. A laborious re-write on the hotel's lavender-tinted paper.

Milan, some months later.

"Have you seen this, G? Under-Secretary of the Min. of Ed. is visiting us tomorrow."

"Why the hell can't they just leave us to get on with it?"

"Well, they *are* paying for the show."

"Okay, but I'm not treating that bureaucrat to lunch."

"Oh, yes, you jolly well are. It goes with the job."

Apparently educated guys, even with amazingly high IQs, do eat, and all went well until we reached the espresso stage, when I heard myself saying . . .

"Do you know, I re-wrote your official script in a day, on a bed in a Montreal hotel? Not bad for a bloke who got nought out of ten for English and left school, if you can call it that, at the age of fourteen."

Pushy little twerp, thinks he, but must be polite.

"And what was the name of your school?"

"It didn't rate a NAME," I replied, "A common school where the Wembley brats were taught the 3Rs."

"Its name?" he queried – obviously a one-track mind.

"If it's of interest, it was off a side road named Park Lane."

"Well I'll be damned!" he exclaimed offering his hand, as an old Etonian would when meeting a classmate, "I went there!" *Touché.*

And so, back to the drawing board

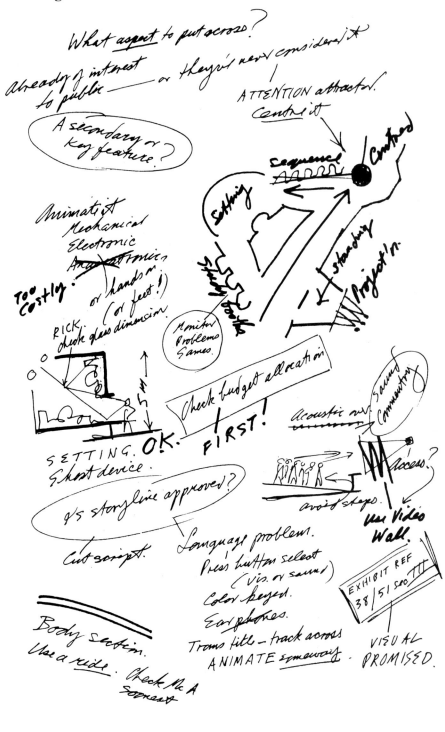

351

Margaret Thatcher – milk snatcher

One morning Mehitabel put on an upstage pose to announce that Margaret Thatcher had invited me to Downing Street for lunch. Joke over, I went back to my desk, but Mehitabel wasn't joking, and she flashed a card, "It's to dine with Manley, our ex-buddy, Prime Minister of Jamaica." Then the penny dropped.

Some time back I had been dispatched to Jamaica by UNESCO, all expenses paid, as 'Cultural Technical Aid' – a human sacrifice to heal the wound caused by British lack of interest in Jamaican affairs, or so I guessed. Arriving at Kingston Airport Mehitabel and I, sighting a welcoming committee from the consulate waiting to pounce, took evasive action and crept out by the goods exit. It took them two days to catch up with us, by which time friend Manley had manipulated the situation by announcing on TV and radio that I was there to design an important museum on Jamaican culture.

This was not in my bureaucratic brief, which I interpreted as finding a place in the shade from which to give *advice,* while Mehitabel lazed in the sun.

Now I was to put on a show in the slave quarters of a planter's house. No culture in sight, I thought it best to invent some. Result, a jolly time depicting Jamaica's turgid, hair-raising history.

A detail from the museum. Columbus' ships, stranded on his last voyage, the crew beleaguered for two years.
Visiting the beach, no sign of wreckage which must be buried deep in the sand.

Title: VISITORS TO JAMAICA

Arawaks contentedly swatting flies when not fishing. **First:**

Arrival of Spanish, who introduce murder by the sword and ship the natives to the mainland as slaves. The few islanders that remain prefer to commit genocide.

Planters from England arrive, bringing in Irish labour. The latter can't take the heat and get drunk on rum. Planters replace them with acclimatized slaves from Africa. These don't adapt to the European 'work ethic' and so are treated as animals. **Next:**

Many take to the hills and murder planters as a hobby. March into town with a live, white baby on a stake. Strong administrator sent over with troops; results in ambushes, killings and mayhem. **Then:**

A vicar from St John's Wood arrives to teach the blacks Christianity. They like it. A wealthy man cannot get through the needle's eye into Heaven? So God don't like them plantation bosses. **Response:**

A tough, acquisitive governor is sent in to make the best of it: profit for City gents and sanctimonious churchmen at home. **Result:**

Situation gets out of control. Morgan, the notorious pirate, obligingly hauls down his skull and crossbones, to be made Governor. **Crisis:**

He clamps down on anything that moves; introduces gambling, drunkenness and whoring. He also amasses an immense fortune.

A violent earthquake tosses Morgan's gang, with their 'pieces-of-eight', into the sea. Hopeless Government back home, to save face, gives slaves their freedom . . . (freedom to compete for a minimum wage). Most become indigent layabouts, leaving their women to do the work. **God loses patience:**

Shedding responsibility, the UK government eventually gives Jamaica her independence.

My theme – slave-chains, greedy Governors, mayhem and inept do-gooders – struck me as a pretty fair rendering of civilisation, when examined well away from the PR spotlights. Not exactly what Manley had in mind. He was a busy guy and I doubt he really cared. But, the British Consul had accused me of being anti-British, so I made for 10 Downing Street with some misgivings.

I needn't have worried. I was soon tossing a salad with the young Winston Churchill and passing the mustard to the Foreign Secretary. I decided Maggie would make a perfect character actress, playing hostess in a stately home whodunit; charming to guests and not at all pushy.

The PM and I had already met when we played a crazy game of cops and robbers with a mechanical cow.

The Brain Drain

This was triggered off when some press guy noticed that British scientists were flying over to the USA for better pay, and called it the 'Brain Drain'. Once the phenomenon was named, politicians woke up and even made speeches about it. Margaret Thatcher (while wearing her 'science' hat) decided to be seen

A visual for the area dealing with undersea exploration.

354

doing something about it by putting on an exhibition of scientific research – from the detection of sub-atomic particles like quarks, to useful tricks like growing pea-plants without any leaves, but which still produced fat peas.

The job of sorting out suitable topics and putting the show up was passed to me (the rabbit-out-of-a-hat syndrome again). This entailed sitting in sessions with five research councils, (who allocated the funds), then zigzagging around the country to chat up boffins for success stories.

I also had fun observing my new client, later termed the 'Iron Lady', at close quarters.

It would go like this. Robbie, one of those Ministry moles who concocts replies to 'Questions in the House', found time to assemble a page of wordy titles for the show, such as:

'AN EXHIBITION OF RESEARCH PROJECTS CURRENTLY FUNDED BY THE GOVERNMENT THROUGH THE SCIENCE RESEARCH COUNCILS'

I suggested a shorter one, **'SEARCH'**. Maggie put her tick against the concise title. Maybe she had doctorates in Biology and Law, but she could think simple.

When I presented my scheme, I was accompanied by this Robbie guy (ordinaries are never let loose near the inner sanctum). First an ante-room, so hushed by the near presence we might have been waiting for an audience in the White House. Two natty young men came out of her door, were called back, then came out again in a flurry. There was a long interval while Robbie, obviously a believer, grinned nervously and straightened his tie for the fifth time. This annoyed me. "She's probably pulling her knickers up," I remarked, in an anything but hushed voice, with the result that he was blushing a beautiful pink when we entered her room.

When I could find a chair on which to open my folio, I found that she was sufficiently on-the-ball to understand how I proposed demonstrating the birth of our galaxy, three-dimensionally, by projecting controlled lighting through a web of fibre optics. Anyone who has tried to explain practicalities

SEARCH CARTOONERY
Scientists enjoy my poking fun at other laboratories – but rarely their own.

The minutiae of fish-scales.

I have it! It's 'Medusaitis'.

A day's stint at the weather centre.

to politicians will consider this sufficiently remarkable. She said that she looked forward to seeing it in operation, and added, "That is, if I am still in office when the show opens." Two good marks: first, for cottoning on to how the device operated and, second, for admitting to an outsider that her political office could fold, just like that.

These august research councils were made up of middle-aged boffins – all teetering on the edge of becoming Nobel Prize winners, or being put out to grass. When I (modestly) pointed out to Maggie how even I could see that some notions put forward by the Medical Council probably dated from their own student days, she told me to go ahead under my own steam. Terrific!

Some research men can be quite sensitive. There was a rather self-important lab. director named Professor Swallow, who closed the doors to me after I had addressed my 'thank you' letter to him as Mr Bird. (Fortunately his staff let me in by the side door.)

The animal that caused the battle was brought into the show when I realised that a cow is a mobile processing plant – grass in at one end and milk out of the other, but we know not exactly how. To make this newsworthy, I had a full-size reproduction of its insides constructed from an assembly of 'found objects'. In the process I discovered the answer to a structural problem that had always worried me. When a cow stands, looking at nothing, ruminating, its neck appears to be much too short for its head ever to reach the ground. A simple answer. The hinge-point is not at the top of the thick neck, as one would suppose, but near the base. That technical point cleared up, I could take a deep breath and get on with selecting its inner organs: a football bladder for a heart (pumping), a bellows for lungs (heaving in and out), three stomachs – one of which was tartan bagpipes, and so on. Then came the item that triggered off the battle – a specially-blown glass udder with its four dangling teats. The visitor pressed a button, an impulse flashed back to its womb, a sweet little calf dropped, a sponge, representing its lactic gland, contracted and – bingo – the teat squirted milk.

It had not occurred to me that there was a link between

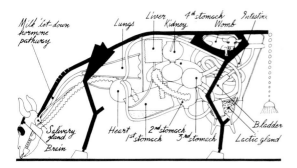

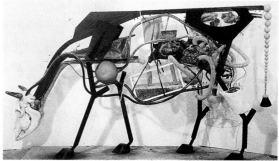

*The cow, as plotted on the drawing board
and the completed, animated device,
as assembled by Derek Freeborn.*

Maggie and milk. When her party came into power, each Minister was instructed to make savings. Maggie made the mistake of cutting free milk for primary schools. Education is a sticky subject closely watched by parents. How else could they get the children off their hands for five hours a day? Result, banner headlines in the popular press:

MAGGIE THATCHER – MILK SNATCHER

I was somewhat taken aback when a Ministry watchdog instructed me that my cow must not operate. He was having palpitations at the thought of his lady boss walking around on opening day, initiating a jet of milk and the press having a field day. I argued that when she cut the milk hand-out, she was acting in her 'education' capacity, here she was concerned with 'science', but to no avail. Was the man a glue-sniffer?

In the heat of the moment I lost my sense of humour and sent a pompous letter to the Department of Education and Science, directing its attention to three facts: Britain was not yet a police state; civil servants could not introduce political issues into an independent scientific(!) demonstration; and I proposed going ahead with it. Mehitabel said not to send it, and how right she was.

Some days later, when I steered Maggie round the preview and the cow obligingly squirted, I told her what "those idiots from the Ministry" had said. There was little she could do but reply, "How foolish." But the Whitehall 'mafia' was ahead of me; they sequestered the key to the pump. Although I had other problems, I gunned my car to Parliament Square and had I owned a gun, I would have carried it with me. To my consternation, the guy there just went po-faced and handed me the key. Why? They had sabotaged the mechanism. After a back-aching performance under the platform, we got it working and on the day Maggie did squirt the milk.

The press? They were busy photographing the Duke of Edinburgh.

OPPORTUNITY. *Sketched on the road to Annapolis. Surely there will be a gap in the jigsaw – some place, for me?*

A peek under the carpet

Having joined the flight of boffins across the Atlantic, I am in Manhattan.

A New York cabby who, from the photo on his permit, is probably on parole from Alcatraz, slides his mouth round a thick neck to emit a sound I interpret as, "Your pipe stinks." This was before smoking had been classed as an un-American activity and even Jimmy Carter, the President, smoked a corn-cob. This guy obviously doesn't like limeys and I am not sure that I do, but I can't leave it at that.

A couple of blocks later I risk being chucked out onto the sidewalk, by shouting through the perforated grille, "New York stinks." Redneck swerves, avoids a limousine and, as the taxi bucks a manhole cover, mutters, "You can say dat again." Actually, I rather like New York.

The clerk at the hotel desk wishes us a nice day and hands me a message. It's from a prospective client. *'You are invited to attend a non-negative thinking breakfast meeting at The Plaza Hotel, Monday, 8 a.m.'*

Obviously early birds – that means a working weekend. I look round the stuffy Sixth Avenue hotel room; not a choice place to prepare a scheme. Then I have it and 'phone Mehitabel who is trapped in a similar stuffy room down the corridor. "Chinese laundry here," (our call sign). "Remember the lush offices of that architectural partnership on Park we visited the other day? It'll be empty over the weekend!"

To satisfy the security guy in the elevator lobby, we sign in. Eighteenth floor, acres of air-conditioned work-places bathed in fluorescent light. Mehitabel dodges a rubber plant and settles at a desk with a typewriter. I plump for a draughting board with, gosh, an electric pencil sharpener. Nice set-up. Locating the coffee dispenser and a packet of assorted crackers, she coolly serves a stray member of their staff who is, apparently, also working a weekend stint. Later, in all innocence, he obligingly runs off some dyeline prints for me.

With such walk-in facilities available, why pay rental? Should try the coffee dispenser at the Pentagon next time. A joke? No.

We infiltrate the Army

A month previously, in the Hungry Horse – a Chelsea restaurant – I had the honour of meeting David Bauer, who started the Friends of the Earth, to discuss possible sites for a World Centre. Malta? No. Too insular. Stockholm? No. Way off the map. Bauer then suggested Fort Baker, just over the water from San Francisco. "Isn't that where 'Sergeant Bilko' was stationed?" And it will soon be available, he tells me.

The Army refused to collaborate on grounds of *SECURITY,* so we tried the direct method – Bilko-style. Cross the Golden Gate Bridge – pay off taxi at gate – no duty officer in sight – go ahead. Mehitabel held one end of the surveyor's tape, while I paced out areas. A passing officer, swinging a tennis racquet, sang out, "Have a nice day." We did. Mehitabel gave the impression that she was *not* taking photographs, while I squatted on the front steps of the Commander's HQ, a drawing pad on my knees.

True, it was a weekend but, unchallenged, we didn't even have the fun of *pretending* to be Communist spies. "No wonder the Japs. got away with Pearl Harbor," I grumbled, as we legged it back across the bridge in a deluge of rain.

This project proved to be a non-starter when I discovered that I was expected to solicit sponsors to provide funding for the show.

Women's lib in the football world?

This time a Hall of Fame for the Ivy League took us to Rutgers and Harvard to be indoctrinated, then on to Noter Dame (sic) to meet their coach. Posh office (obviously more important than the President). He slapped me on the back, "So, you're G." Then, obviously impressed by the demure Mehitabel, he steered me into the adjoining room and, indicating a gaggle of ex-cheerleaders tapping at typewriters, made a proposal, "Say, Gees, what about trading three of mine for one of yours?"

MY LAND IT IS OF THEE

Next, a heavy session of game talk – incomprehensible to me – as I crouched in the dark watching a film with the Harvard team, as they dissected the tactics used by Yale in their last battle. Dedication . . . as when Colonel Garbish, (three times 'All American', who married Chrysler's daughter), accosted me on Madison Avenue. Indifferent to the bustling ad. agency guys pressing past us, chasing the dollar, he told me how, prior to going onto the grid, his team would pause for a prayer to God. Tricky decision for God, if the opposing team also happened to be asking for support. Hell. I was not born to be a football fanatic; there were no poppet cheer-leaders to egg *me* on with a, "G-a-r, G-a-r, Gardner – design us a Hall of Fame."

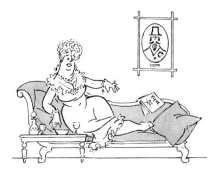

Probably came over in the Mayflower.

Football landed us with the Army again, at West Point, where guys like Eisenhower and MacArthur were programmed, and the shoulder-blades of the young cadets touch, even when saluting a lamppost, "Yes, Sirrr . . . "

By chance, it was passing-out day and, as a visiting officer, albeit from the wrong army, I took my place with Mehitabel on the saluting dais, shoulder to shoulder with the Commander. In the sparkling sunshine we were faced by five hundred cadets lined up like freshly-painted toy soldiers. A silver band struck up 'My Land, it is of Thee' – the Stars and Stripes was hauled up the flag-pole – the Commander saluted – I offered an English salute – the cadets saluted as one, but their eyes were not on the flag – they were all concentrated on the first girl in Maryland wearing a miniskirt.

Alas, that crazy effort came to nothing. My impressive exhibit sequence was okayed, but the New York architect they had engaged proposed a monumental structure that swallowed-up all the funds in monumental preliminary fees. That, as they say, is how the cookie crumbles.

In Maryland – Sir James

Designing a new Science Center in Baltimore, I was invited to the country club. The top lady, who probably came over in the *Mayflower,* but was now reclining on a sofa, graciously gestured me to join her, as our Queen might when asked to be kind to some guy from a banana republic. Honoured, of course. Dry Martinis all round and polite conversation – hard work.

We were interrupted by the arrival of my client, a smiling six-foot-six, Brooks-outfitted, grown-up college boy.

Avoiding the cashew nuts and wineglasses on the low table, he leaned over to offer me a slim envelope, booming in a loud voice, "Your cheque, Sir James. Fee as promised. Okay?" (He insisted on calling me Sir James, much to Mehitabel's amusement.)

In England, to be handed one's fee in public would be unthinkable, but this was the USA.

Jobs now telescoped one into another and, before flying south to try my luck in Alabama, I found myself buzzing over Chesapeake Bay in the plexiglass dome of a pretty little helicopter. I was to design exhibits, in an old tobacco barn, for a Washington lobbyist who aimed to convince doubters that the nearby atomic power plant would not adversely affect the environment. (This was, by the way, before the Three Mile Island incident.)

Important, as this was the breeding ground for tasty Maryland crabs, which had settled in the mud to have sex – sideways – and bring up their young, long before we arrived on the scene. I was to demonstrate how their youngsters, sucked in by the power plant intake, would be filtered out and tossed back into the bay by revolving scoops. I could visualise bored crabs queuing up for the free happening, as if at a brachiopodal funfair.

Eventually, arriving in Alabama, I met Birmingham's (surprise, black) Mayor, who told me his City Council were planning a large museum centre to show the smug Northerners that, "We may be way down South, but are, nevertheless, 'civilised'," – or words to that effect. The rabbit-out-of-hat syndrome again, but a welcome change from college football.

Installed in a vacant storeroom at the rear of the fire station, interrupted spasmodically by inquisitive firemen with Maxwell House coffee in paper cups and the wailing of sirens, was a no-go situation. A quiet place to work? Mehitabel unfolded a map, "Panama City!" she exclaimed. "It's on the Gulf – probably another Old New Orleans!"

How wrong can one get?

A dull day's drive south across flat everglades. Comatose alligators, the only occupants, lazily opened one eye as we passed. We hit the coast to find five miles of honky-tonks, dolled up motels, Disney World-type horrors, rumbustious kids screaming and waving cans of Coke as they tore around in cars with open exhausts. Hell on earth.

Exploring the coast, we located paradise. A private, enclosed domain for the affluent. We hired a neat little house set by a man-made lake with, beyond, a velvety green man-made landscape. No indigenous flora or fauna, only the occasional tycoon gliding from one green to the next in his silent electric buggy.

At last we could settle down to groping for a version of the past that would give the Southerners a new vision of themselves.

After the psychological relief of completing super treatments for the proposed museum, I felt somewhat uncomfortable. Produce ideas to impress visiting New Yorkers, okay, but surely it was somewhat arrogant for an (uncultured) outsider to impose his notions of culture on the locals?

To them, a museum is a cocooned area one enters on tiptoe, as into a cathedral. But Birmingham was already dominated by two towering edifices, as authoritative as any cathedral.

THE SCHLOSS BLAST FURNACES
Now red with rust, dead monuments
to the birth of the city. Floodlit with,
below, a treatment designed to make
them a focal point for exciting activity.

I had already proposed telling the tough story of people and steel in the rolling-mills at their base. Then, in contrast to the pasteurised landscape outside my window, I let rip. Getting out my pastels, I visualised an area where people could let their hair down and enjoy high jinks, games and each other.

Not bad for 'off-the-cuff', thinks I, as, bypassing the overfed golfing gents, we headed back for Birmingham.

My treatments were okayed by the Mayor but, meanwhile, some New York architects took so much in fees, it left nothing in the kitty for exhibits.

Putting it down to experience, I invoiced for minimum expenses – at least the Mayor now had some pretty pictures.

Then, off to Virginia where my world turned a full circle: echoing the bogus Mississippi river-boat on stilts at Battersea – I found myself designing the real thing.

An architect from Virginia, after the doubtful pleasure of crossing the Atlantic on the *QE2*, asked me to collaborate in the design of a new Mississippi river-boat. I paused for a moment, picturing one of those pretty stern-wheelers with smoke bellowing from tall, spiked funnels, then coolly replied, "Happy to," – as though detailing paddle-boats was a daily routine. To myself I said – "Whoops!"

This Virginian had a leisurely practice, designing comfortable one-off residences for comfortable one-off clients, operating from a folksy little township, which was for all the world like the setting for a TV soap opera. An odd-man-out, more interested in the arts than horses and the ball game, he visualised a river-boat with the sleek, authoritative lines of the *QE2*. After all, she would be the Queen of the Southern States.

His old man, who was funding the project, was expecting the more romantic rendering, as pictured on the record sleeve for the Rogers & Hammerstein musical, *Show Boat:* a pretty wedding cake affair with curlicues and tall smoke-stacks – not that wedding cakes have smoke-stacks.

Faced with conflicting commands, I should have gone rigid-mad like one of Pavlov's dogs. Instead, I decided to use my own judgement.

364

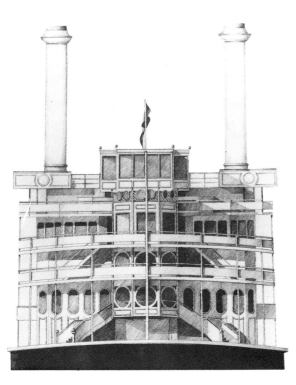

The Mississippi Queen

A philosopher named Le Rochefoucauld – I guess he must have been French – once made a creepy, but profound, remark, "Everyone complains of his memory, but no one of his judgement." Creepy, because a designer starts making judgements as soon as he puts pencil to paper.

How easy it is to slip up. Asked to install a bathroom in a foreign embassy for a Far Eastern princess, I partitioned it with rectangular glass bricks, then in vogue, to admit light to a passageway.

The contractor saved my life by suggesting I come over to view the result. Standing in the passageway one saw hundreds of miniature images – as in a fly's multiple eye – of a grinning workman standing in the lady's bath, aping a grotesque rendering of *Japanese Princess Stroking Thigh*. A lovely idea, but not on . . . so back to the drawing board.

With that warning in mind – to Virginia.

A double breasted turkey?

Our car juddered over cattle-grids and past velvety green pastures where well-groomed horses posed, as though waiting to be painted by Stubbs. We were to stay the night in one of those rare colonial houses that had not *Gone With The Wind*, which gave me the feeling of inadequacy I suffered as a boy when selected to take part in a game of charades.

The Charade

Tiptoeing to the top of a delicate, sweeping stairway, *en route* to the dining room, I had second thoughts, did a quick about-turn to switch my woolly sweater for a creased, but fairly white, shirt. I murmured to Mehitabel, "You look super," but she took no account of this, knowing I was biased, and my remark seemed excessive when we were introduced to our client's lady; a slim, Swedish ex-airline hostess, sheathed in chartreuse silk. Expensive . . . and so was the table-lay.

Candlelight reflected in gold plate – not any old gold plate, but dishes from which George III had actually filled his belly, and still bearing his engraved cipher.

As our host carved the roast, he proudly volunteered that the trussed corpse I referred to as a chicken was not a chicken, but a double-breasted turkey. Stumped, I tried to picture a turkey suckling twin chicks . . . there is the duck-billed platypus, of course . . . ? Meanwhile, I was concerned that he repeatedly addressed me as "Sir James," which induced the delinquent feeling of not having been hatched from a properly certified egg. Too true, I guess.

When coffee was served in the cherry-wood study and our host asked for news of the Royal Family, I decided it was time to come clean. I pointed out that (a) I was not particularly interested in a family which is a cosseted relic of an ancient mafia that parcelled out Europe to their relatives, committing incest and fratricide *en route* – incidentally providing Will Shakespeare with some dramatic theatre, and (b) I am not a Sir, (for which the recipient kneels), but a modest CBE, which is hung around one's neck in a standing position, or words to that effect. By then the temperature in that room had dropped to near zero.

366

But next morning all was bright and beautiful. Mehitabel disappeared, to bounce round the estate on horseback with the lady of the house and, as a genuine 'Englisher', (albeit with some off-beat opinions), I still had the job.

Old style. Upper deck, locals and immigrants. Lower deck, cargo - hogs, pianos, hoop skirts, kegs, or raw cotton for export. These river-boats carried more cargo than all the vessels serving the British Empire.

Groping for know-how

Reading up on river-boat lore, I found that the old craft were occasionally re-vamped to stage bawdy shows, accompanied by drinks and high-jinks; hence the romantic *Show Boat* image. In practice, there were literally thousands of river-boats carrying cargo, maybe nine thousand bales of cotton a trip, down river. Some were built with an elaborate saloon for transporting passengers.

In 1824, an enterprising captain converted a deck into cabins, naming them after States – which coined the term 'stateroom', now used to identify top-class cabins world-wide.

The size of the cabins in our boat would not justify that title, but my architect friend enjoyed the jigsaw game of interlocking cabins, always with the aim of getting one more in. He eventually devised a neat club sandwich of accommodation mounted, nearly down to the water-line, on the flat hull. He treated the interior, including the public rooms, with uncommonly elegant décor, even co-opting an uncommonly elegant calligrapher from The Royal College of Art.

To fulfil the expectations of nostalgic travellers, I designed the exterior as an old-style stern-wheeler steaming up river.

The Washington, 1824.
The first river-boat to be
fitted out with cabins.

The old boats were timber-built, hence those tall smoke-stacks designed to carry the cascade of sparks away from the deck-houses. An owner would consider himself lucky if his boat survived five years before hitting a waterlogged tree trunk (origin of the word 'snag') or going up in flames.

No need to launch lifeboats or sing 'Abide With Me'. As soon as the boat settled on the bottom, passengers would gather on the top deck and shout for help.

To power her with steam was not the original intention, but a river pilot – Mark Twain to the life – demonstrating his navigation needs on a moonlight trip, pointed out, "You see that faint line of slick in the bend ahead? Get stuck on that, reverse on gas turbines and where are you? Still on the mud bank. Now with steam, I can screw down the valves until the boiler sweats and – she's off. Tell your New York gentlemen that." They weren't from New York but, to this river pilot, anyone north of Cincinnati was an outlander.

Meanwhile, I was discovering, to my dismay, that the pretty colour prints were just colour prints. As it was nearly a hundred years since the last authentic stern-wheeler was built, we would have no 'experts' breathing down our necks. Prodding around in a backstreet bookshop in Baltimore, I unearthed a faded paperback *How To Construct A Model Stern-wheeler*, where an enthusiast had made on-the-spot drawings of their construction and rig.

It turned out that the flat timber hulls were mounted with a series of tall poles, cross-braced with ropes to prevent the thrust of the paddle-wheel bending the whole set-up into the shape of a limp banana. No problem. We were building with steel. Question: how light could we get?

The yardman at Louisville, accustomed to building tough bull-nosed tugboats, proposed heavy vertical members to support the upper decks. These would obscure the view, so I took a trip on the Staten Island Ferry and measured its slender stanchions. They had been designed to support only one upper deck, but the yardmen shrugged, as if to say, "It's your baby," and I had my slender stanchions.

"Tall smoke-stacks!" exclaimed a shocked yard-man. "You must be going bananas. First bridge would knock them flat."

368

Damn. It had not occurred to me that there were no bridges in the old days, and my obstinate, "Well, we'll have to telescope them," was not well received. Question: how to drop them quickly when, at the last moment, a pilot realises that he has misjudged the flood level and, then, how to wind them up again not *encrusted with soot?*

Rope and pole bracing, to prevent the hull bending under the thrust of the paddle-wheel.

I doodled for some days with the soot problem, then the solution just presented itself, as answers to design problems often do.

The traditional gangway is hung out dead ahead to act as an aiming point, so the pilot can judge the line the boat is taking. It can also be swung out to the side if, for example, the captain decides to drive along the levee to the next point of call, to play dice with some buddies. This gangway, already over fifty feet long and six feet wide, had to take the Captain's VW Beetle, so I asked a friend at Ove Arup's, who engineered the 1,704 metre span of the Menai Bridge, to detail it.

After a few bosh shots at rigging, I adopted the old model-maker's sketch, although it looked a lash-up to me.

These river-men were encyclopedias of Mississippi lore; when to move over to the slow-water side of the river as it snaked; to back-paddle when the flood thrust them at a mud bank in a new location, the while keeping an eye on the surface for signs of a snag. They lived for the river and did not give a damn for landsmen's smart status patterns.

With the Captain in mind, I proposed a Cunard-style stateroom where he could entertain guests, but was told he would be happier playing 'clapper' with tablespoons in the bar.

"The First Officer? Oh, you mean Hank. Well now, last I saw he was learning some kid to fly a kite, aft."

On the drawing board

Now for the boat. Design of the fore-deck was important, as the passengers' first experience when they stepped on deck set the mood. I introduced a double-serpentine, carpeted stairway with brass risers and side panels in coloured plexiglass. At the stairhead, an octagonal gazebo, the upper level providing a charming nook where passengers could relax, sip afternoon tea and dream. Civilised? "Say, honey, just the place for the kids."

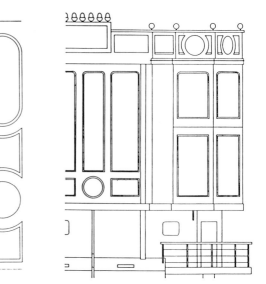

Above, a studio model to check construction aft. For the rest, white paint, mahogany, coloured glass, plexiglass and brass. The acorns up top are traditional river-boat trim.

DEFINITELY NOT THE QE2

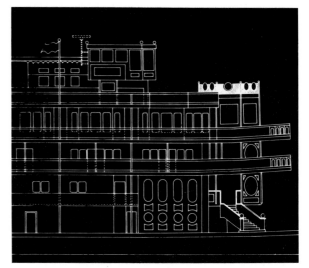

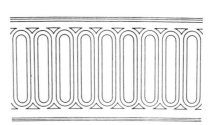

370

Hell. In the aft bar they would be sipping mint juleps.

Most ships start with a graceful prow and terminate as though the designer had tired of the task when he reached her backside. Come to think of it, the same goes for the white-bearded guy on a cloud who was responsible for shaping the elephant – and us, for that matter, though maybe some womanisers might disagree.

Even music composers suffer from this, 'How do I end it?' syndrome; invariably finishing with a series of crashing chords, like a traction engine breaking down half way up a hill. I broke with tradition and, in spite of some raised eyebrows, interrupted her horizontal lines with a vertical two-deck bar aft, a classical pavilion with zigzag side niches, all glazed, so passengers could see the river slowly unwinding as the scarlet paddle-wheel thumped round below, beating a trail of foam. To prevent the close-up view of this monster intruding on river meditation, it would be viewed through pink-tinted glass – nice touch. In the wetted area above the wheel, boxes planted with mint. Mint? For the mint juleps, of course.

Traditionally, river-boats talk to each other in passing with friendly hoots. Our boat would do more than this, announcing her approach with a splatter of boiler-water and sound from a range of steam whistles called a 'calliope'. This sound would echo back with a time-lag, resulting in an off-key disharmony faintly resembling some Southern ballad, and definitely 'river-boat'.

Nevertheless, I felt she still needed to express her identity, triumphantly announcing – "I am the Queen of the River."

Remembering the gilded armorial crests on the high stern-castles of old fighting ships, I mounted above her stern two larger-than-life, high-breasted mermaids with flowing hair, gazing serenely down river. To acknowledge the old cotton plantations, I proposed that one of the ladies be black, but our backer said, "No. Two blondes and make them sexy." A trite response from one of those Northerners who won the Civil War.

Birth of a mermaid. First in clay, then a plaster mould, then a skin of metallic fibreglass is cast. Finally, three weeks' burnishing with steel wool and rouge.

371

A pretty model, to encourage ourselves, and the yardmen at Louisville, who are tuned up to build tugboats.

Steering it through

Those sexy mermaids were still being given their metallic sheen by a craftswoman in the UK when Mehitabel and I made our way to the Louisville boat-yard, where the sheer and camber we associate with ocean-going craft are unknown. Flat watermen, slow of speech, pauses for cogitation; it's the Kentucky way.

They had our pile of plans and – a hopeful offering on our part – a model to indicate that she was definitely not just another tugboat.

"Maybe you have something there," they would say. "Maybe we'll take another look at that drawing." A pause, while that burst of communication beds well down, then one of the group heaves himself reluctantly from his chair and moves off. I watch a tired wasp climb the window pane, fail to negotiate the transom, fall on its back, right itself and climb again, like a mechanical toy that hasn't been tooled up for negotiating transoms. My drawing, with its friendly office stamp, is at last unfolded and I point out a 'grace-line' . . . for a guy who attacks sheet steel with a carbon arc.

In a desperate effort to play it slow and cool, I indicate an error of detail on the wheel support-frames. They call in the guy who marks out the plates. I take a deep breath and again point out the discrepancy. He leans heavily over the bench and looks at the drawing with as much recognition as if it were a map of the subway. A pause . . . then, "Well now, I guess you and your little lady are about ready for an iced Coke?" Oh, well, keep on the attack, like that bloody wasp.

Not fifty yards away, moored to the quay alongside a rugged half-completed tug and plicking with cascades of red sparks, where oxy-acetylene cutters are at work, she appears to be coming together as specified, and on time. No dramatic launch down the slipway, as she is built afloat, but a naming ceremony when this top heavy, three-dimensional abstract in grey metal will brave the river as . . . *The Mississippi Queen.*

An error of judgement. British canal boats have much-loved traditional patterns in bright colours, a charming conceit I intended transferring to this boat, only to be told by my collaborator that it was not on – she must be all in white, in the Mississippi tradition. He was, of course, quite right, so she was white as a wedding cake when, some months later, with suppressed excitement, we returned to see her named.

All over bar the shouting

She had been towed across the river to the public quay but, after travelling 2,600 miles to stand on her deck, our progress is barred by a dense crowd – longshoremen's families, teenagers dolled up plantation-style, politicians, helmeted cops on throbbing motorcycles and, weaving in and out of the bystanders legs, barking dogs.

We can just see the slender smoke-stacks of the *Belle of Louisville*, a little local stern-wheeler that has come to pay her respects. Then, a derisive cheer as the sober old *Delta Queen*, the much loved river-boat we are replacing, who has also come to pay *her* respects gets her out-slung gangway tangled with ours.

Steam whistles splutter angrily, as self-appointed masters of ceremony in the crowd shout conflicting orders, paddle-wheels thrash this way and that, when . . . down comes the deluge. Mehitabel, newspaper over head, makes for the nearby hotel restaurant at a run. Following, I drape my limp jacket over a chairback, "Crazy lot. Let's give the naming a miss and have lunch." Mehitabel is already scanning the menu for 'lobster thermidor'.

The town turns out, and we turn up, for the naming ceremony.

An hour later the sun comes out, and so do we, to find that the tangle has been sorted out and there is a sense in the crowd that something is about to happen. We are quickly hustled onto the boat, and why? We are about to experience an event which, as described by Mark Twain, 'Makes a body's liver curl with enjoyment'.

A GREAT RIVER-BOAT RACE

Three proud stern-wheelers pounding up river, bands playing, sirens tooting, choking black smoke billowing from tall smokestacks and drifting across the water, while pounding paddle-wheels thrash up humping waves that race along the levee, chasing over-excited youngsters who skip along in the sparkling sunlight.

I feel a lump in my throat. We are, at this delirious moment, living in a time warp. This is for real and it will never happen again . . . like us.

The last I saw of Albert Pope Hinkley Jr., he was steering a zigzag course into town, arm in arm with the Captain, to the sound of a tipsy Kentucky band, followed by a jostling crowd and assorted stray dogs.

Back at the studio I cut a snippet from one of the popular dailies:

'BAD news for Britain-knockers. The Americans come all the way to Hampstead, London, to ask QE2 *designer James Gardner to create a new Mississippi river-boat. Like asking a 'limey' to design a new cowboy hat.'*

Three days that shook the world

Leisure? Don't make me laugh. Unlike a friend of mine who pops over to 'her little place in Provence', which – to rub it in – *I* helped her find.

Very commendable, but not my cup of tea, thinks I, doodling a dull visual at the drawing board. The 'phone rings. She is there and the sun is shining.

"Surely, you didn't ring just to tell me that?"

Her voice is edged with excitement, "No. Remember that nice ruin we viewed but couldn't get?" (A sign mounted over it had warned, *'Très Dangereuse'.*) "Well, it's now available. Only snag, *Madame* in Marseille needs the money in hard cash, next week, or we lose it."

"We?"

"Well, you, of course."

I hold the 'phone poised. It's now or never and, too quick at decisions, I hear my voice saying, "Hold it then, and expect me in a couple of days with the necessary."

Thus, in an aberrant moment, I adventured blindly into the habitat of French peasants who hunt truffles on dark nights.

Mehitabel and I buzzed happily down the *autoroute*, a briefcase stuffed with money bouncing on the back seat. Periodic diversions to locate banks, so we could change our sterling into local currency. Quite a lot of banks, as our Government had set a limit of £50 for any one trip.

Easing wads of francs into a bulging briefcase, under the quizzical eyes of French bankers, I felt as guilty as a suspect spiv laundering loot.

After a night at Beaune, and money changed, we could relax as we drifted into a world alight with brilliant colours . . . Van Gogh territory; poppies, placid peasants perched on bright blue farm carts, and ragged lines of cypresses dancing in the dazzle.

Well off the beaten track, clinging to the top of a hill at the foot of the Luberon Mountains, an ancient village boasting a

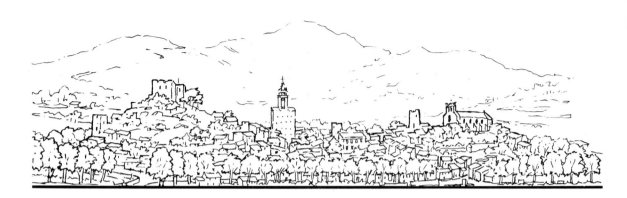

ruined keep and a medieval bell-tower, which always tolls the hour twice in succession, so peasants in the fields have a second chance if they count wrong the first time.

At last, through the flip-flip shadow-pattern cast across the sunlit road by long avenues of pollarded plane trees, we glimpse the bell-tower, poised sedately over a complex tumble of pantile roofs. Slatted shutters, weathered stone and Roman pantiles baking in the sun. A lizard basks on a wall, and, only a hundred yards down, a patisserie in the Place de la Fontaine – crisp baguette loaves and croissants still warm from the oven.

"Picturesque, I suppose," says Mehitabel, "but it doesn't look *you.*"

Innocent as *The Babes in the Wood*, we were naively excited at the fun of purchasing a property . . . . . . but in Provence?

Jinx 1

Anti-climax. My friend's place is deserted. We about-face and drive down to the local café where she has booked us rooms. But she hasn't. An abrupt *mademoiselle* behind the bar tells us, with a dismissive shrug, there is one room available and for one night only.

I hump Mehitabel's bag up the back-stair, then, swinging back the shutters to let in light, announce the good news, "Mehitabel, you've a little balcony all to yourself. A view of café tables below and a deep fish pond shaded by ancient plane trees. Lovely."

Leaving her to admire the view, I pootle around to eventually dump my bags over another cafe eight miles away at Lauris, and return to discover my friend at home. Over supper I am informed we have arrived a day early. Also, that to purchase property I must open a French bank account. No problem. A guy who knows a guy in the consulate had given me the name of a bank in Aix – so first thing tomorrow. Okay?

Jinx 2

The village is in darkness when we return to the café, which now wears a dead pan look, all shutters closed. Obviously, they won't leave their feather beds for those unnatural English – *separate rooms indeed*. It's a do-it-yourself situation, so we stagger with a ladder from a nearby building site, prop it up to Mehitabel's balcony and soon she is smiling down at me in the moonlight, through long fair hair, like Ophelia. Quite romantic.

I make do on a rather bumpy sofa at my friend's place and, come morning – damn – the razor has spent an expensive night in my bag at Lauris. Unshaven, I dash down to the café, collect the key to Mehitabel's room and release her so she can use the loo. "The bank at Aix," I remind her. "Only fifteen miles on the map."

After finding a vacant space to park our car, we stroll down the Via Mirable, the most elegant of main streets under its cathedral-like vault of translucent foliage, mossy fountains and, on the shaded side, The Grindley and Ottoman Bank.

Jinx 3

"I say, it looks rather up-market!" I finger my stubbled chin as we enter; a reminder of the inner sanctum at Cartier in the old days. An expensively-suited gent, sporting garnet cufflinks, and a willowy lady secretary swathed in black; a pair who discreetly manoeuvre money for the French upper crust . . . and that includes Prince Rainier of Monaco, I guess.

Open an account? "Certainly. With pleasure." I flash my wad of notes. "But, *dis-donc*, we cannot accept French currency from a visitor. Tax problems, *comprenez*-vous? It must be in sterling, or a cheque on a French bank."

Hell. So we did the wrong thing.

Two coffees, *grande tasse*, on the sunny side of the street, while the implication of this sinks in. Recovering our car from the parking lot, we realise why there was a vacant space – it is in the forecourt of the *gendarmerie*. Backing out, (very circumspectly), we head back to the café, as Mehitabel's room must be vacated by noon.

A less officious *mademoiselle*, sister of the bar-girl, tells us the room has already been booked for tonight under the name of Gardner. But that's us! How crazy can they get? I hump Mehitabel's bags back up the stairs, peep into a room allocated for me (no bags), then, as we relax for a moment, sipping *pastis* by the fish pond, a revelation.

"Hiram Winterbottom!"

"Hiram what?"

"Not what, who. Grand guy. Lives in a valley just over the Luberon. Well-to-do. He'll give us a cheque on his bank in exchange for those damned francs."

We drive through a rather scary canyon, Mehitabel remarking on the lupins, snap-dragons and Canterbury bells growing along the verges.

"How did they get there?"

"It's where they originally come from," I reply, as we climb over a mountain pass to arrive at Hiram's ultra-modern, white stone house, or should I say temple, hidden in a pine-wood up the next valley.

It is an admirable, intellectual concept, conceived with cool logic. No interior doorways, the rooms being arranged at ascending half-levels; climb a short flight of stone steps to one level, then round and up to the next. Germanic precision, but somewhat marred by excited flies buzzing over greasy dishes at kitchen level; the upper stairways littered with unwashed socks and underpants.

"Obviously a man's house," comments Mehitabel.

"Really?"

Later, returning through the canyon with the desired cheque in my pocket, a near-miss with a post van at a blind U-turn and we arrive to come up against . . .

Jinx 4

My friend has news. I must apply for a Resident's Permit at the *mairie*, where the flag of France hangs limply over a crumbling stone entry.

It's like the replay of a René Claire film.

A trio of identical pillbox-hatted police welcomes us from behind the duty officer's desk. They open up what looks like the wrapping paper from a lump of ossified beeswax, a plan of the village, and indicate a plot. "You are interested in Unit 203, *Monsieur*?" The place is a three-dimensional jigsaw of interlocking habitations. This plan omits someone's cave under part of my ruin and another ancient cave thirty feet below. I generously offer to correct their plan, but they will have none of it. The chief of the trio proudly smooths his moustache, "This, *Monsieur*, is the official plan, registered at Avignon."

Jinx 5

After a liberal use of rubber stamps, I am informed that my site is classified as *un monument ancien*. Any changes I propose must be approved by some archaeological bureaucrats in Paris. I put up my hands and shrug like a Frenchman, then out into the sunlight to start up the car for Aix, when we are flagged down by my artist friend.

Jinx 6

She has been doing research on our behalf. Good. True, we pass the purchase money to the *notaire* by cheque, but – wait for it – only half. The remainder must be handed to *Madame* in cash (the accepted French method for evading tax). Very civilised, don't you agree?

Oh, no! I must now ask Hiram to destroy one cheque and write us another. This would be a casual operation in the UK, but in France a numbered cheque is as unalterable as a marriage contract. Enough. Deserting Mehitabel I breeze off to Lauris to release – and pay for – my bag.

Early next morning I explain our predicament to Hiram over the 'phone, then back through that scary canyon.

Jinx 7

He is not at home. No letter-box in the smart, plate glass door, so we do a circus act. Mehitabel bends, gripping her knees, while I kneel balanced on her back and toss his cheque through the fanlight. We stand mesmerised, as the neat buff envelope sails slowly down this way then that, to finally slide gently under a cardboard box full of waste-paper. All our money, and only a corner of that modest envelope in sight. *Emergency measures are called for.*

Philip, one of my team and exhibit-chaser, who occasionally 'dresses' exhibits for us, is staying with a friend six miles up the mountain. We ring him from a 'phone booth in the nearby town of Apt. Will he please contact Hiram, and tell him where that cheque is? I'll be back later . . .

Only a day and a half to go. Mehitabel has had enough and dives into Hiram's bathing pool to cool off. Fortunately – not always the case – it happens to be filled with water.

Eventually a disgruntled Hiram drives us back to Apt where, after some bureaucratic tut-tutting, I have (a) a French cheque for half the amount and (b) the rest in cash.

A hairy drive back through the gorge and then on to Aix, aiming to get there before that discreet bank closes.

Jinx 8

We don't. It is Friday and they have closed for what the French call *'le weekend'.* Floored.

We sit at a café table and gaze moodily at the smartly dressed locals strolling by, all clearly at peace with the world. Mehitabel doesn't give up, but creeps back to peep through the bank's plate glass frontage. "Useless," I say. "When a bank closes, it is CLOSED."

But no. One of two great Renaissance doors alongside the bank swings slowly open and our friend of the garnet cufflinks smiles at Mehitabel. She smiles back and we are ushered in.

He admires Hiram's cheque (and Mehitabel), asks for three signatures, and I am IN; and so dazed with relief that, making a dignified exit, I walk nose-first slap into that glass window.

"How's your poor nose?" asks a concerned Mehitabel.

"My eyes are watering. Better you drive," I reply.

Who cares – tomorrow the last hurdle, an appointment with *Madame* at the *notaire's* office.

Anxious to settle the matter, we turn up a quarter of an hour early. The sleepy-eyed *notaire* – rather like a bullfrog – points out that we have disturbed his post-lunch siesta and angrily shuts the door. Bad start.

The bell-tower strikes the hour (twice) and we enter the sanctum of this manipulator who, the French having discarded priests, has the local residents dancing on strings.

Jinx 9

Desultory conversation, we in hesitant, mispronounced French. Papers viewed and agreed, then a deadly pause: *Madame* from Marseille fails to appear.

He shrugs, so I shrug, and we are shown out to sit on the coping of the bubbling fountain to wait. After a while the old bullfrog leaves his office and walks off to disappear down the street. Hell. This is the last day.

Gloom in the Place de la Fontaine.

The bell-tower booms us back to life, and there is *Madame*, descending from her sleek red Citrôen.

The *notaire* appears from nowhere, papers agreed and signed, cheque handed over. We wait patiently while *Madame* flips through her wad of notes one by one.

As we leave Mehitabel whispers, "The champagne. It's a must. I'd forgotten! Keep her chatting while I dash round to the Co-op."

The old girl speaks less English than I French. Eventually, after sipping that cheap champagne, it is, *"Bonsoir, Madame, très plaisance,"* and – obligatory – I kiss the dignified matron on both cheeks, one – two – three.

What a relief. We finish the bottle and, by now rather tiddly in the heat, measure up the tumbled-down ruin with a tape, giggling the while. Strange to relate, the dimensions proved to be smack on.

Jinx 10

It was then that I came up with a bright remark, "We haven't started yet, the fun will be making the place livable." I fumbled for an address in my wallet, "Just time to visit a mason; he lives at Pertuis."

"But you always avoid Masons", said Mehitabel.

"That's *Freemasons*. This is a real stonemason, who can do the job – I hope."

We pootled off in the dusk following the signs to Pertuis, a market town up the valley where, after circling a giant plane tree twice and backing out of a one way street, we located his office in a narrow cul-de-sac.

Claude Vigne, on whom my hopes were centred, proved to be a sturdy, squat little man whose office served as stabling for a plump wife and three wide-eyed children. He politely turned off the television and cleared space on a table, littered with the debris of a family meal, for my layout plan which, it soon became apparent, he understood no more than my French.

". . . and that's an ancient defensive wall, goes back to the year dot."

382

The cave under. *Reconstructed upper level.*

Nothing for it but to sketch as I spoke; not an intellectual exercise like Hiram's place, but replicating simple construction as used by the locals. Seeing it drawn bit-by-bit in front of his eyes, as it were, he soon warmed to the idea.

Vigne had never before been responsible for dealing with carpenters, plumbers and glaziers. Under sporadic crossfire from his wife he eventually agreed, but only after an excited period of hand waving with his *Madame*, when he added fifteen per cent for *"la difficulté"*.

As my ruin, an ancient granary, could only be approached by a steep stone alley intended for medieval traffic – donkeys with panniers – definitely not for builders' trucks, I signalled 'okay' and tabled a 'Letter of Intent' I had prepared for him to sign.

A ghastly pause as Vigne sat, immobile, frowning at it.

My heart sank. Was this to be *Jinx 11*? Vigne was battling with a personal problem – he was illiterate. Eventually, taking my pen with a resolute gesture, he signed it with his mark, 'X'.

I almost fainted with relief.

Back at the studio, Simon greeted us with a questioning smile, "So, how did it go?" I held the empty champagne bottle high in the air and gaily replied, "No problem."

383

A stranger? Throw a rock at him

A super specimen of 'Old Man'.
Ancient basalt from the mantle
broken up by intrusions of magma
30,000 million years back.
(Before the Tolpuddle Martyrs.)

The Geological Museum. Bits of dead rock laid out in state in a great echoing gallery; the silence occasionally broken by the squeak of a janitor's boots. When the curators in their hidey-holes heard that Dunning, the Director, had asked an outsider in to jolly the place up *and uncover their secrets*, the reaction was, "like the howling of dogs before an earthquake."

Realising that, though I might be conversant with the make-up of suet puddings, I knew nothing of metamorphic aggregates, Dunning let me in on the act. Apparently, while we had all been avidly following the antics of the first man on the moon on TV, as he teed off a golf ball, geologists had been discovering how our planet ticks.

Exploring the ocean floors, they calculated that the continents were pieces of an ancient jigsaw anchored to the sea bed, which was slowly moving. New material from the mantle, oozing up through rifts on the sea floor would contact the edge of a continent and dive under, pushing up mountain chains. Disturbing the hot mantle, it would occasionally backfire, hence volcanoes.

Thrilling. That explained almost everything . . . Why the UK is a sceptred isle, Everest is up where it is, and why turtles now swim so far to lay their eggs.

Being a geologist, Dunning reckoned that no man can be treated seriously until he has climbed a mountain, like a goat, and chipped bits off it. So, before I had time to buy climbing boots, I was kidnapped and driven up to the wilds of Scotland to do just that, at a place where the earth once sicked up its insides for all to see.

On my return, I jettisoned the glass cases and taking a mould off an impressive rock-face on the desolate road to Skye, replicated it in the museum, so visitors would enter the exhibit through a cleft in a thirty-five foot high rock-face.

To reassure Mehitabel that I was a born survivor, I sent daily reports back to the studio. The following are a few typical pages from this epic, now secure in the archive of the Institute of the Geological Sciences.

The skin of the Earth is as thin – to scale – as the skin on an apple.
Under this it is red-hot, and still molten at the centre.

First night at Kyle of Lochalsh.

View from window.

Problem – some rocks are upside down, and they all look alike.

A wet glen. Dunning hunts for a (rare) txtbook specemin.

Rock slide & pres unexpected

specemin of agregate. Probably not agregate at all! ('A' paper pending.)

↖ British Rail.

Conference table.

Damn. The Chelsea mob get there first.

Looking for specemins with 'eyes' in.

My clothes are now drying on the radiator.

Bog all the way up? I don't believe it.

Only half a mile — the forst bit's the worst.

386

Mountain building is a slow business.

E.E.C. mountain slides up over Greenland baserock. Thrilling.

The crunch.
↑ us.

Influx of didactic German geologists.

Here, it was first discovered the Earth isn't just a big Windsor pudding, but a displaced enigma.

Like bolts of crettone at a Laura Ashley store

Mt. I'madeit.

After flogging up to the top, specemin is found at A.

'Help yourself' at the Altnacealgach Hotel.

(map ref. on request).

The 80's

Meanwhile . . .

Film star voted US President

Youth shoots at Pope – no lightning

Mount St Helens erupts

Israelis invade Lebanon

Argentineans invade Falklands

Torville & Dean dance 'Bolero'

Mikhail Gorbachev takes over USSR

Speilberg's *ET* takes over USA

Brideshead Revisited competes with *Dallas*

Dinosaurs discovered to have had feathers

Michael Jackson sales top 37 million

Pepsi-Cola invades Moscow

Wreck of *Titanic* discovered

Eddy the Eagle comes last in Olympics

Madonna – 'Like a Virgin'

Sketched at El Salvador while awaiting a plane, en route *to hunt butterflies in the rain forest.*

Fraternising with bankers

In the early days, when short of cash, I would dump my pride and joy – a genuine Wheatstone concertina – on the counter of the local pawnshop; a refuge for the impecunious under the sign of the three golden balls, which could be found in every high street. The doorbell's tinkle would alert the old pawnbroker, as a spider is triggered by a fly caught in its web. Peering from under his jeweller's eye-shade, the old spider would shrug, fumble for the money drawer and mutter, "When, I ask myself, can this foolish boy make time to practice on the instrument? And, he expects me to value it at £5?" But, as I parted my hair to one side and looked reasonably tidy, he would hesitantly peel off five crumpled notes and pass them over, with a pawn ticket.

This guy was, at least, a straight dealer; take it or leave it.

I already had the 'per cent men' sized up. Just picture one of those little stone churches, nestling modestly in its setting of verdant trees; there is one in every English village. Romantic?

The bishop would install his agent here, to keep an eye on the illiterate locals, marry them off if there was a pregnancy, name and count the babies and then programme these gifts from heaven to respect JC and the bishop and – wait for it – to collect *tithes* – ten per cent of every man's product. On to a good thing, they would foster music and theme song to keep the tribe together, just as witch-doctors in the jungle had done before them.

The per cent men behind the imposing façade of today's banks have the same objective in view. Just as a rabbit will freeze when mesmerised by a swaying snake, we are seduced by pompous buildings, the well-brushed clothes and manicured finger-nails of the office-holders. But these guys are not straight-dealers, as they trap an innocent with a small loan and a smile like a good fairy. Why not? They have captured him, or her, for life.

I guess my reaction to bankers is on similar lines to that expressed by Jesus Christ and Henry Ford. Nevertheless, the habit of treating a job as a job got me involved in working for them – not just the high street variety, but those top money-manipulators, The London Clearing Banks.

Camouflaged with a white shirt and sporting a tie (which shows how Christmas presents can come in useful) I would be ushered into the inner sanctum to take my place with five characters in City suits, seated at a polished table under a crystal chandelier. The discreet male secretary, circumspect as Jeeves, quietly opens a window (previous experience of my corn-cob pipe). Five pink, dead pan faces turn my way.

The enemy? I am engaged to make these gentlemen's money-making ploys appear altruistic – internationally. Help!

I had already pointed out to their chairman – a character of the old school, who still referred to girls breasts as 'bristols' – that all banks go through exactly the same ritual when processing money and the public, so what is there to exhibit?

Safe in assuming that he would not drop the idea, and so forego first-class air bookings to far away places, I put forward another notion. Why not invest their budget in a series of prestigious exhibits for Britain? This would be good PR for them and, not stated, a more satisfying task for me.

Now I was free to put on shows of my own devising, aimed at the different cultures – if we can call them that – in major cities throughout the world: Zürich, Toronto, Lisbon, Barcelona, and the rest. No two were alike.

São Paulo

Rectangular columns carrying montages made up of segments cut from contemporary posters – so amusing and 'British' that local companies competed to purchase them after the show.

Revolving pop art. Fun with high fashion, low ordinaries, the stiff upper lip rearguard, our British weather, our fascination with crime fiction and other idiosyncrasies.

Sydney

Not the goods and culture we sold *them*, but the goods and culture they sold *us* – such as lambs' tails for dusters, and grain for the pigeons in Trafalgar Square – culture, after all.

Tokyo

Surprise tactics. A map showing the British Isles situated, unexpectedly, off mainland China, then, contrariwise, Japan as an offshore island to Europe. Theme. How alike our national histories and attitudes are . . . which proves, if you try hard enough, you can get away with anything.

The bankers found themselves sponsoring Japanese call-girls, dressed geisha-style and sitting on shantung silk cushions, as they turned delicate ferris wheels, painted in magenta and pink, to tinkling music.

Contretemps. Pre-opening decision. Our contractor in Tokyo 'phones, "These girls you want. We can hire students, three languages, at £1 an hour. Call-girls at £3 an hour. Actresses, which means superior beauties who serve the nobs, £8 an hour. Which?" As it was for the banks, I plumped for the beauties.

When pie-faced Simon, my prim assistant, arrived in Tokyo to vet a queue of girl applicants, he was somewhat taken aback when the first to saunter into his office had a cigarette between her lips, sported a leather miniskirt and kinky boots that revealed fifteen inches of Japanese thigh.

In dear old Hampstead we associated things Japanese with Gilbert & Sullivan opera.

The UK off China.

Euro-Japan.

"Three little girls from school are we," in this outmoded dress, proved to be of interest, even to the modern Japanese!

She opened her Europeanised eyes wide, "Dress up as a geisha? You must be joking!"

Nevertheless, she and the rest eventually agreed to wear the outfit, plus the hired wig, for a thumping extra charge. "But, NO smoking," said Simon.

Alas, at Caracas I fell into the trap of thinking that what interested *me* would interest the Venezuelans, and put on a collection of quixotic inventions; ingenious devices that would probably never be marketed – but fun. Naturally, the locals were at a loss. Did English banks market these odd contrivances?

"You can't win them all," one remarks. A cheery pretence, as every misjudgment strikes home and leaves a scar.

Depression. Then Mehitabel came up with a bright idea. With four days, why not take a flight she's read about which, after dumping people out at a remote mining town, flew on to Angel Falls? Four hundred miles inland, rain forest all the way. That should get the job out of our hair. It did.

The Lost World

No one told us that the waterfall drops from the highest escarpment in the world, or that the excitement on seeing it triggered Conan Doyle to write *The Lost World* – how his fictional hero, Professor Challenger, discovered prehistoric dinosaurs and pterodactyls still surviving way up above the clouds.

While flying over rain forest which, from the air, looked like a continuous bed of parsley, and bored with the interminable treescape drifting slowly by, my mind drifted back to when I was once down there, on that forest floor. This adventure had been triggered off when a real estate guy, who collected butterflies, seeing a rare specimen – a beautiful Yugoslavian assistant – in my studio, pounced, caught and married her.

It was not so long ago when Georgian bucks fought duels for the possession of desirable females on Primrose Hill, only a stone's throw from the studio. But we must observe the conventions, so I attended the elaborate wedding wearing a hired suit and a forced smile. Having seen me at the drawing board, it occurred to this guy that he could as well make money out of butterflies as real estate, and asked me to design a visitor centre, where the public would pay to walk among more than a thousand butterflies in free flight . . . then a novel idea. This stimulated my childhood curiosity concerning insects.

I had found my fat fingers too clumsy to manipulate these exquisite little tools-for-purpose, each a neatly formed assembly of interlocking parts enclosing – somewhere – a minute power pack. Maybe the Japanese have an affinity with insects? Their Suzuki motorcycle being the most insect-like man-made device I can think of. Or it would be if it were miniaturised to the size of a fingernail and had a power pack that would propel it all the way from Canada to Central Mexico . . . a journey which any young monarch butterfly will undertake, off-the-cuff.

This butterfly business had given me the crazy idea of adventuring up the Amazon with a butterfly net, but I soon found these little bits of fragility were too quick off the mark for a townee. They would insolently flutter out of reach in a patch of sunlight, as I tripped over a liana, or stepped on a dead tree trunk which disintegrated at a touch – releasing, in the process, a myriad of creepy-crawlies. Hell.

To justify my intrusive presence, I settled down to sketching a tree stump on which fifteen species of plant had made a home. Then, brushing the last batch of inquisitive ants off my trousers, I made it back to Manaus.

Here I struck gold, locating a working man's eating place overlooking the river, the inner whitewashed wall of which, illuminated at night, attracted hundreds of moths until it was patterned like a decorative cretonne.

Who cares for dignity? Balancing on marble table-tops, to the surprise of the locals, I picked them off one by one.

The butterfly net? I passed it on to some mudlarking urchins who would, no doubt, use it for fishing.

Mehitabel gave me a nudge. "We've arrived!" she exclaimed, pointing down to what looked like the beginning of a hutted visitor camp, that was probably never completed, on a patch of ground by a bend in the Orinoco. A bit primitive, but who cares when it is dwarfed by a great rock-face that rises

Survival tactics,
living on the stump
of a fallen tree.

A contemporary illustration showing how Professor Challenger's party reached the primeval plateau in the sky.

vertically way, way up like a grey curtain until it is lost to sight in the clouds, extending to the north and south as far as the eye can see. As much as to say, the world you know ends here.

The Falls? A room-boy says we must fly to see them, "The Duke. You pay him, he take you up." This Duke, the pilot, is elusive, but eventually discovered in the bar, staggering round the scattered tables with a 'crocodile' of inebriates. He cons me, bleary-eyed, but sober enough to indicate he'll take us up – next morning.

396

I shrug doubtfully at Mehitabel, "He said, yes." We decide to have a cool drink on it and, by the look of this beachcomber character, it may well be our last.

Next morning arrives as expected . . . but Duke doesn't. "Better ask his wife." When found, it is obvious that the word *wife* should be in quotes. Chivvied out of bed, unshaven and somewhat the worse for wear, he looks blearily up into the mist, "Ceiling too low for flying." As we plan to leave next day, I double the fare and he eventually agrees to try it and see. Our risk.

Driving us in an old jalopy to a corner of the airstrip, he pulls a tarpaulin off a prop. plane which, unlike the pilot, is in surprisingly good nick. A native boy tops up the tanks from a jerrycan, pulls away the chocks, gives the prop. a flip, the engine splutters, opens up, and we are off . . . into the mist. Our pilot grumbles, a spittle-stained cigarette still stuck to his lower lip, as we slowly gain height, at full throttle, until we are through the first cloud layer. The rock face, its top blurred by the mist, is still ominously out of sight. (I guess the pilot had a point.) The plane, struggling for altitude, has nearly reached its limit when the rock face sweeps away to form a deep fold. We buzz into it, still struggling to gain altitude, then I see it – a great river is falling off the edge of the world, a white flare of water, a sequence of ever-changing lacy patterns slowly chasing each other as they fall until, at last, the cascade atomises into mist – to condense into a pool way below, where it becomes a great river again.

Having fulfilled his contract, Duke lit another cigarette, one hand on the controls, and pointed ahead – "Okay?" We flew on up into clear sky to skim tree-tops on the top of the world. No dinosaurs, but Duke, now relaxed and pointing down to where I could just make out a faint criss-cross of tracks, shouted, "Mission station." This must be a marker, for we banked sharply to our right and after some minutes he cut out the engine and, in sudden silence, we found ourselves bouncing along a narrow overgrown landing-strip that had been cleared from the jungle.

Holding up a thick manilla envelope, he indicated a shadow-gap in the trees; an objective. Leaving the brave little machine to take care of itself, we followed him past a derelict airport building, now taken over by trees, and came to a cluster of rusting, corrugated iron shacks. "Old diamond diggings," he explained monosyllabically . . . "Owe Jackson a visit."

The angel in the rain forest

This may not be Conan Doyle's dream, but it was a lost world – two irregular lines of deserted, patched-up cabins with a dirt track between; once possibly considered a street. Our pilot shouts, "Jackson." There is a creak as a shutter swings open and a desiccated gaffer's head appears, "Down the store," he barks and the shutter slams shut. Friendly bloke – pure Hitchcock.

Then – or was I dreaming – a battered Jeep came bouncing down the track, surmounted by three grim-faced, bearded toughs, who ignored us completely as we leapt aside. Surely, a pretty townee like Mehitabel can't be that common hereabouts? She followed us, picking each step with care to avoid scuffing the heels of her dainty shoes.

At the 'store', which proved to be just another derelict shack, we were faced by a guy in a startlingly clean shirt. Jackson. He showed no surprise at our appearing out of the blue – but then he must have heard the aircraft. Warm canned beer – no charge. Duke explained that this good-for-nothing interloper earned more loot than any man has a right to, and from what? He grubbed in the old mine-tips for marketable industrial diamonds. That explained the three toughs on the Jeep – I guess they did the dirty work. Solved.

Sipping warm beer, I watched an Amerindian woman in a dazzle-patch of sunlight. She was busily stitching with an old hand-operated Singer sewing machine. On a wire against the wall above her hung four or five missionary dresses. "For sale," said Jackson. "Local currency. Not money, but honey." The dresses, with their puffed sleeves and full ruched skirts, have been made up, so neatly, from cheap but gaily patterned cottons.

I still picture her in my mind, almost with envy . . . to create with pride such pretty things, objects of desire for the naked people of the forest. A lone, dedicated angel – four hundred miles from anywhere.

398

The rotten apple

A stamp issued during the British Occupation, depicting the Citadel at Jerusalem.

Peace. Sunday morning, the place to myself and no bloody 'phone calls. Mug of coffee to hand, I peer at the diagram. Now, how to position a fibre as fine as a spider's web so that a laser beam travelling along it will jump across a four-inch gap to then hit a similar fibre end on, dead centre?

Can't be done.

Guess we'll have to cheat, which will mean putting a fast one over the Science Museum curator . . .

I jump as the 'phone suddenly comes to life. A self-confident American accent, "Karl Katz. The Metropolitan, New York. You know it? Right. Am I speaking to the Gardner responsible for the show at the Geological Museum? Good. I went bananas trying to locate you." The caller seemed aggrieved; American designers are invariably named in three-inch letters in the credits. He continues, "I'm ringing to say I rate your treatments as top class."

"Nice of you to say so."

Back to the problem. Suppose, instead of cutting the fibre, it is looped round the back, out of sight, and a heat sensor is mounted against the gap so, put your hand there and . . . ?

The 'phone again, same guy, "We were cut off. I have a proposition to discuss. Say we get together," pause, "in twenty minutes? Okay?"

"Fine. Look forward to meeting you," I lied.

But, when he turned up, Katz was worth meeting. Up-market trigger-man in the museum world, friend of Jackie Onassis, and with some resemblance to Kissinger, except that he played with intellectual projects for cultivated people, rather than international balls-ups for the White House.

He was involved in a project to be staged on the university campus at Tel Aviv. Not a *museum* in the accepted sense, no artifacts to be mounted in glass cases; in fact, nothing to get hold of. He aimed to put across a CONCEPT.

"Such as?"

PLANNING MEETING No.538

Jewish historians met to argue about the project for eleven years, but got nowhere.

My visitor sat back, pursed his lips, looked into mid-distance and went into professional mode.

"In the past many peoples have been taken over by invaders, or been driven to vacate their settlements and start again some other place. Given time, they invariably assimilate. Problem. After being turned out of Jerusalem by the Romans, and being driven out of Alexandria, Spain, Central Europe, South America – you name it – most Jews have hung onto their ancient tribal beliefs and refuse to assimilate. How come . . . interested?"

Well, that was an unexpected douche of gen. out of the blue. As a few million dollars were involved, the least I could do was make some fresh coffee. Soon I became involved in producing one of the world's great museums and discovered, in the process, that human history, presented in the 'glossies' as a lovely rosy apple, was maggoty inside.

The strip of land marked Palestine on that Sunday School map, now termed Israel, must now be viewed through a biblical distorting mirror.

I have a go

The BA jet waited for take-off, while the steward attempted to bring a gaggle of archaic, bearded characters, muttering prayers and arguing when they should be fastening their seat belts, into the twentieth century.

Karl explained that historians had met on and off for eleven years to argue the project, but had got nowhere. To dampen criticism, they played safe and commissioned a well-known architect to erect a building. Building up and still at a loss – what to put in it? They called in 'Shaike' Weinberg, who managed the local theatre. Theatre, okay, but a museum? Also at a loss, he decided to ask the advice of 'professionals' – us.

400

We inspected the building, which dominated the campus like a great concrete elephant, whose gloomy insides had been gathering dust for years. Picking our way around builders' debris and avoiding gaping voids in the concrete floors, we climbed a stairway that seemed to have no end until, disturbing a flutter of bats whose droppings covered the upper flight, we arrived at the top – to discover that this was the *only* stairway. Mehitabel made a note, *no circulation for visitors unless they jump off the roof,* and we joined the theme-team around a table in a hot builders' hut.

"We're still waiting for the air-conditioning," says Shaike. "This is the Middle East, you know." Ominous.

We discover Karl Katz lying on the table like a plump knight on a medieval tomb. "Slipped disc," he says. "More comfortable on my back."

For five long days these characters played a game of erudite ping-pong; wordmen batting opinions about Jewish history – of which there appeared to be quite a stockpile – across the table. Then to Jerusalem for an input on mysticism by Abba Kovner, the Israeli hero-poet, who had the appearance and crazy ideas of a Harpo Marx – except he took them seriously.

Mehitabel patiently took notes of all this opinionating which, after some judicious overnight editing, we issued as 'MINUTES OF MEETINGS'. When I gave her a day off to relax in the sun Shaike was taken aback, so I informed him she was soliciting to cover her air fare. A heavy hint which had no effect.

Eventually I reminded him that they were paying me to design and, with so much heavy history to digest, could they please find us a quiet spot where I could be alone, to think? They were rather shocked at the notion of my going off with the Jewish spirit under my arm.

Nevertheless, next day found Mehitabel and I settled in little pinewood chalets, where the holiday crowd immediately classified us as a film director and beddable starlet. Nice idea, but, being a troglodyte, I crept into the shade, spread the notes on the floor and tried to think Jewish. I had to battle with concepts that had been fossilized for centuries by rabbis; linear

Bedroom study. Mehitabel takes Hampstead to a chalet in Israel.

401

descendants of those historic PR men – the scribes. Better first to sort out the facts, but I then discovered that the classical world I had been told of at school must be viewed from an unexpected angle. I concentrated on something *concrete* – the building.

By taking out a stairway, filling in a floor, opening a way through the service area and converting the goods lift for public use, the interior was no longer a long climb to nowhere. Good.

With a liberal use of coloured pencils, I attempted to sort out a sequence of exhibitable facts from the scribbled notes, arranging them along a route, some large and some small.

There were no interruptions, just the rhythmic sound of waves tumbling along a beach, the occasional cough of a tethered camel, or Mehitabel, whose slim wet body was offered up to the sun to brown (just as we developed bromide photo-prints in the old do-it-yourself days).

Having located a typewriter that operated from left to right in English, not right to left in Hebrew, Mehitabel was soon tapping out the storyline. A pause, as she muttered, "Male chauvinists." Apparently, the Jewish life-cycle starts, not with the birth of a baby, but with the circumcision.

On-the-spot sketch of sabbath in the Holy Land; Tel Aviv beach with Jaffa in the distance. Note patrolling gunboat.

402

"So, female babies don't count?"

"Not in their tribal god's book," I reply knowingly, "That is, until the female marries to produce another boy – a potential rabbi."

"No wonder their young men are so cocky," was her response.

She had something there. Having been so propositioned on Tel Aviv beach by pushy young Israelis, she took refuge among the air-conditioning ducts on the hotel roof.

People echo their backgrounds. Nevertheless, forgetting my preconceptions, I produced an acceptable layout, with visuals, and then added numbers to the sections (to give them a spurious logic). Fine. Back in Tel Aviv, we taped the product to the walls of my bedroom, put a neat cover on the typed report, crossed fingers and awaited the arrival of our clients.

Surprised to discover that a project they had been arguing for a decade, in the abstract, had suddenly taken three-dimensional form, they offered us a glass of Israeli wine to celebrate the event – and the job of seeing it through.

The Museum of the Diaspora, as it became known, took three years to complete and Israel, that strip of jealously fought over land, became my stamping ground.

To Jerusalem

Katz gave me an introduction to one of the greatest men living, Teddy Kollek, the Mayor of Jerusalem, as I needed a permit to take moulds off the massive stone blocks which were laid in Herodian times at the Citadel – they would make a dramatic introduction to the Museum.

ENTRY TO THE SEQUENCE
Herodian blocks, moulded in fibreglass
– in stone they would crash through
the concrete floor.

As our taxi dodged its way through the Arab quarter, an anthill of narrow crowded streets, a bomb detonated . . . and we couldn't see the entry to the Mayor's office for dust. Our driver swore, switched off his cassette (which was playing Mahler), swung the wheel to avoid the screaming crowd and bounced us up a side way to the rear entrance.

Teddy Kollek, in his shirt-sleeves, brushed dust off Mehitabel's shoulder, then coolly served us with English tea, only interrupting our discussion to press the intercom. "How many casualties?" he asked. Not known yet. "Tell the Press to report the incident in low-key. We don't want to excite retribution." Then, back with us, he signed a permit and presented us with a book of Jewish jokes. Only a man as cool as he could keep internecine tensions in the Holy City from sectorial strife. Once, in a moment of frustration, Kollek said he was so bedevilled by religious bodies – Greek Orthodox, Fundamentalists, Moslem factions, Scottish Presbyterians and the rest, plus the United Nations and the archaeologists – that one day he would set himself on fire in the street. He was letting off steam, of course, but years later, when working on a project for Kollek in Jerusalem's Citadel, with religious characters breathing down our necks, I got a measure of his dedication to the City.

Viewing Herod's great masonry blocks and those added later by the Crusaders, the Turks and, eventually, by the British, I noted that they became progressively smaller – a record in stone of the steadily diminishing power of the bosses over the workers. (Or, if you see it thataway, the liberation of the workers from the authority of the bosses.) Craftsmen still used the same tools, but they lacked our preoccupation with TIME.

To Tiberius

Next day, with time in mind, I drove over the mountains in a little hired Renault with Lyn Kramer, an adept modeller, to match colour tabs against an ancient mosaic on a hill overlooking the sea of Galilee.

We had to check these on-the-spot as, where colours are concerned, the camera *does* lie. The journeyman who had put together this assembly of stone chippings had used delicate pastel shades, marble fragments from many sites – some far away. Probably a gentile from Antioch working for the Jews. We were gentiles from Londinium working for the Jews but, to produce our mosaic, used an Italian product which came in standard sheets like postage stamps, and with the same limited colour range. This posed one whale of a problem, but we couldn't solve it there. So back to Tel Aviv.

Rounding a sharp bend we came to a village that had been knocked to bits by high-velocity shells. Not able to read Hebrew, we turned off onto a track which, as it turned out, took us . . .

The mosaic at Tiberius.

. . . to Jericho

It soon became apparent that this was a restricted military track leading along the recently fought over West Bank. To our left, across the escarpment of the river Jordan, was a sunlit panorama of 'enemy territory', but we saw it through a high, wire fence backed by a tank ditch. On our right were barren limestone heights, which concealed, I supposed, Israeli observation posts – but we were too concerned with our near-empty fuel tank to care. A refuelling pump? Don't make me laugh.

Pulling slowly up each hill, then coasting down to the next, passing shot-up Arab hamlets with cock-eyed water tanks reclining at odd angles, I remembered how, some time back, the debonair Sir Mortimer Wheeler had described a Stone Age dig at this same Jericho for a reconstruction I was preparing.

Apparently, Stone Age blokes had not lived in dried mud huts, as expected, but had built stone fortresses complete with towers and chiselled stairways. They had neatly plastered the inner walls and floors, one of which showed the imprint of a woven reed mat, like one I could buy in Hampstead today. Sir Mortimer had described how the walls of their living chambers met the floor in a gentle curve, and no one could think of a reason for it.

But I could – and told him immediately, "No furniture. So, that curve in the wall would act as a backrest for Stone Age man when reclining." Nice to impress the great man – but the handsome old stallion's heavy-lidded eyes were locked with purposeful intensity on Mehitabel – and my bright idea was lost in thin air.

Nevertheless, I looked forward to seeing Jericho . . . if we could get that far.

The fuel indicator had long passed the red mark when the track swung inland and we free-wheeled down to a cluster of dusty buildings, to pull up at a decrepit fuel pump. A cheeky Arab urchin, after pumping at the handle, scampered off, bare-footed, to return with a wide grin and a beautiful white narcissus, which he offered to Lyn. I guess a sense of poetry helped neutralise the rust-coloured dust and the flies round his eyes. The dump turned out to be Jericho.

History is what you make it

The romance of research: a sick story of prayer, mayhem and mass murder. How the credulous were bombarded by blinkered manipulators, priests, rabbis, and the mullahs who called prayers from pretty minarets. Priests are not my cup of tea, and rabbis? Need it be said. Rather than enter an aircraft loo just vacated by an orthodox rabbi, one waits for the next 'vacant' booth. Instinctive reaction, as on spotting a large spider.

Fortunately, there were none of these guys with little round caps on the back of their heads on our committee. True, I have on occasion needed to work with the odd prince, sultan, paramount chief, football coach, even with a black mayor in Alabama, and a Washington lobbyist, but Shaike Weinberg, who was now attempting to control me, was just a nice guy.

Discussing photo images
with Cornell Capa, in New York.

406

I found him sinking lower and lower in his chair under the pressure of administrative happenings. There was something appealing in the way he rested his head in his hands, like a small boy in trouble with the workings of a complicated toy that keeps shooting off in the wrong direction then coming to a standstill. Meanwhile, the local blokes had knotted up the air-conditioning ducts and our films melted in the projectors. The elevator sported a label in Hebrew that meant 'not working', which went for most of the labour force, who were compulsive chatterers.

He looked up despondently from a cluttered desk.

"G, I have a problem."

"So?"

"Abba Kovner insists you delete the Christian crosses on the domes in your Byzantine mural."

"But it's based on an original of the period."

"Maybe. We're not dealing with facts, but with *people*. Many Israelis find the Christian cross to be as disturbing as the Nazi swastika would be – even to you."

I happen to consider the Nazi symbol to be one of the most effective logos in advertising history, but . . .

"Okay. All crosses out."

"Bound to be problems, G. Our historian asks why the tails on the mounts of those Mamluk horsemen – the ones blowing trumpets – are knotted."

"Because that detail comes from an original manuscript, so tell that historian to get knotted."

Shaike shrugs, then, "The animated film of Benjamin of

DESIGNED IN THE ISLAMIC MANNER
Section of cartoon for a wall painting telling the story of the rise of Ibn Shaprut, from a local apothecary to become the king's chief adviser. Tenth century Spain.

A diorama of the harbour at Alexandria,
AD 100. We show the Pharos lighthouse, as
no details of the other structures remain.

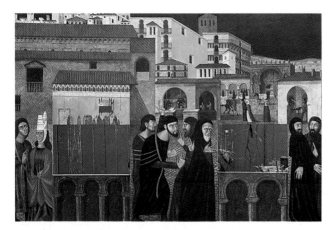

Artwork, good enough for the Prado
in Madrid, shows conflict between the
orthodox and assimilated intellectuals.
By Barry Evans.

A painted ceiling in Poland, now destroyed.
Reconstructed from amateur black and white
photographs, by a team in Covent Garden.

Tudela . . ." he fiddles with his papers for the 'storyboard', but fails to find it. "The picture has him writing from left to right. He would have been writing in Hebrew . . . "

"Right to left," I interject. Damn. The animator, a knowledgeable guy, should have thought of that. "This will need a remake. Cost from the contingency allocation, I guess?"

"This isn't a contingency, G. It's a damned silly mistake."

"Okay," I say resignedly, "Take it out of our fee. Next?"

Occasionally we took purposeful risks, as when we invented a missing head on a replica of a Roman relief – which neither Shaike's historian, nor a guy from the Metropolitan, noticed. One up to us in this 'potted history' game.

The bits the text books miss

Back in the studio, living in a stop-frame sequence of incongruous incidents, I check the different bits of jigsaw to ensure that when in place they will look, not like an assembly of bits, but (as Jacques Cartier once described that Chinese lacquered table) "a unity poised in its own space and time."

I'm flipping through colour swatches for a Coptic embroidery by a needlewoman from Guernsey, who has one day in London to purchase the skeins of dyed wool, when a visiting modeller asks me to specify colours for the costumes of three toga-dressed figurines. Right.

The intellectual Greek will be in white, but he can give it the traditional key pattern border. The Greek's son is at the show-off age and has just returned from Rome, so he can wear saffron yellow, which I am told was the in-thing for young men a hundred years after Christ. The seated figure, who is a Jew, must have two stripes down his toga and, as he is also a dyer, a piece of royal purple cloth tucked over his ear as a mark of high status. By the way, their purple was what we now call scarlet.

A Professor Narkiss is now breathing in my ear, so, to fend off more opinion on this detail, I remind him how he told us that the medieval European Jew wore a distinctive, pointed, 'lampshade' hat, like a Chippendale Chinaman. Question: "Was it made from leather, canvas, basketwork, horn . . .?" The Professor gives a cheerful grin, "No one has a clue." In truth,

A stylised rendering of Joseph, King of the Khazars, dictating a letter to his scribe.

no one has had occasion to think about it. So, it's over to me – and this goes for a great deal of what is called 'research' when it comes to the nitty-gritty of making things.

We are interrupted by a four-letter word and the slam of an oven door – Philip has just been on the verge of over-baking a fake book. The product looks quite authentic – and what a resounding title, *Maimonides' Guide To The Perplexed.*

A pity I wasn't advised at art school that faking is not only fun, but also a most lucrative form of art. After all, at least a third of the paintings in the American collections are fakes – just as much of our story is suspect – all, doubtless, a part of the rich tapestry of life.

How simple it would be to design one object, say a coffin, then spend one's life just replicating it, knowing that bodies will be arriving at one's door as steadily as baggage tumbling onto an airport carousel.

A change of pace

Jobs come by chance, so, while orchestrating the deep notes of the Jewish diaspora, I got involved in a much lighter situation to a USA theme, 'The American Way of Life'.

I found myself six-thousand miles away at Cape Canaveral, lifting up the skirt of a pretty Puerto Rican immigrant . . . so a pernickety Washington senator could take a peep at her posterior.

I should note that the lady in question was made of fibreglass. I had given her the plump backside the Caribbeans so admire – a bit of realism.

Not to this senator. Sweating in the heat, I took a slice off her behind with a hack-saw, dropped the skirt and gave it a gentle pat.

"Okay, now . . . sir?" All things to all men.

Exciting climax or damp squib?

Back in Tel Aviv, slightly fazed by jet lag, I prowled around the dim galleries, acutely aware of the difference between what I had imagined and what I now experienced; an added sensation of voids. The space I had passed through was still there behind me, more above, more feeling its way around that corner ahead – a sense of anticipation. Two shadowy figures had apparently found a way in through a 'No Entry' barrier. They resolved into the editor of the *Encyclopedia Judaica* and Abba Kovner, who could be a chain-smoking buddy one moment, then drop his eyelids and take the form of a prophet with a hot line to God the next. He was out of his depth and worried. Surely the walls of this area would not remain dark brown? Also, they were unable to read the lettering in the 'Culture' section, which was in white relief on white. I gave my stock answer, "It'll be right on the day."

True, the show looked depressing – just like a night-club in the cold light of morning when the cleaners were at work, but, as for a night-club, this affair had been designed for controlled lighting and until that was set by the dimmers, it didn't mean a thing. I spent the last five days working quietly round the galleries with a practical professional who was willing to balance with one foot on a ladder (while burning his fingers on a hot fitting) to adjust a shadow effect. We focused a spot here, 'niggered' another to cut a reflection, softened a flood with a tinted filter – two greys, or chocolate? Then we decided to eliminate some light sources altogether. This went on until we had achieved a mile of coherent lighting.

Suddenly, bingo! Everyone, including the committee, said, "It's marvellous." I was not so happy – all I could see was what might have been.

As usual, I evaded the pompous opening ceremony and, with the contractor and my assistants, had a riotous dinner in a replica we had constructed, of an ancient stone synagogue somewhere in Poland, after temporarily removing the candles and sacred books.

Meanwhile, the official guests were doing what was considered 'proper' in an auditorium on the floor below.

Preparing a multi-plane glass painting – religious conflict at Toledo.

Delicate modelling for a group of figurines. By Philip Kemp.

Artists in Covent Garden, working on a reconstruction of a painted ceiling.

The Museum of the Diaspora opened officially, on time, and took its place as one of the world's top museums, but then I am not a person who visits museums unless it is for some particular purpose. Such as designing one? Sure, have a go at designing anything . . .

As the glass doors swung silently behind us to the watchman's, "Shalom," I looked into the Tel Aviv night sky and took a deep breath of fresh air. "So, that's the end of that," I remarked to Mehitabel. "Just think of it, we'll be on the plane tomorrow morning."

"Not so," said Mehitabel, reminding me, very pointedly, that Karl Katz had invited both of us to join him for lunch next day with Teddy Kollek and Jacqueline Onassis.

Nevertheless, early next morning she joined me, with a rueful smile, to queue up at Lod airport for the last time – maybe.

Not again!

Some years back I had an 'affair' with Jerusalem's ancient Citadel; designed to defend the Jaffa Gate. After viewing the modest (dull) display of broken pots it then housed, Mehitabel, asking for the loo, was informed that there was an Arab one, but its concrete floor was used for making the local bread. Urgent, so I hailed a taxi to the posh International Hotel, visible a mile away on a hilltop. Soft carpet, air-conditioning, super. Coffee on the terrace.

On leaving, the uniformed doorman, taking us to be guests, had us driven back to the Citadel in the hotel's limousine. Very nice.

Unfortunately, archaeologists insisted that, before anything was done, they must dig the site over. This took seven years.

Back in the UK, a message arrived at the studio. Teddy Kollek, who had long dreamed of mounting exhibits depicting the 'History of Jerusalem', asked me to take the job on. To please him, I did a crazy thing and agreed, though the Citadel had been specifically designed *not* to house exhibits, but so a defender could take a bead on the enemy through slots in the thick walls, from little chambers with narrow entries.

City of dreams, in stone

TO DETER THE INFIDEL. *A rather doubtful visual – how the Citadel was built under Herod.*

413

THE CITADEL
Two thousand years of rebuilding over thirty feet of accumulated rubble.

Darius makes a proclamation. Segment of a fifteen foot relief, designed to illustrate the Captivity in Babylon.

A pagan effigy being removed from the disused Temple after the Romans left. A back-lit, multiplane glass painting.

To present an acceptable history of this beautiful city of dreams would need the exercise of . . . let's call it, judicious selectivity. Not as difficult as one might suppose. People are happy to believe what they wish to believe – a tempting opportunity for romantic reconstructions by artist-craftsmen. Darius and Babylon, the Roman cohorts, Crusaders as brave emblems of chivalry, examples of Islamic artistry, and a varying mix of peoples in their picturesque garb, strange beliefs . . . and an occasional camel.

In the event, I would have to manoeuvre around local historians and archaeologists jealous of any interpretation of history other than their own. Watching from the sidelines, would be a 'Religious Susceptibilities Committee' to check I didn't knock any of their supposed beliefs. Then there would be the problems of presenting the history of this 'City of Peace', without revealing that it is the most bitterly fought over bit of blood-soaked ground on earth. When the Crusaders eventually sacked the city and had murdered every occupant, including women and children, their priest ascended the Mount, lined deep in corpses, and raised the Cross of Christ on high. What price religious susceptibilities? Meanwhile, some Christians buried a bit of the 'True Cross' under the site of the Holy Sepulchre to fool Empress Caroline – PR tactics.

Our reconstruction of the notorious Temple set problems. The porch at the entry, flanked by two bronze columns, (introduced, not for use but for status), was too wide for a stone lintel. We introduced timber beams, with others set horizontally in the walls. The purpose of the latter, we guessed, would be to give stability to the roughly cut stonework. It had not occurred to the archaeologists that this Temple would need to be roofed, to keep the rain out. Again, we opted for heavy timbers. In the result our model proved to be so similar to the local Canaanite Temples and unlike the dream, we were asked to display it as a hologram - to give the expected ethereal look.

Surprising to discover that when the Jews had passed long years as captives, 'Weeping by the rivers of Babylon', King Darius, at last, released them to return to Jerusalem, only a few Zealots took up the option. So, the bulk of David's people remained to assimilate, I guessed, as Arabs in Mesopotamia?

414

Delving deeply into the subject I lost my cool and attempted a reconstruction of the Ark of the Covenant, as described in Exodus.

Supposing that Moses had it made in Egypt for the desert trek, I was excited to discover that a royal casket, excavated from Tutankhamun's tomb, fitted the description – except it did not have two seraphim facing each other across the lid, wings touching. This stalled me, so I asked London's Chief Rabbi for the official interpretation. He sent me a photo of a silver box, which might well have contained cigarettes on an executive's desk, with two Renaissance cupids on the lid. Renaissance!

In those times, craftsmen did not 'create' motifs,
invariably replicating traditional forms.

I scouted around various experts, and the British Museum, to end up with the only early rendering of sacred beasts with wings swept forward – and it was Egyptian; those dog-faced guardians of the nether world with beautiful feathered wings. Solved.

Dr Barnett, the leading authority on Middle Eastern antiquities, though ill at the time, tendered advice; thought our proposal was probably valid . . . he would think on it. Then he died in his bed. Stalled.

Are these people mad?

To check, I showed our reconstruction to the Head of Judaic Studies at the University of Jerusalem. After a long pause, the following response.

'This may be an archaeological reconstruction, but it is unacceptable. Yes, probably well researched, but that isn't the point. If a polaroid photograph had been taken of the Ark when it was made for Moses, and it was exactly like this, you must not exhibit it, *as it does not comply with Rabbinical teaching.'* Many highly respected professors live in Cloud-cuckoo-land.

G VERSION
THE ARK OF THE COVENANT

I eventually exhibited our Ark, beautifully gilded, in a museum at Detroit, where the rabbi proudly shows it off to visitors.

Working in Israel, one has the problem of getting in and, even more difficult, getting out, as one is subject to intensive security inspections at the airport. Fair enough – who wants to be hijacked?

It can be amusing, as when the inspectors, discovering some weighty packages concealed under a model of the Mount, insisted on taking me to a security room to open them up. They discovered a tinned steak pudding, butter, bacon and a jar of Oxford marmalade. I pointed out that I found Israeli food rather depressing.

On a later occasion it was far from amusing. Eve, from the studio, opened her bag, fluttered her eyelashes and said, "Clothes." The security guy then found, in addition to clothes, a wrapped package with, alongside it, an electronic timing device. Unwrapping the package he found a heavy, black block, on the face of which had been lettered . . .

MECHANISM FOR
THE DESTRUCTION
OF JERUSALEM

Under the eye of a camouflaged guy with a hand-gun, it took many hours and telephone calls before poor Eve could convince security that it was a device for controlling the 'effects' in a museum setting – depicting the Roman seige of Jerusalem prior to its destruction, in the year AD 79.

Preliminary sketch for the setting, which had animated 'smoke' and sound – hence the electronic timing device.

Skating on thin ice

Adventuring into the past on the drawing board can give one a false sense of controlling the situation, but I must tread carefully, as this is disputed territory.

Professor A. J. P. Taylor, the historian, pointed out, and he should know, that no historian would take on the heavy load of research involved unless he had an axe to grind. Fair enough.

It is refreshing to discover that archaeologists are quite human, each tending to 'find' exactly what he is looking for. The Germans – specimens that can be chronologically dated. Americans – an eye-catching antique for a museum. The Israelis – 'proofs' of the old biblical testaments. The French – a 'find' that will contribute to the glory of France. The English – bits of bric-à-brac that will give clues to how the ancients may have lived. Then some guy in a white coat comes along and turns everything on its head with carbon dating.

Me? I say, "No 'phone calls please," dip impatiently into books, flagged at the appropriate pages, and attempt to visualise a moment in the past as we might have seen it, had we been *there*. I soon discovered that what we accept as history is a hop, skip and jump affair, and the gaps . . . . are tremendous.

For example, I decided to fabricate an impressive relief to show a *yeshiva* near ancient Babylon (the first 'open university') in the Sessanean style. As a guide to style I could only find reference to two tiles, one showing a camel, the other a chunk of moulding from a cornice. Difficult to guess how these Semites rendered images of people, so I enticed Philip Kemp, a top artist-modeller to go out into space, and invent a bogus, but convincing, Sessanean style. Lovely job. A colonnaded courtyard filled with Semitic types, all peering myopically at a learned scribe, guys with camels in the background and, in the foreground, an exilarch (boss).

SORTING OUT ARCHAEOLOGY
The corner of the Temple at Jerusalem in Roman Times. The area now occupied by the 'Wailing Wall'.

THE EXILARCH
Portrait of a leader who could well have had a double chin and a beer belly.

It looked really authentic – so convincing that a picture of our bogus exilarch was inserted in a recently published history as if it were a genuine artefact.

The obsessive archaeologist

Better the real thing. I was lured into the Negev Desert by an archaeologist who – unusually – was a specialist in metallurgy.

Beno, the archaeologist, had been hunting for clues in a no-go area, so waterless and dead that – as history records – the nomadic tribes had attempted to deter Lawrence from crossing it on his epic race to Aqaba. In that part of the desert they call the sun 'The Hammer of God'.

It took more than that to deter Beno. He had located a spot where Stone Age Man, using *flint* tools, had mined for a material not yet used by Man – copper.

The towering rock escarpments that bound the area are riddled at their base with tunnels, like a Swiss cheese, which the Israeli savants referred to as 'King Solomon's Mines'. To their chagrin, Beno, who was not out for popularity, said, "No. No scion of David ever went near the place."

When, still digging in the heat, he reported that he had unearthed traces of a temple dedicated to the pagan goddess Hathor – battle commenced. But, while opponents were busy writing papers in the comfort of their libraries, he located, high up on a rock face, an incised rendering of Rameses II making an offering to the lady. Game, set and match to Beno.

It was then he asked me to think up a scheme for developing the area and reconstructing some of the ancient workings, so that Timna would be acknowledged, world-wide, as the spot where a great breakthrough occurred: Chalcolithic man discovered copper, which the Egyptians later mined in a big way to produce bronze . . . *the inception of the Bronze Age!*

I bounced around the area in a Land Rover for three days, armed with bottles of drinking water (which I normally avoid) against being desiccated by the hammer of god.

Abstract rock formations – rose pink and white – awe inspiring, threatening, but always beautiful – up canyons, "You're not drinking enough water, G," – clambering rock-faces – slithering down screes – Mehitabel disappearing into black holes on all fours – primitive pin-men with bows and arrows scratched on the rocks – chariots! "Drink your water, G." Meanwhile, a non-stop lecture by the agile Beno as he shows off his baby; Mehitabel climbing rocks while taking notes.

Back in the cool of Hampstead, I spread out the hundred or more photographs and site sketches, and prepared a layout. At the entrance to the valley, I introduced a pavilion displaying Beno's 'finds' and fronted it with a sculpted figure. King Solomon? No, the elegant goddess, Hathor, in her clinging shift, a horned moon on her head.

TIMNA
Elevation of the pavilion, faced with local stone to blend in with the rockscape.

419

The mix, as before

In the old Duke Street days, Carlton Studio's smart lady rep. – the friendly blonde with magenta fingernails – decided that young G, who lived from job-to-sketch, needed managing. Nice to have a classy rep. around but, after a month, she gave up. How to plan ahead, when the unforeseen could come up the stairs anytime, point a finger at G and say, "Dance!" She married a handsome New Zealand sheep-farmer; the behaviour of sheep being, after all, as predictable as the Establishment.

So I danced, and that included undertaking the research until my mind was filled with extracts from encyclopedias, laboratories, wizards and egg-heads, with no index – a bag of odd pieces from other peoples' jigsaws . . .

It might be gemstones and prisms to be displayed in a Crystal Pavilion in the Austrian Alps.

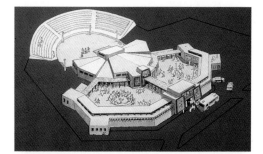

The Aztec life-style for a learning centre in Mexico. A novel theatre which has a stage that can face two ways.

A study of prejudice and hate to jerk the people of Los Angeles into facing their ethnic problems.

Hans Christian Andersen in 3D for exhibiting in Copenhagen.

Young Kay is enamoured of the beautiful Snow Queen in her ice palace.

The princess, who detected the presence of a pea under a pile of quilts. Proof – the actual pea is preserved under this glass dome.

Visuals produced in an hotel bedroom in Crete, while Mehitabel sunned herself.

Hopeful guesswork

When working on that well-aired topic, energy, I heard that traces of a Roman water-mill had recently been discovered in the South of France. Roman? That's something new. The site had not yet been surveyed, so off I went to Arles to see what I could make of it. Disappointing.

A cutting up a steep slope, scattered with stones and broken pantiles. At the top an aqueduct, at the base a little stone foot-bridge over a culvert. Twelve feet up the slope, stone bearings to take a large water-wheel – indications of others above it, which, if evenly spaced, would make for eight wheels – impossible? To one side, traces of steep steps and below, bits of stone foundation peeking through the dry grasses.

As it turned out, I only had the half of it. Years later a proper survey revealed there had been two tiers of eight wheels, set side-by-side. Nevertheless, a good try.

Clonmacnoise, a medieval relic

Archaeological reconstruction? Great fun – that is, if one doesn't profess to be a professor.

Take Clonmacnoise, a medieval relic as haunting as its name, sited in the centre of Ireland by a bend in the River Shannon and surrounded by bogs. Difficult to believe that in the ninth and tenth centuries, this desolate spot was the most important centre of learning in Europe.

Midwinter, under a lowering sky, dark stones are silhouetted against the snow. A ruined chapel, crumbling sections of defensive wall, and what might be mistaken for the chimney of an old mine working but was, in fact, a watch-tower. Such a site would be sacked many times, even by aggressive Vikings in longboats. A clue to the occupants – great granite crosses, rearing up at odd angles in the snow.

Bringing a corpse to life

Roads being near impassable, they would have used the river, so a quay, storage and fishermen's huts. Quarters for the scribes and laymen. An 'A' frame house under construction. A Scandinavian-style fence being replaced with a defensive one. Braziers set on raised platforms, with fuel, to give warning of approaching marauders.

They needed to be self-sufficient, so smallholdings to the north, along an 'esker' (a long mound left by the last glaciation). Hay stacked round poles, as for a damp climate. Men flailing corn, and a grain store. A prehistoric stone barrow, used as a pigsty. Nice touch.

Activity. Guards on watch. Fundamentalists arguing godly notions, women gossiping while one feeds her hens. Female slaves humping loads. Middens heaped in available corners.

Outside the main gate I risked introducing a hostelry; the bush hanging over it – traditional sign that wine is on tap. Stabling, vegetable plots, beehives, hogs, a pigeon loft, a tethered goat.

I like to think that a medieval visitor would have accepted all this as normal. The Irish historian who mattered, gave it a 'pass'! Nice guys, the Irish!

Pie in the sky

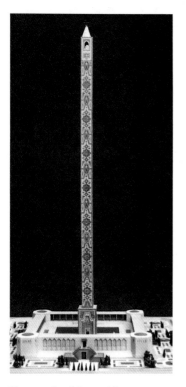

Photographs of the model

The height of ambition

A competition to design an Eighth Wonder of the World.

The Royals of Saudi Arabia okayed my scheme, the highest tower ever; a slender 'pencil' pointing to the heavens.

For its plinth, a block half as high as the Eiffel Tower and, above that, a slender column only twenty metres square extending, well almost, forever.

I constructed it from a column of interlocking concrete blocks, which would stand the pressure and, so it would flex in the wind, threaded them like a necklace on a network of pre-stressed cables anchored to a great buried foundation. Ove Arup, the engineers, put it on their computer, realigned my cables and gave it a tentative okay.

The tower would rise from the centre of a rectangular lake bordered by a colonnade, with a pavilion at each corner. These would represent Poetry, Chivalry (which, by the way, we learned from the Arabs) the Sword of Islam, and the State. The complex would be contained in a high wall, set off by a garden with the characteristic canals and fountains.

The Royals approved and after we had produced a ten foot model . . . the bottom dropped out of the oil market, so no monument. A pity as, even if it collapsed, it would be nice to be known as the guy who *attempted* to beat gravity.

It would be clad in Islamic tiles, which, I guessed, would employ all the tile-makers in the Middle East for five years.

424

Competing with the best

An enthusiastic, but pragmatic guy from the Mexican Government provided me with a draughting table in one of their top hotels and gave me five days to design a museum. This was to be a twentieth century presentation of Mexico's mineral wealth, to contrast with the world-renowned Museum of Anthropology, mounted in Mexico City's central park and fronted by a wide, paved concourse. Not to be beaten, I introduced a similar concourse opposite, where visitors could look down to see, fifteen feet below, a large relief model of Mexico carved from the indigenous rock – a glint of silver and gold, set in a mirror-like pool. Super.

Beyond the concourse, a great black pyramid (Aztec), clad with the rough volcanic lava found locally, and surrounded by a dry moat. To enter, visitors would ascend a ramp in a slot in its face. Dramatic. Once inside, they would descend by a series of curved ramps and a travolator, to exit at the lower level.

To make it visually memorable, the highest flag-pole mounted with the largest flag in the world – high to catch the wind, as Mexico City suffers from atmospheric inversion.

All went well, even to our ultimate completion of their bureaucratic forms, then . . . a change in government, so no museum. But, in my mind, the pyramid is there, a whiff of smoke drifting from its peak. I haven't returned to be disabused.

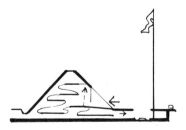

Section through the pyramid.

425

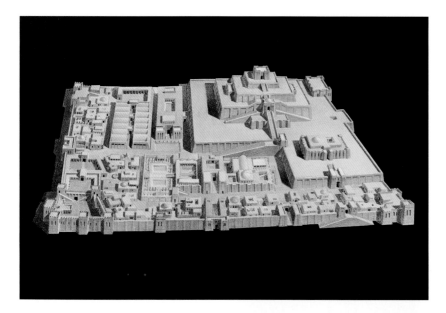

THE CITY OF UR
The central mount occupied by the controlling establishment.

King, priest and scribes.

Grain store and garrison.

Stages in a sequence. Buildings give clues to class divisions – prototype for the evolution of cities.

People – the providers en masse.

The great City of Ur, on the Euphrates

The reconstruction attempted here is based on the 'not exactly, but like what might have been' principle, *not* favoured by scholars. In reference books I found parts of the city's footprint, but to visualise the above-ground structures I had a vast stockpile of sun-baked bricks, what is known of the period – five thousand years back – and a box of crayons.

The more important buildings would have been faced with coloured, glazed bricks, which I omitted, as making the buildings stand up from the paper, with shade and shadow, was complicated enough.

The temple mount, shown here with its defensive wall, was man-made and sited on a flat plain by the river. In addition to the temple, with its processional approaches, would be quarters for the priests and scribes. Linked to the mount would be a library – storehouse for tax returns on clay tablets – and, to its left, the vaulted grain store, with stabling for camels where, today, we would site the car-park. The large structure below the mount contained the king's council chambers with, adjoining it, the queen's palace, recognised by its garden and pools, with a private entry.

Within the mount's defensive wall would be residences for the king's relatives and officers, each with an inner courtyard.

On the wall to the left, the citadel, with areas for exercising and stabling.

Beyond the area shown here was a vast jigsaw of small, interlocking habitations for the workers and traders. Markets, and ways through to the harbour, with fortified gates in an outer wall. Beyond that again, a wide, cultivated zone, patterned with neat irrigation channels.

This great city was flourishing for more than twice as long as our civilisation, if we date it from the birth of Christ – time for development, such as extending the temple to form a great ziggurat. Ur is described in some detail, as its layout reveals the segmentation of people into classes, similar to the social pattern adopted to this day – climax to the next chapter, which deals with MAN.

Flying an oriental kite

The biggest job ever

Here we go – another opening ceremony.

At school I was taught to name this place Formosa (Beautiful Island), but today it calls itself Taiwan. The sun is shining on a wide, paved concourse where well-drilled boys, decked out in yellow, are performing gymnastics to the beat of an off-key silver band. Swaying in the wind, because it is made of plastic and filled with air, a pink dinosaur peers down at the show, pie-faced.

Standing head and shoulders above the chattering crowd of Chinese look-alikes, I must say, a museum of Life Science seems out of kilter with that nearby temple; its elaborately-tiled roofs curling up at the corners like stale, off-the-shelf sandwiches and topped off, not with dinosaurs, but grimacing dragons. The occasional sound of a gong.

How on earth did I become involved with this uncontrolled population explosion? Some months back a *femme fatale*, with a low-cut dress and high pretensions, accosted me archly with the bright remark, "How clever of you . . . You *are* James Gardner? . . . To land such a super job, and for the Chinese, of all people," under the impression that I had been fishing for it, like the little man in the 'lampshade' hat who sits on the end of a punt on the willow pattern plate. It wasn't like that at all.

The door to many splendoured things

Three years back, a Chinese professor, going by the name of Pao-teh Han, had been zigzagging back and forth across the United States (he hated flying), seeking some experts who could design and produce a large museum from scratch. He carried with him a dream of something wonderful – *the elegances of the natural world combined with the beauty of art.*

Han had already learned to avoid using the word 'beauty' – something of its meaning seemed to be lost in the translation. He was depressed.

He had been allocated some derelict paddy-fields at the edge of Taichung, and three years to produce the museum. If he failed, professor or not, he was for the CHOP.

Victorian parlour maid.

As a last hope, he approached a contractor in New Jersey who, by chance, had worked with me in the past. "Not in our ballpark," was the response. "The man you want is James Gardner. No, not in New York. His studio is in Hampstead. You know, London."

So, one wet morning, without any warning, this worried guy landed on our doorstep . . .

Extract from a report by learned Chinese Professor who, in the Year of the Pig, entered the sanctum of Western Visualiser.

Translated from Mandarin:

"The door to many splendoured things. When I entered his Studio I felt that I had already found the man I was looking for. The place was not the slick interior designers normally opt for, but a domain of fantasy. The mannequin of a Victorian parlourmaid stood by a window, a faint light shines on a miniature southern Sung Dynasty cup, and the place was full of things he had designed, from works of art to strange devices; a wire model for a robot, a working steam engine, and ships.

In his early eighties, Gardner has white hair and bright eyes, a designer with a free spirit. A brilliant conversationalist, he immediately addressed me by name and I felt suddenly uplifted. Someone who shared his ideals had been fulfilled by a stranger from the other side of the world.

Later, as I lay in my hotel room, I had a problem. This was a very big project to entrust to one man and I had only met Gardner and his secretary . . ."

Was I surprised on reading this.

Not being accustomed to the nuances of Chinese body-language, I had thought the inscrutable professor somewhat reserved.

We got the job.

To be entrusted with tipping ideas out of my head and setting them up to be understood by people brought up on rice and 'Confucius he say' – and being given the money to do it – was like the finger of fate touching me on a sensitive spot and saying, "Now do what I've trained you to do, and stop carping."

"Mehitabel. Two tickets to Taiwan, Club Class, and better signal that guy Han our ETA."

Fishing in an oriental pool

As our plane reversed thrust along the runway at Chiang Kai-shek airport, I felt reasonably optimistic. Refreshing to step back in time and work person-to-person with a motivated guy who trusts me. In contrast with our Western World, where the talkers have now taken over, drifting from committee to committee, where each non-person puts in his poke to justify his expenses. The longer action is side-tracked, the longer he can gather with the other clubby talkers, so, top marks for delaying tactics.

True, the Chinese invented bureaucracy but, after three visits and ten months evading the issue, their money-mandarins eventually risked placing the contract with a guy in a roll-neck sweater. It was in millions of dollars.

We were now left with two years to lay out the show, design over 2,000 exhibits, load them on a slow boat to China, and then, with the help of forty UK workmen and assorted specialists, get it up.

It's all in my head, if I can sort it

"Mum, look what I've done!"

To be a professional is not enough. Like a young boy, one needs motivation; the approval of a person one respects. In this case, a romantic Chinaman who would be tending his collection of bonsai trees and still a little worried. Will that man Gardner pull it off?

First, as we would say in the Army, "What is the object of the exercise?"

The stories of an all-seeing God, dished out by Sunday School teachers, had never really sunk in; although, as proof, a varnished map of Palestine (where his son had apparently got into trouble) hung on the class-room wall. At that time I was more interested in building rabbit hutches.

Nature abhors a vacuum, so a sense of loneliness and wonder caused me to slowly concoct a jigsaw of this strange universe and how it ticks. After all, here I am on this planet and what else is there to do? My head may be no larger than a coconut, but it has space for more than I was ever able to put into it, from the life cycle of the tobacco mosaic virus and how

A little worried . . .

431

inbred camels mate, to how a fast-breeder nuclear-reactor operates and the statutory length of a public bus in Dublin.

Having presented a glossy, illustrated version of this model – updated and omitting the reactor and bus – to the professor, I was asked to explain it to fifteen curators-to-be, as though I were a modern Marco Polo come to reveal the secrets of the Western World.

An hour later, as we left the university campus, I remarked, with some relief. "It went down well, don't you think?"

"Really, G," said Mehitabel. "The Chinese always put on a polite smile if they're nonplussed, or about to yank the carpet out from under you."

A pause for thought. "Oh well," I replied, "they appeared to be impressed . . . the way I said it?"

"Maybe." Mehitabel grinned cheekily as she waved her handbag at an approaching Taiwan taxi.

In the event they didn't question a thing.

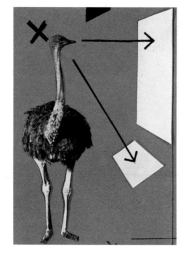

The importance of a viewer's eye level.
For the Chinese we lower it four inches.

I plan for this to be the first museum in the world which explains, in a continuous sequence, how life on earth evolved, from its start to today. To keep these hyperactive people interested in a mile or more of exhibits, I will need to use every trick in the book.

Professor Han warned me the Taiwanese have yet to learn how to behave in a museum. I must dampen them down; lead them to think coolly about a reality and forget the population explosion outside, buzzing with activity, as though someone has kicked over an ants' nest.

The locals appeared to be disinterested in the occasional temples, now as flyblown and dusty as the ancient gods they represented. On the other hand, I was so impressed by the exceptionally wide span of the airport arrivals' concourse, I asked Mehitabel to guard our bags while I paced it out. The Chinese architect didn't bat an eyelid when I gave him the dimension, and devised a series of fifteen wide galleries of uninterrupted space, sufficient to build a small town in . . . or G notions of *cause and effect.*

This museum, being the latest *'effect',* would, I hoped, have a shelf-life of thirty years or so.

'In the beginning'

One Chinese myth starts life, not in a garden, but in an egg. Good show. So, to first cool the visitors down, I laid out a series of white, egg-shaped chambers, with ghosted renderings of biological cell patterns floating slowly up the walls – an idea I got from the Electric Circus in Manhattan.

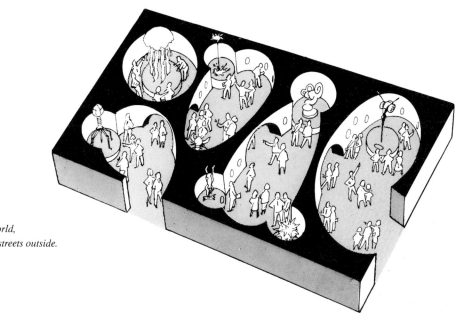

Visitors enter another world,
a contrast with the busy streets outside.

Spotlit, a few examples of the most elegant works of Nature-the-designer; magnified in scale to dominate the visitor. The head of a beetle, with its multiple eyes, poised over a fifteen foot proboscis; as authoritative as an Egyptian god/king.

An abstract sculptural fantasy is slowly rotating. It proves to be the bone formation in the human ear, enlarged 300 times. Suspended from high above, the tentacles of a greatly enlarged jellyfish. Looking up, one sees the fragile, symmetrical nerve system deep in its jelly-like body. (An exhibit so sensitive that a number of specialists refused to attempt it.) Then, an ant's foot, enlarged 83,000 times. A meaningful mechanism which, by comparison, makes the human foot with its reduced toes, first developed for grasping tree branches, a meaty deformity.

433

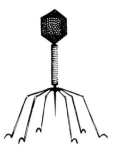

Micro virus.　　*Bird god.*　　*Athene.*　　*Buddha.*　　*Maggots from dung. No eggs – NIL.*

In the final egg-shaped chamber, is a spaceman from H.G. Wells' *The War of the Worlds*. A virus which, in actuality, is so minute that one can only 'see' it electronically. We can even count the molecules that form its tetrahedron-shaped body. It is armed with a syringe which it uses to inject its DNA into another living cell which, instead of going about its business, starts to produce hundreds of little viruses which will then inject other cells.

Frightening, but, in the order of things, even the AIDS virus is a successful form of life.

These were beautiful exhibits to make and I hope that after seeing them, visitors will no longer take such natural devices for granted. Something, somewhere must be making it happen?

I then display a mix of the ghostly gods, invented by witch-doctors and priests to explain away the problem.

Next, how some practical guys, seeing maggots wriggling out of dung heaps, thought *that* must be how life started – until Louis Pasteur proved that a horse-fly had to lay its eggs there first. Stalemate.

The micro-world

To find the real answer we take the visitor way back in time . . . before there was such a thing as life on our planet. Attracted by a rumbling sound, they pass into a wide, Pre-Cambrian landscape, a great erupting volcano – flowing magma – shuddering floor – meteors thumping down on the caked lava – but dead as the moon. Sniff at the sniffer and there's a smell like rotten eggs. There ain't no oxygen, so . . . no life as we know it.

How did life start? That's more than interesting, but the real business goes on at a minute scale, so we invite the visitor into

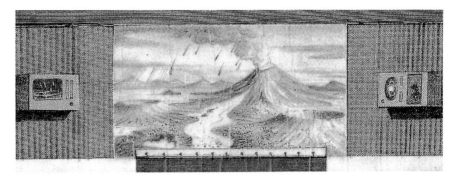

a projection theatre, where they can enjoy a personal peep into the micro-universe which energises life.

Imagine, for a moment, that some egg-heads from the blackness of outer space are approaching our planet. They see points of light in clusters on the Earth's shadow side, like ganglia pulsing out radio signals and linked to each other by a web of electric wiring. Nerve fibres? Approaching closer, they can make out a network of narrow channels, along which thousands of little metallic capsules are flowing to and from the nerve-centres, like blood corpuscles. They might, quite logically, surmise that our planet is a highly developed organism . . . circling the sun for warmth?

STORY SEQUENCE IN ONE OF THE 17 GALLERIES

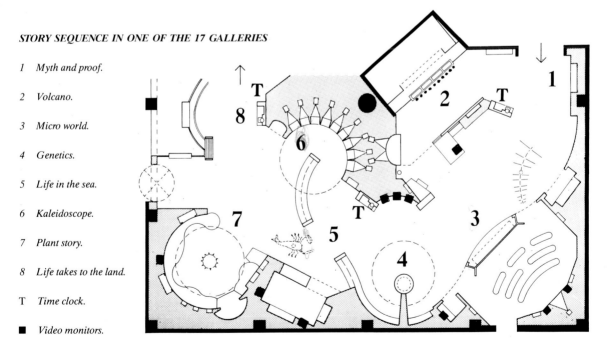

1 Myth and proof.

2 Volcano.

3 Micro world.

4 Genetics.

5 Life in the sea.

6 Kaleidoscope.

7 Plant story.

8 Life takes to the land.

T Time clock.

■ *Video monitors.*

435

To remain sterile like the moon,
or come to life.

"Will you won't you, will you won't you, won't you join the dance?"

Space travel nonsense of course but, scale-wise, comparable to our body, a vast assembly of microscopic molecules playing at chemistry – a complex game of put-and-take. What makes them active? Billions of even more minute electrons and other particles buzzing around, playing their game of push-and-pull.

The happening was bound to take place, given time, in a soupy sea busy with minute molecules all dancing to the Brownian Motion. Some were left-handed and others right-handed, which made the choice of partners selective. Other pairs would find one was happy in water, while the other rejected it, but they clung obstinately together, as delicate liquid crystal membranes drifting through the dancing crowd to occasionally engulf a mixed bag, even maybe a lively protein which would shove – if it hit trouble, or grab – if its membrane touched another.

Meanwhile, a string of carbon atoms, which have a happy habit of joining together in long hokey cokey chains, gathering others as they go, happened to touch its tail to become a loop. Now it was very difficult to break apart . . . survival. Flipped around by the jostling molecules, it became twisted into a spiral. Free dancers, attracted to this neat spiral, clung to it particle by particle – twins. Heavy going, so it split apart and then there were two. It had replicated, and went on and on replicating as a way of life . . . LIFE.

(Apologies to micro-biologists for this hop, skip and jump version of what may, or may not, have happened. After all, it was a long time ago.)

There were numerous groups playing this game, but only a few made it to provide templates for today's plants and animals. Nevertheless, it was a rather acidic existence in that soupy sea, the status quo broken occasionally by violent electric storms under a yellowish sky.

Stop the Earth, I want to get off

Most visitors' sense of time only goes back to their granddads, but life evolved over millions of years, which need to be measured as geological periods. The time it took for the shells of minute diatoms to sink to the sea floor to build up the White Cliffs of Dover was, geologically, only a flash in the pan.

We punctuate the story with geological time-clocks; a globe showing the orientation of land masses and weather reports. Necessary, as our planet wobbles on its axis like a slow gyroscope. (The North Pole was once centred on Milan.)

Meanwhile, to complicate things further, the continents have been slowly drifting around on the sea bed, like rafts, linking together and then breaking apart.

Thus, there was a continual change of climate – sometimes abrupt, if we were hit by an asteroid – so life forms had to adapt, or face the consequences.

Continents drift, guided by magnets under the sea floor.

Health warning – most became extinct.

For millions of years the only activity would be found in the seas. Soft creatures supported by the water before they wrapped around a skeletal frame – even the shark, a survivor from early times, hasn't yet developed a skeleton. Why? He's so successful he doesn't need one.

But no animals could adventure onto the land until there were plants to feed on. The first plants? This presented an opportunity to construct my favourite setting . . . our world before there were eyes to see it.

Imagine yourself back in time, standing in a desolate landscape of barren lava. The waters are covered with humps of matted blue-green algae, (like the green slime on a wet pavement), which cling to the wet rocks. As a side effect of

Behind – a geological clock.

437

ONE OF THE FIFTEEN GALLERIES

To the left, the DNA code.
Overhead, a ferocious sea scorpion.

The most primitive
and elementary life forms.
Behind – the nematode story.

A kaleidoscope of undersea life,
and soft-bodied creatures.

their survival mechanism, plants breath out oxygen and so, after millions of boring years, the sky – slowly – became – blue. Oxygen! Now, thanks to that green slime, the show becomes visitor-friendly; life as we know it could get going.

The world as laid out for vegetarians

We relate happenings to our own sense of time, which seems to speed up as we grow older. Insects and birds, on the other hand, live and react to a faster tempo than us mammals, whilst plants . . . ? True, they smell better than us, but they can't even *see*. Most visitors will view them as the background furnishing used by Nature to fill in the gaps between cities. But plants are quite active to *their own time-scale*. To excite interest, I introduced speeded-up film clips – buds burst open, seeds are shot explosively into the wind, tendrils search blindly for something to hang on to, while rootlets probe underground like purposeful worms.

Being non-mobile, plants take happily to captivity and this led to a novel concept. I planned a shaded walkway, where the visitor could stroll through a living sequence, representing the evolution of plant life.

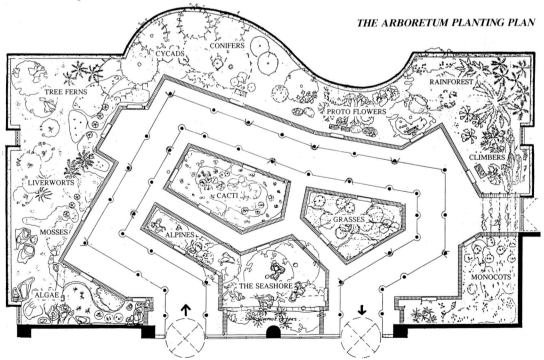

THE ARBORETUM PLANTING PLAN

CONIFERS

CYCADS

RAINFOREST

TREE FERNS

PROTO FLOWERS

CLIMBERS

LIVERWORTS

CACTI

GRASSES

MOSSES

ALPINES

MONOCOTS

ALGAE

THE SEASHORE

439

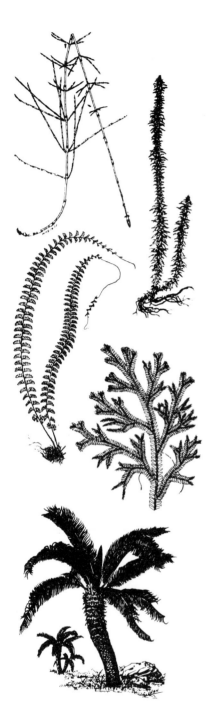

First, our friend the blue-green algae, on a wet stone, then mosses, liverworts that introduced stalks, tree ferns, cycads – those tough, spiky-leaved plants that the dinosaurs had to develop vast bellies to digest – then conifers and a myriad of intricate leaf patterns, delicate photo-film fans poised to catch the sunlight. Climax – lush rain forest with elegant fan-palms forty feet high.

Terrific, it had never been attempted before but, when I specified grass, the Chinese nurseryman, who had been up in the mountains hunting for rare specimens, was taken aback – he spent much of his life weeding out grass.

With the help of a translator, I made the point that it was only recently, after the ice-cap retreated and grasslands took over, that herds of grazing animals developed.

As soon as plants colonised the land, the first creatures to follow them were insects, the Earth's first owner-occupiers. We had fun reconstructing hairy spiders, with bodies the size of footballs, giant millipedes, two metres long, and giant WORMS. To clear away the cobweb of ancient myths, we back up our story with proofs – the faeces of a dinosaur, the nerve-system of a cat (in spirits), and, in this case, fossilized worm-casts.

It's not a small world, to a nematode

With worms in mind, a diversion to Cambridge, where the discovery of the DNA helix shook the world.

Mehitabel backs the car into a vacant space (which turns out to be the perk of a hospital matron from the adjoining building) and we make our way up to a research laboratory squeezed into angled attics under the roof. We intrude on three bearded biologists and a pallid, blonde assistant with shadows under her eyes.

One guy regretfully deserts his computer and leads us to a bench littered with micro-pics. taken with an electron-microscope.

These guys have spent the last six years counting and mapping the cells of the nematode, which is no bigger than this ☞ – and found by the thousand in any patch of earth, or a potato, for that matter. Nevertheless, these research guys can cut each little worm into sixty or more slices, sections which reveal how its minute cells organise themselves.

He indicates a complex line diagram with professional satisfaction, "That's its nervous-system. Only twenty-seven ganglia."

Gosh, thinks I, it could almost be a politician!

Micro-section through a nematode.

Next we see a minor epic on video, which he announces with pride, *The World of the Nematodes.* Live shots, enormously enlarged, of that other world where the little monsters nibble at root tips and, in close-up, a couple having sex. Gosh, romance in a potato; and the fuss *we* make of our mammalian sexual appetites.

Then we are clattering down the stairs to the sound of an irate matron honking her horn in the car-park.

"Silly cow," says Mehitabel. Females can be quite cruel to their own kind.

Who cares, when we have just been on the inside with guys who probe into the unknown to discover why seed (a) develops into a frog, while seed (b) ends up as the log. But these research guys still have a long way to go.

So have we – to Santa Rosa, where a specialist is about to replicate a Jurassic Forest for us. He turns up macho cowboy-style in an open Land Rover with a showy screech of tyres and a, "Howdy." Climbing in, I observe a thick book nestling against the manual gear-shift. "The Good Book," he comments. "Wouldn't trek any place without it."

Crazy? No – it's a giggle when some pompous ass pretends to logic, which is just the tip of the iceberg – our brains have schizophrenia built in. I long ago discovered that human behaviour depends, at any one time, on which segment of the mental pie-chart is being activated.

Sunday is prayer, let's be altruistic – Monday, suing a neighbour – Tuesday, closing a dicey deal – Wednesday, golf – Thursday, being unconsciously racist – Friday, getting pissed as a newt at a stag-party. This guy? It's Saturday and, biblical-segment quiescent, he is about to spend months working on an exhibit demonstrating . . . a RATIONAL view of life.

Is this all a waste of time? I guess so. Nevertheless, we

make our way to Salt Lake City for casts of the skeleton of a giant dinosaur, who had got there first and died in a swamp. After filling time risking a Mormon haircut, I inspect a shed full of bones and arrange for a set to be shipped to Denmark, for assembly by a guy who knows how. Fine. Only then am I given the latest stop-press news. The *camarasaurus* didn't curve its tail, as represented on all the reconstructions made to date, but held it out stiff to balance its neck. Hell. Then how am I to get this eighteen metre long monster into the hall? Back to the drawing-board.

Sitting on a camarasaurus, *thigh bone, Mehitabel lists its bone count.*

Can dinosaurs fly?

In this hazardous business one is open to surprises. I decided to suspend a group of *pterodactyls* so they sailed around, way up, in the manner of a mobile. Looked good on the sketch, until I discovered that the one with a head like a boomerang, the *pteranodon,* had a wing-span as big as a glider. Nothing for it but to cross fingers and hope the roof-bolts hold.

The slow gyration of this mobile will be watched by a moody guy in a T-shirt, leaning against the balcony rail at a higher level. When visitors approach they will be surprised to discover he is a dinosaur and, believe it or not, speaks in mandarin. Turning his head, he says, "You humans annoy me. You make a big thing of the fact that we became extinct. For your information, we lived here for a hundred and sixty million years. Your lot have only been around for 4,000 years and are already making a mess of things." He coolly turns his head away to gaze back at the *pterodactyls.*

But dinosaurs did not become extinct. Some small warm-blooded ones developed a coat of feathers to keep out the cold and to their, and the larger dinosaurs', surprise, found they could fly. We now call them birds.

I intended to give one of these little dinosaurs, the size of a chicken, primitive feathers, but our adviser (ex-British Museum of Natural History and a smart script-writer) said she would resign if I insisted on inventing my own Natural History.

I dodged that one by introducing a lively cartoon film showing how a little feathered dinosaur named Archie, chased

442

A *mobile of* pterodactyls.

A quetzalcoatlus *on its cliff-top nest.*

by others who were jealous, discovered that he could fly, "we-wee-weee . . ." He landed in the mud, to be dug up by a German fossil-hunter who named him *archaeopteryx.*

Some months later a small dinosaur fossil was found to have primitive feathers. So there we go.

Most academics, not being designers, are nervous of deviating from the party line and end up in a time-lag. I would not be surprised if one day some professor informs me that I am a normal *Homo sapiens*, when it is obvious that I was sent here, as punishment, from an advanced planet in outer space.

As a recent arrival from outer space, in the business of constructing mechanisms, I am fascinated. All these creatures of different types, yet having one thing in common – what a strange method of reproduction they have adopted.

If a designer has a new idea (rare) he can try it out on the drawing-board. But Nature is unable to do this trick of producing a rabbit out of a hat – cannot, for example, use the wheel – but must go back to square one and re-enact the past as it happened, step-by-step.

Rather as though Henry Ford, having decided to launch a new model, went right back to the first Model 'T', then ran through a sequence of prototypes covering every car produced so far until, finally on track, he tooled up for the latest model.

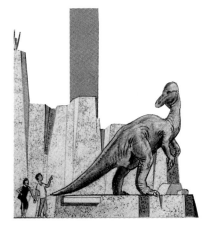

A *duck-billed* corythosaurus *calmly turns to quiz the visitors as they approach.*

THE DINOSAURS.

Dinosaurs writ large

We overstated the importance of dinosaurs, as Professor Han, quite correctly, appreciated that this would attract the crowds.

Visitors followed a dinosaur's footprints along a dark cave, to peep through the legs of an apatosaurus *in a group browsing on cycads. A sound of munching and the beast's head comes into view, chewing the tough spines. After a sequence of peep-shows showing their evolution in time, visitors pass through a Jurassic forest to enter the Dinosaur Gallery, shown to the right.*

Through windows giving on to the park, they see two giant dinosaurs in battle.

Below is a visual for the model-maker with, to the right, a detail of a completed reconstruction.

To the far right, a group of dinosaurs is enjoying breakfast in a Jurassic forest. They are fully animated, set off by an infra-red detector. Conversation: the herbivore says he is ". . . getting larger and fatter eating vegetables." The carnivore to the left interjects, ". . . and slower and slower. We eat meat," showing his teeth. Such animations not only excite the visitor, but put the story across in a memorable way.

A VISUAL FOR THE MODELLER.

Up to flight.

Surely, not the simplest way?

The productivity of the Taiwanese is so great, it is estimated that, in twenty years' time there will be standing-room only on the island.

On site, one of my partners in crime has been allocated a bedroom entirely furnished in black, even to synthetic black fur on the ceiling. Okay.

Returning one afternoon to retrieve a note-pad, he surprised a naked couple copulating like mad on his bed. Helped pay for the room, I guess, but, apart from the undignified antics we mammals go through . . .

The undignified antics of Homo sapiens.

. . . how does conservative Nature get back to square one?

The ancient Pre-Cambrian sea is replaced by a saline lake carried about by us land animals in a little bag (the womb). Pockets of molecules arrive, to zigzag around in this mini-sea, flexing their threadlike tails (the sperm).

Then Nature goes through a series of old models, in embryo. First it could be the prototype for a fish, as gill slits and two black, fishy eyes take form while it rests snugly in the curve of its tail.

Then four little buds appear (it is to become a mammal), which will later shape up as limbs, then a spine right round to the tip of its tail. No tail required for this latest model, so it reduces to a stump (which we sit on).

This is the code for *Homo sapiens,* but there is a stock of

446

basic templates, all starting from a fishy blob, but deviating to produce the current models now in service. (There were once many, many more, but these are the few that have avoided being cancelled out by events.) It's like a pack of cards. One carries the imprint for mammal, a set of 'Lego' units which make up complete skeletons. As we show in the museum, they can be put together for an alligator, a shrew, a mole or a man.

There can be an occasional jinx in this process – a physical mischance; molecules may be knocked off course. This can cause abnormalities, some of which are useful and become normalities . . . like the overdeveloped human brain.

Nevertheless, Nature's code can be very precise; the common dragon-fly has replicated to the original elegant detail for over 300 million years. Far more exciting than those witch-doctors' myths.

"Lecture over," as my wife used to say, so . . .

On with the show

Having become inured to the evasive double-talk and hype of experts in committee, it was a relief to know exactly what we wanted and to go straight to it.

Our tight little group at the studio had now increased to twenty-six; production activated by Alex, an ex-assistant with an abrasive Scottish accent, effective when trouble-shooting. Almost every top artist-craftsman in the UK was now working for us, against time. None of them let us down – it was the Battle of Britain all over again.

Eve, who had joined us in the old Duke Street days, was checking who paid who what, when and why.

"The Queen was in her parlour counting out the money."

Item 763. Letter of intent to mural artist A – An advance for canvas – Progress payment? Guess he's worth it – Main contract to set designer B – Three progress payments – Transport an extra? – Release final payment to B – He passes on agreed percentage to A – A then reimburses our advances – Add copyright fees to photo library – Estimate time on site plus expenses – Add transport and insurance – Pause for coffee – Only a few hundred more to go.

Watch it! More money out than in. Assistance from Barclays Bank? You must be joking! Nevertheless we made it.

Embryo car.

Embryo you.

A set of 'Lego'.

447

Getting everything – a scatter of dinosaurs, a thirty-five foot replica of a human gut, animations and kaleidoscopes, and 1,500 species of insects (from Penang) – into containers and shipped on a slow boat to Taiwan, was comparable to a military operation. How Noah managed to get all the animals into the ark defeats me. At least he had no call to label a giant *Orang-utan* as an 'antelope', to get it through customs.

Wheedling the remains of Peking Man from mainland China, then enemy territory, required re-routing them in the manner of an illicit arms dealer, but that is another story.

While our electronics egg-heads were carefully threading thirty kilometres of wire through the museum to serve videos, sound and projections, two of our workmen were seducing, or being seduced by and marrying, Taiwanese girls – one of whom ran a bar. We did, as a side effect, spread a little English culture in the Far East, as the following remark by a local handler, "I ain't no bloody Chinese Chink!"

Meanwhile Professor Han, something of a mandarin who refused to communicate with non-boss types, decided to lay out an unauthorised garden on the roof. Came a downpour and a soup of Taiwan mud cascaded into one of our galleries – fortunately, the more delicate exhibits were protected with polythene.

In the UK, two half-completed dinosaurs were destroyed by fire, to be completely remade, while an ingenious Danish model-maker produced a perfect replica of a beautiful Rhinoceros Beetle, scaled up to the size of a family car.

A surprise shock for the visitors – who tend to judge everything to their own scale.

This completely took over his living-room, with no way to get it out. "Then you'll have to get down to dismembering it," barked Alex, with a dour Scots grin.

A little-known species.

Next, a museum specialist delivers an elegant model of a horsefly (*Hybornitra affinis)*. We had asked him for a housefly *(Musca domestica)*. In this race against time, a sense of humour was essential.

Han had asked for, "the beauty of Nature," so the exhibit must not only tell a story, but be elegant. How gills were adapted to lungs, and limbs from belly-crawling to leaping and – flying. Animals driven by the imperative to breed resulted in their filling every available niche in our planet, even to the dark ocean abysses, where creatures emit infra-red signals to detect their prey, like fighter aircraft.

Too many FACTS. So, for light relief, I introduced a sweet flying pig to give the viewers a gentle shock.

Excluding the pig, we have a delicately-balanced pattern of active living units, each unconsciously playing its part in a great orchestrated symphony . . . that is, until I am faced with the duck-billed platypus; a mammal that lays eggs, basks in the mud and has a duck's bill. He just doesn't fit the pattern, so I have him, as an interloper, reclining at ease on a satin-covered, Chinese footstool. Delightful.

I now have another odd-bod to deal with, a mammal which visitors will anticipate as the final CLIMAX . . .

us

. . . an important event which Nature had planned for all along. Impossible to disabuse people in one afternoon. Nevertheless, I peg on.

After finding their way through a G rendering of a rain forest, the trees being cutout line drawings set out in depth, the black and white emphasising the fur and feather of its inhabitants with, finally, a parrot that speaks mandarin introducing Man.

'Lucy In The Sky With Diamonds'

The first lady of whom we have record would be unlikely to get a job as a receptionist. She is about one metre high and somewhat hairy. She stands, one hand grasping the branch of a tree and (shock) her beady black eyes move to scan a wide setting of the African veldt. By a distant bluff she sees a small tent and a Land Rover, while, nearby, archaeologists are unearthing her fossilized skeleton.

By the tent, a miniature transistor set is playing the Beatles song 'Lucy In The Sky With Diamonds', so she has been honoured with the name 'Lucy'.

Next, a diorama shows a straggling group making their lonely way, past patches of bog and snow, across a bleak landscape under a lowering sky. The last Ice Age has recently retreated and they are migrating . . . to eventually scatter their progeny across the continents.

Those who survived the cold, heat and microbe attacks have embedded their stamina and resistance in our genes.

Perhaps, if we examine Early Man, we will find clues to some unplanned aspects of human behaviour . . .

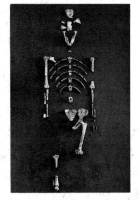

Fossil clues to 'Lucy'.

Sigmund Freud? He ignored our ancestry

Our predecessors, living in small self-supporting groups for millions of years have, I guess, passed on in our DNA behaviour patterns now buried deep in our unconscious. A group will take to violence to protect their totem or religion. Intrusion by outsiders from other groups is barely tolerated.

Our behaviour? There's no need to borrow theories from academics. We can examine a group of hunter-gatherers, who are living in a time-warp, as it were, in Africa.

Placing one foot well back for balance, I tension the six foot long-bow. No rabbits in view, so I take a bead on a rabbi strolling down the other side of the street, but no-go. I haven't the muscle to draw the slender arrow more than half-way back and am ashamed to realise that my arm muscles are as soft as the white pith one finds on a peeled orange.

This beautiful weapon was gifted by a group of primitive Hadza hunter-gatherers, the 'click' people. With the arrows had been a deadly poison, wrapped in a leaf, for arming the arrow-heads. "Don't touch it," warned the eccentric ethnologist who had enticed the group to give us examples of their few possessions for the museum. Few, because they only owned essential items they could carry. To my surprise, the collection included a miniature bow and arrow. A toy? No, the young must train for survival by developing their little biceps at an early age.

For thousands of years men have subsisted by collecting available edibles from a piece of territory and then moving on – as, come to think of it, do grazing animals.

The 'click' women collect sufficient berries or nuts and roots for the day in two hours. The men go off, to return some time later with a young monkey – brought down after three or four mis-shots.

All this was to be expected, but a surprise! The men, having time on their hands, would spend long hours playing a game of chance, tossing pieces of bark in the air to land this or that way up – just as I tossed cigarette cards in the school playground.

A DIORAMA SETTING
The last Ice Age is retreating.
A family group is migrating,
very much alone in a wide,
uninhabited landscape.

451

The preliminary sketch.

We then show how, as soon as these groups settled, the balance changed.

A wide diorama shows early settlers behind their stockade and a modelled air-view of a cluster of bee-hive huts in a clearing patterned with cultivation patches. This could well have terminated this sequence on Man, but I decided to go beyond the accepted brief and take the story to the next stage.

Interesting to observe the developing pattern objectively, as one would a community of ants tooled-up for feeding, fighting and breeding.

But, unlike the ants, Man's behaviour became unpredictable – he had an overdeveloped brain and individuals communicated mental images with words. For this aspect of the story I introduced an audio-visual theatre.

A completed detail.

The powerhouse of civilisation

The presence of Man is revealed, as with monkeys in the jungle, by a constant chattering. How words soon took over. Words were no longer used to parallel reality, but to describe imagined images and happenings, so men ended up living in a dream-world. Men make things: so some guy must have made us and the world we live in. What a guy! The word-men soon became dominant, inventing concepts like 'sin', (Nature's mechanism for procreation), which gave them the spurious authority once only enjoyed by witch-doctors.

As H.G. Wells once said, when giving a lecture at Oxford University. "Once a mental notion is given a name, it puts on the garment of reality."

For millions of years Man was lazy and aggressive by turn, sustained by the mothering instinct of the females. (Women's Lib. please note.) The behaviour of boys in the playground is revealing as setting the pattern for evolving society, as they compete and bully for status, often in packs. When an outsider attacks a man's lifestyle, he will happily take to group violence.

Man may not be interested in the stern-end of a hippopotamus, but he will be triggered off by the backside of a female of his own species . . . Nature's imperative. I guess we are all motivated by these same subconscious drives.

My schoolboy hero, Mungo Park, the first man to cross the African continent, found every habitation fenced by a high prickly hedge or stockade.

This was not so much for the protection of the inhabitants, as their possessions. Outsiders would risk (even enjoy) a fight to get their hands on wealth without working for it.

The ancient hill top villages, which had acted as staging-posts on my tramp down Italy, had been built for defence, which indicated that bands of marauders preying on the producers went on . . . I guess it still goes on, in the accepted guise of banking and corporate crime, by well-dressed gents in those air-conditioned skyscraper blocks.

TECHNOLOGY
Flint scrapers.
Needles.
Toggles.
Basket-work.
Clay pots.
Nets.
Fish-hooks.
Traps.
Leather thongs.
Rope.
Weaving.
Dyes.
Glass beads.
Wattle fences.

Bosses, fighters and workers

Using a sequence of models, coupled to film and commentary, I was able to describe how the cluster of round huts in a clearing could *develop* - in spite of attacks and the occasional genocide – into a great conurbation like the ancient City of Ur.

On a map of today this would be classed as a sizeable city, a dense spread of low rectangular dwellings in a bend of the Euphrates River . . .

On a mount dominating its centre, you would find the top man and his priests, with a store of grain and a well-trained bodyguard on call.

The top guy was probably illiterate, writing being a secret craft known only to the scribes. The priest would act as his PR man – giving him a godlike authority, with the help of artist-craftsmen, while his scribes would supervise tax gathering, in the course of which they invented writing, for tax records. And very nice, too.

The million or more underclass workers, when not producing babies, would cultivate, develop sophisticated irrigation canals, travelling far and wide, and hold markets for the exchange of produce. On occasion, the defensive army would equate their weapons with power and go on the offensive, subduing and sequestering the possessions of neighbouring communities – as do fighter-ants.

The mounds, called '*tells*' in the Middle East, show how city after city was destroyed, rebuilt and destroyed again and again; the works of artist-craftsmen just thin layers of dust.

As time passed, scribes became a power in the land, using a restricted written code to maintain their authority (religious leaders and lawyers). So, men were already grouped into a class structure. Then a guy invented printing, so the scribes lost much of their power and the cat was among the pigeons.

With their penchant for gambling, the men played a game with physics and numbers based on *cause* and *effect* . . . and hit the jackpot. That is, until Einstein introduced a new game based on space and TIME. This again set the cat among the pigeons and we terminate our story with a demonstration of the strange effects of his special theory of relativity.

A long walk from that rendering of a Pre-Cambrian volcano, but all aspects of the flowering of LIFE.

The pay-off

As a final fling, in a large gallery devoted to the workings of the human body, I built the story around the flexible tube we have in common with the not so simple worm.

A thirty-five foot long rendering of the human gut, designed to shock the visitor into appreciating how it engulfs material from the outside world. Not for the pleasure of owners of 'diners cards', but to supply millions of minute molecules so that they can interact and, as a side effect, keep our great bodies poised on two legs.

How did these inscrutable Chinese react? After the first hectic rush, 15,000 visitors now find their way through the mile or so of exhibits every day.

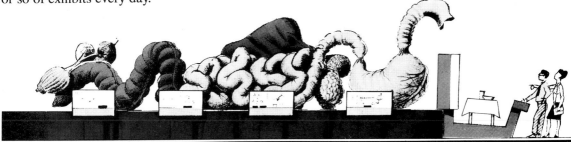

I may ask myself, does what I do justify the non-stop game of put-and-take being played non-stop in the vast micro-universe? I guess not. Just a toss of the dice, as are the millions of near replicas coming down the conveyor belt – populating our planet with ten billion centres of selfish activity. Chance happenings, but each one a little universe that can mirror itself in its mind – even grope for and invent an . . .

IMAGINED PURPOSE

Maybe the drink-induced chant of the football fans, "We're here because we're here . . ." has the answer, after all.

A few of the hundreds of creative artists and craftsmen
who dedicated a slice of their lives to converting
my visuals to a reality.

Rowland Emmett
Barry Evans
William Kempster
David Gentleman
Lawrence Scarfe
Barbara Jones
John Piper
Laurie Barr
Henry Moore
Lewitt & Him
Charles Longbottom
Pauline Whitehouse
Herbert Westbrook
Derek & Pat Freeborn
Kit Freeborn
Philip Kemp
Bridget Kempster
Pat & Jim Turner
Bruce Angrave
Ethelwyn Baker
Nicholas Bently
Ferdinand Bellan
Barbara Campbell
Michael Copus
Bob Simpson
Peter French
Eric Frazer
David Gillespie
Peter Judge
Simon & Sally Dray
Warner & Lena Cook
Simon Beer
Lyn Kramer
Astrid Zydower
Bernard Kramer
Lisa Kramer
Bill Philby
Ken Gillham
Ian Cairnie
Peter Whiteman
Richard Taylor
John Revell
Malcolm Lewis
R.G. Adnitt
Anthony Barton
Kirsten Broen
Peter Boys
Derek Fields

Fidelma Massey
Lin Chien-Ch'eng
Derek Frampton
John Holmes
Neil Wood
Richard Glassborow
Jenny Tylden-Wright
David Willrich
Donal Lyons
David Bergen
David Coutts
Sally Lecky-Thomson
Roy Wiltshire
Stuart Smith
Ralph Steadman
Will Wilson
Elizabeth Wilson
Peter Parr
Fred White
Philip Dimmick
Dennis King
Arnold Machin
Keith New
Jon Bannenburg
Russell Page
Howard Phillips
Robin Prater
E. Ragazini
Phyllis Richards
Denzil Skinner
Graham Sutherland
Norman Weaver
Kim Allen
Martin Bainbridge
A.J. Carter
Cornell Capa
Charmaine Wood
Gerry Dadds
Derek Stewart
Zahava Schachor
G.A. Wingrove
Nick Peters
Bo Bindel
Roby Braun
Nick Rayburn
Bryan Kneale
Jeremy Hunt
Carol Betera

Frances Crowe
Jamie Shuttleworth
Caroline Shuttleworth
Fred Funk
Jeppe Mohl
Philip Jackson
Margaret Oliphant
Anthony Parks
Diane Radford
Lyndsey Ball
James Hollis Hoff
Julia Serbon
Drew Takahashi
Simon Rice-Oxley
Howard Wilman
Gary Hincks
Mike McCabe
Robert Fawcett
Martin Beacom
Jon Barron
Ron Holthuijsen
Dave Thomas
John Coppinger
James Madsen, Jr.
Tim Cooksey
Bob Farrow
John Flynn
Bob Godfrey
Mollie Holt
Magnus Irvin
Gerry Judah
John Lansdell
Kim Lane
Conrad Lanham
Andre Tammes
Sheila Lintel
Juliette Nissen
Eric de Mare
Chris Melling
Liz Moore
Dustin Mortimer
Gerald Nash
John Fraser
Steve Billinger
Graham High
Paul Trainer
Fergus Bourke
Jacinta Fitzgerald

Index

458

459

460

How to evade those negative periods termed 'leisure'.
Key projects designed by the author, or for which he was the controlling designer.

London	'How They Fly' Exhibition
Kensington	'Britain Can Make It' Exhibition
Edinburgh	Enterprise Scotland
Heathrow	BA aircraft interiors
South Bank	Festival of Britain
Battersea	Festival Gardens
New Delhi	'Young India' Pavilion
Kent	Lydd Airport
Brussels	UK Pavilion and exhibits
Milan	Triennale educational exhibit
Gothenberg	Fashion show
Kensington	Commonwealth Exhibition
St Helens	Glass Museum
Eindhoven	The Evoluon Museum
Sheffield	Industrial Exhibition
New York	British Trade Fair
Glasgow	The *QE2*
Montreal	'Britain Today'
Bradford	Museum of Colour
London	'TV History', IBA
Syon Park	Garden Centre complex
Brunei	The Churchill Museum
Stockholm	Atomic Pavilion
Geneva	Peaceful Uses of Atomic Energy
Kensington	'Search' Scientific Exhibition
London	'The Story of the Earth'
Louisville	Mississippi Riverboat
Baltimore	Science Centre
Chesapeake Bay	Environmental Exhibition
Tsukuba	Asian Development Bank Pavilion

York	Heritage Museum
Dublin	'Options' Conservation Exhibition
Tel Aviv	Museum of the Diaspora
Cape Canaveral	USA Bicentennial Exhibition
Detroit	Holocaust Museum
Copenhagen	Ship Museum
Jamaica	Cultural Heritage Museum
Jerusalem	The Citadel Museum
Fort Lauderdale	'Butterfly World'
Taiwan	The National Museum of Natural Science
Los Angeles	Museum of Intolerance

The author has also been responsible for overseas prestige and trade exhibits at:

Barcelona – Bahrain – Basle – Brussels – Caracas – Geneva – Gothenberg – Hanover – Helsinki – Lisbon – Milan – Moscow – New York – Osaka – Oslo – Rome – São Paolo – Sydney – Singapore – Stockholm – Toronto – Zürich

THE FUTURE IS ON THE DRAWING BOARD. WHERE ARE THE COMPUTERS? UPSTAIRS.

Acknowledgements

Page 5 – Portrait of the author by Ralph Steadman. **Page 11** – Marlene Dietrich in The Blue Angel: Popperfoto. **Page 20** – Rembrandt self-portrait, aged 63 (detail): Reproduced by courtesy of the Trustees, The National Gallery, London. **Page 21 (top)** – The Madonna and Child with St John and Angels (The Manchester Madonna), (detail), ascribed to Michelangelo: Reproduced by courtesy of the Trustees, The National Gallery, London. **Page 21 (middle)** – Fruit and Flowers, (detail), Brussel: Reproduced by courtesy of the Trustees, The National Gallery, London. **Page 21 (bottom)** – The Watermills at Singraven near Denekamp, (detail), Hobbema: Reproduced by courtesy of the Trustees, The National Gallery, London. **Page 24 (right)** – Cartier jewellery: Sotheby's, Geneva. **Page 27** – Poster by E. McKnight Kauffer (reconstruction): Courtesy of the Board of Trustees of the V & A. **Page 38** – Imperial Airways Poster, (detail): British Airways. **Page 44** – Cellini's Perseus, (detail): The Conway Library, Courtauld Institute of Art. **Page 78** – Harry Gordon Selfridge, (detail): National Portrait Gallery, London. **Page 81** – "Canopus" Flying-boat: Short Brothers Ltd. **Page 82** – Imperial Airways Poster: British Airways. **Page 83** – Shell Poster: Shell UK Ltd. **Page 92** – "Jane" cartoons: © 1993 Mirror Group Newspapers Ltd. distributed by North America Syndicate Inc. **Pages 116/117** – Dummy Tanks and Gun: Imperial War Museum, London. **Page 121** – "Big Bobs" Dummy Landing-craft: Imperial War Museum, London. **Pages 131/136 (top)** – "Britain Can Make It" Exhibition, 1947: The Design Council. **Page 136 (bottom)** – "Britain Can Make It" Exhibition, 1947: The Design Council/Perstorp Warerite Ltd. **Pages 137/8** – "Britain Can Make It" Exhibition, 1947: The Design Council. **Page 139** – "Britain Can Make It" Exhibition, 1947: The Design Council/The New York Times. **Page 155** – The Sistine Chapel Ceiling (detail), Michelangelo: The Bridgeman Art Library. **Page 167** – The Crystal Palace, Hyde Park: The British Architectural Library, RIBA, London. **Page 172** – Vauxhall Gardens showing the Grand Walk: Guildhall Library, City of London. **Page 176 (bottom)** – Jacob Epstein, sculptor, at work, (detail): Hulton Deutsch. **Page 177** – Henry Moore, sculptor, at work, (detail): Art Gallery of Ontario. **Page 190** – Girls on Ride at Funfair: Hulton Deutsch. **Page 315** – The Garden of Earthly Delights, (detail), Bosch: © Museo del Prado, Madrid. **Page 321** – Landscape with the Marriage of Isaac and Rebekah ("The Mill"), (detail), Claude: Reproduced by courtesy of the Trustees, The National Gallery, London. **Page 328** – Portrait of Madame Récamier, (detail), François Gérard: Musée de la Ville de Paris, Musée Carnavalet/Giraudon. **Page 344/6** – Courtesy of Astrid Zydower. **Page 347** – Young Man Among Roses, Nicholas Hilliard: Courtesy of the Board of Trustees of the V & A. **Page 348** – Courtesy of Astrid Zydower. **Page 367** – Delta Queen Steamboat Co. **Page 385 (top left)** – The Natural History Museum, London. **Page 393 (bottom)** – The Mikado 1989 tour, The D'Oyly Carte Opera Company: Savoy Theatre Archives/Bob Workman (Photographer). **Page 420 (bottom)** – Courtesy of Simon Wiesenthal Center/Jim Mendenhall, 1992 (Photographer). **Page 438** Courtesy of Photobition Ltd. **Page 450 (bottom)** – "Lucy" skeleton: The Cleveland Museum of Natural History. **Pages 429, 437, 445 (bottom left), 445 (bottom right), 449, 450 (top), 451 and 452 (bottom)** – Nicholas Sinclair, 1988 (Photographer). All other illustrations are either the work of the author, or from his own collection/archives.